3 Italian Conductors
7 'Viennese' Sopranos

Discographies
compiled by John Hunt

1991

Contents

9   Arturo Toscanini

135 Guido Cantelli

163 Carlo Maria Giulini

203 Elisabeth Schwarzkopf

303 Irmgard Seefried

343 Elisabeth Grümmer

369 Sena Jurinac

397 Hilde Güden

423 Lisa Della Casa

445 Rita Streich

3 Italian Conductors
Published by John Hunt.
Designed by Richard Chluparty
© 1991 John Hunt
reprinted 2009
ISBN 978-0-951026-83-0

Published 1991 by John Hunt

Designed by Richard Chlupaty, London

Copyright 1991 John Hunt

Sole distributors:
Travis & Emery,
17 Cecil Court,
London, WC2N 4EZ,
United Kingdom.
(+44) 20 7 459 2129.
sales@travis-and-emery.com

Acknowledgement

This publication has been made possible by generous support from the following:

Yoshihiro Asada, Osaka

Andrew Barker, Rochester

Edward Chibas, Caracas

Geoffrey Gammon, Surbiton

Eugene Kaskey, New York

Ernst Lumpe, Soest

James Read, Morecambe

Göran Söderwall, Stockholm

Yoshihiko Suzuki, Tokyo

Richard Ames, New Barnet

Mike Ashman, Cardiff

Jonathan Brown, Turner (Australia)

John Derry, Newcastle-upon-Tyne

Erik Dervos, London

Robert Donaldson, Edinburgh

Christopher Dowling, London

Gustav Fenyo, Glasgow

Bruce Morrison, Gillingham

Gregory Page-Turner, Bridport

C. Pemberton, London

Gordon Reeves, Birmingham

John Squire, Nether Stowey

Neville Sumpter, Northolt

Hermann Wendel, Frankfurt-am-Main

Foreword

These discographies are intended to be a guide to record collectors and to students of a particular interpreter's art. They list, alphabetically under composers, all the artist's commercially published recordings, plus any known commercial recordings which have not been published together with the many unofficially published recordings taken from live performance or radio broadcast.

The 3-column layout gives place, year and, where possible, month of recording (column 1), orchestra and other main participating artists (column 2) and catalogue numbers for the most important published editions of each recording (column 3). The information in this third column indicates first issue, on 78rpm or LP record, in the country of origin or in the country of the parent record company (for example, Decca's recordings with the Vienna Philharmonic in Vienna are given their British Decca catalogue numbers); the first issue is then followed by important reissues both on LP and compact disc; some, but by no means all, issues in the 45rpm format between the late 1940s and early 1960s are included; finally, commercially published video recordings are included in their VHS format, with laser discs due to follow in many instances at the time of going to press.

My approach differs considerably from the conventional discography which lists an artist's recordings chronologically and also includes matrix details for pre-LP material: I have yet to be convinced that these details are sufficiently important for the general collector. Furthermore, as the discography is being produced in UK, there is bias throughout to British catalogue numbers rather than their European or American equivalents. Recording venues within a city often varied considerably, and I have therefore felt it sufficient to name the city without specifying which hall or studio might have been used.

The listings are supplemented by the reproduction of concert or opera programmes and record company advertising for the artist concerned. This helps to place the recording activity within the context of the performer's career in general.
The programmes are from my own collection, but additional Toscanini material has been made available by Clive Pearsall.

Any exceptions to the guidelines described above are mentioned in the introduction to the individual discography.

I wish to acknowledge the generous help in checking and supplying information which I have received from the following friends, colleagues and collectors: first and foremost Clifford Elkin, Glasgow, who has patiently subjected himself to my constant questions concerning the singer discographies; and then, in alphabetical order:

Keith Bennett, Woodbridge
Ray Burford, London
Ed Chichura, San Francisco
Simon Clark, Bedford
Mathias Erhard, Berlin
Henry Fogel, Chicago
Ray and Marleen Hall, London
Pam Hancox, London
Alfred Kaine, Hamburg
Susan Kessler, London
David Lampon, Marlpool
Luis Luna, Berlin
Geoffrey Parsons, London
Clive Pearsall, Malta
Mario Vicentini, Varese

Caricatures are by R.P. Bauer, taken from the book "Im Konzertsaal karikiert" (Langen-Müller, Munich 1959).

Vocal works are listed in most cases in their original language (exceptions being made for Slav and Scandinavian languages), with an indication if the work is sung in a language other than the original.

A list of abbreviations used is to be found overleaf.

John Hunt

Abbreviations

Bamberg SO	Bamberg Symphony Orchestra
Bavarian RO	Bavarian Radio Symphony Orchestra
BBCSO	BBC Symphony Orchestra (London)
BPO	Berlin Philharmonic Orchestra
Berlin RO	Berlin Radio Orchestra (sometimes confused with RIAS Orchestra)
Berlin SO	Berlin Symphony Orchestra
Boston SO	Boston Symphony Orchestra
Canadian RO	Canadian Radio Orchestra (Toronto)
CSO	Chicago Symphony Orchestra
Detroit SO	Detroit Symphony Orchestra
LAPO	Los Angeles Philharmonic Orchestra
Leipzig GO	Leipzig Gewandhaus Orchestra
LPO	London Philharmonic Orchestra
LSO	London Symphony Orchestra
NBC	NBC Symphony Orchestra (New York)
NDR Orchestra	North German Radio Orchestra (Hamburg)
NYPO	New York Philharmonic Orchestra/Philharmonic Symphony Orchestra
VPO	Vienna Philharmonic Orchestra/Vienna State Opera Orchestra
VSO	Vienna Symphony Orchestra
WDR Orchestra	West German Radio Orchestra (Cologne)
np	Not published (recordings which were allocated a catalogue number but subsequently not released)

3 Italian Conductors

Toscanini
Cantelli
Giulini

Discographies
compiled by John Hunt

John Hunt

John Hunt was born in Windsor and graduated from University College London in German Langauage and Literature. He has worked in personnel administration, classical record retailing and bibliographic research. Now on the lecture panel of the Federation of Recorded Music Societies, he has presented programmes for music clubs all over the UK and in Ireland; his subjects include the Salzburg Summer and Easter Festivals, which he visited regularly for over 30 years, and the careers of a number of prominent conductors and singers.

John Hunt is also Chairman of the Wilhelm Furtwängler Society UK, and his previously published discographies include Furtwängler (already in its 3rd edition), Karajan and, in conjunction with Stephen J. Pettitt, the complete recordings of the Philharmonia Orchestra.

Why 3 Italian conductors ?

My previous discographical efforts having been concentrated on artists from the northern half of Europe, I felt that it was time to look at some interpreters from warmer climes, whose work has been preserved with reasonable success, both in action in the concert hall and in the more analytical atmosphere of the studio.

The survey comprises the man who must be regarded as Italy's foremost interpretive artist, then the protégé who may well have developed into his equal - and also into a serious rival to Herbert von Karajan - if fate had not intervened; and, to complete the trio, a modern conductor who also has his roots in Italy's great past but who is probably less well appreciated than he deserves to be because of his own reticence in the face of the publicity machines.

The recordings in these 3 discographies cover the entire 70-year period during which serious attempts have been made to record important conductors in charge of a symphony orchestra: from Toscanini's first sessions whilst visiting the USA in 1920-21 to Giulini's Vienna Philharmonic sessions in April 1991. Only the handful of recordings by Artur Nikisch pre-date this period, otherwise a reduced orchestra was only needed before the primitive recording horn in order to accompany a singer.

Arturo Toscanini
Discography

Compiled by John Hunt
1991

Recording Toscanini

Arturo Toscanini began his recording career, 34 years after his début as a conductor, on 17 December 1920. On that day he recorded the third movement of the Mozart Symphony No 39; the fourth movement was to follow on 20 December. He conducted the La Scala Orchestra, with which he was on an American tour, and the recordings were made in Camden, New Jersey, for the Victor Talking Machine Company. The sessions, ending in March 1921, also yielded the Donizetti "Don Pasquale" Overture, the fourth movements of Beethoven Symphonies 1 and 5, Scherzo and Wedding March from Mendelssohn "A Midsummer Night's Dream" and pieces by Berlioz, Bizet, Massenet, Wolf-Ferrari, Galilei and Pizetti.

The last recording, some 34 years later, was made on 5 June 1954. This was to re-record certain sections of "Aida" for insertion into the 1949 broadcast recording of the complete opera, making it suitable for commercial release. The recently disbanded NBC Symphony Orchestra was reassembled for this last session and it was also to be the last time that Toscanini conducted an orchestra.

The 1920-21 series of La Scala Orchestra recordings are, in my opinion, unjustly neglected, for they preserve some of the best orchestral sound made by the acoustic process. There have been two reissues of these records so far, both on LP. RCA (Japan) AT 1076 is best, with more immediate sound and close to the originals, and without the added echo of RCA VL 46024.

Toscanini's next recording was not to be until February 1926, and by then electrical recording was in its infancy. In this, his one and only excursion from the RCA Victor/HMV fold, he recorded with the Philharmonic Symphony Orchestra of New York the Nocturne and Scherzo from "A Midsummer Night's Dream". Although he allowed its release Toscanini was, it seems, unhappy with this record, and 3 years were to pass before the Victor Company could lure him back to face the recording microphone.

Thus began a famous, if not to say historic, series of recordings. From 1929 until 1936 he recorded for Victor with the Philharmonic Symphony Orchestra in Carnegie Hall, New York, and from 1937 to 1939 for HMV with the BBC Symphony Orchestra in Queen's Hall, London. Many of these were considered to be demonstration discs in their day and still sound, when properly reproduced, remarkably fine.

This is, sadly, not the case with the early recordings Toscanini made with the NBC Symphony Orchestra in Studio 8-H, Radio City, New York. For all the sonic splendours of the 1929-36 records, it appears that he wanted us to hear the music as it sounded to him on the podium. To this end the engineers were required to record with microphones close up to the orchestra. This can be observed on the newly-released video/laserdisc recordings of some NBC Studio 8-H concerts, where microphones are clearly seen suspended over the Maestro's head. This technique leaves the recordings short on ambience or on the sound of the hall itself, but gives us great clarity. Everything can be clearly heard, unclouded by excessive reverberation. This is above all, I am sure, how Toscanini wished his recordings to sound. However, it was not all the engineers' doing: I am told by those who attended his concerts that clarity was one of the hallmarks of a Toscanini performance.

The same, or very similar, microphone technique was, I am convinced, used for both broadcast concerts and recording sessions. Extra microphones were, however, sometimes used and this can be seen on RCA video 790.355. This is the televsion concert from Carnegie Hall on 3 November 1951, with the NBC Symphony playing Weber's "Euryanthe" Overture and Brahms Symphony No 1. An extra microphone on a tall stand is placed in front of the woodwind, for extra clarity no doubt.

Toscanini began conducting the NBC Symphony in December 1937, and by around 1950 some very good recordings were being made, even in Studio 8-H. The Dukas "Sorcerer's Apprentice" recorded there on 19 March 1950 is a good example: heard on RCA compact disc RD 86205 it sounds quite splendid, the sound having tremendous impact and, of course, great clarity. Matters were improved even further when Toscanini and his NBC Symphony moved to Carnegie Hall for recording sessions.

This kind of recorded sound is, however, not to everyone's taste and it is unfortunate that some reject Toscanini recordings on their recorded sound alone. On any commercial recording I have heard the ear soon and readily adjusts and hears through the sound, as such, to the music itself. But many attempts have been made, doubtless in order to placate the sonically perturbed, to "improve" the sound. Filtering, artificial echo and electronic stereo techniques have all been tried. Not all these attempts have, in my view, been entirely unsuccessful. Try, if you can, for example RCA Victor LP LM 1833 with Debussy "La Mer" and "Ibéria". The record sleeve and label bear the legend "enhanced sound" - at least they are honest about it - but fear not, it has been done in a very subtle way, giving the effect of more space around the orchestra. "Enhanced sound" maybe, but this is not the sound Toscanini approved for release. For that we must go back to the original release of any particular recording.

It is therefore very gratifying that RCA has chosen Arthur Fierro, who worked closely with Walter Toscanini, the Maestro's son, on the preservation of his father's recordings, to supervise the remastering of most of the recordings for compact disc release. Mr Fierro has chosen, most wisely, to go right back - wherever possible - to the original session tapes or broadcast transcriptions, avoiding all the many attempted "improvements" en route. So that, in virtually all cases, we can hear the sound that Toscanini approved. Just in time, it seems, for some of the tapes, now over 40 years old, are showing signs of deterioration. Due to Mr Fierro's stirling efforts the recordings are now preserved in digital format but, even more importantly, as close as possible to the originals. Sadly this is not always the case elsewhere: historical recordings are being reissued with imagined improvements and ignoring the original sound. After the original has deteriorated beyond redemption all that will be left is an "improved" version on which to make further "improvements", the original lost forever.

Mr Fierro has, nevertheless, sometimes deviated from the "sound as Toscanini approved it" rule. Most splendidly in the CD release of the Beethoven Leonore No 3 Overture from the NBC Symphony concert, broadcast from Studio 8-H on 4 November 1939. The original HMV 78 release - DB 5703-4, for some reason only issued in UK - was, to put it mildly, brash and noisy. Another source (probably Voice of America transcription discs) was found for its issue on CD, RCA GD 60255. The result is quite remarkable. The basic sound is the same, but all the noise and distortion has gone. This is, in my opinion, one of the truly great Toscanini recordings and we hear it now as if new minted. I am certain that the Maestro would have approved.

Toscanini was incredibly self-critical. During the few years left to him in retirement he spent many hours listening, with his son Walter, to recordings of his broadcast concerts. The aim was to see how many, with Toscanini's approval, were suitable for commercial release. Only a small amount of his vast output was deemed fit. Previously unissued recording sessions were also reviewed. Out of this Toscanini gave approval for release of some of the famous recordings he made with the Philadelphia Orchestra in 1941 and 1942. The Schubert 9th Symphony and Strauss' Death and Transfiguration were approved but sadly, due to technical reasons, were not issued until after Toscanini's death. The entire series was eventually released some years later.

Now some do not agree with the Maestro's view and countless "pirate" issues of his broadcasts and performances have been issued for sale. I, like many, am in two minds about this vexed question. To publish these recordings is mostly illegal, and Toscanini did not approve them on artistic grounds anyway. They are, in the main, badly done, with poor sound from dubious sources. But it is fascinating to hear a great conductor at work, as it were, warts and all.

The whole "pirate" problem could, I suppose, be solved overnight if RCA chose to release this material itself. It would at least be done professionally. Yet they are no doubt bound to issue only recordings Toscanini approved for them to release. Thank goodness the rule was recently broken when, with the approval of the Toscanini family, the television concerts 1948-52 were released on video and laserdisc. Perhaps in the future they will allow further material, of obvious artistic merit, to be heard.

The discography will, therefore, be a most valuable guide to those wishing to learn of currently available and out-of-print recordings by one of the gramophone's most distinguished sons, Arturo Toscanini.

Clive Pearsall
Malta, March 1991

Compiler's note

For the Toscanini discography precise recording dates within a month are given, as commercial versions and broadcasts of the same work exist, often recorded only a few days apart. LPs issued with the prefix AT include the internationally-released Toscanini Edition (3-digit numbers) and the high-quality Japanese edition (4-digit numbers); LPs with prefix ATS cover the unofficial American Toscanini Society issues (4-digit numbers) and the limited private edition published in UK in the 1980s by Michael G. Thomas (3-digit numbers); in each case the 3- and 4-digit number is entered on the same line of the listing. LPs with prefix VL include the last LP series issued in UK as well as various separate versions published only in Italy under licence from RCA.

All the operas which Toscanini played at the 1937 Salzburg Festival (Fidelio, Falstaff, Zauberflöte and Meistersinger) were relayed by Austrian Radio and recorded on a machine known as the Selenophone, which cut a vertical recording into 8mm acetate film. According to Toscanini's biographer Harvey Sachs, NBC requested copies of these recordings, but through a clerical error Fidelio was omitted from the list and the omission was not noticed for several years, by which time the originals were probably destroyed or lost. As there has been confusion over which performance of each opera was broadcast, various pirate issues of the Selenophone tapes have had conflicting dates; and in the case of Fidelio, all we have is the incomplete Act I from a previous broadcast in 1936.

V-Discs were 12-inch 78rpm records pressed on vinylite for distribution to American forces at home and abroad between 1944 and 1949. The Toscanini items were taken from NBC acetates; they were not available commercially and the masters were eventually destroyed; they also appear to have been haphazardly dated in some cases, with the same number often allocated to more than one item. AFRS (Armed Forces Radio Service) material was, on the other hand, not available to individual service personnel but was distributed to forces radio stations on 16-inch 33 1/3 rpm discs for re-broadcast at a later date.

THE WHITE HOUSE
WASHINGTON

April 30, 1936

My dear Signor Toscanini:

    I have just read with regret that last evening in New York you brought to a close your career as head of the New York Philharmonic Orchestra. May I add my word of appreciation for all that you have done for music during your stay among us. I wish you Godspeed as you leave our shores.

Very sincerely yours,

Franklin D Roosevelt

Signor Arturo Toscanini,
Astor Hotel,
New York, N. Y.

Atterberg

Symphony No 6

New York 21 November 1943	NBC	LP: Toscanini Society ATS 1005-9 CD: Dell' Arte DA 9019

Bach

Brandenburg Concerto No 2

New York 30 January 1936	NYPO	LP: Toscanini Society ATS 104
New York 29 October 1938	NBC	45: Musicians' Foundation No 3 LP: Toscanini Society ATS 1040-3 LP: Movimento Musica 01.025

Orchestral Suite No 3

New York 22 November 1947	NBC	LP: Toscanini Society ATS 1040-3

Air (Orchestral Suite No 3)

New York 8 April 1946	NBC	78: HMV DB 21235 78: RCA Victor M 1080/DM 1080 45: RCA Victor WDM 1080 LP: RCA Victor LM 7032 LP: RCA RB 6606 LP: RCA AT 1070 CD: RCA GD 60308

Passacaglia and Fugue in C minor (arr. Respighi)

New York 14 October 1939	NBC	LP: Music and Arts ATRA 3011
New York 22 November 1947	NBC	45: Musicians' Foundation No 3 LP: Toscanini Society ATS 1040-3 LP: Movimento Musica 01.025 CD: Memories HR 4168

Toccata and Fugue in D minor (arr. Wood)

New York 23 February 1936	NYPO	LP: Toscanini Society ATS 104

Saint Matthew Passion: Excerpt (Final Chorus)

New York 1 April 1945	NBC NBC Chorus	LP: Toscanini Society ATS 1040-3

Barber

Adagio for strings

New York 5 November 1938 World premiere	NBC	LP: Toscanini Society ATS 1093-6 np LP: Toscanini Society ATS 101
New York 13 December 1941	NBC	CD: Memories HR 4199
New York 19 March 1942	NBC	78: RCA Victor 11-8287 78: HMV DB 6180 LP: RCA Victor LM 7032 LP: RCA RB 6607 LP: RCA AT 1069

Essay for orchestra

New York 5 November 1938	NBC	LP: Toscanini Society ATS 101 CD: Memories HR 4199
New York 24 January 1942	NBC	LP: Toscanini Society ATS 1093-6 np

Bazzini

Saul, Overture

New York 14 January 1939	NBC	LP: Toscanini Society ATS 1070 np LP: Toscanini Society ATS 102

Beethoven

Symphony No 1

Camden NJ 30 March 1921 <u>Fourth movement only</u>	La Scala Orchestra	78: Victor Talking Machine VTM 74690/6300 78: HMV DB 417 LP: RCA AT 1076 LP: RCA VL 46024
New York 23 February 1936	NYPO	LP: Toscanini Society ATS 1016-24
London 25 October 1937	BBCSO	78: HMV DB 3537-40/8520-3 auto 78: RCA Victor M 507/DM 507 45: RCA Victor WCT 49 LP: RCA Victor LCT 1023 LP: World Records SH 134 LP: Seraphim IC 6015 LP: EMI EX 29 09303/29 12253 <u>Third movement</u> 78: HMV DB 3350
New York 28 October 1939	NBC	LP: Toscanini Society ATS 1113 LP: Music and Arts ATRA 3011 CD: Relief CR 1861 CD: Nuova Era 2243-8 CD: Palette PAL 1061
Lucerne 7 July 1946	La Scala Orchestra	LP: Relief RL 811 CD: Palette PAL 1067
New York 21 December 1951	NBC	45: RCA Victor WDM 6009 LP: RCA Victor LM 6009/6900/6901 LP: HMV ALP 1040 LP: RCA RB 16101 LP: RCA Victor VIC 8000 LP: RCA VIC 1654 LP: RCA VCM 1 LP: RCA AT 117/600/1008 LP: RCA VL 46020/45822 CD: RCA RD 87197 CD: RCA GD 60252/60324

Symphony No 2

New York 4 November 1939	NBC	LP: Toscanini Society ATS 1113 LP: Music and Arts ATRA 3011 CD: Nuova Era 2243-8 CD: Melodram MEL 28031 CD: Relief CR 1871 CD: Palette PAL 1066
New York 3 December 1944	NBC	LP: Toscanini Society ATS 1048-54
New York 18 December 1944	NBC	RCA unpublished
New York 7 November 1949 (First movement) & 5 October 1951	NBC	45: RCA Victor WDM 1723 LP: RCA Victor LM 1723/6900/6901 LP: HMV ALP 1145 LP: RCA RB 16101 LP: RCA Victor 8000 LP: RCA VCM 1 LP: RCA VIC 1654 LP: RCA AT 117/600/1008 LP: RCA VL 46020/45822 CD: RCA (Japan) R32C-1015 CD: RCA RD 87198 CD: RCA GD 60253/60324

Symphony No 3 "Eroica"

New York 3 December 1938	NBC	LP: Toscanini Society ATS 1016-24 CD: Music and Arts ATRA 264
New York 28 October 1939	NBC	78: HMV DB 5946-52/8904-10 auto 78: RCA Victor M 765 LP: Toscanini Society ATS 1114 LP: RCA AT 1078 LP: Franklin Mint CD: Nuova Era 2243-8
New York 5 November 1944	NBC	LP: Toscanini Society ATS 120
New York 28 November and 5 December 1949	NBC	78: RCA Victor M 1375 45: RCA Victor WDM 1375 LP: RCA Victor LM 1042/6900/6901 LP: HMV ALP 1008 LP: RCA RB 16102 LP: RCA AT 1009 CD: RCA RD 87197 CD: RCA GD 60252/60328
New York 6 December 1953	NBC	LP: RCA Victor LM 2387 LP: RCA Victor 8000 LP: RCA VIC 1655 LP: RCA VCM 1 LP: RCA AT 121/600/1010 LP: RCA VL 46020/45808 CD: RCA (Japan) RCCD 1002

Symphony No 4

New York   NYPO   LP: Toscanini Society ATS 1016
2 February 1936   LP: Relief RL 821
                                    CD: Palette PAL 1063

London   BBCSO   78: HMV DB 3896-99/8733-6 auto
1 June 1939   78: RCA Victor M 676
                                    LP: HMV ALP 1598
                                    LP: World Records SH 134
                                    LP: Seraphim IC 6015
                                    LP: EMI EX 29 09303/29 12253

New York   NBC   LP: Toscanini Society ATS 1115
4 November 1939   LP: Music and Arts ATRA 3011
                                    CD: Relief CR 1861
                                    CD: Nuova Era 2243-8
                                    CD: Palette PAL 1061

New York   NBC   45: RCA Victor WDM 1723
3 February 1951   LP: RCA Victor LM 1723/6900/6901
                                    LP: HMV ALP 1145
                                    LP: RCA RB 16103
                                    LP: RCA Victor 8000
                                    LP: RCA VIC 1656
                                    LP: RCA VCM 1
                                    LP: RCA AT 128/600/1011
                                    LP: RCA VL 46020/45818
                                    CD: RCA (Japan) R32C-1016
                                    CD: RCA GD 60254/60324

Symphony No 5

Camden NJ 23 December 1920 Fourth movement only	La Scala Orchestra	78: Victor Talking Machine 74769-70/6304 78: HMV DB 420 LP: RCA AT 1076 LP: RCA VL 46024
New York 4 March 1931	NYPO	RCA unpublished
New York 9 April 1933	NYPO	LP: Toscanini Society ATS 1016-24 LP: Relief RL 821 LP: Music and Arts ATRA 3010 CD: Palette PAL 1063 CD: Pearl GEMMCDS 9373
New York 27 February and 1 & 29 March 1939	NBC	78: HMV DB 3822-5/8691-4 auto 78: RCA Victor M 640 45: RCA Victor WCT 67 LP: RCA Victor LCT 1041 LP: RCA AT 1015 LP: Franklin Mint
New York 11 November 1939	NBC	LP: Toscanini Society ATS 1115 CD: Nuova Era 2243-8 CD: Palette PAL 1066 CD: Relief CR 1871
New York 22 March 1952	NBC	45: RCA Victor WDM 1757 LP: RCA Victor LM 1757/6900/6901 LP: HMV ALP 1108 LP: RCA RB 16103 LP: RCA Victor 8000 LP: RCA VIC 1648 LP: RCA AT 128/600/1011 LP: RCA VL 46020/45818 CD: RCA (Japan) RCCD 1003 LP: RCA RD 85753 CD: RCA GD 60255/60324 VHS Video: RCA 790.357

Symphony No 6 "Pastoral"

London 21 and 22 October 1937	BBCSO	78: HMV DB 3333-7/8369-73 auto 78: RCA Victor M 417/DM 417 45: RCA Victor WCT 70 LP: RCA Victor LCT 1042 LP: HMV ALP 1664 LP: Seraphim IC 6015 LP: World Records SH 112 LP: BBC Records BBC 4001 LP: EMI EX 29 09303/29 12253 CD: EMI (Italy) CDC 880454
New York 8 January 1938	NBC	LP: Toscanini Society ATS 1048-54
New York 11 November 1939	NBC	LP: Toscanini Society ATS 1116 CD: Nuova Era 2243-8
New York 12 January 1952	NBC	Reference Recording unpublished
New York 14 January 1952	NBC	45: RCA Victor WDM 1755 LP: RCA Victor LM 1755/6900/6901 LP: HMV ALP 1129 LP: RCA RB 16104 LP: RCA Victor 8000 LP: RCA VIC 1657 LP: RCA VCM 2 LP: RCA AT 133/600/1012 LP: RCA VL 46020/45801 CD: RCA (Japan) RCCD 1004 CD: RCA GD 60254/60324

Symphony No 7

London 14 June 1935	BBCSO		LP: EMI EX 29 09303/29 12253

New York   NYPO   78: HMV DB 2986-90/8190-4 auto
9 & 10 April 1936   78: RCA Victor M 317
                                  45: RCA Victor WCT 17
                                  LP: RCA Victor LCT 1013
                                  LP: RCA Camden CAL 352/CDM 1028
                                  LP: RCA VIC 1502
                                  LP: RCA AT 1072
                                  LP: Franklin Mint
                                  CD: Pearl GEMMCDS 9373
                                  CD: RCA GD 60329

New York   NBC   LP: Toscanini Society ATS 1117
18 November 1939   CD: Nuova Era 2243-8
                                  CD: Relief CR 1885

New York   NBC   AFRS: 85
19 November 1944

New York   NBC   RCA unpublished
19 July 1945

New York   NBC   LP: Toscanini Society ATS 1048-54
25 October 1947

New York   NBC   RCA unpublished
27 October 1947

New York   NBC   45: RCA Victor WDM 1756
9 November 1951   LP: RCA Victor LM 1756/6900/6901
                                  LP: HMV ALP 1119
                                  LP: RCA RB 16105
                                  LP: RCA Victor 8000
                                  LP: RCA VIC 1658
                                  LP: RCA VCM 2
                                  LP: RCA AT 140/600/1013
                                  LP: RCA VL 46020/45813
                                  CD: RCA (Japan) R32C-1017
                                  CD: RCA RD 87198
                                  CD: RCA GD 60253/60324
                                  CD: Melodram MEL 28031
                                  CD: Hunt CDLSMH 34007

Symphony No 8

New York 8 March 1936	NYPO	LP: Toscanini Society ATS 1019-20
New York 17 April 1939	NBC	78: HMV DB 6160-2/8957-9 auto 78: RCA Victor M 908 /DM 908 LP: RCA AT 1079
New York 25 November 1939	NBC	LP: Toscanini Society ATS 1118 CD: Nuova Era 2243-8
New York 8 November 1952	NBC	CD: Hunt CDLSMH 34007
New York 10 November 1952	NBC	45: RCA Victor WDM 1757 LP: RCA Victor LM 1757/6900/6901 LP: HMV ALP 1108 LP: RCA RB 16106 LP: RCA Victor 8000 LP: RCA VIC 1656 LP: RCA VCM 2 LP: RCA AT 140/600/1013 LP: RCA VL 46020/45831 CD: RCA (Japan) R32C-1016 CD: RCA GD 60255/60324

Symphony No 9 "Choral"

New York 8 March 1936	NYPO Schola Cantorum Tentoni, Bampton, Kullmann, Pinza	LP: Toscanini Society ATS 1019-20
New York 6 February 1938	NBC Schola Cantorum Bovy, Thorborg, Peerce, Pinza	LP: Music and Arts ATRA 3007 CD: Music and Arts ATRA 3007
New York 2 December 1939	NBC Westminster Choir Novotna, Thorborg, Peerce, Moscona	LP: Toscanini Society ATS 1118-9 CD: Nuova Era 2243-8 CD: Legato Classics LCD 136 CD: Relief CR 1891 Legato issue incorrectly dated 1944
Buenos Aires 24 July 1941	Teatro Colon Chorus & Orchestra Hedwig, Kindermann, Maison, Kipnis	LP: Toscanini Society ATS 118-9
New York 3 April 1948	NBC Collegiate Chorale McKnight, Hobson, Dillon, Scott	LP: Toscanini Society ATS 1048-54 VHS Video: RCA 790.347
New York 31 March and 1 April 1952	NBC Shaw Chorale Farrell, Merriman, Peerce, Scott	45: RCA Victor WDM 6009 LP: RCA Victor LM 6009/6900/6901 LP: HMV ALP 1039-40 LP: RCA RB 16106-7 LP: RCA Victor 8000 LP: RCA VIC 1607 LP: RCA VCM 2 LP: RCA AT 143/600/1014 LP: RCA VL 46020/45831-2 LP: Franklin Mint CD: RCA (Japan) RCCD 1005 CD: RCA RD 85936 CD: RCA GD 60256/60324 Fourth movement only 45: RCA Victor ERB 7046 LP: RCA Victor LRM 7046 Rehearsal extracts LP: Musicians' Foundation No 1 LP: CLS MDRL 12821

Missa Solemnis

New York 28 April 1935	NYPO Schola Cantorum Rethberg, Telva, Martinelli, Pinza	LP: Toscanini Society ATS 1048-54 LP: GRP Records GRP 1001 LP: HRE Records HRE 259
New York 28 December 1940	NBC Westminster Choir Milanov, Castagna, Björling, Kipnis	LP: Toscanini Society ATS 1023-4 LP: Melodram MEL 006 CD: Music and Arts ATRA 259 CD: Melodram MEL 38006 CD: Palette PAL 3004-6 CD: AS-Disc AS 307 CD: Greenline 3CLC 4003
New York 30 & 31 March and 2 April 1953	NBC Shaw Chorale Marshall, Merriman, Conley, Hines	45: RCA Victor ERG 6013 LP: RCA Victor LM 6013 LP: HMV ALP 1182-3 LP: RCA RB 16133-4 LP: RCA AT 200 LP: RCA VCM 9 LP: RCA AT 200/1020-1 CD: RCA GD 60272

Choral Fantasia

New York 2 December 1939	NBC Westminster Choir Dorfman	LP: Toscanini Society ATS 1016-24 LP: Music and Arts ATRA 3010 CD: Music and Arts ATRA 259 CD: Nuova Era 2243-8 CD: Melodram MEL 28031

Violin Concerto

New York 11 March 1940	NBC Heifetz	78: HMV DB 5724-8 78: RCA Victor M 705/DM 705 45: RCA Victor WCT 14 LP: RCA Victor LCT 1010 LP: RCA DPS 2006 LP: RCA AT 1019 LP: Franklin Mint CD: RCA RD 85756 CD: RCA GD 60261 Third movement 78: RCA VIctor M 1064

Triple Concerto

New York 16 April 1933 Third movement only	NYPO Carreras, Piastro, Wallenstein	LP: Toscanini Society ATS 1048-54
New York 1 May 1942	NYPO Dorfman, Piastro, Schuster	LP: Toscanini Society ATS 1016-24

Piano Concerto No 1

New York 9 August 1945	NBC Dorfman	78: RCA Victor M 1036/DM 1036 45: RCA Victor WDM 1036 LP: RCA Victor LM 1039 LP: RCA VIC 1521 LP: RCA AT 106/1015

Piano Concerto No 3

New York 29 August 1944	NBC Rubinstein	78: RCA Victor M 1016/DM 1016 45: RCA Victor WCT 13 LP: RCA Victor LCT 1009 LP: RCA RL 42860 LP: RCA AT 1016 LP: Franklin Mint CD: RCA RD 85756 CD: RCA GD 60261
New York 24 November 1946	NBC Hess	LP: Toscanini Society ATS 1016-24 CD: Melodram MEL 28031

Piano Concerto No 4

New York 23 February 1936	NYPO Serkin	LP: Toscanini Society ATS 1048-54
New York 26 November 1944	NBC Serkin	LP: RCA Victor LM 2797 LP: RCA RB 6628 LP: RCA AT 106

Septet

New York 18 November 1939	NBC	LP: Toscanini Society ATS 1112 CD: Memories CR 1885
New York 26 November 1951	NBC	45: RCA Victor WDM 1745 LP: RCA Victor LM 1745 LP: HMV ALP 1106 LP: RCA Victor 8000 LP: RCA VCM 1 LP: RCA AT 144/600/1018 CD: RCA (Japan) R32C-1017

Septet: Excerpts (movements 1, 4 and 6)

New York 3 December 1944	NBC	LP: Toscanini Society ATS 1048-54

Adagio and Scherzo (String Quartet No 16)

New York 1 January 1938	NBC	CD: Music and Arts ATRA 264 CD: Melodram MEL 28031
New York 8 March 1938	NBC	78: RCA Victor M 590 78: HMV DB 3904 (Adagio) 78: HMV DB 3858 (Scherzo) 45: RCA Victor WCT 65 LP: RCA Victor LCT 1041 LP: RCA Victor 8000 LP: RCA VCM 2 LP: RCA AT 144/600/1018
New York 25 November 1939	NBC	LP: Toscanini Society ATS 1112
New York 25 October 1947	NBC	LP: Toscanini Society ATS 1048-54

Cavatina (String Quartet No 13)

New York 26 November 1944	NBC	LP: Toscanini Society ATS 1016-24

Fugue (String Quartet No 9)

New York 26 November 1944	NBC	LP: Toscanini Society ATS 1016-24

Fidelio

Salzburg 31 August 1935 <u>Incomplete</u> <u>recording of Act 1</u> <u>only</u>	VPO Vienna Opera Chorus Lehmann, Helletsgruber, Gallos, Jerger, Baumann	LP: Unique Opera Recordings UORC 218
New York 10 & 17 December 1944 and 14 June 1945	NBC NBC Chorus Bampton, Steber, Peerce, Laderoute, Belarsky, Janssen, Moscona	LP: RCA Victor LM 6025 LP: HMV ALP 1304-5 LP: RCA AT 204 LP: RCA VCM 9 LP: RCA AT 204/1099-1100 Excerpts LP: Franklin Mint Overture only LP: RCA AT 136 LP: RCA VL 46020/45827 CD: RCA GD 60273

Fidelio, Overture

New York 28 October 1939	NBC	LP: Toscanini Society ATS 1111 LP: Music and Arts ATRA 3011 CD: Relief CR 1861 CD: Nuova Era 2243-8

Consecration of the House, Overture

New York 16 March 1947	NBC	CD: Music and Arts ATRA 264 CD: Melodram MEL 28031
New York 25 October 1947	NBC	LP: Toscanini Society ATS 1048-54
New York 16 December 1947	NBC	78: HMV DB 21234-5 78: RCA Victor M 1287/DM 1287 45: RCA Victor WDM 1287 LP: RCA Victor LM 6/9022 LP: RCA Victor 8000 LP: RCA VCM 1 LP: RCA AT 136/1019 LP: RCA VL 46020/45827
New York 19 March 1939	NBC	LP: Music and Arts ATRA 3010

Coriolan, Overture

New York 2 February 1936	NYPO	LP: Toscanini Society ATS 1019-20
London 1 June 1939	BBCSO	EMI unpublished
New York 11 November 1939	NBC	LP: Toscanini Society ATS 1111 CD: Nuova Era 2243-8
New York 26 November 1944	NBC	CD: Melodram MEL 28031 <u>Rehearsal extract</u> LP: Morgan MOR 001
New York 1 June 1945	NBC	78: RCA Victor 11-9023 45: RCA Victor ERA 91 LP: RCA Victor 8000 LP: RCA VCM 1 LP: RCA AT 136/1019 LP: RCA VL 46020/45827
New York 6 December 1953	NBC	LP: Toscanini Society ATS 1016-24 LP: Music and Arts ATRA 3007

Egmont, Overture

New York 18 November 1939	NBC	78: HMV DB 5705 LP: Music and Arts ATRA 3011 LP: Toscanini Society ATS 1111 LP: RCA AT 1079 LP: Music and Arts ATRA 3011 CD: Nuova Era 2243-8 CD: Relief CR 1885
Lucerne 7 July 1946	La Scala Orchestra	LP: Relief RL 811 CD: Palette PAL 1067
New York 19 January 1953	NBC	45: RCA Victor ERA 249 LP: RCA Victor LM 1834 LP: HMV ALP 1235 LP: RCA Victor 8000 LP: RCA VCM 1 LP: RCA VIC 1010/1658 LP: RCA AT 136/1019 LP: RCA VL 46020/45827 CD: RCA (Japan) RCCD 1002

Leonore No 1, Overture

London 1 June 1939	BBCSO	78: HMV DB 3846 78: RCA Victor 15945 45: RCA Victor WCT 65 LP: RCA Victor LCT 1041 LP: HMV ALP 1598 LP: EMI XLP 30079 LP: Seraphim 60150/IC 6015 LP: EMI EX 29 09303/29 12253
New York 25 November 1939	NBC	LP: Toscanini Society ATS 1111 CD: Nuova Era 2243-8
New York 29 October 1944	NBC	V-Disc: 392 LP: Toscanini Society ATS 118-9

Leonore No 2, Overture

New York 25 November 1939	NBC	78: HMV DA 1753-4 LP: Toscanini Society ATS 1111 LP: RCA AT 1079 LP: Franklin Mint CD: Nuova Era 2243-8
New York 19 November 1944	NBC	LP: Toscanini Society ATS 118-9
New York 12 January 1952	NBC	RCA unpublished
New York 7 March 1954	NBC	LP: Toscanini Society ATS 1016-24

Leonore No 3, Overture

New York 26 April 1936	NYPO	LP: Toscanini Society ATS 1090-1 np LP: Toscanini Society ATS 109-10
New York 4 November 1939	NBC	78: HMV DB 5703-4 LP: RCA VIC 1521 LP: Toscanini Society ATS 1111 LP: RCA Victor AT 1079 CD: Nuova Era 2243-8 CD: RCA RD 85753 CD: RCA GD 60255/60324
New York 19 December 1944	NBC	LP: Toscanini Society ATS 118-9 <u>Presumably intended for inclusion in the complete Fidelio recording, but not used</u>
New York 1 June 1945	NBC	78: RCA Victor SP 2/M 1098 45: RCA Victor WDM 1098/ERB 7023 LP: RCA Victor LRM 7023/LM 1043/LVT 1025 LP: RCA AT 136/1019 LP: RCA VL 46020/45827 CD: RCA (Japan) RCCD 1004 <u>Included in complete Fidelio recording</u>
New York 6 March 1948	NBC	AFRS: 105

La Damnation de Faust: Excerpt (Scene 7)

New York 16 February 1947	NBC NBC Chorus Harrell, Moscona	LP: Toscanini Society ATS 1055-9 LP: Music and Arts ATRA 3001

La Damnation de Faust: Excerpt (Hungarian March)

Camden NJ 24 December 1920	La Scala Orchestra	78: Victor Talking Machine VTM 76495/6300 78: HMV DB 417 LP: RCA AT 1076 LP: RCA VL 46024
New York 5 April 1941	NBC	CD: Music and Arts ATRA 614
New York 14 May 1941	NBC	RCA unpublished
New York 2 September 1945	NBC	LP: RCA Victor LM 6026 LP: RCA VIC 1321 LP: RCA AT 124/1036 LP: Franklin Mint CD: RCA (Japan) R32C-1105 CD: RCA RD 85755

La Damnation de Faust: Excerpt (Dance of the sylphs)

New York 16 February 1947	NBC	LP: Toscanini Society ATS 1055-9 LP: Music and Arts ATRA 3001
New York 16 December 1947	NBC	RCA unpublished

Les francs juges, Overture

New York 5 April 1941	NBC	LP: Toscanini Society ATS 1055-9 LP: Music and Arts ATRA 3001 CD: Music and Arts ATRA 614

Roman Carnival, Overture

New York 10 January 1953	NBC	CD: Curcio-Hunt CON 11
New York 19 January 1953	NBC	LP: RCA Victor LM 1834 LP: HMV ALP 1235 LP: RCA VIC 1010/1244 LP: RCA AT 100/1036 LP: Franklin Mint LP: RCA VL 45821 CD: RCA (Japan) R32C-1019/1105 CD: RCA RD 85755

Bizet

Carmen, Suite No 1

New York 19 September 1943	NBC	LP: Toscanini Society ATS 1082 np LP: Toscanini Society ATS 108 <u>Toreadors' March only</u> V-Disc: 53
New York 2 August 1952	NBC	LP: Dell' Arte DA 9010 CD: Memories HR 4185
New York 5 August 1952	NBC	45: RCA Victor ERB 7013 LP: RCA Victor LRM 7013/LM 6026 LP: HMV ALP 1417 LP: RCA VIC 1263 LP: RCA AT 109/124/1066 LP: Franklin Mint CD: RCA (Japan) R32C-1018 <u>R32C-1018 incorrectly dated 5 April 1952</u>

Carmen, Suite No 1: Excerpt (Act 4 Prelude)

Camden NJ 31 March 1921	La Scala Orchestra	78: Victor Talking Machine VTM 64999/839 78: HMV DA 374 LP: RCA AT 1076 LP: RCA VL 46024

L'Arlésienne, Suite No 1 and Pastorale (Suite No 2)

New York 19 September 1943	NBC	LP: Toscanini Society ATS 1082 np LP: Fonit Cetra ARK 11 LP: Music and Arts ATRA 3001 LP: Franklin Mint CD: Memories HR 4185 <u>Carillon only</u> V-Disc: 53

L'Arlésienne, Suite No 2: Excerpt (Farandole)

Camden NJ 11 March 1921	La Scala Orchestra	78: Victor Talking Machine 64986/839 78: HMV DA 374 LP: RCA AT 1076 LP: RCA VL 46024

The Fair Maid of Perth, Suite

New York 19 September 1943	NBC	LP: Toscanini Society ATS 1082 np LP: Fonit Cetra ARK 11 LP: Music and Arts ATRA 3001 CD: Memories HR 4185

Boccherini

Quartet in D op 6 no 1

New York 19 November 1949	NBC	LP: Toscanini Society ATS 104

Minuet in A (Quartet op 13 no 3)

New York 4 April 1943	NBC	LP: Toscanini Society ATS 1036 V-Disc: 226

Boito

Mefistofele, Prologue

New York 2 December 1945	NBC NBC Chorus Moscona	CD: Melodram MEL 18021
Milan 11 May 1946	La Scala Chorus & Orchestra Pasero	LP: HRE Records HRE 243 LP: Discoreale DR 10004-5 CD: Legato SRO 802
Milan 10 June 1948	La Scala Chorus and Orchestra Siepi	LP: Hope Records HOPE 222
New York 14 March 1954	NBC Shaw Chorale Columbus Boys Choir Moscona	LP: RCA Victor LM 1849 LP: HMV ALP 1363 LP: RCA VIC 1398 LP: RCA VCM 6 LP: RCA AT 131/1052 LP: Franklin Mint CD: RCA GD 60276

Mefistofele, Act 3

Milan 10 June 1948	La Scala Chorus and Orchestra Prandelli, G.Nelli, Siepi	LP: Hope Records HOPE 222 CD: Legato SRO 802

Nerone, Act 3 and Act 4, Scene 2

Milan 10 June 1948	La Scala Chorus and Orchestra Nelli, Simionato, Ticozzi, Guarrera, Siepi, Nessi	LP: Hope Records HOPE 222 CD: Legato SRO 802

NERONE
TRAGEDIA IN QUATTRO ATTI
PAROLE E MUSICA DI
ARRIGO BOITO
(Proprietà G. Ricordi & C.)

PRIMA ESECUZIONE
MILANO
TEATRO ALLA SCALA
1 Maggio 1924

PERSONAGGI

NERONE	Sig. Aureliano Pertile
SIMON MAGO	» Marcello Journet
FANUÊL	» Carlo Galeffi
ASTERIA	Sig.ª Rosa Raisa
RUBRIA	» Luisa Bertana
TIGELLINO	Sig. Ezio Pinza
GOBRIAS	» Giuseppe Nessi
DOSITÊO	» Carlo Walter
PÈRSIDE	Sig.ª Mita Vasari
CERINTO	» Maria Doria
IL TEMPIERE	Sig. Emilio Venturini
PRIMO VIANDANTE	» Alfredo Tedeschi
SECONDO VIANDANTE	» Giuseppe Menni
LO SCHIAVO AMMONITORE	» Aristide Baracchi
TERPNOS	» N. N.

MAESTRO DIRETTORE E CONCERTATORE
ARTURO TOSCANINI

Maestri sostituti: FERRUCCIO CALUSIO - PIETRO CLAUSETTI - EDUARDO FORNARINI
MARIO FRIGERIO - GUIDO RAGNI - EMILIO ROSSI - VITTORIO RUFFO - ANTONINO VOTTO
Maestro del Coro: VITTORE VENEZIANI - Maestro della Banda: ALESSIO MORRONE
Maestri suggeritori: ARMANDO PETRUCCI e EMILIO DELENDE
Coreografo: GIOVANNI PRATESI - Prima ballerina: CIA FORNAROLI
Direttore della messa in scena: GIOVACCHINO FORZANO
Direttore dell'allestimento scenico: CARAMBA

Scene, costumi ed attrezzi su bozzetti di LODOVICO POGLIAGHI
Scenografo: EDOARDO MARCHIORO colla collaborazione di ALESSANDRO MAGNONI

First performance of Boito's "Nerone" at La Scala Milan in 1924

Bolzoni

Minuet

New York NBC LP: Toscanini Society ATS 1098 np
20 June 1943

Al castello mediovale

New York NBC LP: Toscanini Society ATS 1099 np
18 July 1943 LP: Toscanini Society ATS 102

Borodin

Symphony No 2

New York NBC LP: Toscanini Society ATS 1060
26 February 1938 LP: Toscanini Society ATS 106

Bossi

Intermezzi Goldoniani

New York NBC LP: Toscanini Society ATS 1088 np
3 September 1944 LP: Toscanini Society ATS 102

Brahms

Symphony No 1

New York 25 December 1937	NBC	LP: Toscanini Society ATS 1079-80 np CD: Myto MCD 89009
New York 6 May 1940	NBC	LP: Melodram MEL 229 CD: Palette PAL 1062 CD: Melodram MEL 18011
New York 10 March 1941	NBC	78: HMV DB 6124-8/8939-43 auto 78: RCA Victor M 875 LP: RCA AT 1080
New York 3 November 1951	NBC	LP: GDS Records GDS 5001 CD: Nuova Era 013.6315 CD: Hunt CD 706 VHS Video: RCA 790.355
New York 6 November 1951	NBC	78: HMV DB 9768-72 45: RCA Victor WDM 1702 LP: RCA Victor LM 1702/6108 LP: HMV ALP 1012 LP: RCA RB 16097 LP: RCA Victor 6400 LP: RCA VCM 3 LP: RCA AT 115/305/1037 LP: RCA VL 45828 CD: RCA (Japan) RCCD 1006 CD: RCA GD 60257/60325
London 29 September 1952	Philharmonia	LP: Toscanini Society ATS 1030-3 LP: Turnabout THS 65027-30 LP: Fonit Cetra LO 511 LP: Fonit Cetra DOC 52 CD: Hunt CD 524 CD: Fonit Cetra CDE 1016

Symphony No 2

London 10 June 1938	BBCSO	EMI unpublished
New York 10 February 1951	NBC	LP: Toscanini Society ATS 1044 CD: Hunt CD 706
New York 11 February 1952	NBC	78: HMV DB 9773-6 45: RCA Victor WDM 1731 LP: RCA Victor LM 1731/6108 LP: HMV ALP 1013 LP: RCA RB 16098 LP: RCA Victor 6400 LP: RCA VCM 3 LP: RCA AT 132/305/1038 LP: RCA VL 45815 LP: Franklin Mint CD: RCA GD 60258/60325
London 29 September 1952	Philharmonia	LP: Toscanini Society ATS 1030-3 LP: Turnabout THS 65027-30 LP: Fonit Cetra LO 511 LP: Fonit Cetra DOC 52 LP: Longanesi Periodici GCL 65 CD: Hunt CD 524 CD: Fonit Cetra CDE 1040

Symphony No 3

Stockholm 3 December 1933 Excerpt from 2nd movement	Stockholm Philharmonic Orchestra	CD: BIS CD 421-4
New York 15 October 1938	NBC	LP: Toscanini Society ATS 114
London 1 October 1952	Philharmonia	LP: Toscanini Society ATS 1030-3 LP: Turnabout THS 65027-30 LP: Fonit Cetra LO 511 LP: Fonit Cetra DOC 52 CD: Hunt CD 524 CD: Fonit Cetra CDE 1040
New York 1 November 1952	NBC	LP: Toscanini Society ATS 1086 CD: Hunt CD 706 Hunt incorrectly dated February 1952
New York 4 November 1952	NBC	LP: RCA Victor LM 1836/6108 LP: HMV ALP 1166 LP: RCA RB 16099 LP: RCA Victor 6400 LP: RCA VCM 3 LP: RCA AT 137/305/1039 LP: RCA VL 45824 CD: RCA (Japan) R32C-1021 CD: RCA GD 60259/60325

Symphony No 4

London 3 & 5 June 1935	BBCSO		LP: Toscanini Society ATS 1005-9 CD: EMI CDH 769 7832
New York 27 November 1948	NBC		Unpublished
New York 3 December 1951	NBC		45: RCA Victor WDM 1713 LP: RCA Victor LM 1713/6108 LP: HMV ALP 1029 LP: RCA RB 16100 LP: RCA Victor 6400 LP: RCA VCM 3 LP: RCA AT 146/305/1040 LP: RCA VL 45805 LP: Franklin Mint CD: RCA GD 60260/60325
New York 29 December 1951	NBC		CD: Hunt CD 706 Incorrectly dated 22 December
London 1 October 1952	Philharmonia		LP: Toscanini Society ATS 1030-3 LP: Turnabout THS 65027-30 LP: Fonit Cetra LO 511 LP: Fonit Cetra DOC 52 CD: Hunt CD 524 CD: Fonit Cetra CDE 1031

Violin Concerto

New York 24 February 1935 First and second movements only	NYPO Heifetz		LP: Strad-Heifetz 1-2

Double Concerto

New York 13 November 1948	NBC Mischakoff, Miller		LP: RCA Victor LM 2178 LP: RCA RB 16066 LP: RCA AT 125/1042 CD: RCA GD 60259/60325 VHS Video: RCA 790.352

MONDAY, 29 SEPTEMBER 1952

Programme

Tragic Overture, Op. 81   *Brahms*

Symphony No. 1 in C minor, Op. 68   *Brahms*

Un poco sostenuto—Allegro
Andante sostenuto
Un poco allegretto e grazioso
Adagio più andante—Allegro non troppo

INTERVAL

Symphony No. 2 in D major, Op. 73   *Brahms*

Allegro non troppo
Adagio non troppo
Allegretto grazioso (quasi andantino)
Allegro con spirito

1952 concerts in London with the Philharmonia Orchestra

WEDNESDAY, 1 OCTOBER 1952

Programme

Variations on a Theme of Joseph Haydn, Op. 56a   *Brahms*

Symphony No. 3 in F major, Op. 90   *Brahms*

Allegro con brio
Andante
Poco allegretto
Allegro

INTERVAL

Symphony No. 4 in E minor, Op. 98   *Brahms*

Allegro non troppo
Andante moderato
Allegro giocoso
Allegro energico e passionato

NO SMOKING—NOT EVEN ABDULLA

Piano Concerto No 1

New York 17 March 1935	NYPO Horowitz	LP: Toscanini Society ATS 112-3

Piano Concerto No 2

New York 2 February 1936	NYPO Casadesus	LP: Toscanini Society ATS 112-3
New York 6 May 1940	NBC Horowitz	LP: Melodram MEL 229
New York 9 May 1940	NBC Horowitz	78: HMV DB 5861-6/8884-9 auto 78: RCA Victor M 740/DM 740 45: RCA Victor WCT 38 LP: RCA Victor LCT 1025 LP: RCA AT 103/1041 LP: RCA VH 019/400
New York 23 October 1948	NBC Horowitz	CD: Stradivarius 13595 CD: Classical Society CSCD 103 CD: Bellaphon Viola 689-24-002 Bellaphon Viola incorrectly dated May 1941

Ein deutsches Requiem

New York 24 January 1943	NBC Westminster Choir Della Chiesa, Janssen	LP: Toscanini Society ATS 1001-4 CD: Memories HR 4164

Gesang der Parzen

New York 27 November 1948	NBC Shaw Chorale	LP: RCA Victor LM 6711 LP: RCA AT 125/1043 CD: RCA GD 60260/60325

Liebeslieder-Walzer op 52

New York 13 November 1948	Chorus Balsam, Kahn	LP: RCA Victor LM 6711 LP: RCA AT 1043 CD: RCA GD 60260/60325 VHS Video: RCA 790.352

Serenade No 1: Excerpt (First movement: Allegro molto)

New York 17 January 1943	NBC	CD: Dell' Arte DA 9022
New York 23 October 1948	NBC	LP: Toscanini Society ATS 1083 np LP: Melodram MEL 229 CD: Melodram MEL 18011

Serenade No 1: Excerpt (Fourth movement: Menuetto I - Menuetto II)

New York 9 March 1947	NBC	LP: Toscanini Society ATS 1083 np
New York 6 November 1948	NBC	CD: Dell' Arte DA 9022

Serenade No 2

New York 27 December 1942	NBC	LP: RCA Victor LM 6711 LP: RCA AT 152/1042

Variations and Fugue on a theme of Handel (orch. Rubbra)

New York 7 January 1939	NBC	LP: Toscanini Society ATS 1001-4 CD: Dell' Arte DA 9020

Haydn Variations (Variations on St Antoni Chorale)

New York 10 April 1936	NYPO	78: HMV DB 3031-2 78: RCA Victor M 355 45: RCA Victor WCT 36 LP: RCA Victor LCT 1023 LP: RCA Camden CAL 326/CDM 1055 LP: RCA AT 1073 CD: Pearl GEMMCDS 9373 CD: RCA GD 60329
New York 26 February 1938	NBC	LP: Toscanini Society ATS 114
New York 17 November 1946	NBC	AFRS: 65
New York 4 February 1952	NBC	45: RCA Victor WDM 1725 LP: RCA Victor LM 1725 LP: HMV ALP 1204 LP: RCA RB 16092 LP: RCA VIC 1001/6400 LP: RCA VCM 3 LP: RCA AT 125/1040 LP: Franklin Mint CD: RCA (Japan) RCCD 1006 CD: RCA GD 60258/60325 CD: AS-Disc AS 113
London 1 October 1952	Philharmonia	LP: Toscanini Society ATS 1030-3 LP: Turnabout THS 65027-30 LP: Fonit Cetra LO 511 LP: Fonit Cetra DOC 52 LP: Longanesi Periodici GCL 65 CD: Hunt CD 524

Academic Festival Overture

New York   NBC   LP: RCA Victor LM 7026
6 November 1948   LP: RCA Victor 6400
                                            LP: RCA VCM 3
                                            LP: RCA AT 152
                                            LP: Franklin Mint
                                            CD: RCA (Japan) RCCD 1020
                                            CD: RCA GD 60257/60325

Tragic Overture

London   BBCSO   78: HMV DB 3349-50
25 October 1937   78: RCA Victor M 507
                                            45: RCA Victor WCT 49
                                            LP: EMI XLP 30079
                                            LP: Seraphim 60150
                                            CD: EMI CDH 769 7832

London   Philharmonia   LP: Toscanini Society ATS 1030-3
29 September 1952   LP: Turnabout THS 65027-30
                                            LP: Fonit Cetra LO 511
                                            LP: Fonit Cetra DOC 52
                                            CD: Hunt CD 524
                                            CD: Fonit Cetra CDE 1016

New York   NBC   LP: RCA Victor LM 7026
22 November 1953   LP: RCA Victor 6400
                                            LP: RCA VCM 3
                                            LP: RCA AT 125/1039
                                            LP: Franklin Mint
                                            CD: RCA (Japan) R32C-1022
                                            CD: RCA GD 60258/60325

Hungarian Dance No 1

New York   NBC   V-Disc: 593
10 January 1943

New York   NBC   LP: Toscanini Society ATS 107
13 November 1948   VHS Video: RCA 790.352

Hungarian Dances Nos 1, 17, 20 and 21

New York   NBC   LP: RCA Victor LM 1834
17 February 1953   LP: HMV ALP 1235
                                            LP: RCA VIC 1010/1321
                                            LP: RCA AT 118/1043
                                            LP: Franklin Mint
                                            CD: RCA (Japan) R32C-1019
                                            CD: RCA GD 60257/60325

Hungarian Dances Nos 17, 20 and 21

New York   NBC   LP: Toscanini Society ATS 1100 np
2 July 1944

Busoni

Berceuse élégiaque

New York 13 March 1948	NBC	LP: Toscanini Society ATS 1077 np
New York 10 December 1949	NBC	LP: Toscanini Society ATS 1039

Rondo arlecchinesco

New York 10 December 1949	NBC	LP: Toscanini Society ATS 1039

Castelnuovo-Tedesco

Fairy Tale, Overture

New York 25 November 1945	NBC	V-Disc: 607 LP: Toscanini Society ATS 1078 np LP: Toscanini Society ATS 103

The Taming of the Shrew, Overture

New York 30 March 1940	NBC	LP: Toscanini Society ATS 1078 np
New York 26 March 1944	NBC	LP: Toscanini Society ATS 103

Catalani

La Wally, Act 4 Prelude

New York 2 August 1952	NBC	LP: Dell' Arte DA 9010 CD: Memories HR 4198
New York 5 August 1952	NBC	45: RCA Victor ERA 101 LP: RCA Victor LM 6026 LP: RCA AT 116 LP: RCA VL 45829 LP: Franklin Mint

Dance of the water nymphs (Loreley)

New York 2 August 1952	NBC	LP: Dell' Arte DA 9010 CD: Memories HR 4198
New York 5 August 1952	NBC	45: RCA Victor ERA 101 LP: RCA Victor LM 6026 LP: RCA VIC 1263 LP: RCA AT 109 LP: RCA VL 46017/45829 LP: Franklin Mint

Cherubini

Requiem in C minor

New York 18 February 1950	NBC Shaw Chorale	LP: RCA Victor LM 2000 LP: HMV ALP 1412 LP: RCA VCM 10 LP: RCA AT 147/1029 CD: RCA GD 60272 CD: Memories HR 4186

Symphony in D

New York 10 March 1952	NBC	45: RCA Victor WDM 1745 LP: RCA Victor LM 1745 LP: HMV ALP 1106 LP: RCA AT 135/1030 LP: Franklin Mint Rehearsal extract LP: CLS MDRL 12821

Scherzo (String Quartet No 1)

New York 4 April 1943	NBC	LP: Toscanini Society ATS 1036

Ali Baba, Overture

New York 3 December 1949	NBC	LP: RCA Victor LM 7026 LP: RCA RB 6573 LP: RCA AT 135/1030

Anacréon, Overture

Den Haag 23 March 1938	Residentie Orchestra	LP: Dell' Arte DA 9007
Lucerne 27 August 1938	Elite Orchestra	LP: Relief RL 811
New York 21 March 1953	NBC	LP: RCA Victor LM 7026 LP: RCA RB 6573 LP: RCA AT 135/1030 CD: Stradivarius STR 13593

Médée, Overture

New York 18 February 1950	NBC	LP: RCA Victor LM 7026 LP: RCA AT 135/1030 LP: RCA VL 45817

Cimarosa

Il matrimonio per raggiro, Overture

New York NBC
12 November 1949

LP: RCA Victor LM 7026
LP: RCA RB 6573
LP: RCA VCM 6
LP: RCA AT 134/1032

Il matrimonio segreto, Overture

New York NBC
14 November 1943

LP: RCA Victor LM 7026
LP: RCA RB 6573
LP: RCA VCM 6
LP: RCA AT 116/1032

Copland

El salon mexico

New York NBC
14 March 1942

LP: Toscanini Society ATS 1093-6 np
LP: Toscanini Society ATS 101
CD: Memories HR 4199

Creston

Choric Dance No 2

New York NBC
1 November 1942

LP: Toscanini Society ATS 1093-6 np

Frontiers

New York NBC
25 November 1945
World premiere

LP: Toscanini Society ATS 1093-6 np

Debussy

Ibéria (Images)

New York 5 November 1938	NBC	LP: Music and Arts ATRA 3011
New York 13 April 1940	NBC	LP: Toscanini Society ATS 1106-7
Philadelphia 18 November 1941	Philadelphia Orchestra	LP: RCA RL 01900 CD: RCA GD 60311/60328
New York 2 June 1950	NBC	LP: RCA Victor LM 1833 LP: RCA VIC 1052/1246 LP: RCA AT 111/1059 LP: RCA VL 45823 CD: RCA GD 60265
New York 14 February 1953	NBC	LP: Fonit Cetra DOC 18 CD: Hunt CD 529 CD: Nuova Era 013.6328 CD: Fonit Cetra CDE 1028 CD: Curcio-Hunt CON 29

La Mer

London 12 June 1935	BBCSO	LP: EMI EH 29 13451 CD: EMI CDH 763 0442/769 7842
New York 13 April 1940	NBC	LP: Toscanini Society ATS 1106-7
Philadelphia 8 & 9 February 1942	Philadelphia Orchestra	LP: RCA RL 01900 CD: RCA GD 60311/60328
New York 4 March and 2 December 1947	NBC	RCA unpublished
New York 29 September 1947	NBC	AFRS: 66
New York 1 June 1950	NBC	45: RCA Victor WDM 1583/ERB 17/ERB 48 LP: RCA Victor LM 1221/1833 LP: HMV ALP 1070 LP: RCA VIC 1246 LP: RCA AT 111/1059 LP: RCA VL 45823 LP: Franklin Mint CD: RCA GD 60265 <u>Rehearsal extract</u> LP: Morgan MOR 001
New York 14 February 1953	NBC	LP: Fonit Cetra DOC 18 CD: Hunt CD 529 CD: Fonit Cetra CDE 1028 CD: Nuova Era 013.6328

Danse (orch. Ravel)

New York 13 April 1940	NBC	LP: Toscanini Society ATS 1106-7 LP: Music and Arts ATRA 3001

Marche écossaise

New York 13 April 1940	NBC	LP: Toscanini Society ATS 1106-7 LP: Music and Arts ATRA 3001 CD: Dell' Arte DA 9021

Nuages et fêtes (Nocturnes)

New York 13 April 1940	NBC	LP: Toscanini Society ATS 1106-7
New York 15 March 1952	NBC	LP: Toscanini Society ATS 1046 LP: Music and Arts ATRA 3001 LP: Franklin Mint CD: Hunt CD 529 CD: RCA GD 60265 VHS Video: RCA 790.353

Prélude à l'après midi d'un faune

New York 1 March 1936	NYPO	LP: Toscanini Society ATS 1089 np
Den Haag 23 March 1938	Residentie Orchestra	LP: Dell' Arte DA 9007
New York 20 June 1943	NBC	LP: Toscanini Society ATS 1098 np
New York 11 February 1945	NBC	V-Disc: 708
New York 27 March 1948	NBC	LP: Toscanini Society ATS 1011-15
New York 17 February 1951	NBC	LP: Toscanini Society ATS 1045
New York 14 February 1953	NBC	LP: Fonit Cetra DOC 18 LP: Music and Arts ATRA 3001 LP: Franklin Mint CD: Hunt CD 529 CD: Fonit Cetra CDE 1028 CD: RCA GD 60265
New York 17 February 1953	NBC	RCA unpublished

La demoiselle élue

New York 13 April 1940	NBC Chorus Novotna	LP: Toscanini Society ATS 1106-7 LP: Music and Arts ATRA 3001

Donizetti

Don Pasquale, Overture

Camden NJ 29 & 30 March 1921	La Scala Orchestra	78: Victor Talking Machine VTM 66030-1/841 78: HMV DA 376 LP: RCA AT 1076 LP: RCA VL 46024
New York 20 June 1943	NBC	LP: Toscanini Society ATS 1098 np
New York 13 March 1948	NBC	LP: Toscanini Society ATS 1077 np CD: Memories HR 4202
New York 5 October 1951	NBC	45: RCA Victor ERB 7028 LP: RCA Victor LRM 7028/LM 6026 LP: HMV ALP 1417 LP: RCA VCM 6 LP: RCA AT 134/1032 LP: RCA VL 45817 LP: Franklin Mint

Dukas

L'apprenti sorcier

New York 18 March 1929	NYPO	78: HMV D 1689 78: RCA Victor 7021 LP: RCA Camden CAL 309/CDM 1027 LP: RCA AT 1073 CD: Pearl GEMMCDS 9373 CD: RCA GD 60329
New York 12 February 1938	NBC	CD: Memories HR 4182
Den Haag 23 March 1938	Residentie Orchestra	LP: Dell' Arte DA 9007
New York 20 June 1943	NBC	LP: Toscanini Society ATS 1098 np
New York 19 March 1950	NBC	78: RCA Victor DM 1416 45: RCA Victor WDM 1416 LP: RCA Victor LM 1118/LM 2056 LP: HMV ALP 1432 LP: RCA VIC 1189/1267 LP: RCA AT 142/1066 LP: RCA VL 45803 LP: Franklin Mint CD: RCA (Japan) RCCD 1009 CD: RCA RD 86205

Ariane et Barbe-bleue, Suite

New York 2 March 1947	NBC Chorus	V-Disc: 836-7 LP: Toscanini Society ATS 1011-15 LP: Fonit Cetra ARK 11 LP: Music and Arts ATRA 3001 CD: Memories HR 4167

Dvorak

Symphony No 9 "From the New World"

New York 5 November 1938	NBC	LP: Music and Arts ATRA 3011
New York 31 January 1953	NBC	CD: Nuova Era 013.6311-2 CD: Hunt CDLSMH 34017 CD: AS-Disc AS 111 CD: Virtuoso 269.7012/269.9142 CD: Memories HR 4209 CD: Greenline 3CLC 40Q4 Greenline incorrectly dated 3 January
New York 2 February 1953	NBC	45: RCA Victor ERC 1 LP: RCA Victor LM 1778 LP: HMV ALP 1222 LP: RCA RB 16116 LP: RCA VIC 1249/1187 LP: RCA AT 114/1062 LP: RCA VL 45812 LP: Franklin Mint CD: RCA (Japan) RCCD 1008 CD: RCA GD 60279

Cello Concerto

New York 28 January 1945	NBC Kurtz	LP: Toscanini Society ATS 1011-15 LP: Music and Arts ATRA 3005

Symphonic Variations

New York 4 December 1948	NBC	LP: Toscanini Society ATS 1025-9 VHS Video: RCA 790.354
New York 17 November 1951	NBC	LP: Fonit Cetra ARK 10 LP: Dell' Arte DA 9008 CD: Memories HR 4209 CD: Hunt CDLSMH 34017

Scherzo capriccioso

New York 20 April 1940	NBC	LP: Toscanini Society ATS 1011-5 LP: Music and Arts ATRA 3005 Rehearsal extracts LP: Music and Arts ATRA 3005
New York 28 January 1945	NBC	CD: Memories HR 4209

Elgar

Enigma Variations

London 3 June 1935	BBCSO	LP: EMI EH 29 13451 CD: EMI CDH 769 7842
New York 18 November 1945 Variation 7 only	NBC	V-Disc: 606
New York 17 February 1951	NBC	LP: Toscanini Society ATS 1045
New York 10 December 1951	NBC	45: RCA Victor WDM 1725 LP: RCA Victor LM 1725 LP: HMV ALP 1204 LP: RCA VIC 1001/1344 LP: RCA AT 1070 CD: RCA GD 60287

Introduction and Allegro for strings

New York 20 April 1940	NBC	LP: Toscanini Society ATS 1055-9

Enescu

Rumanian Rhapsody No 1

New York 14 December 1940	NBC	LP: Toscanini Society ATS 107
New York 13 January 1946	NBC	LP: Toscanini Society ATS 1038 CD: Memories HR 4182

Falla

El amor brujo

New York 28 January 1939	NBC Burzio	LP: Toscanini Society ATS 1092 np LP: Toscanini Society ATS 103 CD: Memories HR 4165

El amor brujo: Excerpts (Fire Dance; Dance of Terror)

New York 3 September 1944	NBC	LP: Toscanini Society ATS 1088 np LP: Toscanini Society ATS 103

Fernandez

Batuque (Reisado do pastoreio)

Washington	NBC	LP: Toscanini Society ATS 1092 np
14 May 1940		LP: Toscanini Society ATS 103

Foroni

Overture in C minor

New York	NBC	LP: Toscanini Society ATS 1070 np
2 September 1945		LP: Toscanini Society ATS 102

Franchetti

Nocturne (Cristoforo Colombo)

New York	NBC	LP: Toscanini Society ATS 1070 np
14 December 1940	Horne	LP: Toscanini Society ATS 102

Franck

Symphony in D minor

New York 14 December 1940	NBC	LP: Franklin Mint CD: Music and Arts ATRA 274 <u>Franklin Mint version contains second and third movements from this performance, but first movement is taken from the 1946 performance</u>
New York 24 March 1946	NBC	LP: Toscanini Society ATS 1055-9 CD: Dell' Arte DA 9021

Les Eolides

New York 12 November 1938	NBC	CD: Music and Arts ATRA 274
New York 2 July 1944	NBC	LP: Toscanini Society ATS 1100 np
New York 5 March 1949	NBC	LP: Toscanini Society ATS 1055-9
New York 13 December 1953	NBC	LP: Toscanini Society ATS 1047 LP: Music and Arts ATRA 3001

Psyché et Eros

New York 5 January 1952	NBC	CD: Music and Arts ATRA 274
New York 7 January 1952	NBC	LP: Franklin Mint 1838 LP: HMV ALP 1218 LP: RCA VIC 1246 LP: RCA AT 142/1066

Le sommeil de Psyché

New York 14 January 1939	NBC	LP: Music and Arts ATRA 3001

Rédemption, Symphonic Interlude

New York 2 March 1947	NBC	LP: Toscanini Society ATS 108 <u>Incorrectly dated 15 March 1952</u>
New York 15 March 1952	NBC	LP: Toscanini Society ATS 1046 LP: Fonit Cetra ARK 11 LP: Music and Arts ATRA 3001 CD: Music and Arts ATRA 274 VHS Video: RCA 790.353

Geminiani

Concerto Grosso op 3 no 2

London 12 June 1935	BBCSO	EMI unpublished

Gershwin

An American in Paris

New York 14 November 1943	NBC	LP: Fonit Cetra ARK 4 CD: Hunt CD 534
New York 18 May 1945	NBC	45: RCA Victor WDM 1657 LP: RCA Victor LM 9020 LP: HMV ALP 1107 LP: RCA AT 129 /1069 LP: Franklin Mint

Piano Concerto in F

New York 2 April 1944	NBC Levant	LP: Toscanini Society ATS 1093-6 np LP: Fonit Cetra ARK 4 CD: Hunt CD 534 Fonit Cetra incorrectly dated 2 March 194

Rhapsody in Blue

New York 1 November 1942	NBC Wild	LP: Toscanini Society ATS 1093-6 np LP: Fonit Cetra ARK 4 CD: Hunt CD 534

Gilbert

Comedy Overture on Negro themes

New York 1 November 1942	NBC	LP: Toscanini Society ATS 1093-6 np

Gillis

Symphony No 5½

New York 21 September 1947	NBC	V-Disc: 826 LP: Toscanini Society ATS 1093-6 np

Giordano

Dance of the Moor (Il Rè)

New York   NBC   LP: Toscanini Society ATS 1039
10 December 1949

Siberia, Act 2 Prelude

New York   NBC   LP: Toscanini Society ATS 1039
10 December 1949   CD: Memories HR 4198

Glinka

Jota aragonesa

New York   NBC   V-Disc: 593
7 November 1943   LP: Toscanini Society ATS 1097 np
     LP: Dell' Arte DA 9011
     CD: Relief CR 1886

New York   NBC   LP: Toscanini Society ATS 1088 np
3 September 1944   CD: Memories HR 4182

New York   NBC   V-Disc: 593
4 November 1945   LP: Toscanini Society ATS 1025-9

New York   NBC   LP: Franklin Mint
4 March 1950   CD: RCA GD 60308

     V-Disc 593 has both dates 7 November 1943 and 4 November 1945

Kamarinskaya, Waltz-Fantasy

New York   NBC   LP: RCA Victor LM 6026
21 December 1940   LP: HMV ALP 1418
     LP: RCA VIC 1245
     LP: RCA AT 124/1066
     CD: Memories HR 4213

Gluck

Orfeo ed Euridice, Act 2

New York 1 April 1945	NBC NBC Chorus Merriman, Philips	LP: Toscanini Society ATS 1040
New York 22 November 1952	NBC Shaw Chorale Merriman, Gibson	LP: RCA Victor LM 1850/LVT 1041 LP: HMV ALP 1357 LP: RCA AT 127/1006 LP: RCA (France) GM 43348 CD: Memories HR 4213

Orfeo ed Euridice: Excerpt (Dance of the blessed spirits)

New York 21 November 1929	NYPO	78: HMV D 1784 78: RCA Victor M 65/DM 65 LP: RCA AT 1081 CD: Pearl GEMMCDS 9373 CD: RCA GD 60329
New York 4 November 1946	NBC	78: RCA Victor M 1172/DM 1505 45: RCA Victor WDM 1172/1505 LP: RCA Victor LM 7032 LP: RCA RB 6607 LP: RCA AT 1007

Iphigénie en Aulide, Overture

New York 28 January 1939	NBC	LP: Toscanini Society ATS 122
New York 22 November 1952	NBC	LP: RCA Victor LM 7026 LP: RCA RB 6573 LP: RCA AT 1007 LP: RCA (France) GM 43348 CD: Memories HR 4213

Goldmark

Rustic Wedding, Symphony: Excerpts (In the garden; Serenade)

New York 3 September 1944	NBC	LP: Toscanini Society ATS 1088 np LP: Toscanini Society ATS 100

Rustic Wedding, Symphony: Excerpt (Scherzo)

New York 1 March 1936	NYPO	LP: Toscanini Society ATS 1089 np

Gould

Lincoln Legend

New York 1 November 1942 World premiere	NBC	LP: Toscanini Society ATS 1093-6 np CD: Memories HR 4199

Grieg

Holberg Suite

New York 27 April 1940	NBC	LP: Toscanini Society ATS 1055-9

Griffes

The White Peacock (Roman Sketches)

New York 7 February 1943	NBC	LP: Toscanini Society ATS 1093-6 np

Grofé

Grand Canyon, Suite

New York 11 September 1945	NBC	78: RCA Victor M 1038 45: RCA Victor WDM 1038/ERC 3/ERA 15 LP: RCA Victor LM 1004 LP: HMV ALP 1232 LP: RCA AT 129/1069 Excerpts 45: HMV 7ER 5012

Grand Canyon, Suite: Excerpts (On the trail; Cloudburst)

New York 7 February 1943	NBC	V-Disc: 561 CD: Memories HR 4199

Handel

Concerto Grosso op 6 no 12

New York 19 February 1938	NBC	LP: Toscanini Society ATS 104
New York 22 November 1947	NBC	LP: Toscanini Society ATS 1041

Minuet (Concerto Grosso op 6 no 5)

New York 20 June 1943	NBC	LP: Toscanini Society ATS 1098 np

Susannah, Overture

New York 15 March 1936	NYPO	LP: Toscanini Society ATS 104

Harris

Symphony No 3

New York 16 March 1940	NBC	LP: Toscanini Society ATS 101 CD: Dell' Arte DA 9020

Haydn

Symphony No 31 "Horn Signal"

New York   NBC   LP: Toscanini Society ATS 1042
29 October 1938   LP: Relief RL 842
                               CD: Relief CR 1842
                               CD: Palette PAL 1062
                               CD: Memories HR 4201

Symphony No 88

New York   NBC   LP: Toscanini Society ATS 1001-4
19 February 1938   LP: Toscanini Society ATS 124-5

New York   NBC   78: HMV DB 3515-7/8497-9 auto
8 March 1938   78: RCA Victor M 454
                               45: RCA Victor WCT 29
                               LP: RCA Victor LCT 7
                               LP: RCA AT 130/1001

Symphony No 92 "Oxford"

New York   NBC   LP: Toscanini Society ATS 1055-9
19 March 1944

Symphony No 94 "Surprise"

New York   NBC   LP: Toscanini Society ATS 1098 np
20 June 1943   LP: Toscanini Society ATS 124-5

New York   NBC   LP: RCA Victor LM 1789
26 January 1953   LP: RCA RB 16138
                               LP: RCA VIC 1262
                               LP: RCA VCM 7
                               LP: RCA AT 120/1002
                               LP: RCA VL 45816

Symphony No 98

New York   NBC   LP: Toscanini Society ATS 1055-9
22 January 1938   LP: Relief RL 842
                               CD: Relief CR 1842
                               CD: Palette PAL 1062

New York   NBC   78: RCA Victor M 1025
25 May 1945   LP: RCA AT 1077
                               LP: Franklin Mint

Symphony No 99

New York 1 February 1941	NBC	LP: Toscanini Society ATS 124-5
New York 2 July 1944	NBC	LP: Toscanini Society ATS 1100 np
New York 12 March 1949	NBC	LP: RCA Victor LM 6711 LP: RCA AT 149/1001

Symphony No 101 "Clock"

New York 29 & 30 March 1929	NYPO	78: HMV D 1668-71/7667-70 auto 78: RCA Victor M 57 LP: RCA Camden CAL 375/CDM 1054 LP: RCA AT 130/1073 CD: Pearl GEMMCDS 9373 CD: RCA GD 60329
Den Haag 23 March 1938	Residentie Orchestra	LP: Dell' Arte DA 9007
New York 13 January 1945	NYPO	LP: Toscanini Society ATS 1034-5 LP: Music and Arts ATRA 3009 CD: AS-Disc AS 600
New York 9 October and 6 November 1946 & 12 June 1947	NBC	78: RCA Victor DM 1368 45: RCA Victor WDM 1368 LP: RCA Victor LM 1038 LP: RCA RB 16138 LP: RCA VIC 1262 LP: RCA VCM 7 LP: RCA AT 120/1002

Symphony No 104 "London"

New York 31 October 1943	NBC	LP: Toscanini Society ATS 1001-4 LP: Toscanini Society ATS 124-5

Sinfonia Concertante op 84

New York 14 October 1939	NBC Mischakoff, Miller, Bloom, Polisi	LP: Music and Arts ATRA 3011
New York 6 March 1948	NBC Mischakoff, Miller, Renzi, Sharrow	LP: RCA Victor LM 6711 LP: RCA AT 149/1001 LP: Franklin Mint CD: Memories HR 4201

 # AUGUSTEO

I.
(631. dalla Fondazione dei Concerti).

Sabato 29 Novembre 1920, ore 21

PRIMO CONCERTO
DIRETTO DA
ARTURO TOSCANINI
(ORCHESTRA TOSCANINI)

Programma.

1. **Vivaldi** . . - *Concerto* in *la min.* per archi.
   - Allegro moderato.
   - Adagio.
   - Allegro.

2. **Beethoven** . - *Quinta Sinfonia.*
   - Allegro con brio.
   - Andante con moto.
   - Scherzo.
   - Finale.

3a. **Block** . . . - *Danza* (dai *tre Poemi ebraici*).
 b. **Tomassini** . - *Serenata* dai (" *Chiari di Luna* „).

4. **Respighi** . - *Le fontane di Roma.* - Poema sinfonico.
   - La fontana di Valle Giulia all'alba.
   - La fontana del Tritone al mattino.
   - La fontana di Trevi al meriggio.
   - La fontana di Villa Medici al tramonto.

5. **Debussy** . . - *Iberia* Images pour orchestre.
   - I. Par les rues et par les chemins.
   - II. Les parfums de la nuit.
   - III. Les matins d'un jour de fête.

6. **Wagner** . . - *Tanhäuser* Ouverture.

The Philharmonic Society of New York

FOUNDED 1842

| 1925 | EIGHTY-FOURTH SEASON | 1926 |

CARNEGIE HALL

Thursday Evening, January 14, 1926
AT EIGHT-THIRTY
Friday Afternoon, January 15, 1926
AT TWO-THIRTY

2036TH AND 2037TH CONCERTS

Under the Direction of
ARTURO TOSCANINI

MR. TOSCANINI'S FIRST APPEARANCE
with the
PHILHARMONIC SOCIETY

PROGRAM

1. HAYDN..................Symphony in D major (B. & H. No. 4)
   - I. Adagio; Presto
   - II. Andante
   - III. Menuetto: Allegro
   - IV. Finale: Vivace

2. RESPIGHI..................Symphonic Poem, "The Pines of Rome"
   - I. The Pines of the Villa Borghese
   - II. The Pines near a Catacomb
   - III. The Pines of the Janiculum*
   - IV. The Pines of the Appian Way
     (First time in New York)

INTERMISSION

3. SIBELIUS..................Tone-Poem, "The Swan of Tuonela"

4. WAGNER..................Siegfried's Death and Funeral Music, from Götterdämmerung

5. WEBER..................Overture to "Euryanthe"

---

* The Nightingale's Song in the third movement of Respighi's work is reproduced on a Brunswick Panatrope

ARTHUR JUDSON, Manager
EDWARD ERVIN, Associate Manager
THE STEINWAY is the Official Piano of The Philharmonic Society

Any of the works on this program can be obtained for home study at the 58th Street Branch of the New York Public Library, 121 East 58th Street.

Toscanini's first concert with the Philharmonic Symphony Orchestra

Serenade (String Quartet op 3 no 5)

New York 4 April 1943	NBC	LP: Toscanini Society ATS 1036
New York 27 August 1944	NBC	LP: Toscanini Society ATS 124-5 CD: Relief CR 1842 CD: Palette PAL 1062 CD: Memories HR 4201 Memories incorrectly dated 4 April 1943

Hérold

Zampa, Overture

New York 4 April 1943	NBC	V-Disc: 95 LP: Toscanini Society ATS 1036
New York 27 August 1944	NBC	LP: Toscanini Society ATS 108
New York 2 August 1952	NBC	LP: Dell' Arte DA 9010 CD: Memories HR 4202
New York 5 August 1952	NBC	45: RCA Victor ERB 7014 LP: RCA Victor LM 1834/LRM 7014 LP: HMV ALP 1235 LP: RCA VIC 1010 LP: RCA AT 124/1071 LP: RCA VL 45817 LP: Franklin Mint CD: RCA (Japan) R32C-1018

Humperdinck

Hänsel und Gretel, Overture

New York 13 January 1946	NBC	LP: Toscanini Society ATS 1038
New York 2 August 1952	NBC	LP: Dell' Arte DA 9010 CD: Memories HR 4202
New York 5 August 1952	NBC	45: RCA Victor ERB 7014 LP: RCA Victor LM 6026/LRM 7014 LP: HMV ALP 1418 LP: RCA AT 1071 LP: Franklin Mint

Königskinder, Act 3 Prelude

New York 17 November 1946	NBC	LP: Toscanini Society ATS 1084 np

Kabalevsky

Symphony No 2

New York 8 November 1942	NBC	LP: Toscanini Society ATS 106
New York 25 March 1945	NBC	LP: Melodiya 33C 10 05291-2
New York 26 February 1949	NBC	LP: Toscanini Society ATS 1081 np

Colas Breugnon, Overture

New York 11 April 1943	NBC	LP: Toscanini Society ATS 106 CD: Dell' Arte DA 9020
New York 21 January 1945	NBC	V-Disc: 675
New York 7 April 1946	NBC	LP: Toscanini Society ATS 1081 np
New York 8 April 1946	NBC	78: RCA Victor M 1178/DM 1416 45: RCA Victor WDM 1178/WDM 1416 LP: RCA Victor LM 7032 LP: RCA RB 6607 LP: RCA AT 124/1066 LP: Franklin Mint

Kalinnikov

Symphony No 1

New York 7 November 1943	NBC	LP: Toscanini Society ATS 1097 np LP: Dell' Arte DA 9011 CD: Relief CR 1886

Kennan

Night Soliloquy

New York 7 February 1943	NBC	LP: Toscanini Society ATS 1093-6 np

Kodaly

Hary Janos, Suite

New York 29 November 1947	NBC	LP: RCA Victor LM 1973 LP: RCA AT 122/1064 LP: Franklin Mint CD: RCA GD 60279

Marosszek Dances

New York 8 February 1941	NBC	LP: Toscanini Society ATS 107 CD: Memories HR 4165

Kozeluh

Andante and Allegro (String Quartet No 2)

New York 15 March 1936	NYPO	LP: Toscanini Society ATS 104

Liadov

Kikimora

New York 7 November 1943	NBC	LP: Toscanini Society ATS 1097 np
New York 13 January 1946	NBC	LP: Toscanini Society ATS 1038
New York 11 December 1948	NBC	CD: Memories HR 4200
New York 26 July 1952	NBC	LP: Dell' Arte DA 9014 CD: Relief CR 1886
New York 29 July 1952	NBC	45: RCA Victor ERB 7014 LP: RCA Victor LM 2056/LRM 7014 LP: RCA VIC 1245 LP: RCA AT 124/1066 LP: Franklin Mint

Liszt

Hungarian Rhapsody No 2

New York 4 April 1943	NBC	LP: Toscanini Society ATS 1036 CD: Memories HR 4182

Orpheus

New York 26 November 1938	NBC	LP: Toscanini Society ATS 1084 np LP: Toscanini Society ATS 100

Von der Wiege bis zum Grabe

New York 8 February 1941	NBC	LP: Toscanini Society ATS 1084 np LP: Toscanini Society ATS 100

Mancinelli

Fuga degli amanti (Scene veneziane)

New York 13 January 1946	NBC	LP: Toscanini Society ATS 1038
New York 13 March 1948	NBC	LP: Toscanini Society ATS 1077 np

Massenet

Scènes alsaciennes

New York 18 July 1943	NBC	LP: Toscanini Society ATS 1099 np LP: Music and Arts ATRA 3001 CD: Memories HR 4166

Fête bohème (Scènes pittoresques)

Camden NJ 3 March 1921	La Scala Orchestra	78: Victor Talking Machine VTM 74725/6301 78: HMV DB 418 LP: RCA AT 1076 LP: RCA VL 46024

Martucci

Symphony No 1

New York	NBC	LP: Toscanini Society ATS 1071-4
26 November 1938		LP: Paragon 2LB 53001

Symphony No 2

New York	NBC	LP: Toscanini Society ATS 1071-4
30 March 1940		LP: Paragon 2LB 53001

Piano Concerto in B flat minor

New York	NBC	LP: Toscanini Society ATS 1071-4
20 January 1946	D'Attili	LP: Paragon 2LB 53008
New York	NBC	LP: Dell' Arte DA 9017
17 January 1953	Horszowski	

Canzoni dei ricordi

New York	NBC	LP: Toscanini Society ATS 1071-4
29 March 1941	Castagna	LP: Paragon 2LB 53008

Danza (Tarantella)

New York	NBC	LP: Toscanini Society ATS 1071-4
19 February 1938		LP: Paragon 2LB 53008

Notturno

New York	NBC	LP: Toscanini Society ATS 1071-4
15 October 1938		LP: Paragon 2LB 53008

Noveletta

New York	NBC	LP: Toscanini Society ATS 1071-4
15 October 1938		LP: Paragon 2LB 53008
New York	NBC	V-Disc: 848
13 March 1948		LP: Toscanini Society ATS 1077 np

Mendelssohn

Symphony No 3 "Scotch"

New York 5 April 1941	NBC	LP: Toscanini Society ATS 1025-9 LP: Music and Arts ATRA 3004 CD: Music and Arts ATRA 268

Symphony No 4 "Italian"

New York 5 February 1938	NBC	LP: Toscanini Society ATS 1075
New York 14 March 1942	NBC	CD: Music and Arts ATRA 268
New York 27 February 1954	NBC	LP: RCA Victor LM 1851 LP: HMV ALP 1267 LP: RCA VIC 1341 LP: RCA AT 101/1026 LP: RCA VL 45809 LP: Franklin Mint CD: RCA (Japan) RCCD 1007 Fourth movement taken from 28 February performance
New York 28 February 1954	NBC	CD: Nuova Era 013.6311-2 CD: Melodram MEL 18013 CD: Memories HR 4184 Nuova Era incorrectly dated 27 February 1954

Symphony No 5 "Reformation"

New York 8 November 1942	NBC	CD: Music and Arts ATRA 268
New York 13 December 1953		LP: RCA Victor LM 1851 LP: HMV ALP 1267 LP: RCA VL 45809 LP: RCA AT 123/1026 CD: RCA (Japan) RCCD 1007 CD: Memories HR 4184

Violin Concerto

New York 1936 Incomplete	NYPO Milstein	LP: Toscanini Society ATS 109-110
New York 9 April 1944	NBC Heifetz	LP: Toscanini Society ATS 1075 np LP: Fonit Cetra ARK 10 CD: Melodram MEL 18013

The Fair Melusine, Overture

New York 11 January 1947	NBC	LP: Toscanini Society ATS 1037 LP: Music and Arts ATRA 3004 CD: Melodram MEL 18013
New York 11 December 1948	NBC	LP: Toscanini Society ATS 1011-5

The Hebrides, Overture

New York 4 November 1945	NBC	LP: Toscanini Society ATS 1025-9 LP: Music and Arts ATRA 3004 CD: Melodram MEL 18013

A Midsummer Night's Dream, Overture

Philadelphia 11 and 12 January 1942	Philadelphia Orchestra	LP: RCA RL 01900 CD: RCA GD 60314/60328
New York 27 January 1942	NBC	LP: Toscanini Society ATS 107
New York 1 November 1947	NBC	LP: Toscanini Society ATS 1037 CD: Music and Arts ATRA 268
New York 4 November 1947	NBC	78: RCA Victor M 1280 45: RCA Victor WDM 1280 LP: RCA Victor LM 1221 LP: RCA VIC 1337 LP: RCA AT 138/1027 LP: Franklin Mint
New York 10 February 1951	NBC	LP: Toscanini Society ATS 1044

Intermezzo (A Midsummer Night's Dream)

Philadelphia 11 and 12 January 1942	Philadelphia Orchestra	LP: RCA RL 01900 CD: RCA GD 60314/60328
New York 1 November 1947	NBC	LP: Toscanini Society ATS 1037 CD: Music and Arts ATRA 268
New York 4 November 1947	NBC	78: RCA Victor M 1280 45: RCA Victor WDM 1280 LP: RCA Victor LM 1221 LP: RCA VIC 1337 LP: RCA AT 138/1027 LP: Franklin Mint

Scherzo (A Midsummer Night's Dream)

Camden NJ 9 March 1921	La Scala Orchestra	78: HMV DB 191 LP: RCA AT 1076 LP: RCA VL 46024
New York February 1926	NYPO	78: Brunswick 50074/50161 78: Polydor 595008 LP: RCA AT 1081 CD: Pearl GEMMCDS 9373 CD: RCA GD 60329
New York 30 March 1929	NYPO	78: HMV D 1671 78: RCA Victor M 57 LP: RCA Victor CAL 326/CDM 1055 LP: RCA AT 1073 CD: Pearl GEMMCDS 9373 CD: RCA GD 60329
Philadelphia 11 and 12 January 1942	Philadelphia Orchestra	LP: RCA RL 01900 CD: RCA GD 60314/60328
New York 6 November 1946	NBC	78: RCA Victor M 1167/DM 1368 45: RCA Victor WDM 1167/WDM 1368 LP: RCA Victor LM 7032 LP: RCA AT 1025
New York 1 November 1947	NBC	LP: Toscanini Society ATA 1037 CD: Music and Arts ATRA 268
New York 4 November 1947	NBC	78: RCA Victor M 1280 45: RCA Victor WDM 1280 LP: RCA Victor LM 1221 LP: RCA RB 6606 LP: RCA VIC 1337 LP: RCA AT 138/1027 LP: Franklin Mint

Nocturne (A Midsummer Night's Dream)

New York February 1926	NYPO	78: Brunswick 50074 78: Polydor 595008 LP: RCA AT 1081 CD: Pearl GEMMCDS 9373 CD: RCA GD 60329
Philadelphia 11 and 12 January 1942	Philadelphia Orchestra	LP: RCA RL 01900 CD: RCA GD 60314/60328
New York 1 November 1947	NBC	LP: Toscanini Society ATS 1037 CD: Music and Arts ATRA 268
New York 4 November 1947	NBC	78: RCA Victor M 1280 45: RCA Victor WDM 1280 LP: RCA Victor LM 1221 LP: RCA VIC 1337 LP: RCA AT 138/1027 LP: Franklin Mint

Ye spotted snakes (A Midsummer Night's Dream)

Philadelphia 11 and 12 January 1942	Philadelphia Orchestra Pennsylvania Glee Club Eustis, Kirk	LP: RCA RL 01900 CD: RCA GD 60314/60328
New York 1 November 1947	NBC Chorus Philips, Warner	LP: Toscanini Society ATS 1037 LP: Music and Arts ATRA 3004 CD: Music and Arts ATRA 268
New York 4 November 1947	NBC Chorus Philips, Warner	RCA unpublished

Wedding March (A Midsummer Night's Dream)

Camden NJ 11 March 1921	La Scala Orchestra	78: Victor Talking Machine VTM 74745/6302 78: HMV DB 191´ LP: RCA AT 1076 LP: RCA VL 46024
Philadelphia 11 and 12 January 1942	Philadelphia Orchestra	LP: RCA RL 01900 CD: RCA GD 60314/60328
New York 1 November 1947	NBC	LP: Toscanini Society ATS 1037 CD: Music and Arts ATRA 268
New York 4 November 1947	NBC	78: RCA Victor M 1280 45: RCA Victor WDM 1280 LP: RCA Victor LM 1221 LP: RCA VIC 1337 LP: RCA AT 138 /1027 LP: Franklin Mint

Finale (A Midsummer Night's Dream)

Philadelphia 11 and 12 January 1942	Philadelphia Orchestra Pennsylvania Glee Club Eustis, Kirk	LP: RCA RL 01900 CD: RCA GD 60314/60328
New York 1 November 1947	NBC Chorus Philips, Warner	LP: Toscanini Society ATS 1037 CD: Music and Arts ATRA 268
New York 4 November 1947	NBC Chorus Philips, Warner	78: RCA Victor M 1280 45: RCA Victor WDM 1280 LP: RCA Victor LM 1221 LP: RCA VIC 1337 LP: RCA AT 138 /1027 LP: Franklin Mint

Octet

New York   NBC   LP: RCA Victor LM 1869
30 March 1947   LP: RCA AT 1027

Scherzo (Octet)

New York   NBC   78: RCA Victor M 1025
1 June 1945   LP: RCA AT 1077

Adagio and Lento (String Quintet in B flat)

New York   NBC   LP: Toscanini Society ATS 1037
1 November 1947   LP: Music and Arts ATRA 3004
                                     CD: Melodram MEL 18013

Meyerbeer

Dinorah, Overture

New York   NBC   LP: Toscanini Society ATS 1070
12 November 1938   Chorus   LP: Music and Arts ATRA 3001
                                     CD: Dell' Arte DA 9021

L'Etoile du nord, Overture

New York   NBC   LP: Music and Arts ATRA 3001
2 November 1951

Mignone

Fantasia Brasiliera

New York   NBC   LP: Toscanini Society ATS 103
14 November 1943   Segal, piano

Festa das Igrejas

New York   NBC   LP: Toscanini Society ATS 1070 np
2 April 1944   LP: Dell' Arte DA 9017

Leopold Mozart

Toy Symphony

New York   NBC   LP: RCA Victor LM 6711
15 February 1941   LP: RCA AT 141/1002
                                     CD: RCA GD 60308

Mozart

Symphony No 29

New York 3 September 1944	NBC	LP: Toscanini Society ATS 1011-15 LP: Relief RL 841 CD: Palette PAL 1065 Relief incorrectly dated 3 September 1934

Symphony No 35 "Haffner"

New York 30 March and 4 & 5 April 1929	NYPO	78: HMV D 1782-4/7402-4 auto 78: RCA Victor M 65 LP: RCA Camden CAL 326/CDM 1055 LP: RCA AT 1072 CD: Pearl GEMMCDS 9373 CD: RCA GD 60329
London 14 June 1935	BBCSO	EMI unpublished
New York 3 November 1946	NBC	LP: Toscanini Society ATS 1043 CD: Memories HR 4187 Rehearsal extracts LP: CLS MDRL 12821 LP: Relief RL 831
New York 4 and 6 November 1946	NBC	78: RCA Victor M 1172 45: RCA Victor WDM 1172 LP: RCA Victor LM 1038 LP: RCA RB 16137 LP: RCA VCM 7 LP: RCA AT 126/1003 LP: RCA VL 4509005

Symphony No 38 "Prague"

New York 4 February 1939	NBC	LP: Toscanini Society ATS 1007 LP: Turnabout THS 65033-5 LP: Relief RL 841 CD: Palette PAL 1065

Symphony No 39

Camden NJ 17 and 20 December 1920 Third and fourth movements	La Scala Orchestra	78: Victor Talking Machine VTM 74668-9/6303 78: HMV DB 419 LP: RCA AT 1076 LP: RCA VL 46024
New York 6 March 1948	NBC	LP: RCA Victor LM 2001 LP: HMV ALP 1492 LP: RCA VIC 1330 LP: RCA VCM 7 LP: RCA AT 126/1003 CD: Memories HR 4211

Symphony No 40

New York 26 April 1936	NYPO	LP: Toscanini Society ATS 1090-1 np LP: Toscanini Society ATS 109-10
New York 25 December 1937	NBC	LP: Toscanini Society ATS 1079-80 np CD: Myto MCD 89009
New York 7 March 1938 and 27 February 1939	NBC	78: HMV DB 3790-2/8679-81 auto 78: RCA Victor M 631 LP: RCA AT 1077
New York 27 January 1946 First movement	NBC	V-Disc: 638
New York 4 December 1948	NBC	VHS Video: RCA 790.354
New York 12 March 1950	NBC	LP: RCA Victor LM 1789 LP: RCA RB 16137 LP: RCA VIC 1330 LP: RCA VCM 7 LP: RCA AT 110/1004 LP: RCA VL 45816/46003 LP: Franklin Mint CD: RCA (Japan) RCCD 1001
New York 21 March 1953	NBC	LP: GDS Records GDS 5011 CD: Stradivarius STR 13593 CD: Melodram MEL 37040 CD: AS-Disc AS 112 CD: Memories HR 4211

Symphony No 41 "Jupiter"

New York 4 February 1945	NBC	CD: Memories HR 4187
New York 22 June 1945	NBC	78: RCA Victor M 1080 45: RCA Victor WDM 1080 LP: RCA Victor LM 1030 LP: RCA VCM 7 LP: RCA AT 110/1004 LP: RCA VL 46014 CD: RCA (Japan) RCCD 1001

Piano Concerto No 27

New York 23 February 1936	NYPO Serkin	LP: Toscanini Society ATS 1011-15

Bassoon Concerto

New York 8 November 1947	NBC Sharrow	CD: Memories HR 4201
New York 18 November 1947	NBC Sharrow	78: RCA Victor M 1304 45: RCA Victor WDM 1304 LP: RCA Victor LM 1030 LP: RCA AT 141/1005

Sinfonia Concertante K364

New York 15 February 1941	NBC Mischakoff, Cooley	LP: Toscanini Society ATS 1005-9

Divertimento in B flat K287

New York 3 November 1946	NBC	LP: Toscanini Society ATS 1043
New York 8 November 1947	NBC	CD: Memories HR 4187
New York 18 November 1947	NBC	78: RCA Victor DM 1355 45: RCA Victor WDM 1355 LP: RCA Victor LM 13/LM 2001 LP: HMV ALP 1492 LP: RCA VCM 7 LP: RCA AT 141/1005

Don Giovanni, Overture

New York 27 January 1946	NBC	LP: RCA Victor LM 7026 LP: RCA AT 134

Le Nozze di Figaro, Overture

New York 5 December 1943	NBC	LP: RCA Victor LM 7026 LP: RCA VCM 7 LP: RCA AT 116/1007 All wrongly dated 8 November 1947
New York 8 November 1947	NBC	LP: Relief RL 841 CD: Palette PAL 1065 CD: Memories HR 4211

Die Zauberflöte

Salzburg 30 July 1937	VPO Vienna Opera Chorus Novotna, Osvath, Komarek, Roswaenge, Domgraf-Fassbänder, Kipnis, Jerger	LP: Toscanini Society ATS 1025-7 LP: MRF Records MRF 71 LP: Estro Armonico EA 056 LP: Fonit Cetra LO 44 CD: Melodram MEL 37040 Excerpts LP: Pearl GEMM 261-2/277-8 CD: Amadeo 427 0892

Die Zauberflöte, Overture

London 2 June 1938	BBCSO	78: HMV DB 3550 78: RCA Victor 15190 45: RCA Victor WEPR 14/ERA 14 LP: EMI XLP 30079 LP: Seraphim 60150/IC 6015
New York 3 November 1946	NBC	LP: Toscanini Society ATS 1043
New York 5 November 1947 Rehearsal extract	NBC	LP: Musicians' Foundation No. 1
New York 8 November 1947	NBC	AFRS: 60
New York 26 November 1949	NBC	LP: RCA Victor LM 7026 LP: RCA RB 6573 LP: RCA VCM 7 LP: RCA AT 134/1007 LP: RCA VL 45817 CD: RCA (Japan) 1001

Mussorgsky

Pictures at an Exhibition

New York 29 January 1938	NBC	LP: Toscanini Society ATS 115
New York 14 February 1948	NBC	LP: Toscanini Society ATS 1085 np
Milan 16 September 1948	La Scala Orchestra	LP: Fonit Cetra LO 523 LP: Relief RL 822 CD: Palette PAL 2003-4
New York 24 January 1953	NBC	CD: Nuova Era 013.6312 CD: Fonit Cetra CDE 1031 CD: Virtuoso 269.7012/269.9142 CD: Memories HR 4200 CD: Greenline 3CLC 4003
New York 26 January 1953	NBC	45: RCA Victor ERB 35 LP: RCA Victor LM 1838 LP: HMV ALP 1218 LP: RCA VIC 1273/1189 LP: RCA AT 107/1064 LP: RCA VL 45810 LP: Franklin Mint CD: RCA (Japan) RCCD 1009 CD: RCA GD 60287

Boris Godunov, Act 3 Introduction and Polonaise

New York 4 April 1943	NBC	LP: Toscanini Society ATS 1036 LP: Dell' Arte DA 9011 CD: Memories HR 4200

Khovantschina, Prelude

New York 13 December 1953	NBC	LP: Toscanini Society ATS 1047 LP: Dell' Arte DA 9014 CD: Relief CR 1886 CD: Memories HR 4200

Nicolai

The Merry Wives of Windsor, Overture

New York 18 July 1943	NBC	LP: Toscanini Society ATS 1099 np LP: Toscanini Society ATS 107 CD: Memories HR 4202

Paganini

Moto perpetuo (arr. Toscanini)

New York 29 January 1938	NBC	LP: Toscanini Society ATS 107 CD: Memories HR 4182
New York 17 April 1939	NBC	78: HMV DB 3858 78: RCA Victor M 590/DM 590 LP: RCA Victor LM 7032 LP: RCA RB 6606 LP: RCA VIC 1321 LP: RCA AT 1070 LP: Franklin Mint CD: RCA GD 60308
New York 16 March 1940	NBC	CD: Dell' Arte DA 9020

Pizzetti

The Port of Famagusta (La pisanelle)

Camden NJ 20 December 1920	La Scala Orchestra	78: Victor Talking Machine VTM 64952/840 78: HMV DA 375 LP: RCA AT 1076 LP: RCA VL 46024

Ponchielli

La Gioconda, Dance of the hours

New York 4 April 1943	NBC	V-Disc: 63 LP: Toscanini Society ATS 1036 CD: Memories HR 4198
New York 29 July 1952	NBC	78: HMV DB 21587 45: RCA Victor ERB 7005 LP: RCA Victor LRM 7005/LM 1834/LM 2574 LP: HMV ALP 1235 LP: RCA VIC 1010/1263 LP: RCA AT 109/1052 LP: RCA VL 45829/46017 LP: Franklin Mint CD: RCA (Japan) R32C-1018 CD: RCA GD 60308

Prokofiev

Symphony No 1 "Classical"

New York 25 June 1944	NBC	V-Disc: 481 LP: Toscanini Society ATS 115
New York 13 January 1946	NBC	LP: Toscanini Society ATS 1038
New York 15 November 1947	NBC	AFRS: 61
New York 25 March 1950	NBC	Fabbri GSDM Series
New York 15 October 1951	NBC	45: RCA Victor WDM 9020 LP: RCA Victor LM 9020 LP: HMV ALP 1107 LP: RCA AT 122/1070 LP: RCA VL 45826 LP: Franklin Mint

Puccini

La Bohème

New York 3 and 10 February 1946	NBC NBC Chorus Albanese, McKnight, Peerce, Valentino, Cehanovsky, Baccaloni	45: RCA Victor WDM 1646 LP: RCA Victor LM 6006 LP: HMV ALP 1081-2 LP: RCA VIC 6019 LP: RCA AT 203/1097-8 CD: RCA GD 60288 CD: Memories HR 4142-3 Excerpts V-Disc: 654 LP: RCA Victor LM 1844 LP: Franklin Mint

Manon Lescaut, Act 3

Milan 11 May 1946	La Scala Chorus and Orchestra Favero, Malipiero, Nessi, Stabile, Pasero, Forti	LP: Toscanini Society ATS 1010 LP: HRE Records HRE 243 LP: Ed Smith EJS 434 LP: Discoreale DR 10004-5 CD: Legato SRO 802

Manon Lescaut, Intermezzo

New York 2 July 1944	NBC	LP: Toscanini Society ATS 1100 np LP: Franklin Mint
Milan 11 May 1946	La Scala Orchestra	LP: Toscanini Society ATS 1010 LP: HRE Records HRE 243 LP: Ed Smith EJS 434 LP: Discoreale DR 10004-5 CD: Legato SRO 802
New York 10 December 1949	NBC	LP: Toscanini Society ATS 1039

Manon Lescaut, Act 2 Minuet

New York 2 July 1944	NBC	LP: Toscanini Society ATS 1100 np

Ravel

Daphnis et Chloë, 2nd Suite

New York 26 November 1938	NBC	CD: Memories HR 4166
New York 19 November 1949	NBC	LP: Toscanini Society ATS 1055-9 LP: Toscanini Society ATS 108
New York 21 November 1949	NBC	78: RCA Victor DM 1374 45: RCA Victor WDM 1374 LP: RCA Victor LM 1043/6113/7032 LP: RCA Victor LVT 1025 LP: HMV ALP 1070 LP: RCA RB 6606 LP: RCA VIC 1273 LP: RCA AT 107/1060 LP: Franklin Mint

Bolero

New York 21 January 1939	NBC	LP: Discocorp RR 526 CD: Memories HR 4166

La valse

New York 27 April 1940	NBC	LP: Toscanini Society ATS 1055-9
New York 21 November 1943	NBC	LP: Fonit Cetra ARK 11 LP: Music and Arts ATRA 3001 CD: Memories HR 4166

THE NATIONAL BROADCASTING COMPANY

Presents

ARTURO TOSCANINI
Conducting
THE NBC SYMPHONY ORCHESTRA

CHRISTMAS NIGHT
Saturday, December 25, 1937
10:00 to 11:30 P.M., EST.
In NBC Studio 8-H—Radio City

Program

Concerto Grosso in D Minor, Opus 3, No. 11	Vivaldi
Symphony in G Minor	Mozart
Symphony No. 1, in C Minor	Brahms

These programs are broadcast over the
combined NBC Blue and Red Networks.

Since the modern microphone is extremely sensitive, your co-operation in maintaining strict silence during the music is urgently requested.

PROGRAM FOR NEW YEAR'S NIGHT
JANUARY 1, 1938

Symphony in C Major	Schubert
Two Movements from String Quartet in F Major, Opus 135	Beethoven
(a) Lento Assai, Cantante e tranquillo	
(b) Vivace	
"Death and Transfiguration"	Richard Strauss

TEATRO ALLA SCALA
(ENTE AUTONOMO)

STAGIONE SINFONICA MAGGIO - GIUGNO 1946

Concerto N. 1   N. 1 d'abbonamento

SABATO 11 MAGGIO 1946 alle ore 21 precise

INAUGURAZIONE DELLA RICOSTRUITA SALA DEL TEATRO

CONCERTO DIRETTO DA

ARTURO TOSCANINI

PROGRAMMA
PARTE PRIMA

G. ROSSINI	La Gazza Ladra	Ouverture
	Guglielmo Tell	Coro dell'Imeneo
		Danze dell'opera (passo a sei atto 1° e ballabile dei soldati atto 3°)
	Mosè	Preghiera RENATA TEBALDI - JOLANDA GARDINO GIOVANNI MALIPIERO - TANCREDI PASERO
G. VERDI	Nabucco	Ouverture
		Coro degli schiavi
	Vespri Siciliani	Ouverture
	Te Deum	

PARTE SECONDA

G. PUCCINI	Manon Lescaut	Intermezzo e atto III
		MAFALDA FAVERO - GIOVANNI MALIPIERO - GIUSEPPE NESSI MARIANO STABILE - TANCREDI PASERO - CARLO FORTI

PARTE TERZA

A. BOITO	Mefistofele	Prologo	TANCREDI PASERO

SOLISTI:
MAFALDA FAVERO - RENATA TEBALDI - JOLANDA GARDINO
GIOVANNI MALIPIERO - TANCREDI PASERO - MARIANO STABILE - GIUSEPPE NESSI - CARLO FORTI

ORCHESTRA E CORO DELLA SCALA

Maestro del Coro:

VITTORE VENEZIANI

PREZZI

Palchi e Poltrone di Platea *esauriti*	Ingresso ai Palchi . . . . L. 1000
Poltrone di Prima Galleria . . L. 2000	Ingresso alla Prima Galleria . » 350
Poltrone di Seconda Galleria . » 1000	Ingresso alla Seconda Galleria » 150
(compreso l'ingresso, escluse le tasse)	(escluse le tasse)

IN PLATEA NON VI SONO POSTI IN PIEDI

Durante l'esecuzione del Concerto è vietato accedere alla Platea e alle Gallerie. E' pure vietato muoversi dal proprio posto prima della fine di ogni pezzo.
Gli indumenti e gli altri oggetti depositati alle guardarobe non possono essere ritirati che negli intervalli o alla fine del Concerto.
Ragioni d'ordine e d'arte hanno indotto la Direzione a vietare le repliche dei pezzi. Il Pubblico è pregato di uniformarsi a tale disposizione.
La Biglietteria del Teatro si apre alle ore 10 di ciascun giorno per la vendita e prenotazione dei posti e per la vendita dei biglietti d'ingresso.
Per disposizione di S. E. il Prefetto è assolutamente vietato agli spettatori di accedere a qualsiasi posto della Sala (Platea e Gallerie) con cappelli, soprabiti, pellicce, bastoni, ombrelli e simili.
Per disposizione del Regolamento sulla vigilanza dei Teatri il pubblico può lasciare la sala, alla fine dello spettacolo, da tutte indistintamente le porte d'uscita.
Il Teatro si apre alle ore 20½ - Le Gallerie alle ore 19,30

Respighi

Feste romane

New York 30 March 1940	NBC	CD: Memories HR 4168
Philadelphia 19 November 1941	Philadelphia Orchestra	LP: RCA RL 01900 CD: RCA GD 60311/60328
New York 12 December 1949	NBC	78: HMV DB 21487-9 45: RCA Victor WDM 1490 LP: RCA Victor LM 55/LM 1973 LP: HMV BLP 1011 LP: RCA VIC 1344 LP: RCA AT 142/1060 LP: RCA VL 46000 LP: Franklin Mint CD: RCA (Japan) RCCD 1010 CD: RCA GD 60262

Fontane di Roma

New York 17 February 1951	NBC	LP: Toscanini Society ATS 1045
New York 17 December 1951	NBC	45: RCA Victor WDM 1768 LP: RCA Victor LM 1768 LP: HMV ALP 1101 LP: RCA RB 16108 LP: RCA VIC 1188/1244 LP: RCA AT 100/1061 LP: RCA VL 45814/46000 LP: Franklin Mint CD: RCA (Japan) RCCD 1010 CD: RCA GD 60262
New York 22 December 1951	NBC	CD: Memories HR 4168

Pini di Roma

New York 13 January 1945	NYPO	LP: Toscanini Society ATS 1034-5 LP: Music and Arts ATRA 3009 CD: As-Disc AS 600
New York 22 March 1952	NBC	VHS Video: RCA 790.357
New York 14 March 1953	NBC	CD: Memories HR 4168
New York 17 March 1953	NBC	45: RCA Victor WDM 1768/ERB 58 LP: RCA Victor LM 1768 LP: HMV ALP 1101 LP: RCA RB 16108 LP: RCA VIC 1188/1244 LP: RCA AT 100/1061 LP: RCA VL 45814/46000 LP: Franklin Mint CD: RCA (Japan) RCCD 1010 CD: RCA GD 60262

Gagliarda (Ancient Airs and Dances, Suite No 1)

Camden NJ 18 December 1920	La Scala Orchestra	78: Victor Talking Machine VTM 74672 78: HMV DB 418 LP: RCA AT 1076 LP: RCA VL 46024

Rieti

Symphony No 4 "Sinfonia tripartita"

New York 25 November 1945	NBC	LP: Toscanini Society ATS 1078 np

Roger-Ducasse

Sarabande

New York 7 April 1946	NBC NBC Chorus	LP: Toscanini Society ATS 1011-15 LP: Music and Arts ATRA 3001 CD: Dell' Arte DA 9020

Rossini

L'Assiedo di Corinto, Overture

New York 14 June 1945	NBC	LP: RCA Victor LM 7026 LP: RCA RB 6573 LP: RCA VIC 1248 LP: RCA VCM 6 LP: RCA AT 134/1032 LP: RCA VL 46006

Il Barbiere di Siviglia, Overture

New York 21 November 1929	NYPO	78: HMV D 1835 78: RCA Victor 7255/M 1063 45: RCA Camden CAE 336 LP: RCA Camden CAL 326/CAL 336/CDM 1055 LP: RCA AT 1074 CD: Pearl GEMMCDS 9373 CD: RCA GD 60329
Stockholm 3 December 1933 <u>Beginning only</u>	Stockholm Philharmonic Orchestra	LP: Orfeus (Sweden) 1-73 CD: BISCD 421-4
New York 21 November 1943	NBC	CD: Relief CR 1884 CD: Classical Society CSCD 104
New York 28 June 1945	NBC	78: RCA Victor V 2/M 1037/M 1063 45: RCA Victor WDM 1037/WEPR 14/ERA 14 LP: RCA Victor LM 1044/LM 2040 LP: HMV ALP 1007 LP: RCA RB 16096 LP: RCA VIC 1274 LP: RCA VCM 6 LP: RCA AT 108/1031 LP: RCA VL 45807/46004 LP: Franklin Mint
New York 21 March 1954	NBC	CD: Nuova Era 6345

La Cenerentola, Overture

New York 22 October 1938	NBC	CD: Relief CR 1884 CD: Classical Society CSCD 104
New York 8 June 1945	NBC	78: RCA Victor V 2/M 1037 45: RCA Victor WDM 1037/WEPR 13/ERA 13 LP: RCA Victor LM 1044/LM 2040 LP: HMV ALP 1007 LP: RCA RB 16096 LP: RCA VIC 1248 LP: RCA VCM 6 LP: RCA AT 108/1031 LP: RCA VL 45807/46004 LP: Franklin Mint

La gazza ladra, Overture

New York 12 April 1941	NBC	V-Disc: 461/241 CD: Relief CR 1884 CD: Classical Society CSCD 104
New York 25 June 1944	NBC	Unpublished but V-Disc 461 also mentions this date
New York 8 June 1945	NBC	78: RCA Victor V 2/M 1037 45: RCA Victor WDM 1037 LP: RCA Victor LM 1044/LM 2040 LP: HMV ALP 1007 LP: RCA RB 16096 LP: RCA VIC 1274 LP: RCA VCM 6 LP: RCA AT 108/1031 LP: RCA VL 45807/46004
Milan 11 May 1946	La Scala Orchestra	LP: HRE Records HRE 243 LP: Discoreale DR 10004-5 CD: Legato SRO 802

L'Italiana in Algeri, Overture

New York 10 April 1936	NYPO	78: HMV DB 2943 78: RCA Victor 14161/M 825/DM 825 LP: RCA AT 1081 CD: Pearl GEMMCDS 9373 CD: RCA GD 60329
New York 14 April 1950	NBC	LP: RCA Victor LM 7026 LP: RCA VIC 1248 LP: RCA VCM 6 LP: RCA AT 116/1032 LP: RCA VL 46006

Mosè: Excerpt (Preghiera)

Milan 11 May 1946	La Scala Chorus and Orchestra Tebaldi, Gardino, Malipiero, Pasero	LP: Toscanini Society ATS 1010 LP: Ed Smith EJS 434 LP: HRE Records HRE 243 LP: Discoreale DR 10004-5 CD: Legato SRO 802

La scala di seta, Overture

London 13 June 1938	BBCSO	78: HMV DB 3541 78: RCA Victor 15191/M 825/DM 825 LP: EMI XLP 30079 LP: Seraphim 60150 CD: EMI CDH 763 0182
Milan 16 September 1948	La Scala Orchestra	LP: Fonit Cetra LO 523 LP: Relief RL 822 CD: Palette PAL 2003-4
New York 5 March 1949	NBC	CD: Relief CR 1884 CD: Classical Society CSCD 104

Guglielmo Tell, Overture

New York 28 January 1939	NBC	LP: Toscanini Society ATS 123
New York 1 March 1939	NBC	78: HMV DA 1695-6 78: RCA Victor M 605 45: RCA Victor WDM 605 LP: RCA Victor LM 14 LP: RCA AT 1071
New York 16 March 1940	NBC	CD: Relief CR 1884 CD: Classical Society CSCD 104
New York 15 March 1952	NBC	LP: Toscanini Society ATS 1046 CD: Nuova Era 6345 VHS Video: RCA 790.353
New York 19 January 1953	NBC	45: RCA Victor ERB 7054 LP: RCA Victor LM 1986/LM 2040 LP: RCA Victor LRY 9000/LRM 7054 LP: HMV ALP 1441 LP: RCA RB 16096 LP: RCA VIC 1274 LP: RCA VCM 6 LP: RCA AT 108/1031 LP: RCA VL 45807/46004 LP: Franklin Mint CD: RCA (Japan) R32C-1018 CD: RCA RD 86205

Guglielmo Tell: Excerpt (Coro dell' Imeneo)

Milan 11 May 1946	La Scala Chorus and Orchestra	LP: Toscanini Society ATS 1010 LP: HRE Records HRE 243 LP: Discoreale DR 10004-5 CD: Legato SRO 802

Guglielmo Tell: Excerpt (Passo a sei)

New York 19 November 1938	NBC	LP: Toscanini Society ATS 123 CD: Relief CR 1884 CD: Classical Society CSCD 104
New York 4 April 1943	NBC	V-Disc: 226 LP: Toscanini Society ATS 1036
New York 8 June 1945	NBC	78: RCA Victor V 2/M 1037 45: RCA Victor WDM 1037/ERB 7005 LP: RCA Victor LRM 7005 /LM 1037 LP: RCA VIC 1274 LP: RCA VCM 6 LP: RCA AT 109/1032 LP: RCA VL 46017
Milan 11 May 1946	La Scala Orchestra	LP: Toscanini Society ATS 1010 LP: HRE Records HRE 243 LP: Discoreale DR 10004-5 CD: Legato SRO 802
New York 5 January 1952	NBC	CD: Memories HR 4198
New York 31 January 1953	NBC	CD: Nuova Era 6345

Guglielmo Tell: Excerpt (Act 3 Ballet)

New York 19 November 1938	NBC	LP: Toscanini Society ATS 123 CD: Relief CR 1884 CD: Classical Society CSCD 104
Milan 11 May 1946	La Scala	LP: Toscanini Society ATS 1010 LP: HRE Records HRE 243 LP: Discoreale DR 10004-5 CD: Legato SRO 802

Semiramide, Overture

London 12 June 1935	BBCSO	EMI unpublished
New York 10 April 1936	NYPO	78: HMV DB 3079-80 78: RCA Victor M 408/825 LP: RCA Camden CAL 309/CDM 1027 CD: Pearl GEMMCDS 9373 CD: RCA GD 60329
New York 5 February 1938	NBC	LP: Toscanini Society ATS 123
New York 13 March 1948	NBC	LP: Toscanini Society ATS 1077 np
New York 28 September 1951	NBC	45: RCA Victor ERB 7054 LP: RCA Victor LM 2040/LRM 7054 LP: RCA RB 16096 LP: RCA VIC 1274 LP: RCA VCM 6 LP: RCA AT 108/1031 LP: RCA VL 46004
New York 17 November 1951	NBC	CD: Nuova Era 6345 CD: Relief CR 1884 CD: Classical Society CSCD 104

Il Signor bruschino, Overture

New York 8 November 1942	NBC	LP: Toscanini Society ATS 123 CD: Nuova Era 6345 CD: Relief CR 1884 CD: Classical Society CSCD 104
New York 8 June 1945	NBC	78: RCA Victor V 2/M 1037 45: RCA Victor WDM 1037 LP: RCA Victor LM 1044/LM 2040 LP: HMV ALP 1007 45: HMV 7ER 5017 LP: RCA RB 16096 LP: RCA VIC 1274 LP: RCA VCM 6 LP: RCA AT 108/1031 LP: RCA VL 45807/46004
New York 11 November 1945	NBC	V-Disc: 637

String Sonata No 3 in C

New York	NBC	45: Musicians' Foundation No. 2
15 November 1952		LP: Movimento Musica 01.025
		LP: Dell' Arte DA 9008
		CD: Stradivarius STR 13595

Roussel

Le festin de l'araignée

New York	NBC	LP: Toscanini Society ATS 1011-5
7 April 1946		LP: Fonit Cetra ARK 11
		LP: Music and Arts ATRA 3001
		CD: Dell' Arte DA 9021

Rubinstein

Valse caprice

New York	NBC	LP: Toscanini Society ATS 100
21 December 1940		CD: Relief CR 1886

Saint-Saëns

Symphony No 3 "Organ"

New York	NBC	LP: RCA Victor LM 1874
15 November 1952	Crook	LP: HMV ALP 1296
		LP: RCA AT 150 /1065
		CD: Memories HR 4161

Danse macabre

New York	NYPO	LP: Toscanini Society ATS 1089 np
1 March 1936		

New York	NBC	CD: Memories HR 4167
8 January 1938		

New York	NBC	78: RCA Victor DM 1505
1 June 1950		45: RCA Victor WDM 1505/WEPR 15/ERA 15
		LP: RCA Victor LM 1118/LM 2056
		LP: HMV ALP 1432
		45: HMV 7ER 5012
		LP: RCA VIC 1244
		LP: RCA AT 150 /1065
		LP: RCA VL 45803/46007
		LP: Franklin Mint
		CD: RCA (Japan) R32C-1019
		CD: RCA RD 86205

D. Scarlatti

The Good-humoured Ladies, Suite (orch. Tommasini)

New York 24 March 1946	NBC	LP: Toscanini Society ATS 1039

Schubert

Symphony No 2

New York 12 November 1938	NBC	LP: Toscanini Society ATS 1025-9 LP: Music and Arts ATRA 3003 CD: Dell' Arte DA 9022
New York 26 March 1944	NBC	CD: Memories HR 4212

Symphony No 5

New York 14 March 1953	NBC	CD: Hunt CDLSMH 34023 CD: Memories HR 4212
New York 17 March 1953	NBC	LP: RCA Victor LM 1869 LP: RCA VIC 1311 LP: RCA AT 123/1022 LP: RCA VL 45804

Symphony No 8 "Unfinished"

New York 14 October 1939	NBC	LP: Music and Arts ATRA 3009 CD: Memories HR 4212
New York 12 March and 8 June 1950	NBC	78: RCA Victor DM 1456 45: RCA Victor WDM 1456 LP: RCA Victor LM 54/LM 9022 LP: HMV BLP 1038 LP: RCA RB 16092 LP: RCA VIC 1311 LP: RCA AT 101/1022 LP: RCA VL 45804/46003 CD: RCA (Japan) RCCD 1003

Symphony No 9 "Great"

New York 26 April 1936	NYPO	LP: Toscanini Society ATS 1090-1 np LP: Toscanini Society ATS 109-1-
Philadelphia 16 November 1941	Philadelphia Orchestra	LP: RCA Victor LD 2663 LP: RCA RB 6549 LP: RCA AT 102/1075 LP: RCA RL 01900 LP: Franklin Mint CD: RCA GD 60313/60328
New York 23 February 1947	NBC	LP: Toscanini Society ATS 1039
New York 25 February 1947	NBC	78: RCA Victor M 1167 45: RCA Victor WDM 1167 LP: RCA Victor LM 1040 LP: HMV ALP 1120 LP: RCA AT 1024
Milan 16 September 1948	La Scala Orchestra	LP: Fonit Cetra LO 523 LP: Relief RL 822 CD: Palette PAL 2003-4
New York 7 February 1953	NBC	CD: Nuova Era 013.6315 CD: Hunt CDLSMH 34023 Incorrectly dated 7 February 1952
New York 9 February 1953	NBC	LP: RCA Victor LM 1835 LP: RCA RB 16079 LP: RCA AT 151/1023 LP: RCA VL 45820

Grand Duo (orch. Joachim; sometimes referred to as Gastein Symphony)

New York 15 February 1941	NBC	LP: Toscanini Society ATS 1083 np LP: HRE Records HRE 285

Schumann

Symphony No 2

New York 29 March 1941	NBC	LP: Toscanini Society ATS 1011-15 LP: Music and Arts ATRA 3003 LP: Fonit Cetra ARK 10
New York 17 March 1946	NBC	CD: Dell' Arte DA 9022

Symphony No 3 "Rhenish"

New York 29 January 1938	NBC	LP: Toscanini Society ATS 122
New York 12 November 1949	NBC	LP: RCA Victor LM 2048 LP: HMV BLP 1095 LP: RCA VIC 1337 LP: RCA AT 138/1025

Manfred, Overture

New York 19 November 1938	NBC	LP: Toscanini Society ATS 122
New York 11 November 1946	NBC	78: RCA Victor M 1287/DM 1287 45: RCA Victor WDM 1287 LP: RCA Victor LM 6/LM 9022 LP: RCA VIC 1249 LP: RCA AT 1025
New York 31 January 1953	NBC	CD: Curcio-Hunt CON 19

Shostakovich

Symphony No 1

New York 14 January 1939	NBC	LP: Music and Arts ATRA 3011
New York 12 March 1944	NBC	LP: RCA Victor LM 6711 LP: RCA AT 205/1067 LP: RCA VL 45826

Symphony No 7 "Leningrad"

New York 19 July 1942 US premiere	NBC	LP: RCA Victor LM 6711 LP: RCA AT 205/1067-8 CD: Memories HR 4183

Sibelius

Symphony No 2

London 10 June 1938	BBCSO	LP: Toscanini Society ATS 1093-6 np CD: EMI CDH 763 3072
New York 18 February 1939	NBC	CD: Dell' Arte DA 9019
New York 7 December 1940	NBC	LP: RCA Victor LM 6711 LP: RCA AT 139/1063 CD: Memories HR 4210

Symphony No 4

New York 27 April 1940	NBC	LP: Toscanini Society ATS 1009 LP: Music and Arts ATRA 3006 CD: Memories HR 4210

En Saga

London 14 June 1937	BBCSO	LP: Toscanini Society ATS 1093-6 np
New York 15 March 1952	NBC	LP: Toscanini Society ATS 1046 LP: Fonit Cetra ARK 10 LP: Music and Arts ATRA 3006 VHS Video: RCA 790.353

Finlandia

New York 18 February 1939	NBC	CD: Memories HR 4169
New York 5 August 1952	NBC	45: RCA Victor ERB 7005 LP: RCA Victor LM 1834/LRM 7005 LP: HMV ALP 1235 LP: RCA VIC 1010/1245 LP: RCA AT 122/1063 LP: RCA VL 46007 CD: RCA (Japan) R32C-1019

Leminkainen's Homecoming

New York 7 December 1940	NBC	LP: Toscanini Society ATS 1034-5 LP: Music and Arts ATRA 3006 CD: Dell' Arte DA 9020 CD: Memories HR 4169

Pohjola's Daughter

New York   NBC   LP: RCA Victor LM 6711
7 December 1940   LP: RCA AT 139/1063
                                    CD: Memories HR 4169

The Swan of Tuonela

New York   NBC   LP: Music and Arts ATRA 3006
18 February 1939

New York   NBC   V-Disc: 333
27 August 1944   LP: Franklin Mint

New York   NYPO   LP: Toscanini Society ATS 1034-5
13 January 1945   LP: Music and Arts ATRA 3009
                                    CD: AS-Disc AS 600

Siegmeister

Western Suite

New York   NBC   LP: Toscanini Society ATS 1093-6 np
25 November 1945
World premiere

Sinigaglia

Le baruffe chiozzotte, Overture

New York   NBC   LP: Toscanini Society ATS 1039
23 February 1947

Smetana

The Bartered Bride, Overture

New York 26 November 1938	NBC	LP: Toscanini Society ATS 107
New York 17 November 1946	NBC	LP: Toscanini Society ATS 1084 np LP: Franklin Mint CD: Memories HR 4202

Vltava (Má Vlast)

New York 13 December 1941	NBC	V-Disc: 113/121
New York 19 March 1950	NBC	78: HMV DB 21496-7 78: RCA Victor DM 1505 45: RCA Victor WDM 1505 LP: RCA Victor LM 1118/2056 LP: HMV ALP 1432 LP: RCA VIC 1245 LP: RCA AT 124 /1062 LP: RCA VL 45810/46007 LP: Franklin Mint CD: RCA (Japan) RCCD 1008 CD: RCA RD 86205 CD: RCA GD 60279
New York 14 March 1953	NBC	CD: Memories HR 4182

Sousa

El capitán

New York 27 August 1944	NBC	LP: Toscanini Society ATS 101 CD: Memories HR 4199
New York 18 May 1945	NBC	LP: RCA Victor LM 7032 LP: RCA RB 6606-7 LP: RCA AT 1069 LP: Franklin Mint

Semper fidelis

New York 27 August 1944	NBC	LP: Toscanini Society ATS 101 CD: Memories HR 4199

Stars and stripes forever

New York 4 April 1943	NBC	V-Disc: 31 LP: Toscanini Society ATS 1036 CD: Memories HR 4199
New York 18 May 1945	NBC	78: RCA Victor 11-9188 45: RCA Victor 49-1082/ERC 3 LP: RCA Victor VCM 7001 LP: RCA AT 1069 LP: Franklin Mint CD: RCA RD 86205

Johann Strauss

An der schönen blauen Donau, Waltz

New York 6 December 1941	NBC	CD: Memories HR 4198
New York 11 December 1941 & 19 March 1942	NBC	78: HMV DB 6171 78: RCA Victor 11-8580 LP: RCA Victor VCM 7001 LP: RCA VIC 1321 LP: RCA AT 118/1071 CD: RCA GD 60308
New York 18 March 1942	NBC	V-Disc: 138

Frühlingsstimmen, Waltz

New York 18 July 1943	NBC	LP: Toscanini Society ATS 1099 np
New York 13 January 1946	NBC	LP: Toscanini Society ATS 1038 CD: Memories HR 4198

Tritsch-Tratsch, Polka

New York 15 February 1941	NBC	CD: Memories HR 4198
New York 6 May 1941	NBC	78: RCA Victor 11-9188 45: RCA Victor 49-1082 LP: RCA Victor LM 7032 LP: RCA RB 6606-7 LP: RCA VIC 1321 LP: RCA AT 118/1071 CD: RCA GD 60308

Richard Strauss

Dance of the 7 Veils (Salome)

New York 14 January 1939	NBC	LP: Toscanini Society ATS 1001-4 LP: Franklin Mint CD: Hunt CD 530

Don Juan

New York 14 October 1939	NBC	LP: Music and Arts ATRA 3011 CD: Music and Arts ATRA 613
Washington 14 May 1940	NBC	CD: Hunt CD 538
New York 14 February 1948	NBC	LP: Toscanini Society ATS 1085 np
New York 10 January 1951	NBC	45: RCA Victor WDM 1563 LP: RCA Victor LM 1157/LM 7032 LP: HMV ALP 1173 LP: RCA RB 6606-7 LP: RCA VIC 1022/1267 LP: RCA AT 105 /1057 LP: Franklin Mint LP: RCA VL 45819
New York 28 February 1954	NBC	CD: Nuova Era 013.6311-2

Don Quixote

London 23 May 1938	BBCSO Feuermann	LP: Fonit Cetra LO 526
New York 22 October 1938	NBC Feuermann	LP: Toscanini Society ATS 1011-15 LP: Discocorp IGI 372 CD: Hunt CD 530 CD: Music and Arts ATRA 613 Hunt incorrectly dated 22 November 1938
New York 11 December 1948	NBC Miller	AFRS: 116
New York 22 November 1953	NBC Miller	LP: RCA Victor LM 2026 LP: HMV ALP 1493 LP: RCA AT 148/1058 LP: RCA VL 45830 CD: RCA GD 60295

Ein Heldenleben

New York 1 February 1941	NBC	LP: Toscanini Society ATS 1001-4 CD: Hunt CD 538 CD: AS-Disc AS 308

Till Eulenspiegels lustige Streiche

New York 16 March 1940	NBC	CD: Hunt CD 538
New York 1 November 1952	NBC	LP: Toscanini Society ATS 1086 np
New York 4 November 1952	NBC	LP: RCA Victor LM 1891 LP: HMV ALP 1404 LP: RCA VIC 1267 LP: RCA AT 105/1057 LP: RCA VL 45819 LP: Franklin Mint CD: RCA (Japan) RCCD 1009

Tod und Verklärung

New York 1 January 1938	NBC	CD: Hunt CD 530 CD: Music and Arts ATRA 613
Den Haag 23 March 1938	Residentie Orchestra	Unpublished
Philadelphia 8 January 1942	Philadelphia Orchestra	LP: RCA RL 01900 CD: RCA GD 60312/60328
New York 17 November 1946	NBC	AFRS: 65 Rehearsal extracts LP: Paragon LB1 53005
New York 8 and 10 March 1952	NBC	LP: RCA Victor LM 1891 LP: HMV ALP 1404 LP: RCA AT 105/1057 LP: Franklin Mint CD: RCA GD 60295 Rehearsal extracts LP: Morgan MOR 001 LP: Toscanini Society ATS 121

Stravinsky

Petrushka: Excerpts (Tableaux 1 and 4)

New York 21 December 1940	NBC	LP: Toscanini Society ATS 1025-9 LP: HRE Records HRE 285 LP: Franklin Mint

Suppé

Poet and Peasant, Overture

New York 18 July 1943	NBC	LP: RCA Victor LM 6026 LP: HMV ALP 1418 LP: RCA AT 124/1071 LP: RCA VL 45817/46007 LP: Franklin Mint CD: RCA GD 60308

Tchaikovsky

Symphony No 6 "Pathétique"

New York 29 October 1938	NBC	LP: Toscanini Society ATS 111
New York 19 April 1941	NBC	LP: Melodram MEL 235 CD: Melodram MEL 18014
Philadelphia 8 February 1942	Philadelphia Orchestra	LP: RCA RL 01900 CD: RCA GD 60312/60328
New York 24 November 1947	NBC	78: RCA Victor V 27/M 1281 45: RCA Victor WDM 1281 LP: RCA Victor LM 1036 LP: RCA VIC 1268 LP: RCA AT 104/1053 LP: Franklin Mint
New York 21 March 1954	NBC	CD: Nuova Era 013.6322 CD: Curcio-Hunt CON 06

Manfred Symphony

New York 21 January 1945	NBC	AFRS: 92
New York 5 December 1949	NBC	78: RCA Victor DM 1372 45: RCA Victor WDM 1372 LP: RCA Victor LM 1037/LVT 1024 LP: RCA RB 16090 LP: RCA VIC 1315 LP: RCA AT 145/1054
New York 10 January 1953	NBC	CD: Music and Arts ATRA 260 CD: Curcio-Hunt CON 30

Piano Concerto No 1

New York 19 April 1941	NBC Horowitz	LP: Melodram MEL 235 CD: Melodram MEL 18014
New York 6 and 14 May 1941	NBC Horowitz	78: HMV DB 5988-91/8922-5 auto 78: RCA Victor M 800 45: RCA Victor WCT 16/ERBT 3 LP: RCA Victor LCT 1012 LP: HMV CSLP 505 LP: RCA VIC 1554 LP: RCA AT 113 (UK only)/1056
New York 25 April 1943	NBC Horowitz	LP: RCA Victor LM 2319 LP: RCA RB 16190 LP: RCA AT 113 (except UK)/1056 LP: RCA VH 015/400 LP: RCA VL 46016 LP: Franklin Mint CD: RCA GD 60449/87992 CD: Memories HR 4197 CD: Classical Society CSCD 103

Eugene Onegin, Waltz

New York	NBC	LP: Toscanini Society ATS 1025-9
27 August 1944		CD: Memories HR 4197

Nutcracker, Suite

New York	NBC	V-Discs: 261-2/501-2
25 April 1943		

New York   NBC
17 November 1951
LP: Melodram MEL 235
CD: Nuova Era 013.6322
CD: Memories HR 4197

New York   NBC
19 November 1951
45: RCA Victor WRY 9000
LP: RCA Victor LM 1986/LRY 9000
LP: RCA VIC 1263
LP: RCA AT 118
LP: RCA VL 45803
LP: Franklin Mint
CD: RCA (Japan) R32C-1019
Waltz only
LP: RCA AT 119/1055
Various excerpts (different takes)
45: RCA Victor SRJ 9050/SPD 1

Romeo and Juliet, Fantasy Overture

New York   NBC
7 April 1946
LP: Toscanini Society ATS 1081 np

New York   NBC
8 April 1946
78: RCA Victor M 1178
45: RCA Victor WDM 1178/ERB 22
LP: RCA Victor LM 1019/LM 7032
LP: HMV ALP 1469
LP: RCA RB 6606-7
LP: RCA VIC 1245
LP: RCA AT 119/1055
LP: Franklin Mint

Milan   La Scala
16 September 1948   Orchestra
LP: Relief RL 822
CD: Palette PAL 2003-4

New York   NBC
21 March 1953
LP: Toscanini Society ATS 1047
LP: GDS Records GDS 5011
LP: Dell' Arte DA 9014
CD: Music and Arts ATRA 260
CD: Stradivarius STR 13593

The Tempest, Overture

New York   NBC
12 March 1944
LP: Toscanini Society ATS 1060
LP: Dell' Arte DA 9014

The Voyevode, Overture

New York   NBC
19 April 1941
LP: Toscanini Society ATS 1060
LP: Melodram MEL 235
LP: Toscanini Society ATS 111

Carl Fischer Study Score Series

HOWARD HANSON,
 Symphony No. 1 ("Nordic") 2.00
 Symphony No. 2 ("Romantic") 2.50
RANDALL THOMPSON,
 String Quartet No. 1 (D Minor) 1.50
Study scores for other important symphonic and instrumental works in preparation.

CARL FISCHER, INC.
Cooper Square, N. Y. 3 • 165 W. 57 St., N. Y. 19

Everyone goes to "HICKS"
for the Finest Sodas — Fresh Fruit Drinks ...in town
Try us for Breakfast, Luncheon Dinner, Cocktails

H. HICKS & SON INC.
30 W. 57 ST. (bet. 5 & 6 Aves.)

CARNEGIE HALL
Season 1948-1949

FIRE NOTICE—Look around *now* and choose the nearest exit to your seat. In case of fire walk (not run) to *that* Exit. Do not try to beat your neighbor to the street.
FRANK J. QUAYLE, *Fire Commissioner*

Wednesday Evening, April 20th, at 8:30 o'clock

TOSCANINI

and

THE NBC SYMPHONY ORCHESTRA

Assisting Artists:
ROSE BAMPTON and SET SVANHOLM

Program Continued on Second Page Following

A Great Victor Recording
WALTON—Concerto for Violin & Orch. Jascha Heifetz & Cincinnati Sym., Goossens, Cond.
DM-868..........................Price $4.75
LIBERTY MUSIC SHOPS 450 MADISON AVE.

PETERS EDITION
EULENBURG MINIATURE SCORES
HINRICHSEN EDITION

NEW RELEASES

CHAMBER MUSIC ORCHESTRAL WORKS
by
Bach
 Beethoven
  Brahms
   Bruckner
    Chopin
     Haydn
      Mozart
       Schubert
        Vivaldi

Catalogs upon request

C. F. PETERS CORPORATION
Carnegie Hall, 881 Seventh Ave., N. Y. 19

Baldwin
Distinguished Recognition

THE BALDWIN PIANO CO.

20 East 54th St.
New York 22
PLaza 3-7136

Queen's Hall

Sole Lessees: Messrs. Chappell and Co., Ltd.

London Music Festival

FOURTH CONCERT

Monday 30 May 1938 at 8.15 p.m.

Te Deum, for Double Chorus and Orchestra   VERDI
1813—1901

INTERVAL

Requiem Mass, for Four Solo Voices,
                 Chorus and Orchestra   VERDI

Zinka Milanov
Kerstin Thorborg
Helge Roswaenge
Nicola Moscona

The B.B.C. Choral Society
(Chorus Master: Leslie Woodgate)

The B.B.C. Symphony Orchestra
Leader: Paul Beard   Organ: Berkeley Mason

CONDUCTOR: Arturo Toscanini

Thomas

Mignon, Overture

New York 14 March 1942	NBC	LP: Toscanini Society ATS 108
New York 19 March 1942	NBC	78: HMV DB 6177 78: RCA Victor 11-8545 LP: RCA AT 1081
New York 29 July 1952	NBC	45: RCA Victor ERB 7013 LP: RCA Victor LRM 7013/LM 6026 LP: RCA AT 116/1066 LP: Franklin Mint

Tommasini

Il carnevale di Venezia

New York 13 March 1948	NBC	LP: Toscanini Society ATS 1077 np

Vaughan Williams

Tallis Fantasia

New York 18 November 1945	NBC	V-Disc: 606-7 LP: Toscanini Society ATS 1055-9 CD: Memories HR 4182

Verdi

Requiem Mass

London 27 May 1938	BBCSO BBC Choral Society Milanov, Thorborg, Roswaenge, Moscona	LP: Vocal Art (no catalogue number) LP: MKR Records MKR 1001-2 LP: UORC Records UORC 108 LP: Toscanini Society ATS 1108-9 CD: Melodram MEL 28022
New York 23 November 1940	NBC Westminster Choir Milanov, Castagna, Björling, Moscona	LP: UORC Records UORC 229 LP: Toscanini Society ATS 1005-6 LP: Melodram MEL 006 CD: Music and Arts ATRA 240 CD: Melodram MEL 38006 CD: Palette PAL 3004-6 CD: Greenline 3CLC 4003
Milan 26 June 1950	La Scala Chorus and Orchestra Tebaldi, Elmo. Prandelli, Siepi	LP: Hope Records HOPE 115 LP: MDP Records MDP 030 CD: GDS Records GDS 2301
New York 27 January 1951	NBC Shaw Chorale Nelli, Barbieri, Di Stefano, Siepi	LP: RCA Victor LM 6018 LP: HMV ALP 1380-1 LP: RCA RB 16131-2 LP: RCA VCM 10 LP: RCA AT 201/1050-1 LP: RCA VL 46010 CD: RCA GD 60299/60326

Te Deum (4 Pezzi sacri)

New York 23 November 1940	NBC Westminster Choir	LP: Toscanini Society ATS 1005-6 CD: Music and Arts ATRA 240
New York 2 December 1945	NBC Westminster Choir	LP: Toscanini Society ATS 1076 CD: Melodram MEL 28022 CD: GDS Records GDS 2301
Milan 11 May 1946	La Scala Chorus and Orchestra	LP: HRE Records HRE 243 LP: Discoreale DR 10004-5 CD: Legato SRO 802
Milan 24 June 1950	La Scala Chorus and Orchestra	LP: ERI/Fabbri 375.477
New York 14 March 1954	NBC Shaw Chorale	LP: RCA Victor LM 1849 LP: HMV ALP 1363 LP: RCA VIC 1331 LP: RCA VCM 10 LP: RCA AT 132/1049 CD: RCA GD 60299/60326

Prestissimo and Scherzo (String Quartet)

New York 27 January 1946	NBC	LP: Toscanini Society ATS 1076 np LP: Toscanini Society ATS 102 CD: Memories HR 4188-9

Aida

New York	NBC	LP: RCA Victor LM 6132
26 March and	Shaw Chorale	LP: RCA RB 16021-3
2 April 1949	Nelli, Gustavson,	LP: RCA VIC 6113
(extra retakes	Tucker, Valdengo,	LP: RCA AT 302 /1089-91
June 1954)	Scott	LP: RCA VL 45833-5/46021
		CD: Nuova Era 2268-70
		CD: RCA GD 60300/60326
		CD: Memories HR 4150-1
		VHS Video: RCA 790.346

Preludes only
LP: RCA AT 304/VL 45825
Ballet Music
LP: RCA AT 109
Excerpts
LP: RCA VL 45806
LP: Franklin Mint
Rehearsal extracts
LP: CLS MDTP 029
Nuova Era and Memories CDs and RCA video do not have the 1954 retakes

Aida: Excerpt (Ritorna vincitor)

New York	NYPO	LP: Toscanini Society ATS 1089 np
1 March 1936	Giannini	LP: Toscanini Society ATS 105

ATS 105 incorrectly pitched

Aida, Overture

New York	NBC	LP: Toscanini Society ATS 1076 np
30 March 1940		LP: Penzance Records 37
World premiere		LP: Morgan MOR 3701
		LP: Laudis 1002
		LP: Movimento Musica 01.002
		CD: Nuova Era 6345
		CD: Melodram MEL 18021
		CD: Movimento Musica 011.008
		CD: GDS Records GDS 2301
		CD: Memories HR 4188-9

Melodram and GDS issues incorrectly dated 25 July 1943

Un ballo in maschera

New York 17 and 24 January and 3 June 1954	NBC Shaw Chorale Nelli, Turner, Haskins, Peerce, Merrill	LP: RCA Victor LM 6112 LP: HMV ALP 1252-4 LP: RCA AT 300 /1085-7 LP: RCA VL 46015 CD: RCA GD 60301 CD: Memories HR 4146-7 Excerpts LP: RCA AT 304 LP: RCA VL 45825 LP: Franklin Mint

Un ballo in maschera: Excerpt (Eri tu)

New York 25 July 1943	NBC Valentino	LP: TD Records TD 504 CD: Melodram MEL 18021 CD: Memories HR 4188-9

An acoustic recording of an aria and ensemble from Un ballo in maschera, with Pertile and other singers of Toscanini's La Scala ensemble, was made in Milan in 1925 by the Fonitipia company, precisely at the time when Toscanini was conducting the work there; it has occasionally been suggested that this record, later published on Parlophone and reissued in various Pertile LP compilations, was conducted by Toscanini, but there is no real evidence to support this

Don Carlo: Excerpt (O don fatale)

New York 25 July 1943	NBC Merriman	V-Disc: 75 LP: TD Records TD 504 CD: Melodram MEL 18021 CD: Memories HR 4188-9

Falstaff

Salzburg 26 July 1937	VPO Vienna Opera Chorus Somigli, Cravcenko, Vasari, Oltrabella, Stabile, Biasini, Borgioli	LP: Penzance Records 37 LP: Morgan MOR 3701 LP: Fonit Cetra LO 46 Act 1 only LP: MR 2003
Salzburg 23 August 1937	Details as above	LP: Toscanini Society ATS 1067-9 np CD: GDS Records GDS 21014
New York 1 and 8 April 1950	NBC Shaw Chorale Nelli, Merriman, Elmo, Stich-Randall, Valdengo, Guarrera, Madasi	LP: RCA Victor LM 6111/6017 LP: HMV ALP 1229-31 LP: RCA RB 16163-5 LP: RCA AT 301/1094-6 LP: RCA VL 45839-41/46023 CD: RCA GD 60251/60326 CD: Memories HR 4140-1 Rehearsal extracts LP: Paragon LB1 53005 CD: Music and Arts ATRA 248

At time of going to press it has not been verified whether the two Salzburg recordings emanate from the same performance; see note on the Selonophone recordings in introduction to the Toscanini discography.

La forza del destino, Overture

New York 28 June 1945	NBC	78: HMV DB 6314 78: RCA Victor 11-9010 45: RCA Victor 49-1175 LP: RCA AT 1081
New York 27 January 1946	NBC	V-Disc: 638 LP: Toscanini Society ATS 1076 np
New York 8 November 1952	NBC	CD: Nuova Era 6345 CD: Legato Classics LCD 136 CD: Memories HR 4188-9 Legato incorrectly dated 11 November 1952
New York 10 November 1952	NBC	45: RCA Victor ERA 125 45: HMV 7ER 5021 LP: RCA Victor LM 6026/6041 LP: HMV ALP 1417/1452 LP: RCA RB 16140 LP: RCA VIC 1248 LP: RCA VCM 6 LP: RCA AT 304/1049 LP: RCA VL 45806/46006 LP: Franklin Mint LP: Movimento Musica 01.002 CD: RCA (Japan) R32C-1010

La forza del destino: Excerpt (Pace, pace)

New York 25 July 1943	NBC Ribla	LP: TD Records TD 504 CD: Melodram MEL 18021 CD: Memories HR 4188-9

Inno delle nazioni

New York 31 January 1943 US premiere	NBC Westminster Choir Peerce	LP: Toscanini Society ATS 1097 LP: Toscanini Society ATS 105
New York 8 and 20 December 1943	NBC Westminster Choir Peerce	LP: RCA Victor LM 6041 LP: HMV ALP 1453 LP: RCA RB 16139 LP: RCA VIC 1331 LP: RCA VCM 10 LP: RCA AT 304/1049 LP: RCA VL 45825 CD: RCA GD 60299/60326

I Lombardi: Excerpt (Qui posa il fianco)

New York 31 January 1943	NBC Della Chiesa, Peerce, Moscona	LP: RCA Victor LM 6041 LP: HMV ALP 1452 LP: RCA RB 16139 LP: RCA VIC 1314 LP: RCA VCM 6 LP: RCA AT 304/1048 CD: RCA GD 60276 CD: Memories HR 4188-9

Luisa Miller, Overture

New York   NBC
25 July 1943

LP: RCA Victor LM 6041
LP: HMV ALP 1452
LP: RCA RB 16140
LP: RCA VIC 1314
LP: RCA VCM 6
LP: RCA AT 304/1048
LP: RCA VL 45806/46006
LP: Franklin Mint
LP: Movimento Musica 01.002
CD: Nuova Era 6345
CD: Legato Classics LCD 136
CD: Melodram MEL 18021
CD: GDS Records GDS 2301
CD: Memories HR 4188-9
Melodram and GDS issues incorrectly dated 30 March 1940

Luisa Miller: Excerpt (Quando le sere)

New York   NBC
25 July 1943   Peerce

LP: RCA Victor LM 6041
LP: HMV ALP 1452
LP: RCA RB 16140
LP: RCA VIC 1314
LP: RCA VCM 6
LP: RCA AT 304/1048
CD: RCA GD 60299/60326
CD: Melodram MEL 18021
CD: Memories HR 4188-9

Nabucco, Overture

Milan   La Scala
11 May 1946   Orchestra

LP: Toscanini Society ATS 1010
LP: HRE Records HRE 243
LP: Discoreale DR 10004-5
CD: Legato SRO 802

Nabucco: Excerpt (Va pensiero)

New York   NBC
31 January 1943   Westminster Choir

LP: RCA Victor LM 6041
LP: HMV ALP 1452
LP: RCA RB 16139
LP: RCA VIC 1331
LP: RCA VCM 10
LP: RCA AT 304/1048
LP: RCA VL 45806/46015
LP: Franklin Mint
CD: RCA GD 60299/60326
CD: Memories HR 4188-9

Milan   La Scala Chorus
11 May 1946   and Orchestra

LP: Toscanini Society ATS 1010
LP: HRE Records HRE 243
LP: Discoreale DR 10004-5
CD: Legato SRO 802

Otello

New York 6 and 13 December 1947	NBC NBC Chorus Nelli, Merriman, Vinay, Valdengo	45: RCA Victor WDM 6107 LP: RCA Victor LM 6107 LP: HMV ALP 1090-2 LP: RCA RB 16093-5 LP: RCA AT 303/1091-3 LP: RCA VL 45836-8 CD: RCA GD 60327 CD: Memories HR 4144-5 Excerpts V-Disc: 847 (Willow Song and Ave Maria) 45: RCA Victor ERA 260 LP: RCA AT 304 LP: RCA VL 45806/45825 LP: Franklin Mint Rehearsal extract LP: CLS MDRL 12821

Otello, Act 3 Ballet Music

New York 27 January 1946	NBC	LP: Toscanini Society ATS 1076
New York 13 March 1948	NBC	LP: RCA Victor LM 6041 LP: HMV ALP 1453 LP: RCA RB 16139 LP: RCA VIC 1321 LP: Toscanini Society ATS 1077 np LP: RCA AT 109/1049 CD: Memories HR 4198
Milan 16 September 1948	La Scala Orchestra	LP: Fonit Cetra LO 523 LP: Relief RL 822 CD: Palette PAL 2003-4

Rigoletto, Act 4

New York 25 July 1943	NBC NBC Chorus Ribla, Merriman, Peerce, Valentino, Moscona	LP: TD Records TD 504 CD: Melodram MEL 28022 Quartet only V-Disc: 75
New York 25 May 1944	NBC NBC Chorus Milanov, Merriman, Peerce, Warren, Moscona	LP: RCA Victor LM 6041 LP: HMV ALP 1453 LP: RCA RB 16140 LP: RCA VIC 1314 LP: RCA AT 304 LP: RCA VCM 6 LP: RCA AT 304/1048 LP: Movimento Musica 01.002 LP: Laudis 1002 LP: Franklin Mint CD: Movimento Musica 011.008 CD: RCA GD 60276 CD: Memories HR 4188-9

La Traviata

New York 1 and 8 December 1946	NBC NBC Chorus Albanese, Peerce, Merrill	78: HMV DB 21360-72 45: RCA Victor WDM 1544 LP: RCA Victor LM 6003 LP: HMV ALP 1072-3 LP: RCA AT 202/1083-4 CD: Memories HR 4148-9 CD: RCA GD 60329

Excerpts
LP: RCA RB 6619
LP: RCA VL 45825/46015
LP: Franklin Mint

Complete final rehearsal
CD: Music and Arts ATRA 271

Rehearsal extracts
LP: Musicians' Foundation No 1
LP: Paragon LB1 53005
LP: Relief RL 812

La Traviata, Preludes Acts 1 and 3

New York 18 March 1929	NYPO	78: HMV D 1672 78: RCA Victor 6994 45: RCA Camden CAE 335 LP: RCA Camden CAL 309/CDM 1027 LP: RCA AT 1074 CD: Pearl GEMMCDS 9373 CD: RCA GD 60329
New York 10 March 1941	NBC	78: HMV DB 5956 78: RCA Victor 18080 78: RCA Victor M 1064 (Act 1 Prelude) LP: RCA Victor LM 6088 (Act 1 Prelude) LP: RCA VIC 1248 LP: RCA VCM 6 LP: RCA 304/1049
New York 31 January 1943 Act 3 Prelude only	NBC	CD: Memories HR 4188-9
Milan 6 and 8 August 1951	La Scala Orchestra	78: RCA (Brazil) V 886-5000

I Vespri siciliani, Overture

New York 24 January 1942	NBC	LP: RCA Victor LM 6041 LP: HMV ALP 1452 LP: RCA RB 16140 LP: RCA VIC 1248 LP: RCA AT 116/AT 304 LP: RCA VCM 6 LP: RCA AT 116/304/1049 LP: RCA VL 45806/46006 LP: Franklin Mint CD: Memories HR 4188-9
Milan 11 May 1946	La Scala Orchestra	LP: Toscanini Society ATS 1010 LP: HRE Records HRE 243 LP: Discoreale DR 10004-5 CD: Legato SRO 802
Milan 5 and 8 August 1951	La Scala Orchestra	Unpublished

Vieuxtemps

Ballade and Polonaise

New York 14 December 1940	NBC	LP: Toscanini Society ATS 100

Vivaldi

Concerto Grosso in D minor op 3 no 11

New York 25 December 1937	NBC	LP: Toscanini Society ATS 1079-80 np CD: Myto MCD 89009
New York 14 March 1954	NBC	45: Musicians' Foundation No 2 LP: Toscanini Society ATS 1042 LP: Movimento Musica 01.025 LP: Dell' Arte DA 9008

Violin Concerto in B flat

New York 22 November 1947	NBC Mischakoff	LP: Toscanini Society ATS 1041

Wagner

A Faust Overture

London 5 June 1935	BBCSO	LP: Toscanini Society ATS 1005-9 CD: EMI CDH 763 0442
New York 5 March 1938	NBC	LP: Toscanini Society ATS 116-7
New York 27 October 1946	NBC	LP: Toscanini Society ATS 1055-9 CD: Memories HR 4161-3
New York 11 November 1946	NBC	78: HMV DB 6545-6 78: RCA Victor M 1135 45: RCA Victor ERB 7023 LP: RCA Victor LM 7032/LRM 7023 LP: RCA RB 6606-7 LP: RCA VIC 1247 LP: RCA AT 400/1044

Der fliegende Holländer, Overture

New York 26 February 1938	NBC	LP: Toscanini Society ATS 1066 np LP: Toscanini Society ATS 116-7 CD: Hunt CDLSMH 34014
New York 25 February 1939	NBC	LP: Music and Arts ATRA 3002
New York 31 March 1946	NBC	CD: Memories HR 4161-3

Götterdämmerung, Dawn, Duet (Zu neuen Taten) and Siegfried's Rhine Journey

New York	NBC	LP: RCA Victor LM 2452
22 February 1941	Traubel, Melchior	LP: RCA RB 16274
		LP: RCA VIC 1369
		LP: RCA VCM 5
		LP: RCA AT 400/1046
		LP: RCA VL 46019
		LP: Franklin Mint
		CD: Memories HR 4161-3

Götterdämmerung, Dawn and Siegfried's Rhine Journey

New York	NYPO	78: HMV DB 2860-1
8 February 1936		78: RCA Victor M 308
		LP: RCA Camden CAL 375/CDM 1054
		LP: RCA AT 1074
		CD: Pearl GEMMCDS 9373
		CD: RCA GD 60329
New York	NBC	LP: Toscanini Society ATS 116-7
5 March 1938		
New York	NBC	78: HMV DB 5994-6
17 March 1941		78: RCA Victor M 853
		LP: RCA AT 1082
New York	NBC	VHS Video: RCA 790.351
20 March 1948		
New York	NBC	45: RCA Victor WDM 1564
22 December 1949		LP: RCA Victor LM 1157/6020
		LP: HMV ALP 1173
		LP: RCA RB 16135
		LP: RCA VIC 1022/1369
		LP: RCA AT 400/1046
		LP: RCA VL 45811
New York	NBC	LP: CLS RPCL 2033
4 April 1954		LP: Fonit Cetra DOC 17
		LP: Music and Arts BWS 3008
		CD: Fonit Cetra CDC 3
		CD: Music and Arts ATRA 3008
		CD: Hunt CDLSMH 34014

Götterdämmerung, Siegfried's Death and Funeral Music

Salzburg 26 August 1934 Funeral Music only	VPO	LP: Melodram MEL 012 LP: Music and Arts ATRA 3008
London 5 June 1935	BBCSO	CD: EMI CDH 763 0442
New York 24 February 1941	NBC	78: HMV DB 5994-6 78: RCA Victor M 853 LP: RCA AT 1082
New York 13 January 1945	NYPO	LP: Toscanini Society ATS 1034-5 LP: Music and Arts ATRA 3009 CD: AS-Disc AS 600
New York 29 December 1951	NBC	VHS Video: RCA 790.356
New York 3 January 1952	NBC	LP: RCA Victor LM 6020 LP: RCA RB 16136 LP: RCA VIC 1316 LP: RCA VCM 5 LP: RCA AT 400/1046 LP: RCA VL 45811/46018 CD: RCA (Japan) R32C-1024
New York 7 March 1953	NBC	LP: Fonit Cetra DOC 17 CD: Fonit Cetra CDC 3 CD: Hunt CD 539 CD: Music and Arts ATRA 601 CD: Curcio-Hunt CON 12

Götterdämmerung, Brünnhilde's Immolation

New York 22 February 1941	NBC Traubel	LP: Toscanini Society ATS 105
New York 24 February 1941	NBC Traubel	78: RCA Victor M 978 45: RCA Victor WCT 1116 LP: RCA Victor LCT 1116/LVT 1004 LP: RCA VIC 1369 LP: RCA VCM 5 LP: RCA AT 400/1047 LP: RCA VL 46019 CD: Memories HR 4161-3 Orchestral finale only V-Disc: 361

Lohengrin, Act 1 Prelude

New York   NYPO   78: HMV DB 2904
9 April 1936   78: RCA Victor M 308
                                       LP: RCA Camden CAL 375/CDM 1054
                                       LP: RCA AT 1074
                                       CD: Pearl GEMMCDS 9373

New York   NBC   LP: Toscanini Society ATS 116-7
5 March 1938

New York   NBC   78: RCA Victor 11-8807/M 1074
24 February and   LP: RCA AT 1082
6 May 1941

New York   NBC   45: RCA Victor ERB 7029
22 October 1951   LP: RCA Victor LRM 7029/LM 6020
                                       LP: RCA RB 16136
                                       LP: RCA VIC 1247
                                       LP: RCA VCM 5
                                       LP: RCA AT 400/1044
                                       LP: RCA VL 46018
                                       LP: Franklin Mint
                                       CD: RCA (Japan) R32C-1023

New York   NBC   CD: Memories HR 4161-3
29 December 1951   CD: Curcio-Hunt CON 12
                                       VHS Video: RCA 790.356

New York   NBC   LP: CLS RPCL 2033
4 April 1954   LP: Fonit Cetra DOC 17
                                       LP: GDS Records GDS 5011
                                       LP: Music and Arts BWS 3008
                                       CD: Fonit Cetra CDC 3
                                       CD: Music and Arts ATRA 3008
                                       CD: Hunt CDLSMH 34014
                                       CD: Rodolphe RPC 32490

Lohengrin, Act 3 Prelude

New York 8 February and 9 April 1936	NYPO	78: HMV DB 2860-1 78: RCA Victor M 308/1064 LP: RCA Camden CAL 375/CDM 1054 LP: RCA AT 1074 CD: Pearl GEMMCDS 9373 CD: RCA GD 60329
New York 1 March 1936	NYPO	LP: Toscanini Society ATS 1089 np
New York 5 March 1938	NBC	LP: Toscanini Society ATS 116-7
Lucerne 7 July 1946	La Scala Orchestra	LP: Relief RL 811 CD: Palette PAL 1067
New York 20 March 1948	NBC	VHS Video: RCA 790.351
New York 22 October 1951	NBC	45: RCA Victor ERB 7029 LP: RCA Victor LRM 7029/LM 6020/6074 LP: RCA RB 16136 LP: RCA VIC 1247 LP: RCA VCM 5 LP: RCA AT 400/1044 LP: RCA VL 45802/46018 LP: Franklin Mint CD: RCA (Japan) R32C-1023
New York 7 March 1953	NBC	LP: Fonit Cetra DOC 17 CD: Fonit Cetra CDC 3 CD: Music and Arts ATRA 601 CD: Curcio-Hunt CON 12 CD: Memories HR 4161-3

Die Meistersinger von Nürnberg

Salzburg 8 August 1936 <u>Act 1 only</u>	VPO Vienna Opera Chorus Lehmann, Thorborg, Kullmann, Sallaba, Nissen, Alsen, Wiedemann	LP: UORC Records UORC 257
Salzburg 5 or 20 August 1937	VPO Vienna Opera Chorus Reining, Thorborg, Noort, Sallaba, Nissen, Alsen, Wiedemann	LP: Toscanini Society ATS 1062-6 np LP: MR 2003 LP: MRF Records MRF 16 LP: Accent ACC 150040 LP: Melodram MEL 012 CD: Melodram MEL 47041 <u>Final scene only</u> LP: MR 2003

Die Meistersinger von Nürnberg, Act 1 Prelude

New York 11 March 1946	NBC	78: RCA Victor 11-9385 45: RCA Victor 49-0297 LP: RCA Victor LM 6020 LP: RCA RB 16136 LP: RCA VIC 1247 LP: RCA VCM 5 LP: RCA AT 400/1044 LP: RCA VL 45802/46018 CD: RCA (Japan) R32C-1023
Lucerne 7 July 1946	La Scala Orchestra	LP: Relief RL 811
New York 7 February 1953	NBC	LP: Fonit Cetra DOC 17 CD: Fonit Cetra CDC 3 CD: Rodolphe RPC 32490 CD: Memories HR 4161-3
New York 4 April 1954	NBC	LP: MRF Records MRF 16 LP: CLS RPCL 2033 LP: Music and Arts BWS 3008 CD: Music and Arts ATRA 3008 CD: Hunt CDLSMH 34014

Die Meistersinger von Nürnberg, Act 3 Prelude

New York 24 November 1951	NBC	CD: Memories HR 4161-3 78: HMV DB 21564
New York 26 November 1951	NBC	45: RCA Victor ERB 7029 LP: RCA Victor LRM 7029/LM 6020 LP: RCA RB 16136 LP: RCA VIC 1247 LP: RCA VCM 5 LP: RCA AT 400/1044 LP: RCA VL 45802/46018 CD: RCA (Japan) R32C-1023

Parsifal, Act 1 Prelude

London 5 June 1935	BBCSO		CD: EMI CDH 763 0442
New York 5 March 1938	NBC		LP: Toscanini Society ATS 116-7
New York 22 December 1949	NBC		78: HMV DB 21270-2 78: RCA Victor DM 1376 45: RCA Victor WDM 1376 LP: RCA Victor LM 15/LM 6020 LP: HMV BLP 1033 LP: RCA RB 16135 LP: RCA VIC 1278 LP: RCA VCM 5 LP: RCA AT 400/1047 LP: RCA VL 45811/46009 CD: RCA (Japan) R32C-1024

Parsifal, Good Friday Music

London 5 June 1938	BBCSO		CD: EMI CDH 763 0442
New York 22 December 1949	NBC		78: HMV DB 21270-2 78: RCA Victor DM 1376 45: RCA Victor WDM 1376 LP: RCA Victor LM 15/LM 6020 LP: HMV BLP 1033 LP: RCA RB 16135 LP: RCA VIC 1278 LP: RCA VCM 5 LP: RCA AT 400/1047 LP: RCA VL 45811/46009 CD: RCA (Japan) R32C-1024

Parsifal, Symphonic Synthesis (Act 2 Prelude; Act 3 Prelude; Klingsor's Magic Garden; Act 3 Finale)

New York 23 March 1940	NBC		LP: Music and Arts ATRA 3002 Incorrectly labelled as Excerpts Act 3

Rienzi, Overture

New York 3 December 1938	NBC		LP: Toscanini Society ATS 1066 np LP: Music and Arts ATRA 3002 CD: Memories HR 4161-3

SALZBURGER FESTSPIELE
1936

DIE MEISTERSINGER VON NÜRNBERG

OPER IN 3 AUFZÜGEN VON
RICHARD WAGNER

DIRIGENT:
ARTURO TOSCANINI

INSZENIERUNG:
HERBERT GRAF

BÜHNENBILD:
ROBERT KAUTSKY

KOSTÜME:
WILLI BAHNER

ORCHESTER:
DIE WIENER PHILHARMONIKER
CHOR UND BALLETT DER WIENER STAATSOPER

SALZBURGER FESTSPIELE 1937

FIDELIO

OPER IN 2 AKTEN VON
L. v. BEETHOVEN

DIRIGENT:
ARTURO TOSCANINI

INSZENIERUNG:
LOTHAR WALLERSTEIN

BÜHNENBILD:
CLEMENS HOLZMEISTER

ORCHESTER:
DIE WIENER PHILHARMONIKER
CHOR DER WIENER STAATSOPER

Siegfried, Forest Murmurs

New York 20 March 1948	NBC	VHS Video: RCA 790.351

New York 29 October 1951	NBC	78: HMV DB 6546/21599 45: RCA Victor ERB 7029 LP: RCA Victor LRM 7029 LP: RCA VIC 1316 LP: RCA VCM 5 LP: RCA AT 400/1046 LP: RCA VL 46008 CD: RCA (Japan) R32C-1024

New York 29 December 1951	NBC	CD: Curcio-Hunt CON 12 CD: Memories HR 4161-3 VHS Video: RCA 790.356

New York 4 April 1954	NBC	LP: CLS RPCL 2033 LP: Music and Arts BWS 3008 LP: Fonit Cetra DOC 17 CD: Fonit Cetra CDC 3 CD: Music and Arts ATRA 3008 CD: Hunt CDLSMH 34014 CD: Rodolophe RPC 32490

Siegfried Idyll

New York 8 February 1936	NYPO	78: HMV DB 2920-1 78: RCA Victor M 308 LP: RCA Camden CAL 309/CDM 1027 LP: RCA AT 1074 CD: Pearl GEMMCDS 9373 CD: RCA GD 60329

New York 11 March 1946	NBC	78: HMV DB 6668-9 78: RCA Victor M1135 45: RCA Victor WCT 1116 LP: RCA Victor LCT 1116/LVT 1004 LP: RCA AT 1082

New York 29 July 1952	NBC	LP: RCA Victor LM 6020 LP: RCA RB 16136 LP: RCA VIC 1247 LP: RCA VCM 5 LP: RCA AT 400/1045 LP: RCA VL 46008 CD: RCA (Japan) R32C-1023 CD: RCA RD 85751

New York 7 March 1953	NBC	LP: Fonit Cetra DOC 17 CD: Fonit Cetra CDC 3 CD: Hunt CD 539 CD: Music and Arts ATRA 601 CD: Curcio-Hunt CON 12 CD: Memories HR 4161-3

Tannhäuser, Overture

New York 5 March 1938	NBC	LP: Toscanini Society ATS 116-7
New York 4 December 1948	NBC	LP: Toscanini Society ATS 1061 CD: Memories HR 4161-3 VHS Video: RCA 790.354

Tannhäuser, Act 3 Prelude

New York 6 January 1946	NBC	LP: Toscanini Society ATS 1061 LP: Music and Arts ATRA 3002 CD: Memories HR 4161-3
New York 29 November 1953	NBC	LP: Toscanini Society ATS 1028 CD: Hunt CD 539

Tannhäuser, Overture and Venusberg Music

Lucerne 7 July 1946	La Scala Orchestra	LP: Relief RL 811 CD: Relief CR 1881 CD: Palette PAL 1067 Rehearsal extract LP: Relief RL 811
New York 20 March 1948	NBC	LP: Toscanini Society ATS 1061 LP: Music and Arts ATRA 3002 VHS Video: RCA 790.351
New York 8 November 1952	NBC	LP: Fonit Cetra DOC 17 LP: Franklin Mint LP: Music and Arts ATRA 601 CD: Fonit Cetra CDC 3 CD: GDS Records GDS 2301 CD: Melodram MEL 47041 CD: Rodolphe RPC 32490
New York 4 April 1954	NBC	LP: CLS RPCL 2033 LP: Music and Arts BWS 3008 CD: Music and Arts ATRA 3008 CD: Hunt CDLSMH 34014 CLS issue contains the broadcast radio interruption due to the conductor's memory lapse

Tannhäuser: Excerpt (Dich, teure Halle)

New York 22 February 1941	NBC Traubel	LP: Toscanini Society ATS 1061 LP: Music and Arts ATRA 3002 LP: Toscanini Society ATS 105 CD: Memories HR 4161-3

Tristan und Isolde, Prelude and Liebestod

New York 5 March 1938	NBC	LP: Toscanini Society ATS 116-7
New York 19 March 1942	NBC	Prelude RCA unpublished Liebestod V-Disc: 361 78: RCA Victor M 978/DM 978 LP: RCA AT 1082
New York 29 December 1951	NBC	VHS Video: RCA 790.356 CD: Curcio-Hunt CON 12
New York 7 January 1952	NBC	LP: RCA Victor LM 6020 LP: RCA RB 16135 LP: RCA VIC 1278 LP: RCA VCM 5 LP: RCA AT 400/1044 LP: RCA VL 45801/46009 LP: Franklin Mint CD: RCA (Japan) R32C-1023 CD: RCA RD 85751 CD: RCA GD 60264 Liebestod only 45: HMV 7ER 5003
New York 7 March 1953	NBC	LP: Fonit Cetra DOC 17 CD: Fonit Cetra CDC 3 CD: Hunt CD 539 CD: Music and Arts ATRA 601 CD: Rodolphe RPC 32490 CD: Memories HR 4161-3

Tristan und Isolde, Prelude

New York 22 February 1941	NBC	LP: Music and Arts ATRA 3002
New York 12 May 1947	NBC	RCA unpublished

Die Walküre, Act 1 Scene 3

New York 22 February 1941	NBC Traubel, Melchior	LP: RCA LM 2452 LP: RCA RB 16224 LP: RCA VIC 1316 LP: RCA VCM 5 LP: RCA AT 400/1045 LP: Franklin Mint CD: RCA (Japan) R32C-1024 CD: RCA RD 85751 CD: RCA GD 60264 CD: Memories HR 4161-3
New York 6 April 1947	NBC Bampton, Svanholm	LP: Edizione Lirica EL 004 LP: HRE Records HRE 5004 LP: Fonit Cetra ARK 12 Rehearsal extracts LP: Fonit Cetra ARK 12 LP: MDTP 029 CD: Myto 90316

Die Walküre, Ride of the Valkyries

New York 5 March 1938	NBC	LP: Toscanini Society ATS 116-7
New York 11 March 1946	NBC	78: HMV DB 6545-6 78: RCA Victor M 1135 45: RCA Victor WDM 1564 LP: RCA AT 1082
New York 20 March 1948	NBC	VHS Video: RCA 790.351 CD: Curcio-Hunt CON 12
New York 29 December 1951	NBC	VHS Video: RCA 790.356 CD: Curcio-Hunt CON 12
New York 3 January 1952	NBC	45: RCA Victor ERA 249 45: HMV 7ER 5003 LP: RCA Victor LM 7032 LP: RCA RB 6606 LP: RCA VIC 1316 LP: RCA AT 400 LP: RCA VCM 5 LP: RCA AT 400/1045 LP: RCA VL 45801/46008 LP: Franklin Mint CD: RCA (Japan) R32C-1023 CD: RCA RD 85751 CD: RCA GD 60264
New York 7 March 1953	NBC	LP: Fonit Cetra DOC 17 CD: Fonit Cetra CDC 3 CD: Hunt CD 539 CD: Rodolphe RPC 32490 CD: Memories HR 4161-3

Waldteufel

Les Patineurs, Waltz

New York 25 June 1944	NBC	CD: Memories HR 4198
New York 28 June 1945	NBC	78: HMV DB 21352 78: RCA Victor 11-8949/M 1062/M 1416 45: HMV 7ER 5017 45: RCA Victor 49-0132, 45: RCA Victor WDM 1416/WEPR 13/ERA 13 LP: RCA Victor LM 14/LRM 1986/LRY 9000 LP: HMV ALP 1441 LP: RCA VIC 1321 LP: RCA AT 118/1071 LP: Franklin Mint CD: RCA (Japan) R32C-1019 CD: RCA GD 60308

Weber

Invitation to the Dance (orch. Berlioz)

London 14 June 1938	BBCSO	78: HMV DB 3542 78: RCA Victor 15192 LP: EMI XLP 30079 LP: Seraphim 60150
New York 28 September 1951	NBC	45: RCA Victor ERA 125 45: HMV 7ER 5021 LP: RCA Victor LM 2056/LM 6113 LP: RCA VIC 1321 LP: RCA AT 118/1028 LP: Franklin Mint CD: RCA (Japan) R32C-1019 CD: RCA GD 60308
New York 13 December 1953	NBC	LP: Toscanini Society ATS 1047 CD: Memories HR 4198

Euryanthe, Overture

New York 13 January 1945	NYPO	LP: Toscanini Society ATS 1034-5 LP: Music and Arts ATRA 3009 CD: AS-Disc AS 600
New York 29 October 1951	NBC	LP: RCA Victor LM 6026 LP: HMV ALP 1417 LP: RCA VIC 1341 LP: RCA AT 134/1028
New York 3 November 1951	NBC	LP: GDS Records GDS 5001 CD: Nuova Era 013.6315 CD: Memories HR 4202 VHS Video: RCA 790.355

Der Freischütz, Overture

New York 1 March 1936	NYPO	LP: Toscanini Society ATS 1089 np
New York 25 May 1945	NBC	78: HMV DB 6331 78: RCA Victor 11-9172 45: RCA Victor 49-1228 LP: RCA AT 1081
New York 3 January 1952	NBC	45: RCA Victor ERB 7028 LP: RCA Victor LRM 7028/LM 6026 LP: HMV ALP 1417 LP: RCA VIC 1341 LP: RCA AT 116/1028 LP: RCA VL 45817 CD: RCA (Japan) R32C-1018
New York 5 January 1952	NBC	CD: Memories HR 4202

Oberon, Overture

New York 2 August 1952	NBC	LP: Dell' Arte DA 9010
New York 5 August 1952	NBC	45: RCA Victor ERB 7028 LP: RCA Victor LRM 7028/LM 6026 LP: RCA VIC 1341 LP: RCA AT 134/1028 LP: Franklin Mint
New York 28 February 1954	NBC	CD: Nuova Era 013.6311-12 CD: AS-Disc AS 308 CD: Memories HR 4202

Wolf-Ferrari

Le donne curiose, Overture

New York 29 November 1947	NBC	LP: Toscanini Society ATS 1039

Il segreto di Susanna, Overture

Camden NJ 10 March 1921	La Scala Orchestra	78: Victor Talking Machine VTM 66081/840 78: HMV DA 375 LP: RCA AT 1076 LP: RCA VL 46024
New York 20 January 1946	NBC	LP: Toscanini Society ATS 1039

Traditional & miscellaneous

British National Anthem

London 29 September and 1 October 1952	Philharmonia	LP: Toscanini Society ATS 1030-3 LP: Turnabout THS 65027-30

The Star-spangled Banner (arr. Toscanini)

New York 19 March 1942	NBC	LP: RCA Victor LM 7032 LP: RCA RB 6606-7 LP: RCA AT 1071 LP: Franklin Mint

L'Internationale (arr. Toscanini)

New York 7 November 1943	NBC	LP: Toscanini Society ATS 1097 np LP: Dell' Arte DA 9011 CD: Relief CR 1886

Garibaldi's War Hymn

New York 9 September 1943	NBC	V-Disc: 31 LP: Toscanini Society ATS 102 Spoken introduction by Walter Toscanini

Dixie

Richmond VA 19 April 1950	NBC	78: RCA Legend

Toscanini : a postscript

Of all the great conductors, Arturo Toscanini is the best known, yet paradoxically the most elusive, his true nature lost behind a blizzard of books, magazine articles, critiques, counter-critiques and anecdotes. The latter in particular have trivialised him into a sort of sacred monster of the podium, forever losing his temper or acting unpredictably and intransigently. He is represented as an anti-intellectual, when in fact he had a most penetrating, all-embracing intellectual grasp of the music he played. Simply to contemplate the scores he knew by heart, down to the last semi-quaver, is to be humbled by his breadth of mind. And depth ? Because he liked to think of himself as a simple Italian musician, many took him at his word; yet those who worked closely with him on complex operas, choral works and symphonies, found he knew all the relevant background material. His favourite singers were those who brought the text of what they sang most vividly alive (one thinks especially of Lehmann and Pertile).

What brings us closer to the Maestro than any written (or spoken) word is his recorded legacy, which is vast and represents him in almost every facet of his even vaster repertoire. We can never recreate the frisson which his very appearance caused in the opera house or concert hall, nor can we realise the full beauty of the sound his simple, eloquent gestures released to set the air quivering around the ears of his hearers. But through his recordings we can at least approach an understanding of why he was so important to the generations who heard him conduct in the flesh. And we can come to appreciate his still-blazing relevance for today's generation - and tomorrow's.

Like most conductors of his time - Koussevitzky and Mengelberg were the outstanding exceptions - Toscanini learnt his trade in the opera house; and being an Italian born and raised in the twilight of the bel canto era, he brought a knowledge and love of singing to all his musicmaking. In the 19th century, as can readily be heard from the recordings of singers like Patti, de Lucia, Battistini and Plancon, the human voice was treated with more care and attention than on today's opera stages. The emphasis was on beauty of tone, articulation and legato, rather than on weight.

If singers in the 19th century opera houses were to be heard, orchestras could not play too loudly. The stringed instruments were all strung with gut, at a slacker tension than today, and the wind and brass instruments were of narrower bore than their modern equivalents, so the entire texture of the orchestra was more transparent. Singers like Caruso, for all that they preserved many of the principles of bel canto, changed all this, responding to the more complex Romantic orchestrations they heard coming from the pit at the turn of the century. As they placed more and more pressure on their tone, so orchestras and conductors felt able to produce more sheer noise - and composers could thicken their scoring still further. The increase in popularity of the purely orchestral concert, going hand in hand with the creation of the great symphony orchestras, allowed composers to indulge their fantasies without reference to the human voice.

At the same time, orchestral standards were abysmal compared with what we would expect now. Toscanini played the major role in raising those standards, through meticulous rehearsal; and he presided over the period in which the modern orchestra, with its thicker, heavier sound, developed. Yet he never forgot his 19th century origins and his "sound" retained its luminosity to the end of his long life. While the bass player Koussevitzky and the organist Stokowski built up massive walls of sound on a foundation of 16 double basses, the cellist Toscanini kept his bass lines light and athletic. The inner parts were treated with unusual respect (the Maestro's viola section in the NBC Symphony, led by Carlton Cooley, included players of the calibre of William Primrose, Louis Kievman and Emanuel Vardi) but they were merely equal parts of a balanced string sound. Toscanini knew many string quartets by heart and loved to hear the Busch Quartet and the Busch Chamber Players rehearse. Not for him the over-emphasis on the cello line that was heard from his fellow cellist Barbirolli; his cello melodies had a singing, sinuous grace - as in Verdi's overtures to "La Forza del Destino" and "I Vespri Siciliani".

Verdi was a major influence on Toscanini, who played in the Orchestra of La Scala under the composer and revered him as man and artist. Time and again, as we read Verdi's admonitions to singers and other musicians in his letters, it could be Toscanini writing. In his later years Verdi was very much against the Romantic rallentandi with which many interpreters distorted his music, and he railed against the liberties they took with his scores. Almost singlehanded, Toscanini campaigned for the sancity of a composer's work - although even he, as a pragmatic musician, made adroit adjustments here and there. He allowed minor departures from the text in Verdi operas, where these were sanctioned by the composer, and could have gone even further in this direction (he was surely being too strict in applying the standards of late Verdi to earlier operas like "La Traviata" and "Rigoletto"). Some of his re-orchestrations, like those in Debussy's "La Mer", were done with the composers' blessings.

One thing Toscanini surely learnt from Verdi was that the impact of a note, or chord, depended on the precision of attack with which it was sounded, rather than on its sheer weight. His chords were like whip-cracks - at the outset of Beethoven's "Eroica" Symphony, for instance - and they generated far more excitement than the sonorous chords of other conductors. The "Eroica", a Toscanini warhorse, could furnish other examples of his strengths: his wonderful sense of rhythm, which buoyed up not just the fast movements but also the Funeral March; his acute judgement of relative tempi; his humour, which heightened the jokes at the start of the finale; and his exhilarating energy, which made the march episode in that finale a triumphant release of animal power. Beethoven also benefited from what one can only call Toscanini's idealism, the sense of striving which he brought to all his work but which was peculiarly appropriate to this composer. Brahms, whose North German sternness was tempered by Toscanini with southern warmth and sensuality, revealed another of the Maestro's strengths: his phrasing, like that of a great singer in that the end of the phrase was always comprehended in its beginning. Similarly the end of an entire movement seemed implicit in the way the conductor launched it, so sure was his grasp of symphonic form.

Like most Italians, Toscanini could not make sense of Mozart, a fault he admitted. It was caused not by slackness of rhythm - the most common fault in Italian Mozartians - but by an inability to express the feminine side of the composer. The conductor who could phrase the question and answer in the slow movement of Beethoven's Fifth Symphony, so that the "answer" became the epitome of consolation and conciliation, could not walk the Mozartian tightrope between grace and drama. With the masculine Haydn, he was more in his element. Likewise he was supreme in all the Beethoven symphonies except the "Pastoral", whose charm and innocence eluded him - the storm was the highlight of his interpretation ! He captured all the dramatic intensity and tenderness of Schubert's "Unfinished" Symphony but the sunnier, Viennese side of this composer was foreign to him; it was characteristic that of the four Brahms Symphonies, the lyrical Third gave him the most trouble. He had other limitations, mostly of repertoire. He remained faithful to the composers he had encountered in his youth: Beethoven, Brahms, Verdi, Wagner, Puccini, Debussy, Strauss - all of them, with the exception of Beethoven, "modern" composers to a man born in 1867. He championed compatriots like Boito, Ponchielli, Respighi and Martucci throughout his life and in his hands, their music seemed twice as good as it really was. In his old age, to fill the rapacious airwaves of the NBC network, he learnt numerous scores which were new to him; but compared with Koussevitzky he made hardly any contribution to promoting new music.

People are still arguing over whether the great violinist Paganini was a genius or a devil - and in some quarters, his fellow Italian Toscanini has stimulated the same debate. At least, in the Maestro's case, we have the recorded evidence on which to make up our own minds; and when all his failings - vanity, impatience, irascibility, stubbornness, superstition - have been thrown into the scales, the pan containing his generosity, warmth, perfectionism and humility is still the heavier. Genius or devil, he was certainly a remarkable man; and his recorded legacy is above all a testament to his human qualities.

Tully Potter 1990

Guido Cantelli
Discography

Compiled by John Hunt
1991

Guido Cantelli with his mentor Arturo Toscanini

Introduction

Looking back at the 1950s one is astounded by the number of exceptional musicians who, by illness or by accident, met their deaths before ever reaching their full maturity. There was the violinist Ginette Neveu, the pianist Dinu Lipatti, horn player Dennis Brain, contralto Kathleen Ferrier - and the conductor Guido Cantelli, tragically killed in 1956 in an air crash at the age of only 36.

In only 7 or 8 years at the top of his profession Cantelli had earned the respect of musicians in his native Italy, in the United States, where he had the good luck to come to the attention of Toscanini, and in London, where a comparatively brief but purposeful series of recording sessions and public concerts with the Philharmonia Orchestra helped bring his extraordinary talent to the widest audience.

Cantelli shared with Carlo Maria Giulini an insistence on only performing music with which he had become familiar after long and careful preparation, and with which he felt fully at ease. Even in standard repertoire he was highly selective, and there were several Beethoven symphonies which he felt himself not yet ready to tackle. He had, however, come to grips with a fair number of contemporary scores, Bartok and Stravinsky in particular, and had demonstrated due interest in some modern composers from his native country.

Nearly all the live recordings of Guido Cantelli emanate from his USA concerts, and it can be expected that still more of these will eventually emerge, officially or unofficially, from the archives of NBC or NYPO to give us further glimpses of a most noble and elegant Italian musician.

John Hunt

Cantelli's last concert

Bach

Sinfonia (Christmas Oratorio)

New York   NBC   CD: AS-Disc AS 618
December 1952

Barber

Adagio for strings

New York   NYPO   CD: AS-Disc AS 515
March 1955

The School for Scandal, Overture

New York   NBC   LP: Toscanini Society ATSGC 1212 np
December 1953   LP: Fonit Cetra LAR 31
                                    CD: AS-Disc AS 515

Bartok

Concerto for orchestra

New York   NBC   LP: Toscanini Society ATSGC 1207 np
February 1952

New York   NYPO   CD: AS-Disc AS 614
March 1953

Music for percussion, strings and celesta

New York   NBC   LP: Toscanini Society ATSGC 1202
December 1952   LP: Baton 1005
                                    CD: AS-Disc AS 614

New York   NYPO   CD: Stradivarius STR 13591
February 1954

Beethoven

Symphony No 1

New York January 1954	NBC	LP: Toscanini Society ATSGC 1203 LP: MDP 037

Symphony No 5

New York February 1954	NBC	LP: Toscanini Society ATSGC 1201 LP: Rococo 2042 LP: MDP 037 CD: Stradivarius STR 10001 CD: AS-Disc AS 616
London May and June 1956	Philharmonia	HMV unpublished (recording incomplete) <u>Second movement</u> LP: HMV ALP 1535 <u>Rehearsal extracts</u> LP: Toscanini Society ATSGC 1201

Symphony No 7

London May 1956	Philharmonia	LP: HMV ALP 1472/ASD 254 LP: Angel 35260 LP: Regal SREG 2011 LP: EMI CFP 103 LP: Seraphim 60038 LP: EMI (Italy) 3C 053 01214

Piano Concerto No 1

New York March 1953	NYPO Serkin	LP: Fonit Cetra DOC 54 CD: Melodram MEL 18010 CD: AS-Disc AS 623

Piano Concerto No 3

New York March 1955	NYPO Firkusny	CD: AS-Disc AS 506

Piano Concerto No 4

New York March 1956	NYPO Backhaus	LP: Toscanini Society ATSGC 1218 np LP: Penzance PR 39 LP: Fonit Cetra LO 520 LP: Fonit Cetra DOC 54 CD: AS-Disc AS 621

Piano Concerto No 5 "Emperor"

New York February 1954	NYPO Serkin	CD: AS-Disc AS 114 CD: Melodram MEL 18010
New York January 1955	NYPO Casadesus	CD: AS-Disc AS 616
New York March 1956	NYPO Gieseking	LP: Fonit Cetra LO 521 LP: Fonit Cetra DOC 54 CD: Stradivarius STR 13594

Berlioz

Hungarian March (La damnation de Faust)

New York   NBC   CD: AS-Disc AS 542
December 1951

Bettinelli

2 invenzioni per orchestra d'archi

New York   NBC   LP: Fonit Cetra LAR 31
December 1953

Brahms

Symphony No 1

New York December 1952	NBC	CD: Stradivarius STR 10007
London May 1953	Philharmonia	LP: HMV ALP 1152 LP: RCA Victor LHMV 1054 LP: EMI ENC 116 LP: EMI XLP 30023 LP: World Records SH 314 <u>Third movement</u> LP: HMV ALP 1535

Symphony No 3

New York December 1951	NBC	LP: CLS MDRL 12822/ARPCL 22022 CD: Stradivarius STR 13591 <u>All issues incorrectly state orchestra to be NYPO</u>
London August 1955	Philharmonia	LP: HMV BLP 1083 LP: EMI XLP 30030 LP: Seraphim 60325 LP: World Records SH 315 LP: EMI 29 05761 CD: EMI CDH 763 0852 <u>First movement</u> LP: HMV ALP 1535 <u>Seraphim was first issue of the stereo version</u>

Piano Concerto No 1

New York April 1956	NYPO Firkusny	CD: AS-Disc AS 506

Alto Rhapsody

New York April 1956	NYPO Westminster Choir Lipton	CD: AS-Disc 621 CD: Stradivarius STR 10007

Tragic Overture

New York January 1951	NBC	CD: AS-Disc 621 CD: Stradivarius STR 10007

Britten

Sinfonia da requiem

New York January 1953	NBC	LP: Toscanini Society ATSGC 1212 np CD: AS-Disc AS 541

Busoni

Berceuse élégiaque

Rome May 1949	Santa Cecilia Orchestra	HMV unpublished
New York March 1954	NYPO	LP: Toscanini Society ATSGC 1216 np LP: Rococo 2042 CD: AS-Disc AS 613

Tanzwalzer

New York March 1954	NYPO	LP: Toscanini Society ATSGC 1216 np CD: AS-Disc AS 613

Casella

Paganiniana

Rome May 1949	Santa Cecilia Orchestra	78: HMV DB 11334-5
New York January 1954	NBC	LP: Toscanini Society ATS 1210 np CD: AS-Disc AS 510

Cherubini

Symphony in D

New York December 1952	NBC	LP: Toscanini Society ATSGC 1211 np CD: AS-Disc AS 615
New York March 1954	NYPO	CD: Claque GM 1005

Copland

El salon mexico

New York March 1955	NYPO	CD: AS-Disc AS 515

Corelli

Concerto Grosso op 6 no 8

New York December 1950	NBC	LP: Toscanini Society ATSGC 1209 np

Creston

2 Choric Dances

New York November 1952	NBC	CD: AS-Disc AS 515

Dance Overture

New York March 1956	NYPO	LP: Penzance PR 39 CD: AS-Disc AS 515

Dallapiccola

Marsia, Suite

New York March 1954	NYPO	CD: AS-Disc AS 510

Debussy

Le martyre de Saint-Sébastien

New York December 1953	NYPO	CD: AS-Disc AS 548
London June 1954	Philharmonia	LP: HMV ALP 1228 LP: World Records SH 374 LP: Pathé 2C 027 03758
Rome November 1954	RAI Rome Orchestra	LP: Fonit Cetra LAR 31

La mer

London September 1954	Philharmonia	LP: HMV ALP 1228 LP: Seraphim 60077 LP: World Records SH 374 LP: Pathé 2C 027 03758
Turin September 1955	RAI Turin Orchestra	CD: AS-Disc AS 548

Nuages et fêtes (Nocturnes)

New York March 1955	NYPO	CD: AS-Disc AS 548
London September 1955	Philharmonia	LP: HMV BLP 1089 45: HMV 7ER 5176 LP: EMI XLP 30092 LP: Angel 35525 LP: Seraphim 60077

Prélude à l'après-midi d'un faune

London June 1954	Philharmonia	LP: HMV ALP 1207 LP: EMI XLP 30092 LP: Angel 35525 LP: Seraphim 60077

Dukas

L'apprenti sorcier

London June 1954	Philharmonia	LP: HMV ALP 1207 LP: EMI XLP 30092
New York January 1955	NYPO	CD: AS-Disc AS 536

Dvorak

<u>Piano Concerto</u>

New York January 1952	NYPO Firkusny	LP: Toscanini Society ATSGC 1216 np CD: AS-Disc AS 536

Falla

<u>El sombrero de 3 picos, Suite</u>

New York January 1954	NBC	LP: Toscanini Society ATSGC 1216 np
London June 1954	Philharmonia	LP: HMV ALP 1207 <u>Danza finale</u> 45: HMV 7ER 5057

Franck

<u>Symphony in D minor</u>

New York January 1954	NBC	CD: AS-Disc AS 542
New York April 1954	NBC	LP: HMV ALP 1219 LP: RCA Victor LM 1852 LP: RCA ARL1-3005 LP: World Records SH 376 LP: RCA AGL1-4083

Frescobaldi

<u>4 pezzi (arr. Ghedini)</u>

New York January 1952	NYPO	CD: AS-Disc AS 618

Gabrieli

Aria della battaglia

New York February 1954	NBC	LP: Toscanini Society ATSGC 1209 np CD: AS-Disc AS 618

Canzona (Sacrae symphoniae)

New York February 1954	NYPO	LP: Toscanini Society ATSGC 1209 np CD: Stradivarius STR 13591 CD: AS-Disc AS 618 Various incorrect dates given

Geminiani

Andante for strings, organ and harp (arr. Marinuzzi)

New York December 1951	NBC	CD: AS-Disc AS 618

Ghedini

Concerto dell' albatro

New York March 1953	NYPO Hambro, Corigliano, Varga, Anderson	CD: AS-Disc AS 507

Partita per orchestra

New York February 1952	NBC	CD: AS-Disc AS 510

Pezzo concertante

New York February 1952	NBC	CD: AS-Disc AS 510
Rome November 1954	RAI Rome Orchestra	LP: Fonit Cetra LAR 31

Handel

Largo (Serse)

New York December 1953	NBC	LP: Toscanini Society ATSGC 1209 np CD: AS-Disc AS 618
New York April 1956	NYPO	CD: AS-Disc AS 618

Messiah, Sinfonia

New York December 1949	NBC	CD: AS-Disc AS 618

Haydn

Symphony No 88

New York December 1952	NBC	CD: AS-Disc AS 537
New York January 1954	NBC	LP: Toscanini Society ATSGC 1202 LP: CLS RPCL 2010

Symphony No 93

New York March 1949	NBC	78: HMV DB 21014-6/9477-9 auto 78: RCA Victor DM 1323 LP: RCA Victor LM 1089 LP: RCA (Italy) A12R-0289
New York March 1955	NYPO	LP: Toscanini Society ATSGC 1213 np CD: AS-Disc AS 537

Hindemith

Concert Music for brass and strings

New York April 1956	NYPO	LP: Toscanini Society ATSGC 1212 np CD: AS-Disc AS 522

Mathis der Maler

New York June 1950	NBC	78: HMV DB 21531-3/9765-7 auto 78: RCA Victor DM 1407 LP: HMV BLP 1010 LP: RCA Victor LM 1089 LP: RCA (Italy) A12R-0289
New York February 1953	NBC	LP: Toscanini Society ATSGC 1213 np CD: AS-Disc AS 522
Rome November 1954	RAI Rome Orchestra	LP: Fonit Cetra LAR 31

Liszt

Piano Concerto No 1

New York January 1952	NYPO Henriot-Schweitzer	CD: AS-Disc AS 509

Piano Concerto No 2

New York March 1953	NYPO Arrau	CD: Music and Arts CD 625 CD: AS-Disc AS 509

GUIDO CANTELLI

"His tragically early death robbed music of one of the very few ... who seem likely ever to reinforce the thinning ranks of undisputedly great conductors." Neville Cardus — *Manchester Guardian*

HERE ARE SOME OF HIS LONG PLAY RECORDS

with the PHILHARMONIA ORCHESTRA

Symphony No. 4 in A ('Italian')
— *Mendelssohn*
Symphony No. 8 in B minor ('Unfinished')
— *Schubert*
ALP1325

Siegfried Idyll — *Wagner*
Romeo and Juliet — Fantasy Overture
— *Tchaikovsky*
ALP1086

Symphony No. 3 in F — *Brahms*
BLP1083

"Daphnis et Chloé" Suite No. 2 — *Ravel*
Lever du jour; Pantomime; Danse générale; also Nocturnes: No. 1, Nuages; No. 2, Fêtes — *Debussy*
BLP1089

Symphony No. 6 in B minor ('Pathétique')—*Tchaikovsky*
ALP1042

Symphony No. 1 in C minor — *Brahms*
ALP1152

TOSCANINI

conducts the
"His Master's Voice"
L.P. Recording ALP1380/81
of Verdi's Requiem in which

FEDORA BARBIERI

sings the
mezzo-soprano rôle.

"HIS MASTER'S VOICE"
LONG PLAY 33⅓ R.P.M. RECORDS

THE GRAMOPHONE CO. LTD.
(RECORD DIVISION)

8-11 GREAT CASTLE STREET
LONDON, W.1.

ROYAL FESTIVAL HALL
General Manager: T. E. BEAN

SUNDAY, JUNE 23rd, 1957

In Memory of Maestro GUIDO CANTELLI, who died in an air-crash on November 23rd, 1956

S. A. GORLINSKY presents

a performance of the

Requiem Mass
GIUSEPPE VERDI (1813 - 1901)

DISMA DE CECCO
(Soprano)

GIACINTO PRANDELLI
(Tenor)

FEDORA BARBIERI
(Contralto)

CARLO CAVA
(Bass)

CROYDON PHILHARMONIC CHOIR
(Chorus Master—Alan J. Kirby)

PHILHARMONIA ORCHESTRA
(Leader—Hugh Bean)

Conductor
ARGEO QUADRI

There will be a brief interval at the conclusion of the DIES IRAE when the artists will remain on the platform and the audience is requested to remain seated

 ★ ★

Cover Photograph by DOUGLAS GLASS

S. A. GORLINSKY LTD.
35 Dover Street, London, W.1

Mendelssohn

Symphony No 4 "Italian"

London October 1951	Philharmonia	HMV unpublished
New York December 1951	NBC	CD: AS-Disc AS 523
London August 1955	Philharmonia	LP: HMV ALP 1325 LP: Angel 35524 LP: Seraphim 60002 LP: World Records SH 290 <u>Second movement</u> LP: HMV ALP 1535

Violin Concerto

New York March 1954	NYPO Heifetz	LP: Rococo 2071 LP: Penzance PR 33 LP: CLS RPCL 2010 CD: AS-Disc 523 CD: Claque GM 1005 CD: Frequenz 041.019

Milhaud

Introduction and Funeral March

New York December 1950	NBC	CD: AS-Disc AS 542

Miller

Procession (Little Suite)

New York November 1952	NBC	CD: AS-Disc AS 515

Monteverdi

Magnificat (arr. Ghedini)

New York April 1956	NYPO Westminster Choir	CD: AS-Disc AS 541

Sonata sopra Sancta Maria

New York February 1952	NBC	CD: AS-Disc AS 541

Mozart

Symphony No 29

New York January 1955	NYPO	CD: AS-Disc AS 537
London June 1956	Philharmonia	LP: HMV ALP 1461 LP: EMI ENC 122 LP: EMI XLP 30034 LP: Pathé 2C 027 03748 Pathé was first issue of stereo version

Piano Concerto No 20

New York March 1953	NYPO Serkin	CD: AS-Disc AS 623

Piano Concerto No 21

New York March 1955	NYPO Gieseking	LP: Toscanini Society ATSGC 1217 np LP: Discocorp IGI 349 LP: Opus MLG 70 LP: CLS MDRL 12823/ARPCL 22022 CD: AS-Disc AS 529 AS-Disc incorrectly dated

Divertimento No 15 K287

New York February 1954	NBC	LP: Toscanini Society ATSGC 1217 np CD: AS-Disc AS 529
New York March 1954	NYPO	LP: Penzance PR 33 CD: Stradivarius STR 13597-9

Ein musikalischer Spass

New York March 1953	NYPO	CD: AS-Disc AS 529
London August 1955	Philharmonia	LP: HMV ALP 1461 LP: EMI XLP 30034 LP: Pathé 2C 027 03748 LP: EMI RLS 7701 Pathé was first issue of stereo version

Così fan tutte

Milan January 1956	La Scala Chorus & Orchestra Schwarzkopf, Sciutti, Merriman, Alva, Panerai, Calabrese	LP: Discocorp IGI 326 LP: Fonit Cetra LO 13 CD: Stradivarius STR 13597-9 <u>Overture only</u> LP: MDP 037

Le Nozze di Figaro, Overture

New York January 1955	NYPO	CD: AS-Disc AS 516

Requiem

Edinburgh September 1950	La Scala Chorus & Orchestra Tebaldi, Barbieri, Prandelli, Siepi	LP: MDP 032 CD: AS-Disc AS 500

Mussorgsky

Pictures from an exhibition

New York January 1951	NBC	LP: HMV BLP 1085 np LP: RCA Victor LM 1719
New York March 1953	NYPO	CD: Stradivarius STR 13594

Piston

Toccata

New York March 1955	NYPO	CD: AS-Disc AS 515

Pizzetti

Preludio ad un altro giorno

New York March 1953	NYPO	LP: Rococo 2042 CD: AS-Disc AS 507

Ravel

Boléro

New York December 1952	NBC	LP: Toscanini Society ATSGC 1206
New York March 1954	NYPO	CD: AS-Disc 547

Daphnis et Chloé, 2nd Suite

New York March 1955	NYPO	CD: AS-Disc AS 547
Rome November 1954	RAI Rome Orchestra	LP: Fonit Cetra LAR 31
London August 1955 and May 1956	Philharmonia	LP: HMV BLP 1089 LP: Angel 35525 LP: EMI XLP 30092

Pavane pour une infante défunte

New York December 1951	NBC	CD: AS-Disc AS 547
London October 1952	Philharmonia	78: HMV DB 21553 45: HMV 7ER 5057 LP: HMV ALP 1207 LP: Angel 35525 LP: EMI XLP 30092

La valse

New York February 1954	NBC	LP: Toscanini Society ATSGC 1206 CD: AS-Disc AS 547

Respighi

Fontane di Roma

Boston December 1954	Boston SO	CD: AS-Disc AS 507

I pini di Roma

Boston December 1954	Boston SO	CD: AS-Disc AS 507

Rossini

L'assiedo di Corinto, Overture

Rome May 1949	Santa Cecilia Orchestra	78: HMV DB 11324
New York February 1953	NBC	LP: Toscanini Society ATSGC 1210 np LP: MDP 037 LP: CLS MDRL 12823/ARPCL 22022 CD: AS-Disc AS 516 CLS incorrectly names orchestra as NYPO

La Cenerentola, Overture

New York February 1954	NBC	LP: Toscanini Society ATSGC 1210 np CD: AS-Disc AS 516 Incorrectly dated March 1954

La gazza ladra, Overture

London October 1952	Philharmonia	HMV unpublished

Semiramide, Overture

Boston January 1953	Boston SO	LP: Toscanini Society ATSGC 1210 np CD: AS-Disc AS 516 Incorrectly dated May 1953

Il signor bruschino, Overture

New York March 1953	NYPO	LP: Toscanini Society ATSGC 1210 np CD: AS-Disc AS 516

Roussel

Sinfonietta

New York December 1951	NBC	CD: AS-Disc AS 536

Schubert

Symphony No 2   NBC   LP: Toscanini Society ATSGC 1211 np
                                                  CD: AS-Disc AS 615
New York
January 1951

Symphony No 8 "Unfinished"

New York   NBC   CD: AS-Disc AS 505
January 1953

London   Philharmonia   LP: HMV ALP 1325
August 1955   LP: Angel 35524
                                                  LP: Seraphim 60002
                                                  LP: World Records SH 290
                                                  First movement
                                                  LP: HMV ALP 1535
                                                  World Records was first issue in stereo

Symphony No 9 "Great"

New York   NBC   LP: Toscanini Society ATSGC 1204
December 1953   CD: AS-Disc AS 505

Schumann

Symphony No 4

New York   NBC   LP: Toscanini Society ATSGC 1203
November 1952   CD: AS-Disc AS 615

London   Philharmonia   LP: HMV BLP 1044
May 1953   LP: RCA Victor LHMV 13
                                                  LP: EMI ENC 122
                                                  LP: EMI XLP 30030
                                                  LP: World Records SH 315
                                                  LP: EMI 29 05761
                                                  CD: EMI CDH 763 0852

Richard Strauss

Don Juan

New York   NYPO   CD: AS-Disc AS 613
March 1956

Tod und Verklärung

New York   NYPO   LP: Baton 1005
March 1954   CD: AS-Disc AS 613

Stravinsky

Le chant du rossignol

New York   NBC   LP: Toscanini Society ATSGC 1214 np
February 1954   CD: Fonit Cetra CDE 1065
                                           CD: AS-Disc AS 530

Fireworks

New York   NBC   LP: Toscanini Society ATSGC 1214 np
January 1951   CD: AS-Disc AS 530

Jeu de cartes

New York   NBC   LP: Toscanini Society ATSGC 1214 np
December 1952   CD: AS-Disc AS 530

Tchaikovsky

Symphony No 4

New York   NBC   CD: AS-Disc AS 620
December 1949
Rehearsals

New York   NBC   LP: Toscanini Society ATSGC 1205
February 1954   LP: CLS ARPCL 32009
                                              CD: Music and Arts CD 602
                                              CD: AS-Disc AS 503-4

Symphony No 5

London   La Scala   78: HMV DB 21187-91/9583-7 auto
September 1950   Orchestra   LP: HMV ALP 1001
                                              LP: RCA Victor LHMV 1003
                                              LP: World Records SHB 52

New York   NBC   LP: Toscanini Society ATSGC 1208 np
March 1952   LP: CLS ARPCL 32009
                                              CD: Music and Arts CD 602
                                              CD: AS-Disc AS 503-4

Symphony No 6 "Pathétique"

London   Philharmonia   LP: HMV ALP 1042
October 1952   LP: RCA Victor LHMV 1047
                                              LP: Pathe 2C 027 03756
                                              LP: World Records SHB 52
                                              CD: EMI CDH 769 7852
                                              Third movement
                                              LP: HMV ALP 1535

New York   NBC   LP: Toscanini Society ATS 1215 np
February 1953   LP: CLS ARPCL 32009
                                              CD: Music and Arts CD 602
                                              CD: AS-Disc AS 503-4

Romeo and Juliet

London   Philharmonia   78: HMV DB 21373-5/9705-7 auto
October 1951   LP: HMV ALP 1086
                                              LP: RCA Victor LM 1719/LHMV 6028
                                              LP: World Records SH 287
                                              CD: EMI CDH 769 7852

New York   NBC   CD: AS-Disc AS 503-4
February 1952

Verdi

Requiem

Boston December 1954	Boston SO New England Conservatory Chorus Nelli, Turner, Conley, Moscona	LP: Discocorp IGI 340 LP: Fonit Cetra LO 503
New York February 1955	NYPO Westminster Choir Nelli, Turner, Tucker, Hines	CD: AS-Disc AS 521

Te deum (4 pezzi sacri)

New York April 1956	NYPO Westminster Choir	LP: Discocorp IGI 340 CD: AS-Disc AS 541

La forza del destino, Overture

New York February 1952	NBC	CD: AS-Disc AS 516 Incorrectly dated February 1955

I vespri siciliani, Overture

New York December 1950	NBC	CD: AS-Disc AS 516

Vivaldi

Le 4 stagioni

New York December 1951	NBC Mischakoff	CD: AS-Disc AS 624 CD: Frequenz 041.016
New York March 1955	NYPO Corigliano	LP: Columbia (USA) ML 5044 LP: Philips ABL 3063 np LP: Philips GBL 5599 LP: Philips (Italy) G 05605 R

Concerto in A flat for 2 violins

New York December 1952	NBC Bolognini, Guilet	LP: Toscanini Society ATSGC 1209 np CD: AS-Disc AS 624

Concerto grosso No 4

New York February 1952	NBC	LP: Toscanini Society ATSGC 1209 np CD: AS-Disc AS 624

Concerto grosso op 3 no 11

New York March 1956	NYPO	CD: AS-Disc AS 624

Wagner

A Faust Overture

New York February 1952	NBC	CD: AS-Disc AS 531
New York March 1953	NYPO	CD: AS-Disc AS 531

Good Friday Music (Parsifal)

New York March and April 1956	NYPO	CD: AS-Disc AS 531

Rienzi, Overture

New York January 1953	NBC	LP: MDP 037 LP: Fonit Cetra LAR 31 CD: AS-Disc AS 531
New York January 1954	NBC	LP: Toscanini Society ATSGC 1206

Siegfried Idyll

London October 1951	Philharmonia	78: HMV DB 21478-9/9746-7 auto LP: HMV ALP 1086 LP: RCA Victor LHMV 13 LP: World Records SH 287

Siegfried's Rhine Journey (Götterdämmerung)

New York March 1953	NYPO	CD: AS-Disc AS 531

Weber

Euryanthe, Overture

New York November 1952	NBC	LP: Toscanini Society ATSGC 1206 LP: MDP 037 CD: AS-Disc AS 623

Carlo Maria Giulini
Discography

Compiled by John Hunt
1991

Introduction

Italian-born conductors of the highest calibre have been tended to be fewer in number than their Northern counterparts. Of those who rose to fame in the post-war era, the scene has been dominated by Carlo Maria Giulini, Claudio Abbado and Riccardo Muti. It is probably still too early for a final assessment of the latter two, whereas Giulini has been a most interesting figure on the music and recording scenes for nearly 40 years.

In the best Italian tradition Giulini was an active man of the theatre in Italy during the 1950s, as is documented by the various live recordings emanating from that period: of these the undoubted highlights are the collaborations at La Scala with Maria Callas.

His gradually deepening interest in music from North of the Alps was probably encouraged by the experience of coming to London in the mid 1950s to perform and record with Walter Legge's Philharmonia Orchestra. Giulini seemed to serve as a mediterranean opposite number to the more austere Klemperer, although their repertoires did overlap in the 4 symphonies of Brahms as well as in the very popular ones by Dvorak ("New World"), Tchaikovsky ("Pathétique") and Franck.

As far as Tchaikovsky is concerned, that "Pathétique" as well as "Romeo and Juliet" and "Francesca da Rimini" are high points of Giulini's Philharmonia discography, where he seems to have captured the turmoil and passion to perfection. It was ironical, therefore, that he could not find a point of contact with the 5th Symphony of Tchaikovsky which would have enabled him to reach convincing interpretation. Although a recording was commenced, under Legge's expert supervision, it had to be abandoned and those tapes remain a torso in EMI's vaults which we will probably never hear.

After that a period of more laid-back activity seems to have set in for Giulini, with at one stage a complete withdrawal from conducting opera in the theatre. Then, in the 1980s, there began the still ongoing indian summer of highly profound interpretations of the German Romantics. The highest achievements seem to have been live performances of Bruckner's 8th Symphony with the Berlin Philharmonic Orchestra, at the personal invitation of Herbert von Karajan, and a series of Bruckner symphony recordings with the Vienna Philharmonic which have become serious contenders for a Bruckner shortlist of great performances. Additionally, Giulini has always displayed special spiritual affinity with the great mainstream choral classics, Beethoven 9th and Missa Solemnis, and the Requiems of Mozart, Brahms and Verdi.

To quote John Holmes in his invaluable reference work "Conductors on Record": "Carlo Maria Giulini is known to musicians as a gentle, gracious man, of impressive suavity and elegance, who beguiles and inspires his players rather than terrifying or bullying them. He keeps to a limited repertoire and feels no necessity to be a missionary for new composers, as his interest is in music that has entered the bloodstream of the people".

John Hunt

Beethoven

Symphony No 3 "Eroica"

Los Angeles November 1978	LAPO	LP: DG 2531 123 LP: DG 413 9791

Symphony No 5

Los Angeles November 1981	LAPO	LP: DG 2532 049 CD: DG 410 0282

Symphony No 6 "Pastoral"

London January and April 1968	New Philharmonia	LP: EMI ASD 2535
Los Angeles November 1979	LAPO	LP: DG 2531 266

Symphony No 7

Chicago March 1971	CSO	LP: EMI ASD 2737 CD: EMI CDM 769 0312

Symphony No 8

London 1972	LSO	LP: EMI SLS 841 CD: EMI CDM 769 0312

Symphony No 9 "Choral"

London 1972	LSO LSO Chorus Armstrong, Reynolds, Tear, Shirley-Quirk	LP: EMI SLS 841
Berlin February 1989 and February 1990	BPO Ernst-Senff-Chor Varady, Nes, K. Lewis, Estes	CD: DG 427 6552

Violin Concerto

London September 1980	Philharmonia Perlman	LP: EMI ASD 4059 CD: EMI CDC 747 0022 VHS Video: EMI MVP 9910 142 Laserdisc: EMI LDA 9910 141

Piano Concerto No 1

Vienna	VSO	LP: DG 2531 302
September 1979	Michelangeli	CD: DG 419 2482

Piano Concerto No 3

London	Philharmonia	LP: Columbia 33CX 1903/SAX 2543
April 1963	Richter-Haaser	LP: Toshiba EAC 30064
Vienna	VSO	CD: DG 423 2302
September 1979	Michelangeli	

Piano Concerto No 5 "Emperor"

Vienna	VSO	LP: DG 2531 385
September 1979	Michelangeli	CD: DG 419 2492

Egmont, Overture

Turin	RAI Turin	LP: Fonit Cetra LAR 46
March 1961	Orchestra	
London	New	LP: EMI ASD 2535
May 1969	Philharmonia	

Missa Solemnis

London	New Philharmonia	CD: Hunt CD 527
May 1966	Orchestra & Chorus	
	Lorengar, Veasey,	
	R.Lewis, Borg	
Rome	RAI Rome	CD: Hunt CD 707
December 1969	Orchestra & Chorus	
	Arroyo, Hamari,	
	Hollweg, El Hage	
London	LPO	LP: EMI SLS 989
1974	New Philharmonia	CD: EMI CZS 762 6932
	Chorus	
	Harper, Baker,	
	Tear, Sotin	

Mass in C

London	New Philharmonia	LP: EMI ASD 2661
September 1970	Orchestra & Chorus	CD: EMI CZS 762 6932
	Ameling, Baker,	
	Altmeyer, Rintzler	

Berlioz

Roméo et Juliette: Orchestral excerpts

Chicago September 1969	CSO	LP: EMI ASD 2606 CD: EMI CDC 747 6162

Bizet

Jeux d'enfants

London October 1955 and October 1956	Philharmonia	LP: Columbia 33CX 1518/SAX 2279 LP: EMI XLP 30067/SXLP 30067

Carmen: Excerpt (La fleur que tu m'avais jetée)

Los Angeles November 1980	LAPO Domingo	LP: DG 2532 009 CD: DG 400 0302

Les pêcheurs de perles: Excerpt (Je crois entendre encore)

Los Angeles November 1980	LAPO Domingo	LP: DG 2532 009 CD: DG 400 0302

Boccherini

Symphony in C minor

London October 1956	Philharmonia	LP: Columbia 33CX 1539
Turin March 1961	RAI Turin Orchestra	LP: Fonit Cetra LAR 46 CD: Hunt CDLSMH 34011

Cello Concerto in B flat (arr. Grützmacher)

London May 1958	Philharmonia Starker	LP: Columbia 33CX 1665 LP: EMI 2M 155 53430-1

Overture in D

London October 1956	Philharmonia	LP: Columbia 33CX 1539

Brahms

Symphony No 1

London January 1961	Philharmonia	LP: Columbia 33CX 1773/SAX 2420 LP: EMI SLS 5241 CD: EMI CZS 252 1682
Los Angeles November 1981	LAPO	LP: DG 2532 056 CD: DG 410 0232 CD: DG 427 8042 CD: DG 431 5912
Vienna April 1991	VPO	DG awaiting publication

Symphony No 2

London October 1962	Philharmonia	LP: Columbia 33CX 1855/SAX 2498 LP: EMI SLS 5241 CD: EMI CZS 252 1682
Los Angeles November 1980	LAPO	LP: DG 2532 014 CD: DG 400 0662
Vienna April 1991	VPO	DG awaiting publication

Symphony No 3

London October and November 1962	Philharmonia	LP: Columbia 33CX 1872/SAX 2516 LP: EMI SLS 5241 CD: EMI CZS 252 1682

Symphony No 4

London April and July 1968	New Philharmonia	LP: EMI SLS 5241 CD: EMI CZS 252 1682
Chicago October 1969	CSO	LP: EMI ASD 2650
Vienna May 1989	VPO	CD: DG 429 4032

Violin Concerto

Chicago November and December 1976	CSO Perlman	LP: EMI ASD 3385 CD: EMI CDC 747 1662

Piano Concerto No 1

London April 1960	Philharmonia Arrau	LP: Columbia 33CX 1739/SAX 2387 LP: EMI CFP 40028 LP: Electrola 1C 187 50266-7 CD: EMI CDM 769 1772
London 1972	LSO Weissenberg	LP: EMI ASD 2992

Piano Concerto No 2

London April 1962	Philharmonia Arrau	LP: Columbia 33CX 1822/SAX 2466 LP: EMI CFP 40034 LP: Electrola 1C 187 50266-7 CD: EMI CDM 769 1782

Ein deutsches Requiem

Vienna June 1987	VPO Vienna Opera Konzertvereinigung Bonney, A.Schmidt	CD: DG 423 5742

Tragic Overture

London October 1962	Philharmonia	LP: Columbia 33CX 1872/SAX 2516 LP: EMI SLS 5241 CD: EMI CZS 252 1682
Vienna May 1989	VPO	CD: DG 429 4032

Variations on St Antoni Chorale (Haydn Variations)

London January 1961	Philharmonia	LP: Columbia 33CX 1778/SAX 2424 LP: EMI SXLP 30278 LP: EMI SLS 5241 CD: EMI CZS 252 1682

Britten

Variations and Fugue on a theme of Purcell (Young person's guide to the orchestra)

| London | Philharmonia | LP: Columbia 33CX 1915/SAX 2555 |
| October 1962 | | LP: EMI SXLP 30240 |

Four Sea Interludes (Peter Grimes)

| London | Philharmonia | LP: Columbia 33CX 1915/SAX 2555 |
| October 1962 | | LP: EMI SXLP 30240 |

Serenade for tenor, horn and strings

| Chicago | CSO | LP: DG 2531 199 |
| April 1977 | Tear, Clevenger | CD: DG 423 2392 |

Les Illuminations

| London | Philharmonia | LP: DG 2531 199 |
| September 1978 | Tear | CD: DG 423 2392 |

Bruckner

Symphony No 2

| Vienna | VSO | LP: EMI ASD 3146 |
| 1974 | | |

Symphony No 7

| Vienna | VPO | LP: DG 419 6271 |
| June 1986 | | CD: DG 419 6272 |

Symphony No 8

| Vienna | VPO | LP: DG 415 1241 |
| May 1984 | | CD: DG 415 1242 |

Symphony No 9

Chicago	CSO	LP: EMI ASD
December 1976		LP: EMI SXLP 30546
		CD: EMI CDC 747 6372

| Vienna | VPO | CD: DG 427 3452 |
| June 1988 | | |

Catalani

La Wally

Milan December 1953	La Scala Chorus & Orchestra Tebaldi, Scotto, Del Monaco, Guelfi, Tozzi	LP: HRE Records HRE 382

Cherubini

Requiem in C minor

Rome 1952	Santa Cecilia Chorus & Orchestra	LP: Columbia 33CX 1075

Les Abencerages

Florence May 1957	Maggio Musicale Chorus & Orchestra Cerquetti, Roney, Misciano, Petri Sung in Italian	LP: MRF Records MRF 52 Also issued on LP by Fonit Cetra

Chopin

Piano Concerto No 1

Los Angeles November 1978	LAPO Zimerman	LP: DG 2531 125 LP: DG 410 9311 CD: DG 415 9702

Piano Concerto No 2

London May 1960	Philharmonia Rubinstein	LP: Replica RPL 2469 CD: Hunt CD 567
Los Angeles November 1979	LAPO Zimerman	LP: DG 2531 126 CD: DG 415 9702

Andante spianato et grande polonaise

Los Angeles November 1979	LAPO Zimerman	LP: DG 2531 126 LP: DG 410 9311 LP: DG 419 0541 CD: DG 419 0542

Cimarosa

Gli orazi e i curiazi

Milan April 1952	RAI Milan Chorus & Orchestra Vercelli, Simionato, Spataro, Del Signore	CD: Melodram CDM 29500

Debussy

La mer

London April 1962	Philharmonia	LP: Columbia 33CX 1818/SAX 2463 LP: EMI SXLP 30146 CD: EMI CDM 769 1842
Los Angeles November 1979	LAPO	LP: DG 2531 264 CD: DG 419 4732 CD: DG 427 2132

Trois Nocturnes

London April 1962	Philharmonia Chorus & Orchestra	LP: Columbia 33CX 1818/SAX 2463 LP: EMI SXLP 30146 CD: EMI CDM 769 1842

Donizetti

Don Sebastiano

Florence May 1953	Teatro Communale Chorus & Orchestra Barbieri, Poggi, Neri, Mascherini	LP: MRF Records MRF 113 LP: Fonit Cetra LO 20

L'Elisir d'amore: Excerpt (Una furtiva lagrima)

Los Angeles November 1980	LAPO Domingo	LP: DG 2532 009 CD: DG 400 0302

Lucia di Lammermoor: Excerpt (Tombe degl' avi miei)

Los Angeles November 1980	LAPO Domingo	LP: DG 2532 009 CD: DG 400 0302

Dvorak

Symphony No 8

London January and April 1962	Philharmonia	LP: Columbia 33CX 1815/SAX 2461 LP: World Records ST 590 LP: Angel AE 34449
Chicago March 1978	CSO	LP: DG 2531 046 LP: DG 413 9801
Amsterdam December 1990	Concertgebouw	Sony awaiting publication

Symphony No 9 "From the New World"

London January 1961	Philharmonia	LP: Columbia 33CX 1759/SAX 2405 LP: EMI SXLP 30163 LP: Angel AE 34449 CD: EMI CDZ 762 5142
Chicago April 1977	CSO	LP: DG 2530 881 CD: DG 423 8822

Cello Concerto

London 1974	LPO Rostropovich	LP: EMI ASD 3452 CD: EMI CDC 749 3062

Scherzo capriccioso

London January 1962	Philharmonia	LP: Columbia 33CX 1815/SAX 2461 LP: World Records ST 590 CD: EMI CDZ 762 5142

Carnival, Overture

London January 1961	Philharmonia	LP: Columbia 33CX 1759/SAX 2405 LP: EMI SXLP 30163

Falla

El amor brujo

London October 1961 and April 1964	Philharmonia De los Angeles	LP: Columbia CX 5265/SAX 5265 LP: EMI SXLP 30140 LP: EMI CFP 4512 CD: EMI CDM 769 0372

The 3-Cornered Hat, Ballet Suite

London July 1957	Philharmonia	LP: Columbia 33CX 1694/SAX 2341 LP: EMI SXLP 30140 LP: EMI CFP 4512 CD: EMI CDM 769 0372 Excerpts 45: Columbia SEL 1635/ESL 6262 45: Columbia SEL 1679/ESL 6284

Fauré

Requiem

London March 1986	Philharmonia Chorus & Orchestra Battle, A.Schmidt	LP: DG 419 2431 CD: DG 419 2432

Franck

Symphony in D minor

London July 1957	Philharmonia	LP: Columbia 33CX 1589 LP: EMI XLP 30055/SXLP 30055
Berlin February 1986	BPO	LP: DG 419 6051 CD: DG 419 6052

Psyché et Eros

London May 1958	Philharmonia	LP: Columbia 33CX 1589 LP: EMI XLP 30055/SXLP 30055
Berlin February 1986	BPO	LP: DG 419 6051 CD: DG 419 6052

Gluck

Alceste

Milan April 1954	La Scala Chorus & Orchestra Callas, Gavarini, Silveri, Panerai, Zaccaria	LP: UORC Records UORC 273 LP: ERR Records ERR 136 LP: Fonit Cetra LO 50 CD: Melodram MEL 26026

Iphigénie en Tauride

Aix-en-Provence 1952	Paris Conservatoire Orchestra Ensemble vocale de Paris Neway, Simoneau, Mollet, Massard	LP: Vox PL 8722 LP: Vox OPBX 212 LP: Pathé DTX 130-2 LP: Electrola 173 1713

Halévy

La Juive: Excerpt (Rachel, quand du seigneur la grace)

Los Angeles November 1980	LAPO Domingo	LP: DG 2532 009 CD: DG 400 0302

Haydn

Symphony No 94 "Surprise"

London October 1956	Philharmonia	LP: Columbia 33CX 1539

Symphony No 104 "London"

Milan March 1965	RAI Milan Orchestra	CD: Fonit Cetra CDE 1063

Cello Concerto in D

London May 1958	Philharmonia Starker	LP: Columbia 33CX 1665 LP: EMI 2M 155 53430-1

PHILHARMONIA CONCERT SOCIETY LTD
Artistic Director: WALTER LEGGE

ROYAL FESTIVAL HALL

MOZART
DON GIOVANNI
(Concert performance)

Monday, February 20, at 7.30 p.m.

Donna Anna	ELISABETH GRÜMMER
Donna Elvira	ELISABETH SCHWARZKOPF
Zerlina	MIRELLA FRENI
Don Giovanni	EBERHARD WÄCHTER
Don Ottavio	ERNST HAEFLIGER
Leporello	GIUSEPPE TADDEI
Masetto	PIERO CAPPUCCILLI
Commendatore	GOTTLOB FRICK

PHILHARMONIA ORCHESTRA
Leader: Hugh Bean

CARLO MARIA GIULINI

Royal Opera House
COVENT GARDEN
HOUSE MANAGER . JOHN COLLINS

THE ROYAL OPERA HOUSE, COVENT GARDEN LIMITED

GENERAL ADMINISTRATOR . SIR DAVID WEBSTER

ASSISTANT GENERAL ADMINISTRATOR . JOHN TOOLEY

in association with the Arts Council of Great Britain

presents

THE COVENT GARDEN OPERA

in

the first performance of a new production of

IL BARBIERE DI SIVIGLIA

OPERA IN TWO ACTS

Music by Gioacchino Rossini

Text by Cesare Sterbini,
founded on Beaumarchais's " Le Barbier de Séville "

Scenery and costumes by JEAN-DENIS MALCLÈS

Conductor : CARLO MARIA GIULINI

Producer : MAURICE SARRAZIN

MONDAY, 16th MAY, 1960

Liszt

Piano Concerto No 1

Vienna	VSO	LP: DG 2530 770
June 1976	Berman	LP: DG 415 8391
		CD: DG 415 8392

Piano Concerto No 2

Vienna	VSO	LP: DG 2530 770
June 1976	Berman	LP: DG 415 8391
		CD: DG 415 8392

Mahler

Symphony No 1 "Titan"

Chicago	CSO	LP: EMI ASD 2722
March 1971		LP: EMI SXLP 30548
		CD: EMI CDC 747 6132

Symphony No 9

Chicago	CSO	LP: DG 2707 097
April 1976		CD: DG 423 9102

Das Lied von der Erde

Berlin	BPO	LP: DG 413 4591
February 1984	Fassbänder, Araiza	CD: DG 413 4592

Malipiero

Monde céleste

Rome	RAI Rome	78: Fonit Cetra
1950	Orchestra	

Meyerbeer

L'Africaine: Excerpt (O paradis)

Los Angeles	LAPO	LP: DG 2532 009
November 1980	Domingo	CD: DG 400 0302

Milhaud

L'Apothéose de Molière

Rome 1950	RAI Rome Orchestra	78: Fonit Cetra

Mozart

Symphony No 40

Turin 1960	RAI Turin Orchestra	CD: Hunt CDLSMH 34011
Milan March 1965	RAI Milan Orchestra	CD: Fonit Cetra CDE 1034
London October and November 1965	New Philharmonia	LP: Decca LXT 6225/SXL 6225 LP: Decca JB 8 CD: Decca 417 7272

Symphony No 41 "Jupiter"

Turin 1960	RAI Turin Orchestra	CD: Hunt CDLSMH 34011
Milan March 1965	RAI Milan Orchestra	CD: Frequenz 041.012 CD: Fonit Cetra CDE 1034
London October and November 1965	New Philharmonia	LP: Decca LXT 6225/SXL 6225 LP: Decca JB 8 CD: Decca 417 7272

Piano Concerto No 9 "Jeunehomme"

Vienna 1978	VSO Weissenberg	LP: Electrola 1C 065 16289

Piano Concerto No 13

Rome December 1951	RAI Rome Orchestra Michelangeli	LP: Fonit Cetra LAR 26

Piano Concerto No 20

Rome December 1951	RAI Rome Orchestra Michelangeli	LP: Fonit Cetra LAR 26

Piano Concerto No 21

Vienna 1978	VSO Weissenberg	LP: Electrola 1C 065 16289

Piano Concerto No 23

Rome December 1951	RAI Rome Orchestra Michelangeli	LP: Fonit Cetra LAR 26 LP: Movimento Musica 01.070
Milan 1987	La Scala Orchestra Horowitz	LP: DG 423 2871 CD: DG 423 2872 VHS Video: DG 072 1153/072 2153 Laserdisc: DG 072 1151/072 2151 Video also contains rehearsal extracts

Violin Concerto No 3

London October 1962	Philharmonia Milstein	Columbia unpublished

Serenade for 13 wind instruments

Rome December 1967	Members of the RAI Rome Orchestra	CD: Fonit Cetra CDE 1063

Eine kleine Nachtmusik

Chicago March 1967	CSO	CD: CSO 90/2 Private Radiothon edition

Requiem

London May 1966	New Philharmonia Chorus & Orchestra Lorengar, Veasey, R.Lewis, Shirley-Quirk	CD: Hunt CD 527
London September 1978	Philharmonia Chorus & Orchestra Donath, C.Ludwig, Tear, Lloyd	LP: EMI ASD 3723 CD: EMI CDZ 762 5182
London April 1989	Philharmonia Chorus & Orchestra Dawson, Nes, K.Lewis, Estes	CD: Sony SK 45577

Thamos, König in Aegypten: Excerpts

Turin 1958	RAI Turin Chorus & Orchestra Meneguzzer, Zilio, Frascati, Monreale, Cajati, Grazia Sung in Italian	LP: Melodram MEL 034 CD: Hunt CDLSMH 34059

Don Giovanni

London October and November 1959	Philharmonia Chorus & Orchestra Schwarzkopf, Sutherland, Sciutti, Alva, Wächter, Taddei, Cappuccilli, Frick	LP: Columbia 33CX 1717-20/SAX 2369-72 LP: EMI SLS 5083 CD: EMI CDS 747 2608 Excerpts LP: Columbia 33CX 1918/SAX 2559 LP: EMI SXLP 30300 CD: EMI CDM 763 0782
Rome May 1970	RAI Rome Chorus & Orchestra Jurinac, Janowitz, Miljakovic, Kraus, Ghiaurov, Petkov, Bruscantini, Monachesi	CD: Melodram MEL 37080 CD: Hunt CDLSMH 34059 CD: Frequenz 043.019 CD: Rodolphe RPV 32675-7

Le Nozze di Figaro

London September and November 1959	Philharmonia Chorus & Orchestra Schwarzkopf, Moffo, Cossotto, Taddei, Wächter, Cappuccilli, Vinco	LP: Columbia 33CX 1732-5/SAX 2381-4 LP: EMI SLS 5152 CD: EMI CMS 763 2662 Excerpts LP: Columbia 33CX 1934/SAX 2573 LP: EMI SXLP 30303

At time of going to press, another version of "Le Nozze di Figaro", recorded in the 1960s in the Netherlands under Giulini, with Schwarzkopf and Prey in the cast, has been announced on Verona CD 27092-4

Mussorgsky

Pictures from an exhibition

Chicago April 1976	CSO	LP: DG 2530 783 LP: DG 410 8381 LP: DG 415 8441 CD: DG 415 8442
Berlin February 1990	BPO	CD: Sony SK 45935

Night on Bare Mountain

London September and October 1956	Philharmonia	LP: Columbia 33CX 1523/SAX 2416 LP: World Records ST 816

Pergolesi

La serva padrona

Milan May and June 1955	La Scala Orchestra Carteri, Rossi-Lemeni	LP: Columbia 33CX 1340 LP: Pathé 2C 063 01335

Prokofiev

Symphony No 1 "Classical"

Chicago April 1976	CSO	LP: DG 2530 783 LP: DG 410 8381

Violin Concerto No 1

London October 1962	Philharmonia Milstein	LP: Columbia CX 5275/SAX 5275 LP: EMI SXLP 30235

Ravel

Alborada del gracioso

London June 1959	Philharmonia	45: Columbia SEL 1684/ESL 6288 LP: Columbia 33CX 1694/SAX 2341 LP: EMI SXLP 30198 LP: EMI EMX 412 0761

Daphnis et Chloé, 2nd Suite

London June 1959	Philharmonia	LP: Columbia 33CX 1694/SAX 2341 LP: EMI SXLP 30198 LP: EMX 412 0761

Ma mère l'oye, Suite

London October 1956	Philharmonia	LP: Columbia 33CX 1518/SAX 2279 LP: EMI XLP 30067/SXLP 30067
Los Angeles November 1979	LAPO	LP: DG 2531 264 LP: DG 415 8441 CD: DG 415 8442
Amsterdam November 1989	Concertgebouw	Sony awaiting publication

Pavane pour une infante défunte

London May 1966	New Philharmonia	LP: Columbia CX 5265/SAX 5265 LP: EMI EMX 412 0761
London March 1986	Philharmonia	LP: DG 419 2431 CD: DG 419 2432

Rapsodie espagnole

London May 1966	New Philharmonia	LP: Columbia CX 5265/SAX 5265 LP: EMI EMX 412 0761
Los Angeles November 1979	LAPO	LP: DG 2531 264 LP: DG 415 8441 CD: DG 415 8442

Rossini

Stabat mater

Rome December 1967	RAI Rome Chorus & Orchestra Zylis-Gara, Verrett, Pavarotti, Zaccaria	LP: Voce 6 CD: Melodram MEL 28012 CD: Hunt CDLSMH 34026 CD: Verona 27060-1 CD: Fonit Cetra CDE 1036
London August 1981	Philharmonia Chorus & Orchestra Ricciarelli, Valentini-Terrani, Gonsalez, R.Raimondi	LP: DG 2532 046 CD: DG 410 0342

Il Barbiere di Siviglia

Milan February 1956	La Scala Chorus & Orchestra Callas, Canali, Alva, Gobbi, Luise, Rossi-Lemeni	LP: MRF Records MRF 101 LP: Estro Armonico EA 015 LP: Fonit Cetra LO 34 LP: Melodram MEL 422 CD: Melodram MEL 26020

Il Barbiere di Siviglia, Overture

London June 1959	Philharmonia	45: Columbia SEL 1696/ESL 6296 LP: Columbia 33CX 1726/SAX 2377 LP: EMI XLP 30094/SXLP 30094 LP: EMI CFP 40379 CD: EMI CDM 769 0422

La Cenerentola, Overture

London April 1964	Philharmonia	LP: Columbia 33CX 1919/SAX 2560 LP: EMI SXLP 30143 CD: EMI CDM 769 0422

La gazza ladra, Overture

London April 1964	Philharmonia	LP: Columbia 33CX 1919/SAX 2560 LP: EMI SXLP 30143 LP: EMI CFP 40379 CD: EMI CDM 769 0422

Guglielmo Tell, Overture

London December 1962	Philharmonia	LP: Columbia 33CX 1919/SAX 2560 LP: EMI SXLP 30143 LP: EMI CFP 40379 CD: EMI CDM 769 0422

Brilliant Recordings by

Carlo Maria Giulini

AND

The Philharmonia Orchestra

'L'OISEAU DE FEU'—Suite (1919)—*Stravinsky*
'JEUX D'ENFANTS'—Suite—*Bizet*
'MA MÈRE L'OYE'—Suite—*Ravel*   33CX1518

SYMPHONY NO. 2 IN C MINOR—('Little Russian')—*Tchaikovsky*
'A NIGHT ON THE BARE MOUNTAIN'—*Moussorgsky orch. Rimsky-Korsakov*

33CX1523

I CONCERTI DELLE STAGIONI—('The Seasons')—*Vivaldi*   33CX1536

COLUMBIA
(Regd. Trade Mark of Columbia Graphophone Co. Ltd)
33⅓ R.P.M. LONG PLAYING RECORDS

E.M.I. RECORDS LTD., 8-11 Great Castle Street, London W.1

ROYAL FESTIVAL HALL
GENERAL MANAGER: T. E. BEAN

PHILHARMONIA CONCERT SOCIETY LTD

ARTISTIC DIRECTOR:
WALTER LEGGE

BEETHOVEN FESTIVAL

PHILHARMONIA
ORCHESTRA
LEADER: HUGH BEAN

GIULINI

Overture, 'Egmont', Op. 84

Symphony No. 6 in F, Op. 68, 'Pastoral'

Symphony No. 5 in C minor, Op. 67

Monday, 27th October, 1958
at 8 p.m.

Programme One Shilling

L'Italiana in Algeri

Milan August 1954	La Scala Chorus & Orchestra Simionato, Sciutti, Valletti, Petri	LP: Columbia 33CX 1215-6 LP: EMI RLS 747

L'Italiana in Algeri, Overture

London June 1959	Philharmonia	45: Columbia SEL 1696/ESL 6296 LP: Columbia 33CX 1726/SAX 2377 LP: EMI XLP 30094/SXLP 30094 LP: EMI CFP 40379 CD: EMI CDM 769 0422

La scala di seta, Overture

London November 1959	Philharmonia	45: Columbia SEL 1699/ESL 6298 LP: Columbia 33CX 1726/SAX 2377 LP: EMI XLP 30094/SXLP 30094 LP: EMI CFP 40379 CD: EMI CDM 769 0422

Semiramide, Overture

London December 1962	Philharmonia	LP: Columbia 33CX 1919/SAX 2560 LP: EMI SXLP 30194 LP: EMI CFP 40379 CD: EMI CDM 769 0422

Il signor bruschino

Rome September 1951	RAI Rome Orchestra Noni, Poli, Bruscantini	LP: Melodram MEL 028 LP: Voce 32

Il signor bruschino, Overture

London June 1959	Philharmonia	LP: Columbia 33CX 1726/SAX 2377 LP: EMI XLP 30094/SXLP 20094 CD: EMI CDM 769 0422

Tancredi, Overture

London April 1964	Philharmonia	LP: Columbia 33CX 1919/SAX 2560 LP: EMI SXLP 30143

Saint-Saëns

Cello Concerto No 1

London September 1957	Philharmonia Starker	LP: Columbia 33CX 1579 LP: World Records ST 529 LP: Toshiba EAC 30163 LP: EMI 2M 155 53430-1
London 1974	LPO Rostropovich	LP: EMI ASD 3452 CD: EMI CDC 749 3062

A. Scarlatti

Il trionfo dell' amore

Milan 1950	RAI Milan Orchestra Zerbini, Zareska, Pini, Berdini, Boriello, Poli	LP: Fonit Cetra LPC 1223

Schubert

Symphony No 4 "Tragic"

Rome December 1967	RAI Rome Orchestra	CD: Fonit Cetra CDE 1057
Chicago March 1978	CSO	LP: DG 2531 047

Symphony No 8 "Unfinished"

London January 1961	Philharmonia	LP: Columbia 33CX 1778/SAX 2424 LP: EMI SXLP 20278
Chicago March 1978	CSO	LP: DG 2531 047 CD: DG 423 8822

Symphony No 9 "Great"

Chicago April 1977	CSO	LP: DG 2530 882

Schumann

Symphony No 3 "Rhenish"

London June 1958	Philharmonia	LP: Columbia 33CX 1662
Turin March 1961	RAI Turin Orchestra	CD: Hunt CDLSMH 34013 CD: Fonit Cetra CDE 1057
Los Angeles December 1980	LAPO	LP: DG 2532 040 CD: DG 400 0622 CD: DG 427 8182

Piano Concerto

Chicago March 1967	CSO Rubinstein	LP: RCA RB 6747/SB 6747 CD: RCA (USA) 6255-2-RC

Cello Concerto

London September 1957	Philharmonia Starker	LP: Columbia 33CX 1579 LP: World Records ST 529 LP: Toshiba EAC 30163 LP: EMI 2M 155 53430-1

Manfred, Overture

London June 1958	Philharmonia	LP: Columbia 33CX 1662
Los Angeles November 1981	LAPO	LP: DG 2532 040 CD: DG 400 0622 CD: DG 427 8042

Stravinsky

L'oiseau de feu, Suite

London October 1956	Philharmonia	LP: Columbia 33CX 1518/SAX 2279 LP: EMI XLP 30067/SXLP 30067 Excerpts 45: Columbia SEL 1635/ESL 6262
Chicago September 1969	CSO	LP: EMI ASD 2614 LP: EMI 102 0701
Amsterdam November 1989	Concertgebouw	CD: Sony SK 45935

Petrushka

Chicago October 1969	CSO	LP: EMI ASD 2614 LP: EMI 102 0701

Tchaikovsky

Symphony No 2 "Little Russian"

London September 1956	Philharmonia	LP: Columbia 33CX 1523/SAX 2416 LP: World Records ST 816 LP: EMI SXLP 30506

Symphony No 5

London April 1962	Philharmonia	Columbia unpublished (recording incomplete)

Symphony No 6 "Pathétique"

London June 1959	Philharmonia	LP: Columbia 33CX 1716/SAX 2368 LP: World Records ST 634 LP: EMI SXLP 30208 CD: EMI CDZ 762 6032
Los Angeles November 1980	LAPO	LP: DG 2532 013 CD: DG 400 0292 CD: DG 427 8232 CD: DG 431 6022

Francesca da Rimini

London April 1962	Philharmonia	LP: Columbia 33CX 1840/SAX 2483 LP: EMI SXLP 30509

Romeo and Juliet, Fantasy Overture

London April 1962	Philharmonia	LP: Columbia 33CX 1840/SAX 2483 CD: EMI CDC 747 6162

Verdi

Aida: Excerpt (Celeste Aida)

Los Angeles November 1980	LAPO Domingo	LP: DG 2632 009 CD: DG 400 0302

Attila

Venice September 1951	Teatro Fenice Chorus & Orchestra Mancini, Penno, Guelfi, Tajo	LP: CLS ARPCL 22024 Also issued on LP by Ed Smith

Don Carlo

London May 1958	Covent Garden Chorus & Orchestra Brouwenstijn, Barbieri, Vickers, Gobbi, Christoff	LP: Paragon DSV 52008 Excerpts LP: Melodram MEL 435
London 1970	Covent Garden Orchestra Ambrosian Chorus Caballé, Verrett, Domingo, Milnes, R.Raimondi	LP: EMI SLS 956 CD: EMI CDS 747 7018

I due foscari

Milan December 1951	RAI Milan Chorus & Orchestra Vitale, Bergonzi, Berzieri, Guelfi	LP: CLS ARPCL 22021 LP: Fonit Cetra LAR 21 CD: Nuova Era 2278-9 Also issued on LP by Morgan Records

Falstaff

Den Haag June 1963	Corena, Capecchi, Alva Orchestra and further cast details not yet available	CD: Verona 27095-6
Los Angeles April 1982	LAPO Los Angeles Master Chorale Ricciarelli, Valentini-Terrani, Boozer, Hendrix, Bruson, Nucci, Gonsalez	LP: DG 2741 020 CD: DG 410 5032
London 1983	Covent Garden Chorus & Orchestra Cast as above	VHS Video: Pioneer Artists (USA) PA 84064 VHS Video: Castle CVI 2001

Ernani: Excerpts (Come rugiada al cespite; Dell' esilio nel dolore; O tu che l'alma adors)

Los Angeles November 1980	LAPO Domingo	LP: DG 2532 009 CD: DG 400 0302

La forza del destino, Overture

London June 1958	Philharmonia	LP: Columbia 33CX 1726/SAX 2377 LP: EMI XLP 30094/SXLP 30094

Rigoletto

Rome November 1966	Rome Opera Chorus & Orchestra Scotto, Pavarotti, Paskalis	LP: Estro Armonico EA 020 CD: Curcio OP 2 CD: Innovations GJ 824 CD: BMCD 001
Vienna September 1979	VPO Vienna Opera Chorus Cotrubas, Domingo, Cappuccilli	LP: DG 2740 225 CD: DG 415 2882 Excerpts LP: DG 2537 057 CD: DG 423 1142

La Traviata

Milan May 1952	RAI Milan Chorus & Orchestra Tebaldi, Prandelli, Orlandi	LP: Stradivarius STR 1001-2 CD: Legato SRO 810 Stradivarius incorrectly dated 1956
Milan May 1955	La Scala Chorus & Orchestra Callas, Di Stefano, Bastianini	LP: MRF Records MRF 87 LP: Fonit Cetra LO 28 LP: Discocorp RR 474 LP: Morgan MOR 5501 LP: Foyer FO 1003 CD: Hunt CD 501 CD: EMI CMS 763 6282
Milan January 1956	La Scala Chorus & Orchestra Callas, G.Raimondi, Bastianini	LP: HRE Records HRE 272 CD: Myto MCD 89003
London April 1967	Covent Garden Chorus & Orchestra Freni, Cioni, Cappuccilli	CD: Frequenz 043.006

La Traviata, Preludes Acts 1 and 3

London May and June 1958	Philharmonia	LP: Columbia 33CX 1726/SAX 2377 LP: EMI XLP 30094/SXLP 30094

Il Trovatore

London November 1964	Covent Garden Chorus & Orchestra Jones, Simionato, Prevedi, Glossop, Rouleau	LP: Legendary LR 175
Rome January 1984	Santa Cecilia Chorus & Orchestra Plowright, Fassbänder, Domingo, Zancanaro, Nesterenko	LP: DG 413 3551 CD: DG 413 3552 Excerpts LP: DG 415 2851 CD: DG 415 2852

Il Trovatore: Excerpt (Ah si, ben mio; Di quella pira)

Los Angeles November 1980	LAPO Wagner Chorale Domingo	LP: DG 2532 009 CD: DG 400 0302

I vespri siciliani, Overture

London June 1958	Philharmonia	LP: Columbia 33CX 1726/SAX 2377 LP: EMI XLP 30094/SXLP 30094

Requiem

London September 1963 and April 1964	Philharmonia Chorus & Orchestra Schwarzkopf, C.Ludwig, Gedda, Ghiaurov	LP: EMI AN 133-4/SAN 133-4 LP: EMI SLS 909 CD: EMI CDS 747 2578
Berlin April and May 1989	BPO Ernst-Senff-Chor Sweet, Quivar, Cole, Estes	CD: DG 423 6742

4 pezzi sacri

London December 1962	Philharmonia Chorus & Orchestra Baker	LP: EMI AN 120/SAN 120 LP: EMI SXLP 30508 CD: EMI CDS 747 2578

Te deum (4 pezzi sacri)

Rome 1962	RAI Rome Chorus & Orchestra	CD: Hunt CDLSMH 34026

Vivaldi

The Four Seasons

London September and October 1955	Philharmonia Parikian	LP: Columbia 33CX 1365 LP: EMI XLP 30058

Weber

Euryanthe

Florence May 1954	Maggio Musicale Chorus & Orchestra Wilfert, Borkh, Kamann, Vanderburg	LP: Fonit Cetra DOC 71

Der Freischütz, Overture

London May 1969	New Philharmonia	EMI unpublished

7 'Viennese' Sopranos

Schwarzkopf
Seefried
Grümmer
Jurinac
Della Casa
Streich
Güden

Discographies
compiled by John Hunt

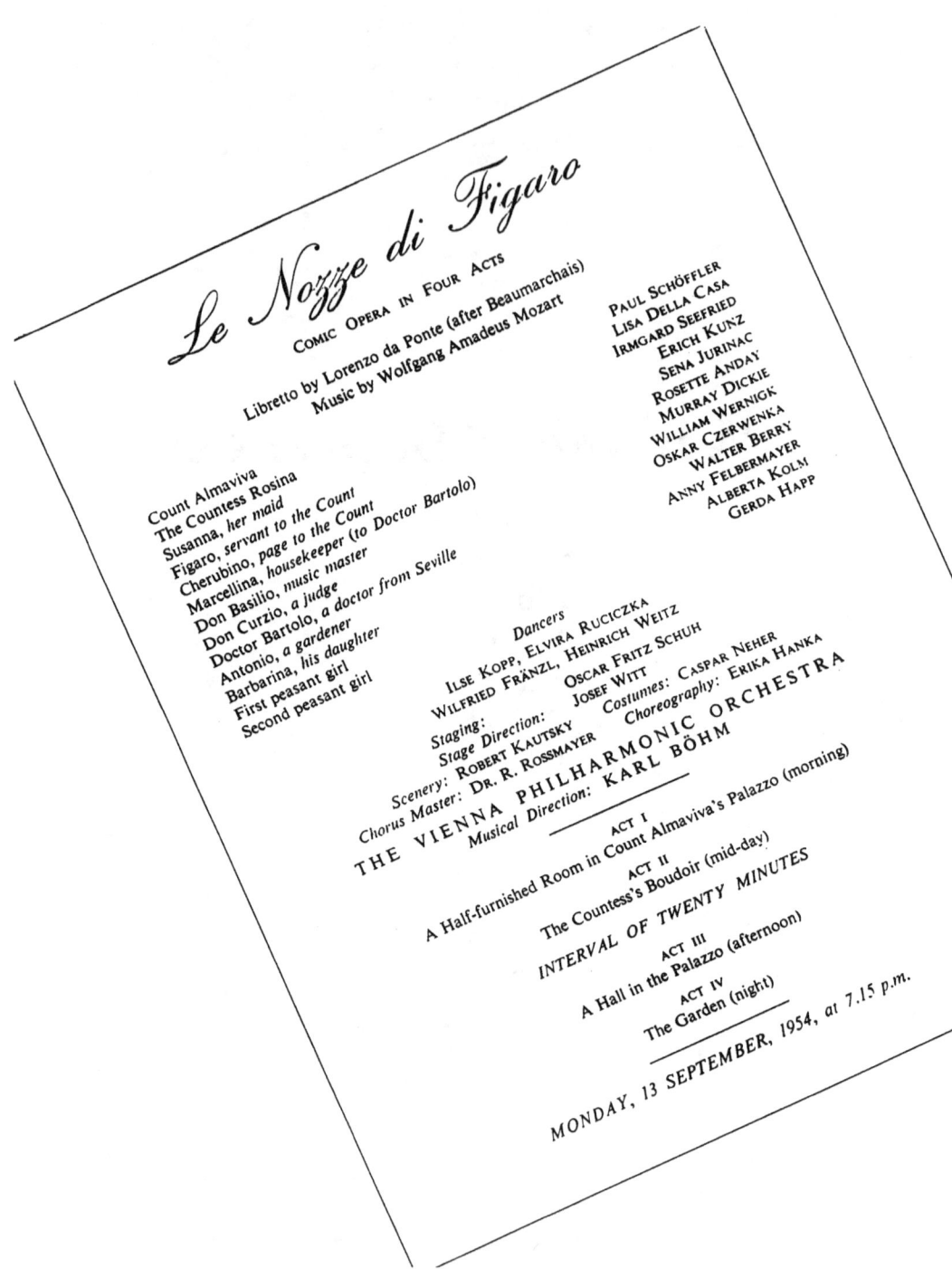

1954 visit to London by the Vienna State Opera

Introduction

The period 1945 to 1965 must surely go down in discographical history as the most productive and successful for the recording of opera from Mozart, through the German classics and romantics, to Wagner and then Viennese operetta. Italian opera did quite well too, although the exploration of early Verdi and rare Rossini and Donizetti seemed to reach full flower in the years after 1965.

If one surveys the profusion of opera recordings from that period, recordings which still dominate the catalogue in 1991 in their CD form, one is struck by the fact that the female roles, falling as they do into the "lyric" category, are dominated by a group of sopranos bred, if not actually born, into the Viennese tradition. They learned their craft in the post-war Vienna opera ensemble or performed there as valued guests during the period from 1943 until well into the 1960s.

Countless attempts have been made to analyse why such a wealth of talent and superb musicianship should have converged on the war-ravaged city of Vienna in the mid 1940, giving exemplary performances of the standard Viennese repertoire whilst all around was ruin and destruction. The need to stay together in times of hardship may have had something to do with it, for here was a group of singers, and not just the sopranos, who were prepared to work long and dedicated hours under the guidance of experienced opera practitioners like the conductors Böhm, Krips and Krauss. In interviews, both Schwarzkopf and Jurinac have emphasised the homogeneity of the Vienna ensemble of those years, where singers of the same voice range would study together and know each others' roles, so that in an emergency they might take on their colleague's part if needed. Our sopranos listened to each other, and as Schwarzkopf stresses, also listened to themselves with critical self-anaysis, in a period before singers became lazy through having access to cassette recordings of themselves. Also, the age of jet travel was still a few years away. Seefried recalled later the importance of unremitting hard work at that time: to the extent that the conductor Krips would expect an eminent exponent of the role of "Salome" to give her performance one evening and yet still be ready, at ten o'clock the next morning, to take part in an intensive ensemble rehearsal for the next evening's opera!

For an analysis of the singers under examination I can do no better than refer the reader to the chapter "Trial by Mozart" in John Steane's indispensable book "The Grand Tradition" (Duckworth 1974). To Steane's shortlist of Viennese sopranos, only one of whom, Hilde Güden, was actually born in the city, I have added the two leading exponents of that same tradition who remained based in the rival city of musical excellence, Berlin: they are Elisabeth Grümmer and Rita Streich.

Where we are more fortunate than John Steane's original 1974 readers is in that those last 17 years have seen the profusion, on the LP and now the CD market, of countless live recordings which supplement, warts and all, the "official" studio documentation of these singers (in the case of at least three of the singers, that "official" representation was, for various reasons, small in any case). Today's younger listeners can therefore now hear with their own ears why some of us older ones view the 1950s and 1960s as such a golden age. Not that I would want to claim that all is gloom in 1991: whilst I see the forbears of our post-war Viennese sopranos as Ivogün, Schumann, Lehmann, Lemnitz and Reining, I also view their successors as Janowitz, Margaret Marshall, Margaret Price, Popp, Varady and Lott.

Ultimately I have to admit that my choice of 7 sopranos is subjective, and that if I were going on the evidence of recordings alone, without my memories of actual performances, I would have had to include that beautiful American artist of the same era, Eleanor Steber.

The repertoire of our sopranos is firmly centred in the lyric field, in the music of Mozart, Weber and Richard Strauss, although it also borders on the soubrette and coloratura, in which Streich and Güden excelled, as well as on the lyric dramatic.

Herbert von Karajan's controversial but epoch-making 1950 version of "Le Nozze di Figaro" boasts Elisabeth Schwarzkopf in the role of Countess, Irmgard Seefried as Susanna and Sena Jurinac as Cherubino. Furtwängler's pirated version of the same opera again has Schwarzkopf and Seefried, with Hilde Güden as Cherubino, while Erich Kleiber, for his 1955 Decca recording, chose Güden for Susanna and Lisa della Casa for Countess. In recordings of "Fidelio", either commercial or pirated, Schwarzkopf, Seefried, Jurinac and della Casa all sang the role of Marzelline, while two of these can be heard venturing into the "Abscheulicher" aria of Leonore, lyric-dramatic territory which only Jurinac kept in her active repertory for a limited time. "Der Freischütz" was recorded with Elisabeth Grümmer as Agathe and Rita Streich as Aennchen, while several of the other sopranos took on, at one time or another, Agathe's arias, those true tests of legato singing.

The finest recorded exponents of Eva in "Meistersinger" in the period in question (by all reports the most captivating on stage as well) were Schwarzkopf, Grümmer and della Casa; the discography of "Arabella" is dominated by complete recordings with della Casa and excerpts with Schwarzkopf. Finally, every collector's shortlist of treasured operetta recordings will include the names of Schwarzkopf, Streich and Güden. And were one to be so bold as to cite one opera recording as summing up the virtues of that great mono LP era of the 1950s, it might well be "Ariadne auf Naxos", produced by Walter Legge and with Schwarzkopf in the title role, Seefried as the Composer and Streich as Zerbinetta.

Even the least recorded of our singers, Sena Jurinac, spanned a range from Cherubino to Leonore, whilst Schwarzkopf and della Casa can both be heard singing arias of all <u>three</u> female leads in "Figaro" (only Güden is heard in published recordings of all three of those roles complete).

At the end of each discography I have added a list of all the roles each singer performed on the stage of the Vienna State Opera or in its temporary homes between 1945 and 1955, the Theater an der Wien and the Volksoper. Listing all the singer's roles adds a perspective to what the artist chose to perform in the recording studio, and I for one cannot deny the secret hope that some of the gems there (Seefried as Liù, della Casa as Queen of Night) might still one day turn up on rediscovered tapes.

In Schwarzkopf and Seefried, our list also includes the two greatest female exponents of the German "Lied", in which capacity I heard them in countless recitals, mainly in London. On the other hand, my regular travels to Salzburg and Vienna enabled me to hear most of the singers in their opera roles. In the period after 1959, when Schwarzkopf last sang opera at Covent Garden (Marschallin), only Jurinac and della Casa returned with any regularity to that house (Seefried, I recall, sang two performances as Octavian in 1962): sad to think that after hosting that first post-war visit of the entire Vienna company in 1947, our Royal Opera House should so sadly have neglected these Viennese sopranos in later years.

<u>John Hunt</u>

Elisabeth Schwarzkopf
Discography

Compiled by John Hunt
1991

Introduction

"Her Master's Voice" is an epithet often applied to Elisabeth Schwarzkopf, referring as it does to the long and fruitful partnership of the artist with her recording producer husband, Walter Legge of EMI; and one of the other sopranos in this discographical survey was once heard to remark that her own recording career had not been so remarkably consistent because she, unlike Schwarzkopf, had "not been married to a recording company" !
I think that this statement is both unjustified and misleading. For one thing, one can hear from the considerable number of recordings made by Schwarzkopf for German radio before 1945 that a very definite musical personality, with a positive style of its own, was already emerging: the makings of am immediately recognisable interpreter, who would have made her imprint on the history of Lieder and German opera even if she had never encountered the man from HMV (Columbia, to be precise).

Not that we can under-estimate Legge's achievement with Schwarzkopf and the many other Columbia recording artists of those 2 postwar decades. Many years earlier he had declared an ambition to marry "the most beautiful singer in the world", and I certainly realised that he had done just this when I first encountered the Schwarzkopf magic in "Falstaff" and "Figaro" at the 1957 Salzburg Festival and then, the following winter, at concerts in London. Her very entrance onto the platform of the Royal Festival Hall aroused an anticipation among the audience that we were about to experience, and moreover enjoy, something really special. And yet, is my description "Schwarzkopf magic" itself perhaps inaccurate ? The soprano's interpretations of Mozart, Strauss and Wolf were the result of sheer long and arduous study, both of the music and the text. It is only the final presentation to an audience which must appear effortless, or, as Richard Strauss put it another way, "it is only the spectators who should be seen to be sweating, not the performers".

Of course we have been able to appreciate, to an even closer degree, what Elisabeth Schwarzkopf was striving for in her stage and platform appearances by observing her, in the years since her retirement from singing, conveying to her students that need for hard and unrelenting work in order to bring a performance to life.

Together with Seefried and Fischer-Dieskau, Schwarzkopf has played a key pioneering role in bringing the German Lied to all 4 corners of the globe, both through recordings and public performance. They presented the literature of German song to audiences worldwide who had no knowledge or background and who, in some cases, had to be won over from an attitude of hostility to all things German. Especially remarkable were the recitals of these 3 artists in the USA in the early 1950s, where they conquered in the same way as they were to later in Japan.

I had the privilege to be involved in the formation, after the singer's retirement, of the Elisabeth Schwarzkopf/ Walter Legge Society, which would promote interest in the vital work carried out for music by this remarkable partnership, and I had hoped that this would be something more than just another "fan club". Instead, I hope that this discography might be my own fitting tribute to a great artist.

As far as Lieder are concerned in the discography, a word of explanation is necessary: although they are listed under composer, I have, within that framework, set them as far as possible in the groups in which they were actually recorded; some particularly popular or frequently recorded songs are listed separately so that one can refer at ease to the different recordings of the same item; finally, in certain instances where a record is shown as unpublished, it is still possible that parts of a particular session were incorporated into the version as eventually published.

John Hunt

Arne

The lass with the delicate air

Berlin 1944	Raucheisen, piano Sung in German	LP: Acanta 40.23557 CD: Acanta 42.43801

When daisies pied

Vienna   Hudez, piano   Columbia unpublished
November 1946

London   Moore, piano   78: Columbia LB 73
October 1947   LP: EMI RLS 763
                                                            LP: EMI RLS 154 6133
                                                            CD: EMI CDM 763 6542/CMS 763 7902

Where the bee sucks

London   Moore, piano   78: Columbia LB 73
October 1947   LP: EMI RLS 763
                                                            LP: EMI RLS 154 6133
                                                            CD: EMI CDM 763 6542/CMS 763 7902

Berlin   Raucheisen, piano   LP: Melodram MEL 082
1958   Recording incorrectly dated 1953

Bach

Mass in B minor

Vienna June 1950	Soprano soloist Ferrier, W.Ludwig, Poell, Schöffler, Singverein VSO Karajan	LP: Foyer FO (number not known) CD: Foyer 2CF-2022 CD: Hunt CDKAR 212 CD: Verona 27073-4 Excerpts CD: Verona 27076 CD: EMI CDM 763 6552/CMS 763 7902 EMI incorrectly states orchestra to be VPO
London July and November 1952	Soprano soloist Höffgen, Gedda, Rehfuss, Singverein Philharmonia Karajan	LP: Columbia 33CX 1121-3 LP: World Records T 854-6 LP: EMI RLS 746 LP: EMI RLS 29 09743 CD: EMI CHS 763 5052 Choruses recorded in Vienna

Saint Matthew Passion

London November 1960, January, April, May and November 1961	Soprano soloist Ludwig, Pears, Gedda, Berry, Fischer-Dieskau, Philharmonia Chorus & Orchestra Klemperer	LP: Columbia 33CX 1799-1803/SAX 2446-50 LP: EMI SLS 827 CD: EMI CMS 763 0582 Excerpts LP: Columbia 33CX 1881/SAX 2526

Cantata No 51 "Jauchzet Gott in allen Landen"

London May 1948 (Columbia)	Soprano soloist Philharmonia Susskind	Columbia unpublished
London October 1950	Soprano soloist Philharmonia Gellhorn	78: Columbia LX 1334-6/8756-8 auto LP: Columbia (USA) ML 4792 LP: Columbia (Germany) C 80628 LP: Seraphim (USA) 60013 LP: EMI RLS 154 6133 CD: EMI CDM 763 2012
Munich October 1951	Soprano soloist Bavarian RO Jochum	LP: Melodram MEL 082 CD: Melodram MEL 16501

Cantata No 199 "Mein Herze schwimmt in Blut"

London May 1957 and May 1958	Soprano soloist Philharmonia Dart	CD: EMI CDM 763 6552/CMS 763 7902

Cantata No 202 "Weichet nur, betrübte Schatten"

Toronto 1955	Soprano soloist Stratford Festival Orchestra Neel	LP: Rococo 5388 Final recitative and aria missing
Amsterdam February 1957	Soprano soloist Concertgebouw Klemperer	LP: Discocorp RR 208 CD: Hunt CD 727 CD: AS-Disc AS 533
London May and June 1957	Soprano soloist Philharmonia Dart	Columbia unpublished

Cantata No 68: Excerpt (Mein gläubiges Herze)

London October 1950	Soprano soloist Parikian, violin Sutcliffe, oboe Clark, cello Jones, organ	78: Columbia LX 1336 LP: Columbia (USA) ML 4792 CD: EMI CDH 763 2012
London May and June 1957 and May 1958	Soprano soloist Philharmonia Dart	Columbia unpublished

Cantata No 92: Excerpt (Meinem Hirten bleib' ich treu)

London May and June 1957 and May 1958	Soprano soloist Philharmonia Dart	Columbia unpublished

Cantata No 208: Excerpt (Schafe können sicher weiden)

Berlin October 1944	Soprano soloist Scheck & Wolf, flutes Schulz, violin Schonecke, cello Raucheisen, piano	CD: Acanta 42.43128
Vienna November 1946	Soprano soloist Niedermayer & Reznicek, flutes Maurer, cello Ahlgrimm, harpsichord	78: Columbia LX 1051 LP: Columbia (USA) ML 4792 LP: EMI ALP 143 5501 CD: EMI CDH 763 2012
London May and June 1957 and May 1958	Soprano soloist Philharmonia Dart	Columbia unpublished

Ave Maria (arr. Gounod)

London October 1947	Pougnet, violin Moore, piano	Columbia unpublished

Bist du bei mir

London September 1952	Moore, piano	78: Columbia LX 1580
London July 1953	Moore, piano	Columbia unpublished
London January 1954	Moore, piano	LP: Columbia 33CX 1044 LP: EMI RLS 763 CD: EMI CDM 763 6542/CMS 763 7902

Beethoven

Symphony No 9 "Choral"

Vienna November and December 1947	Soprano soloist Höngen, Patzak, Hotter, Singverein VPO Karajan	78: Columbia LX 1097-1105/8612-20 auto LP: Toshiba EAC 30101 LP: EMI RLS 7714 LP: EMI 2C 153 03200-5 CD: EMI CDH 761 0762
Bayreuth July 1951	Soprano soloist Höngen, Hopf, Edelmann, Bayreuth Festival Chorus & Orchestra Furtwängler	LP: HMV ALP 1286-7 LP: Electrola 1C 147 00811-2 LP: EMI RLS 727 LP: EMI 2C 151 53678-9 CD: EMI CDC 747 0812 CD: EMI CDH 769 U812/CDHS 763 6062
Lucerne August 1954	Soprano soloist Cavelti, Häfliger, Edelmann, Lucerne Festival Chorus Philharmonia Furtwängler	LP: Furtwängler Series (Japan) MF 18862-3 LP: Fonit Cetra LO 530 LP: Discocorp RR 390 CD: Seven Seas (Japan) K35Y-41 CD: Hunt CDLSMH 34006 CD: Rodolphe RPC 32522-4 Extract from final movement LP: French Furtwängler Society SWF 7701
Vienna July 1955	Soprano soloist Höffgen, Häfliger, Edelmann, Singverein Philharmonia Karajan	LP: Columbia 33CX 1391-2 LP: World Records SH 143-9 LP: Toshiba EAC 37001-19 LP: EMI SLS 5053 CD: EMI CMS 763 3102

Missa Solemnis

Vienna September 1958	Soprano soloist Ludwig, Gedda, Zaccaria, Singverein Philharmonia Karajan	LP: Columbia 33CX 1634-5 LP: World Records ST 914-5 LP: Electrola 1C 191 00627-8 LP: EMI SLS 5198

Ah perfido !

Watford September 1954	Philharmonia Karajan	LP: Columbia 33CX 1278 LP: Toshiba EAC 37001-19 LP: EMI RLS 7715 LP: EMI RLS 154 6133 CD: EMI CDH 763 2012

Fidelio

Salzburg August 1950	Role of Marzelline Flagstad, Patzak, Dermota, Greindl, Schöffler, Braun, Vienna Opera Chorus VPO Furtwängler	LP: MRF Records MRF 50 LP: Morgan MOR 5001 LP: BJR Records BJR 112 LP: Discocorp IGI 328 LP: Fonit Cetra FE 44 CD: Hunt CDWFE 304 CD: Hunt CDWFE 354 CD: Verona 27044-5 Excerpts LP: Melodram MEL 082 CD: Melodram MEL 16501

Fidelio: Excerpt (Abscheulicher, wo eilst du hin ?)

Watford September 1954	Role of Leonore Philharmonia Karajan	LP: Columbia 33CX 1266 LP: Toshiba EAC 37001-19 LP: EMI RLS 7715 LP: EMI RLS 154 6133 CD: EMI CDH 763 2012

Fidelio: Excerpt (Ach wär' ich schon mit dir vereint)

London October 1950	Role of Marzelline Philharmonia Galliera	78: Columbia LX 1410 45: Columbia SCD 2114 LP: EMI EX 769 7411

Fidelio: Excerpt (Mir ist so wunderbar)

London May 1951	Role of Marzelline Flagstad, Stevenson, Gwynne, Covent Garden Orchestra Rankl	LP: Ed Smith EJS 390 Recorded fragments issued on EJS 390 also include Abscheulicher (Flagstad) and dialogue (spoken in English) surrounding both the quartet and aria

Das Geheimnis

Berlin September 1944	Raucheisen, piano	LP: Acanta 40.23557 CD: Acanta 42.43801

Wonne der Wehmut

London April 1952, September 1952 and July 1953	Moore, piano	Columbia unpublished
London January 1954	Moore, piano	LP: Columbia 33CX 1044 LP: EMI RLS 154 6133 CD: EMI CDM 763 6542/CMS 763 7902

Berlioz

La Damnation de Faust

Lucerne August 1950	Role of Marguérite Vroons, Hotter, Pernerstorfer, Lucerne Festival Chorus & Orchestra Furtwängler Sung in German	LP: Fonit Cetra FE 21

Bizet

Carmen: Excerpt (Je dis que rien ne m'épouvante)

London October 1950	Role of Micaela Philharmonia Galliera	78: Columbia LX 1410 45: Columbia SCD 2114 LP: EMI ALP 143 5501

Pastorale

London June 1957	Moore, piano	Columbia unpublished

Bohm

Was i hab'

London June 1957	Moore, piano	Columbia unpublished

Brahms

Ein deutsches Requiem

Lucerne August 1947	Soprano soloist Hotter, Lucerne Festival Chorus & Orchestra Furtwängler	LP: Furtwängler Series (Japan) W 24 Ihr habt nun Traurigkeit LP: Furtwängler Series (Japan) W 22-3
Vienna October 1947	Soprano soloist Hotter, Singverein VPO Karajan	78: Columbia LX 1055-64/8595-8604 auto 78: Columbia (USA) M 755 LP: Toshiba EAC 30103 LP: EMI 2C 153 03200-5 LP: EMI RLS 7714 LP: EMI 2C 051 43176 CD: EMI CDH 761 0102
London March, April and May 1961	Soprano soloist Fischer-Dieskau, Philharmonia Chorus & Orchestra Klemperer	LP: Columbia 33CX 1781-2/SAX 2430-1 LP: EMI SLS 821 CD: EMI CDC 747 2382

Deutsche Volkslieder: Die Sonne scheint nicht mehr; Da unten im Tale; Gunhilde lebt' gar still und fromm; Maria ging aus wandern; Es ging ein Maidlein zarte; Ich stand auf hohem Berge; Es war ein Markgraf überm Rhein; Dort in den Weiden; Och Mod'r ich well en Ding han; Es wohnet ein Fiedler; Schöner Augen schöne Strahlen; Es steht ein Lind; In stiller Nacht; Duets: Jungfräulein, soll ich mit euch gehn?; Feinsliebchen; Wach auf, mein Hort; Schwesterlein; Der Reiter; Sagt mir, o schönste Schäferin mein; Guten Abend; Ach, englische Schäferin; Es ritt ein Ritter; Ach, könnt' ich diesen Abend; Wie komm' ich denn?; Soll sich der Mond nicht heller scheinen; Des Abends kann ich nicht schlafen; Es war eine schöne Jüdin; other songs with Fischer-Dieskau

Berlin August and September 1965	Fischer-Dieskau Moore, piano	LP: EMI AN 163-4/SAN 163-4 LP: Electrola 1C 193 00054-5 CD: EMI CDS 749 5252 Och Mod'r; In stiller Nacht LP: EMI RLS 154 6133 In stiller Nacht CD: EMI CDM 763 6542/CMS 763 7902

In stiller Nacht

London January 1958 and December 1962	Moore, piano	Columbia unpublished

Da unten im Tale

Berlin September 1944	Raucheisen, piano	LP: Acanta 40.23524 LP: Acanta 40.23557 CD: Acanta 42.43801
London November 1951	Moore, piano	Columbia unpublished
London December 1951	Moore, piano	78: Columbia LB 118
London July 1953	Moore, piano	Columbia unpublished
London January 1954	Moore, piano	LP: Columbia 33CX 1044 LP: EMI RLS 763 LP: EMI RLS 154 6133 CD: EMI CDM 763 6532/CMS 763 7902
Hannover March 1962	Reutter, piano	LP: Movimento Musica 02.017 CD: Movimento Musica 051.015 CD: Verona 27075

Och Mod'r ich well en Ding han

London September 1952	Moore, piano	LP: EMI RLS 154 7003
London January 1954	Moore, piano	LP: Columbia 33CX 1044 LP: EMI RLS 763 CD: EMI CDM 763 6532/CMS 763 7902

Lieder: Feldeinsamkeit; Therese; Der Tod, das ist die kühle Nacht; Wiegenlied; Von ewiger Liebe; Wie Melodien; In stiller Nacht; Da unten im Tale; Meine Liebe ist grün; Liebestreu'; Vergebliches Ständchen

Rome February 1954	Fischer, piano	CD: Hunt CD 535

Lieder: Liebestreu'; Ständchen

Hannover March 1962	Reutter, piano	LP: Movimento Musica 02.017 CD: Movimento Musica 051.015 CD: Verona 27075

Lieder: Immer leiser wird mein Schlummer; Wie Melodien; Der Jäger; Liebestreu';
Ständchen

Berlin August and September 1970	Parsons, piano	LP: EMI ASD 2844 Ständchen CD: EMI CDM 763 6542/CMS 763 7902

Lieder: Mädchenlied; Therese; Blinde Kuh

Vienna January 1979	Parsons, piano	LP: Decca SXL 6943 CD: Decca 430 0002

Sandmännchen

London March 1962	Moore, piano	Columbia unpublished

Vergebliches Ständchen

London September 1952	Moore, piano	LP: EMI RLS 154 7003
London January 1954	Moore, piano	LP: Columbia 33CX 1044 LP: EMI RLS 763
New York November 1956	Reeves, piano	CD: EMI CDH 761 0432
Berlin August and September 1970	Parsons, piano	LP: EMI ASD 2844

Von ewiger Liebe

London January 1961 and December 1962	Moore, piano	Columbia unpublished

Wiegenlied

London December 1962	Moore, piano	Columbia unpublished

Busoni

Unter den Linden

Berlin
September 1944

Raucheisen, piano

LP: Acanta 40.23557
CD: Acanta 40.43128

Carissimi

4 Cantatas: Detesta la cativa sorte in amore; Lungi omai; Il mio core; A piè d'un verde alloro

London
May 1955

Seefried
Moore, piano

LP: Columbia 33CX 1331
LP: EMI HLM 7267
CD: EMI CDH 769 7932

Charpentier

Louise: Excerpt (Depuis le jour)

London
May 1950

Role of Louise
Philharmonia
Dobrowen

LP: EMI RLS 763
LP: EMI RLS 154 6133

Chopin

Songs: Maiden's wish; Lithuanian song

Berlin
October 1968

Parsons, piano
Sung in German

LP: EMI ASD 2634

ROYAL ALBERT HALL
(Manager: C. S. Taylor)

PHILHARMONIA ORCHESTRA
(Leader: MANOUG PARIKIAN)

Conductor:
PAUL KLETZKI

ELISABETH SCHWARZKOPF
(Soprano)

Programme

HANDEL-HARTY: Water Music

STRAUSS: First Performance in England of Scenes from Richard Strauss's Operas "Dafne" and "Capriccio"

INTERVAL

MAHLER: Symphony No. 4.

MONDAY, APRIL 9, 1951
at 7.30 p.m.

Management: IBBS & TILLETT LTD., 124 WIGMORE STREET, W.1

A FAMOUS COLUMBIA ARTIST

Elisabeth Schwarzkopf

WITH THE PHILHARMONIA ORCHESTRA

"La Traviata" — *Verdi:* Addio del passato ;
"Madama Butterfly" — *Puccini:* Un bel dì, vedremo LX 1370
"La Bohème" — *Puccini:* Donde lieta uscì ;
"Turandot" — *Puccini:* Signore ascolta! - - - LB 110

ACCOMPANIED BY **GERALD MOORE**

Der Zauberer, K.472 — *Mozart;*
Da unten im tale — *arr. Brahms* · · · · · · · LB 118
Folk Songs: — O du liebs Angeli (Bernese);
Maria auf dem Berge (Silesian); 's Schatzli (Swiss);
Die Beruhigte (Bavarian) · · · · · · · · LB 112

For details of further recordings, see the Columbia Catalogue

Cornelius

Der Barbier von Bagdad

London May 1956	Role of Margiana Hoffman, Gedda, Unger, Wächter, Prey, Chorus Philharmonia Leinsdorf	LP: Columbia 33CX 1400-1 LP: Electrola 1C 147 01448-9M

Duets: Heimatgedenken; Scheiden

Berlin November 1944	Greindl Raucheisen, piano	CD: Acanta 42.43128

Debussy

Pelleas et Melisande

Rome December 1954	Role of Melisande Sciutti, Häfliger, Roux, Petri, Calabrese, RAI Rome Orchestra Karajan	LP: Fonit Cetra ARK 6 LP: Rodolphe RP 12393-5 CD: Hunt CDKAR 218

Mandoline

Berlin August 1965	Moore, piano	LP: Columbia CX 5268/SAX 5268 LP: EMI RLS 154 6133 LP: EMI CDM 763 6542/CMS 763 7902

Dowland

Come again! Sweet love doth now invite

Vienna October 1946	Hudez, piano	LP: EMI ALP 143 5501 LP: EMI RLS 154 6133

Dvorak

Moravian Duets op 32

London	Seefried	LP: Columbia 33CX 1331
May 1955	Moore, piano	LP: EMI HLM 7267
	Sung in German	CD: EMI CDH 769 7932

Songs my mother taught me

London	Moore, piano	LP: Columbia 33CX 1404/SAX 2265
April and May	Sung in English	EP: Columbia SEL 1589/ESL 6255
1956		

Flies

Wiegenlied (attrib. Mozart)

| London | Moore, piano | Columbia unpublished |
| April 1956 | | |

Gieseking

Kinderlieder

| London | Gieseking, piano | CD: EMI CDM 763 6553/CMS 763 7902 |
| April 1955 | | |

Giordani

Caro mio ben

| London | Moore, piano | Columbia unpublished |
| June 1957 | | |

Gluck

Einem Bach der fliesset

Berlin September 1944	Raucheisen, piano	LP: Acanta 40.23557 CD: Acanta 42.43801
London November 1951	Moore, piano	Columbia unpublished
London April 1952	Moore, piano	Columbia unpublished
London September, October and December 1952	Moore, piano	Columbia unpublished
London January 1954	Moore, piano	LP: Columbia 33CX 1044 LP: EMI RLS 763 CD: EMI CDM 763 6532/CMS 763 7902
New York November 1956	Reeves, piano	CD: EMI CHS 761 0432

Grieg

Farmyard Song

London April 1956	Moore, piano Sung in English	LP: Columbia 33CX 1404/SAX 2265 45: Columbia SEL 1600/ESL 6274

Ich liebe dich

London April 1956	Moore, piano Sung in German	LP: Columbia 33CX 1404/SAX 2265 45: Columbia SEL 1600/ESL 6274
Berlin October 1968	Parsons, piano Sung in German	LP: EMI ASD 2634

Ein Schwan

Vienna January 1979	Parsons, piano Sung in German	LP: Decca SXL 6943 CD: Decca 430 0002

Songs: Mit einer Wasserlilie; Letzter Frühling

Berlin October 1968	Parsons, piano Sung in German	LP: EMI ASD 2634

Songs: Erstes Begegnen; Zur Rosenzeit; Mit einer primula veris; Lauf der Welt

Berlin August and September 1970	Parsons, piano Sung in German	LP: EMI ASD 2844

Hahn

Si mers vers avaient des ailes

London April 1956	Moore, piano	LP: Columbia 33CX 1404/SAX 2265 45: Columbia SEL 1589/ESL 6255 LP: EMI RLS 154 6133 CD: EMI CDM 763 6542/CMS 763 7902

Handel

L'Allegro, il pensoroso ed il moderato: Excerpt (Sweet bird)

Vienna November 1946	Niedermayer, flute VPO Krips	78: Columbia LX 1010 LP: EMI ALP 143 5501 LP: EMI RLS 154 6133 CD: EMI CDH 763 2012

Atalanta: Excerpt (Caro selve)

New York November 1956	Reeves, piano	CD: EMI CHS 761 0432

Hercules

Milan December 1958	Role of Iole Barbieri, Corelli, Hines, Bastianini, La Scala Chorus & Orchestra Matacic Sung in Italian	LP: Ed Smith EJS 395 LP: GDS Records GDS 3001

Hercules: Excerpts (Daughter of gods; How blest the maid; Ah, think what ills)

New York December 1960	Role of Iole American Opera Society Chorus & Orchestra Rescigno	LP: Discocorp RR 208

Hercules: Excerpt (My father)

Detroit February 1962	Role of Iole Detroit SO Paray	LP: Rococo 5388

Giulio Cesare: Excerpt (V'adoro pupille)

Detroit February 1962	Role of Cleopatra Detroit SO Paray	LP: Rococo 5388

Messiah

London February- November 1964	Soprano soloist Hoffman, Gedda, Hines, Philharmonia Chorus Philharmonia Klemperer	LP: EMI AN 146-8/SAN 146-8 LP: EMI SLS 915 CD: EMI CMS 763 6212 Excerpts LP: EMI ALP 2288/ASD 2288

Messiah: Excerpt (He shall feed his flock)

Hamburg 1952	Soprano soloist NDR Orchestra Schüchter Sung in German	LP: Melodram MEL 082 LP: Discocorp RR 208 CD: Melodram MEL 16501

Haydn

Scena di Berenice

Amsterdam June 1958	Soprano soloist Netherlands Chamber Orchestra Goldberg	LP: Discocorp RR 208

Trios: An den Vetter; Daphnens einziger Fehler

London February 1967	De los Angeles, Fischer-Dieskau, Moore, piano	LP: EMI SAN 182-3 LP: EMI SLS 926 CD: EMI CDC 749 2382

Heuberger

Der Opernball: Excerpt (Im chambre séparée)

London July 1957	Role of Hortense Philharmonia Ackermann	LP: Columbia 33CX 1570/SAX 2283 LP: EMI ASD 2807 CD: EMI CDC 747 2842

Humperdinck

Hänsel und Gretel

London June and July 1953	Role of Gretel Grümmer, Ilosvay, Schürhoff, Felbermayer, Metternich, Choirs Philharmonia Karajan	LP: Columbia 33CX 1096-7 LP: World Records OC 187-8 LP: EMI SLS 5145 CD: EMI CMS 769 2932 Excerpts LP: Columbia 33CX 1819 LP: World Records OH 189 CD: EMI CDM 763 6572/CMS 763 7902

Hänsel und Gretel: Excerpts (1. Abends will ich schlafen gehen; 2. Der kleine Sandmann bin ich; 3. Suse, liebe Suse...Brüderchen, komm tanz mit mir)

London September 1947	Roles of Gretel and Sandman Seefried, Philharmonia Krips	78: Columbia LX 1036-7 LP: EMI RLS 763 CD: EMI CDH 769 7932 (3)

Winterlied

Berlin November 1944	Raucheisen, piano	LP: Acanta 40.23557 CD: Acanta 42.43128

Jensen

Mürmelndes Lüftchen

London April 1956	Moore, piano Sung in German	LP: Columbia 33CX 1404/SAX 2265 45: Columbia SEL 1600/ESL 6274

Kilpinen

Kleines Lied

Vienna January 1979	Parsons, piano Sung in German	Decca unpublished

Korngold

Die tote Stadt: Excerpt (Glück, das mir verblieb)

Hamburg 1952	Role of Marietta NDR Orchestra Schüchter	LP: Melodram MEL 088

Lehar

Giuditta: Excerpt (Meine Lippen, sie küssen so heiss)

London July 1957	Role of Giuditta Chorus Philharmonia Ackermann	LP: Columbia 33CX 1570/SAX 2283 LP: EMI ASD 2807 CD: EMI CDC 747 2842

Der Graf von Luxemburg: Excerpts (Hoch, Evoë, Angèle Didier; Heut' noch werd' ich Ehefrau)

London July 1957	Role of Angèle Chorus Philharmonia Ackermann	LP: Columbia 33CX 1570/SAX 2283 LP: EMI ASD 2807 CD: EMI CDC 747 2842

Das Land des Lächelns

London April and June 1953	Role of Lisa Loose, Gedda, Kunz, BBC Chorus Philharmonia Ackermann	LP: Columbia 33CX 1114-5 LP: EMI SXDW 3044 CD: EMI CHS 769 5232 Excerpts LP: Columbia 33CX 1712 LP: EMI SLS 5250 LP: EMI RLS 763

Das Land des Lächelns: Selection

Berlin 1940	Role of Lisa Glawitsch, Deutsches Opernhaus Orchestra Lutze	78: Telefunken E 3115 Also published on 45 with same number

Die lustige Witwe

London April 1953	Role of Hanna Loose, Gedda, Kunz, BBC Chorus Philharmonia Ackermann	LP: Columbia 33CX 1051-2 LP: EMI SXDW 3045 CD: EMI CDH 769 5202 Excerpts 78: Columbia LX 1597 LP: Columbia 33CX 1712 45: Columbia SEL 1559 LP: EMI RLS 763 CD: EMI CDM 763 6572/CMS 763 7902
London July 1962	Role of Hanna Steffek, Gedda, Wächter, Philharmonia Chorus & Orchestra Matacic	LP: EMI AN 101-2/SAN 101-2 LP: EMI SLS 823 CD: EMI CDS 747 1788 Excerpts LP: EMI ALP 2252/ASD 2252

Paganini: Selection

Berlin 1940	Glawitsch Deutsches Opernhaus Orchestra Otto	78: Telefunken E 3041 LP: Capitol (USA) P 8033

Der Zarewitsch: Excerpt (Einer wird kommen)

London July 1957 (Columbia)	Role of Sonja Philharmonia Ackermann	LP: Columbia 33CX 1570/SAX 2283 LP: EMI ASD 2807 CD: EMI CDC 747 2842

Leveridge

This great world is a trouble

Berlin 1944	Raucheisen, piano Sung in German	LP: Acanta 40.23557 CD: Acanta 42.43801

Liszt

O lieb' so lang du lieben kannst

London June 1957	Moore, piano	Columbia unpublished

Die 3 Zigeuner

Berlin October 1968	Parsons, piano	LP: EMI ASD 2634

Loewe

Lieder: 1. O süsse Mutter; 2. Blume der Ergebung; 3. Abendstunde; 4. Frühlingsankunft; 5. Frühling; 6. Ihr Spaziergang; 7. Vogelgesang; 8. Die verliebte Schäferin; 9. Die Sylphide; 10. Das Glockenspiel

Berlin March 1943	Raucheisen, piano	LP: Melodiya M10 41285-6 (1,2,3,4,5) LP: Discocorp IGI 385 (1,2,3,4,5) LP: Melodram MEL 082 (4,5) LP: Discocorp RR 208 (1,2,3,4,5) LP: Acanta 40.23534 LP: Acanta 40.23557 (3,4,9) CD: Acanta 42.43801 (3)

Duets: 1. Sonnenlicht; 2. Liebesliedchen; 3. März; 4. Abschied; 5. Die Freude; 6. An Sami

Berlin June 1942	Piltti Raucheisen, piano	LP: Melodiya M10 41285-6 (1,2,3,4) LP: Discocorp IGI 385 (1,2,3,4) LP: Melodram MEL 082 (6) LP: Melodram MEL 088 (3) LP: Discocorp RR 208 (1,2,3,4) LP: Acanta 40.23534 (3,5,6)

Lieder: Zeislein; Irrlichter; Kind und Mädchen

Berlin January 1945	Raucheisen, piano	LP: Acanta 40.23534

Kleiner Haushalt

Berlin October 1968	Parsons, piano	LP: EMI ASD 2634 CD: EMI CDM 763 6542/CMS 763 7902

Tom der Reimer

Vienna January 1979	Parsons, piano	Decca unpublished

Die wandelnde Glocke

Vienna January 1979	Parsons, piano	LP: Decca SXL 6943 CD: Decca 430 0002

Mahler

Symphony No 2 "Resurrection"

London November 1961 and March 1962	Soprano soloist Rössl-Majdan, Philharmonia Chorus & Orchestra Klemperer	LP: Columbia 33CX 1929-30/SAX 2473-4 LP: EMI SLS 806 CD: EMI CDM 769 6622

Symphony No 4

Vienna May 1960	Soprano soloist VPO Walter	LP: Discocorp BWS 705 CD: Music and Arts 50C37-7914-5 4th movement only CD: Verona 27075
London April 1961	Soprano soloist Philharmonia Klemperer	LP: Columbia 33CX 1793/SAX 2441 LP: EMI ASD 2799 CD: EMI CDM 769 6672

Des Knaben Wunderhorn: Das irdische Leben; Rheinlegendchen; Lob des hohen Verstandes; Duets: Verlor'ne Müh'; Der Schildwache Nachtlied; Lied des Verfolgten im Turm; Wo die schönen Trompeten blasen; other songs without Schwarzkopf

London March 1968	Soprano soloist Fischer-Dieskau, LSO Szell	LP: EMI SAN 218 LP: EMI ASD 143 4424 CD: EMI CDC 747 2772

Lieder: Wo die schönen Trompeten blasen; Ich atmet' einen linden Duft; Ich bin der Welt abhanden gekommen

Vienna May 1960	VPO Walter	LP: Discocorp BWS 705 LP: Discocorp RR 208 CD: Music and Arts 50C37 7914-5 CD: Verona 27075

Lieder: 1. Ich atmet' einen linden Duft; 2. Des Antonius Fischpredigt; 3. Lob des hohen Verstandes

Berlin April 1966	Parsons, piano	LP: EMI ASD 2404 CD: EMI CDM 763 6542/CMS 763 7902 (1,2)

Um schlimme Kinder artig zu machen

Berlin October 1968	Parsons, piano	LP: EMI ASD 2634 CD: EMI CDM 763 6542/CMS 763 7902

Martini

Plaisir d'amour

London April 1956	Moore, piano	LP: Columbia 33CX 1404/SAX 2265 45: Columbia SEL 1589/ESL 6255 LP: EMI RLS 154 6133 CD: EMI CDM 763 6542/CMS 763 7902

Marx

Venezianisches Wiegenlied

Vienna January 1979	Parsons, piano	Decca unpublished

Medtner

Songs: 1. The Muse; 2. So tanzet; 3. The Waltz; 4. Einsamkeit; 5. Präludium; 6. Winternacht

London October 1950	Medtner, piano 1 & 3 sung in English	78: Columbia LX 1425 (1,2,3) 78: Columbia LX 1426 (4,5,6)

Songs: 1. The Rose; 2. When roses fade; 3. Im Vorübergehen; 4. Elfenliedchen; 5. Meeresstille; 6. Glückliche Fahrt; 7. Die Quelle; 8. Selbstbetrug

London November 1950	Medtner, piano 1 & 2 sung in English	78: Columbia LX 1423 (1,2,3,4) 78: Columbia LX 1424 (5,6,7,8)

Saturday, 28th October, 1950

MANON

OPERA IN FIVE ACTS

Libretto by Henri Meilhac and Philippe Gille

From the Novel "Manon Lescaut" by the Abbé Prévost

Music by Jules Massenet

English Version by Norman Feasey

Costumes and scenery by James Bailey

CONDUCTOR - WARWICK BRAITHWAITE

THE COVENT GARDEN OPERA CHORUS
Chorus Master - Douglas Robinson

THE COVENT GARDEN ORCHESTRA
Leader - Thomas Matthews

JULES MASSENET, 1842 - 1912

This opera was first produced on 19th January, 1884, at the Opéra-Comique, Paris. It was first performed in England at Liverpool on 17th January 1885, in English. It was performed at Covent Garden 19th May, 1891, in French.

CHARACTERS IN ORDER OF APPEARANCE

GUILLOT de MORFONTAINE, a libertine	PARRY JONES
BRETIGNY, a libertine	ERNEST DAVIES
POUSSETTE ⎫	ADELE LEIGH
JAVOTTE ⎬ Friends of Guillot	IRIS KELLS
ROSETTE ⎭	MONICA SINCLAIR
THE INNKEEPER	KENNETH STEVENSON
LESCAUT, cousin to Manon	GERAINT EVANS
TWO GUARDS	HUBERT LITTLEWOOD, CHARLES MORRIS
MANON LESCAUT	ELISABETH SCHWARZKOPF
THE CHEVALIER des GRIEUX	WALTER MIDGLEY
THE MAIDSERVANT	ELIZABETH GOODALL
THE COUNT des GRIEUX, father to the Chevalier	JESS WALTERS
THREE GAMBLERS	HECTOR THOMAS, AFAN DAVIES, ALAN HOBSON
A POLICE OFFICER	HUBERT LITTLEWOOD

The Audience is asked not to applaud at the end of each Act until the Orchestra has finished playing.

Saturday, 25th November, 1950

THE MAGIC FLUTE

OPERA IN TWO ACTS

Words by Emanuel Schikaneder and Karl Ludwig Giesecke

Music by Wolfgang Amadeus Mozart

English version by Edward J. Dent

Costumes, settings and visual effects devised by Oliver Messel

CONDUCTOR · PETER GELLHORN

THE COVENT GARDEN OPERA CHORUS

Chorus Master · Douglas Robinson

THE COVENT GARDEN ORCHESTRA

Leader · Thomas Matthews

WOLFGANG AMADEUS MOZART, 1756-1791

This opera was first produced on 30th September, 1791, at the Theater auf der Wieden, Vienna. First performed in London, in Italian, at the Haymarket Theatre on 6th June, 1811. First performed in English at Norwich in 1829 and in London at Drury Lane on 10th March, 1838.

CHARACTERS IN ORDER OF APPEARANCE

TAMINO, an Egyptian Prince		RICHARD LEWIS
FIRST LADY ⎫	attending the	ROSINA RAISBECK
SECOND LADY ⎬	Queen of Night	ELISABETH ABERCROMBIE
THIRD LADY ⎭		JEAN WATSON
PAPAGENO, a bird catcher		JESS WALTERS
THE QUEEN OF THE NIGHT		WILMA LIPP
FIRST BOY ⎫		ADELE LEIGH
SECOND BOY ⎬	Genii of the Temple	PATRICIA HOWARD
THIRD BOY ⎭		MONICA SINCLAIR
FIRST SLAVE		ERNEST ROSSER
SECOND SLAVE		STANFORD THOMAS
THIRD SLAVE		RONALD LEWIS
MONOSTATOS, a Moor in Sarastro's service		PARRY JONES
PAMINA, daughter of the Queen of Night		ELISABETH SCHWARZKOPF
THE SPEAKER OF THE TEMPLE		JOHN CAMERON
SARASTRO, High Priest of the Temple		MARIAN NOWAKOWSKI
FIRST PRIEST		EDGAR EVANS
SECOND PRIEST		RHYDDERCH DAVIES
THIRD PRIEST		RONALD FIRMAGER
FOURTH PRIEST		BASIL HEMMING
PAPAGENA, Papageno's sweetheart		IRIS KELLS
FIRST MAN IN ARMOUR		EDGAR EVANS
SECOND MAN IN ARMOUR		RHYDDERCH DAVIES

The Audience is asked not to applaud at the end of each Act until the Orchestra has finished playing.

Tuesday, 15th May, 1951

LA BOHÈME

OPERA IN FOUR ACTS

Words by Giuseppe Giacosa and Luigi Illica
from the novel "Scènes de la vie de Bohème" by
Henri Murger

Music by Giacomo Puccini
(Property of G. Ricordi & Co.)

English version by W. Grist and Percy Pinkerton

CONDUCTOR - PETER GELLHORN

PRODUCER - CHRISTOPHER WEST

THE COVENT GARDEN OPERA CHORUS
Chorus Master - Douglas Robinson

THE COVENT GARDEN ORCHESTRA
Leader - Thomas Matthews

GIACOMO PUCCINI, 1858 - 1924.

This opera was first produced at the Teatro Regio, Turin, on 1st February, 1896. It was first performed in England at Manchester on 22nd April, 1897, and at Covent Garden on 2nd October, 1897, on both occasions in English. It was not performed in England, in Italian, until 1st July, 1899 at Covent Garden.

CHARACTERS IN ORDER OF APPEARANCE

MARCEL, a painter	JESS WALTERS
RUDOLPH, a poet	WALTER MIDGLEY
COLLINE, a philosopher	MARIAN NOWAKOWSKI
SCHAUNARD, a musician	GERAINT EVANS
BENOIT, their landlord	GRAHAME CLIFFORD
MIMI	ELISABETH SCHWARZKOPF
PARPIGNOL, a toy-seller	JAMES JONES
MUSETTA	AUDREY BOWMAN
ALCINDORO, a councillor of state	DAVID TREE
A CUSTOMS OFFICER	HUBERT LITTLEWOOD
A SERGEANT	JAMES McCLUSKEY

The Audience is asked not to applaud at the end of each Act until the Orchestra has finished playing.

Mendelssohn

Auf Flügeln des Gesanges

London April 1956	Moore, piano	LP: Columbia 33CX 1404/SAX 2265 45: Columbia SEL 1589/ESL 6255

Millöcker

Die Dubarry: Excerpts (Ich schenk' mein Herz; Was ich im Leben beginne)

London July 1957	Role of Jeanne Chorus Philharmonia Ackermann	LP: Columbia 33CX 1570/SAX 2283 LP: EMI ASD 2807 CD: EMI CDC 747 2842

Monteverdi

4 Madrigals: Io son pur vezzosetta pastorella; Ardo e scoprir; Baci cari; Dialogo di ninfa e pastore

London May 1955	Seefried Moore, piano	LP: Columbia 33CX 1331 LP: EMI HLM 7267 CD: EMI CDH 769 7932

Morley

It was a lover and his lass

Vienna November 1946	Hudez, piano	Columbia unpublished

Mozart

Exsultate, jubilate

Vienna November 1946	Soprano soloist VPO Krips	Columbia unpublished
London May 1948	Soprano soloist Philharmonia Susskind	78: Columbia LX 1196-7 LP: Columbia (USA) ML 4649 LP: Columbia (Germany) C 80628 LP: Seraphim (USA) 60013 LP: EMI RLS 154 6133 CD: EMI CDH 763 2012
London September 1952	Soprano soloist Philharmonia Pritchard	Columbia unpublished
Toronto 1955	Soprano soloist Stratford Festival Orchestra Neel	LP: Rococo 5388

Concert arias: Vado, ma dove; Alma grande e nobil core

London March 1968	LSO Szell	LP: EMI ASD 2493 CD: EMI CDC 747 9502 CD: EMI CDH 763 7022

Ch'io mi scordi di te?

London May 1955	Anda, piano Philharmonia Ackermann	Columbia unpublished
London March 1968	Brendel, piano LSO Szell	LP: EMI ASD 2493 CD: EMI CDH 747 9502 CD: EMI CDH 763 7022

Nehmt meinen Dank

London April 1955	Gieseking, piano	Columbia unpublished
London April 1955	Philharmonia Galliera	CD: EMI CDM 763 6552/CMS 763 7902
London March 1968	LSO Szell	LP: EMI ASD 2493 CD: EMI CDC 747 9502 CD: EMI CDH 763 7022

La betulia liberata

Turin May 1952	Role of Amital Pirazzini, Valletti, Christoff, Turin RAI Chorus & Orchestra Rossi	LP: Melodram MEL 211 CD: Nuova Era 2377 CD: Memories HR 4222

Così fan tutte

London July and November 1954	Role of Fiordiligi Merriman, Otto, Simoneau, Panerai, Bruscantini, Chorus Philharmonia Karajan	LP: Columbia 33CX 1262-4 LP: World Records SOC 195-7 LP: Electrola 1C 197 54200-8M LP: EMI RLS 7709 CD: EMI CHS 769 6352 Excerpts LP: World Records OH 198 CD: EMI CDM 763 6572/CMS 763 7902
Milan January 1956	Role of Fiordiligi Merriman, Sciutti, Alva, Panerai, Calabrese, La Scala Chorus & Orchestra Cantelli	LP: Discocorp LP: Fonit Cetra LO 13 CD: Stradivarius STR 13597-9
Salzburg July 1960	Role of Fiordiligi Ludwig, Sciutti, Kmennt, Prey, Dönch, Vienna Opera Chorus VPO Böhm	LP: Melodram MEL 708 Excerpts LP: Melodram MEL 082 LP: Melodram MEL 088 CD: Melodram MEL 16501
London September 1962	Role of Fiordiligi Ludwig, Steffek, Kraus, Taddei, Berry, Philharmonia Chorus & Orchestra Böhm	LP: EMI AN 103-6/SAN 103-6 LP: EMI SLS 5028 CD: EMI CMS 769 3302 Excerpts LP: EMI ALP 2265/ASD 2265 LP: EMI SXLP 30457

Così fan tutte: Excerpts (Ah, guarda sorella; Soave sia il vento; Come scoglio; Per pietà; Richiamati da regio contrordine; other excerpts without Schwarzkopf

Salzburg August 1958	Role of Fiordiligi Ludwig, Sciutti, Alva, Panerai, Schmidt, Vienna Opera Chorus VPO Böhm	LP: Gioielli della lirica GML 052

Così fan tutte: Excerpt (Come scoglio)

New York	Role of Fiordiligi	CD: EMI CHS 761 0432
November 1956	Reeves, piano	

Così fan tutte: Excerpt (Amore è un ladroncello)

Blossom	Role of Dorabella	LP: Rococo 5388
July 1968	Cleveland Orchestra	
	Szell	

Die Entführung aus dem Serail

Vienna	Role of Konstanze	LP: Melodram MEL 047
1945	Loose, Dermota,	Excerpts
	Klein, Alsen,	LP: Rococo 5388
	Austrian Radio	LP: Melodram MEL 082
	Chorus & Orchestra	LP: Melodram MEL 088
	Moralt	LP: Acanta BB 23.119
		CD: Melodram MEL 16501

Die Entführung aus dem Serail: Excerpt (Martern aller Arten)

Vienna	Role of Konstanze	LP: Saga XIG 8011
October 1946	VPO	LP: EMI RLS 763
	Karajan	LP: EMI RLS 7714
		LP: EMI RLS 154 6133
		CD: EMI CDH 763 7082
		Saga edition incorrectly identified the singer as Maria Cebotari

Die Entführung aus dem Serail: Excerpt (Welcher Kummer herrscht in meiner Seele)

Vienna	Role of Konstanze	78: Columbia LX 1249
October 1946	VPO	LP: Columbia (USA) ML 4649
	Krips	LP: EMI RLS 763
		LP: EMI RLS 154 6133
		CD: EMI CDH 763 7082

Idomeneo: Excerpt (Zeffiretti lusinghieri)

London	Role of Ilia	LP: Columbia 33CX 1069
September 1952	Philharmonia	45: Columbia SEL 1515
	Pritchard	LP: World Records T 583
		LP: EMI 2C 051 43222
		CD: EMI CDC 747 9502
		CD: EMI CDH 763 7082
Turin	Role of Ilia	LP: Fonit Cetra LMR 5018
December 1952	RAI Turin	LP: Melodram MEL 088
	Orchestra	LP: Discocorp RR 208
	Rossi	LP: Melodram MEL 047
		CD: EMI CDH 763 7082

Don Giovanni

Salzburg July-August 1950	Role of Elvira Welitsch, Seefried, Dermota, Gobbi, Greindl, Kunz, Poell, Vienna Opera Chorus VPO Furtwängler	LP: Ed Smith EJS 419 LP: Olympic 9109 LP: Discocorp RR 407 LP: Turnabout THS 65154-6 LP: Melodram MEL 713 CD: Priceless D 16581 CD: Laudis LCD 34001 Excerpts LP: Melodram MEL 082 LP: Melodram MEL 088 CD: Melodram MEL 16501 Part of side 3 of Olympic edition derives from the 1954 Furtwängler performance
Salzburg July 1953	Role of Elvira Grümmer, Berger, Dermota, Siepi, Edelmann, Arié, Berry, Vienna Opera Chorus VPO Furtwängler	CD: Rodolphe RPC 32527-30 CD: Virtuoso 269.9052
Salzburg August 1954	Role of Elvira Grümmer, Berger, Dermota, Siepi, Edelmann, Ernster, Berry, Vienna Opera Chorus VPO Furtwängler	LP: Morgan MOR 5302 LP: Discocorp MORG 003 LP: Fonit Cetra LO 7 LP: Foyer FO 1017 LP: Fonit Cetra FE 23 LP: EMI EX 29 06673 CD: Music and Arts CD 003 CD: Hunt CD 509 CD: EMI CMS 763 8602 Excerpts LP: Gioielli della lirica GML 05 Final scene missing from this 1954 recording: final scene from the 1953 version has been spliced in

Prolonged confusion over the Austrian Radio tapes of the 1953 and 1954 Salzburg recordings has hopefully been resolved by Edward Chibas in an article in Newsletter No. 105 (December 1990) of the Wilhelm Furtwängler Society UK

London October 1959	Role of Elvira Sutherland, Sciutti, Alva, Wächter, Taddei, Cappuccilli, Frick, Philharmonia Chorus & Orchestra Klemperer	Columbia unpublished (recording incomplete)

Don Giovanni (continued)

London October and November 1959	Role of Elvira Sutherland, Sciutti, Alva, Wächter, Taddei, Cappuccilli, Frick, Philharmonia Chorus and Orchestra Giulini	LP: Columbia 33CX 1717-20/SAX 2369-72 LP: EMI SLS 5083 CD: EMI CDS 747 2608 Excerpts LP: Columbia 33CX 1918/SAX 2559 LP: EMI SXLP 30300 CD: EMI CDM 763 0782
Salzburg August 1960	Role of Elvira Price, Sciutti, Valletti, Wächter, Berry, Panerai, Zaccaria, Vienna Opera Chorus VPO Karajan	LP: HRE Records HRE 247 LP: Movimento Musica 03.001 CD: Movimento Musica 013.6012 CD: Curcio OP 6

Don Giovanni: Excerpt (Mi tradi)

London September 1947	Role of Elvira Philharmonia Krips	78: Columbia LX 1210 45: Columbia SEL 1511 LP: EMI RLS 763
London September 1952	Role of Elvira Philharmonia Pritchard	Columbia unpublished
Turin December 1952	Role of Elvira RAI Turin Orchestra Rossi	LP: Fonit Cetra LMR 5018 LP: Discocorp RR 208
Blossom July 1968	Role of Elvira Cleveland Orchestra Szell	LP: Rococo 5388

Don Giovanni: Excerpt (Non mi dir)

London July 1952	Role of Anna Philharmonia Pritchard	LP: Columbia 33CX 1069 45: Columbia SEL 1515 LP: World Records T 583 LP: EMI RLS 763 LP: EMI 2C 051 43222 CD: EMI CDC 747 9502 CD: EMI CDH 763 7082

Don Giovanni: Excerpts (Batti, batti; Vedrai carino)

London July 1952	Role of Zerlina Philharmonia Pritchard	78: Columbia LB 145 LP: Columbia 33CX 1069 45: Columbia SEL 1511 LP: World Records T 583 LP: EMI 2C 051 43222 CD: EMI CDC 747 9502 CD: EMI CDH 763 7082

Le Nozze di Figaro

Vienna June and October 1950	Role of Countess Seefried, Kunz, Jurinac, London, Vienna Opera Chorus VPO Karajan	78: Columbia LWX 410-425 LP: Columbia 33CX 1007-9 LP: Electrola 1C 197 54200-8M CD: EMI CMS 769 6392 Excerpts 78: Columbia LX 1575 (Dove sono) LP: Columbia 33CX 1558 LP: EMI RLS 764 CD: EMI CDM 763 6572/CMS 763 7902
Salzburg August 1953	Role of Countess Seefried, Kunz, Güden, Schöffler, Vienna Opera Chorus VPO Furtwängler <u>Sung in German</u>	LP: Ed Smith GMR 999 LP: Discocorp IGI 343 LP: Fonit Cetra LO 8 LP: Fonit Cetra FE 27 CD: Rodolphe RPC 32527-30 Excerpts LP: Melodram MEL 082 CD: Melodram MEL 16501
Milan February 1954	Role of Countess Seefried, Panerai, Jurinac, Petri, La Scala Chorus & Orchestra Karajan	LP: Fonit Cetra LO 70 CD: Hunt CDKAR 225 CD: Melodram MEL 37075 Excerpts LP: Gioielli della lirica GML 30
Salzburg July 1957	Role of Countess Seefried, Kunz, Ludwig, Fischer-Dieskau, Vienna Opera Chorus VPO Böhm	LP: Melodram MEL 709 CD: GDS Records GDS 31019 Excerpts LP: Melodram MEL 047 CD: Virtuoso 269.7152
London September and November 1959	Role of Countess Moffo, Taddei, Cossotto, Wächter, Philharmonia Chorus & Orchestra Giulini	LP: Columbia 33CX 1732-5/SAX 2381-4 LP: EMI SLS 5152 CD: EMI CMS 763 2662 Excerpts LP: Columbia 33CX 1934/SAX 2573 LP: EMI SXLP 30303

<u>At time of going to press, another version of "Le Nozze di Figaro", recorded in the 1960s in the Netherlands under Giulini, with Schwarzkopf and Prey in the cast, has been announced on Verona CD 27092-4</u>

Le Nozze di Figaro: Excerpt (Ah, la cieca gelosia)

Milan December 1948	Role of Countess Seefried, Höfermeyer, VPO Karajan	LP: Melodram MEL 088

Le Nozze di Figaro: Excerpt (Porgi amor)

London July 1952	Role of Countess Philharmonia Pritchard	LP: Columbia 33CX 1069 LP: World Records T 583 LP: EMI RLS 763 LP: EMI 2C 051 43222 CD: EMI CDH 763 7082
Hamburg 1952	Role of Countess NDR Orchestra Schüchter	LP: Melodram MEL 082

Le Nozze di Figaro: Excerpt (Dove sono)

London September 1952	Role of Countess Philharmonia Pritchard	LP: Columbia 33CX 1069 LP: World Records T 583 LP: EMI RLS 763 LP: EMI 2C 051 43222 CD: EMI CDH 763 7082

Le Nozze di Figaro: Excerpt (Deh vieni, non tardar)

London July 1952	Role of Susanna Philharmonia Pritchard	LP: Columbia 33CX 1069 LP: World Records T 583 LP: EMI RLS 763 LP: EMI 2C 051 43222 CD: EMI CDC 747 6502 CD: EMI CDH 763 7082
Blossom July 1968	Role of Susanna Cleveland Orchestra Szell	LP: Rococo 5388

Le Nozze di Figaro: Excerpts (Voi che sapete; Non so più)

London July 1952	Role of Cherubino Philharmonia Pritchard	LP: Columbia 33CX 1069 LP: World Records T 583 LP: EMI 2C 051 43222 CD: EMI CDC 747 6502 CD: EMI CDH 763 7082

Le Nozze di Figaro: Excerpt (Voi che sapete)

London 1958	Role of Cherubino Orchestra Mackerras	LP: Voce VOCE 116 Ornamented version of the aria

Il Rè Pastore: Excerpt (L'amerò, sarò costante)

Vienna November 1946	Role of Aminta Sedlak, violin VPO Krips	78: Columbia LX 1096 LP: EMI RLS 763

Die Zauberflöte

Rome December 1953	Role of Pamina Streich, Gedda, Taddei, Petri, Rome RAI Chorus & Orchestra Karajan Sung in Italian	CD: Myto 89007 Excerpts CD: Hunt CD 535
London March and April 1964	Role of First Lady Janowitz, Ludwig, Gedda, Berry, Frick, Philharmonia Chorus & Orchestra Klemperer	LP: EMI AN 137-9/SAN 137-9 LP: EMI SLS 912 CD: EMI CMS 769 9712 Excerpts LP: EMI ALP 2314/ASD 2314 LP: EMI ESD 100 3261 CD: EMI CDM 769 0562

Die Zauberflöte: Excerpt (Ach, ich fühl's)

London April 1948	Role of Pamina Philharmonia Braithwaite Sung in English	LP: EMI ALP 143 5501 LP: EMI RLS 154 6133 CD: EMI CDH 763 7082
London July 1952	Role of Pamina Philharmonia Pritchard	Columbia unpublished
Turin December 1952	Role of Pamina RAI Turin Orchestra Rossi	LP: Fonit Cetra LMR 5018 LP: Melodram MEL 088 LP: Melodram MEL 047 LP: Discocorp RR 208

Die Zauberflöte: Excerpt (Bei Männern, welche Liebe fühlen)

Vienna December 1947	Role of Pamina Kunz, VPO Karajan	Columbia unpublished

Trios: 1. La partenza; 2. Più non si trovano

London February 1967	De los Angeles, Fischer-Dieskau, Moore, piano	LP: EMI SAN 182-3 LP: EMI SLS 926 CD: EMI CDC 749 2382 (2)

Abendempfindung

London September 1952	Moore, piano	78: Columbia LX 1580
London July 1953	Moore, piano	Columbia unpublished
London January 1954	Moore, piano	LP: Columbia 33CX 1044 LP: EMI RLS 763
Berlin August and September 1970	Parsons, piano	LP: EMI ASD 2844

Meine Wünsche

Berlin October 1967	Parsons, piano	LP: EMI ASD 2404

Oiseaux, si tous les ans; Die Verschweigung

Berlin September 1944	Raucheisen, piano Oiseaux, si tous les ans sung in German	LP: Acanta 40.23557 CD: Acanta 42.43801

Das Veilchen

London May 1948	Moore, piano	Columbia unpublished
Berlin October 1967	Parsons, piano	LP: EMI ASD 2404

Warnung

London October 1947	Moore, piano	78: Columbia LB 73 LP: Columbia (USA) ML 4649
London June 1957	Moore, piano	Columbia unpublished
Toronto February 1970	Newmark, piano	LP: Rococo 5388

Der Zauberer

London November 1951	Moore, piano	78: Columbia LB 118
London July 1953	Moore, piano	Columbia unpublished
London January 1954	Moore, piano	LP: Columbia 33CX 1044 LP: EMI RLS 763
Berlin August and September 1970	Parsons, piano	LP: EMI ASD 2844

Lieder: 1. Ridente la calma; 2. Oiseaux, si tous les ans; 3. Dans un bois solitaire; 4. Die kleine Spinnerin; 5. Als Luise die Briefe; 6. Abendempfindung; 7. Das Kinderspiel; 8. Die Alte; 9. Das Traumbild; 10. Das Veilchen; 11. Der Zauberer; 12. Im Frühlingsanfange; 13. Das Lied der Trennung; 14. Die Zufriedenheit; 15. An Chloë; 16. Sehnsucht nach dem Frühlinge; 17. Die Verschweigung

London April 1955	Gieseking, piano	LP: Columbia 33CX 1321 (1-16) LP: EMI ASD 3858 (1-16) LP: Toshiba EAC 81060 (1-17) CD: EMI CDC 747 3262 (1,2,4,5,6,7,11,12,14,15,16) CD: EMI CDH 763 7022 (1-16)

Lieder: Un moto gi gioia; Warnung

London April 1955	Gieseking, piano	Columbia unpublished

Lieder: Dans un bois solitaire; Als Luise die Briefe; Dans un bois solitaire; Un moto di gioia

New York November 1956	Reeves, piano	CD: EMI CDH 761 0432

Lieder: Als Luise die Briefe; Un moto di gioia

Hilversum 1957	De Nobel, piano	CD: Verona 27021

Mussorgsky

Boris Godunov: Excerpt (Death of Boris)

London May 1949	Role of Feodor Christoff, Covent Garden Chorus Philharmonia Dobrowen Sung in Russian	78: HMV DB 21097 LP: HMV BLP 1003 LP: Electrola 1C 147 03336-7M LP: EMI RLS 735

Among the mushrooms

Berlin October 1967	Parsons, piano Sung in German	LP: EMI ASD 2404

Offenbach

Les Contes d'Hoffmann

Paris September and October 1964	Role of Giulietta D'Angelo, Gedda, De los Angeles, London, Blanc, Duclos Choir Paris Conservatoire Orchestra Cluytens	LP: EMI AN 154-6/SAN 154-6 LP: Electrola 1C 157 00045-7 CD: EMI CMS 763 2222 Excerpts LP: Electrola 1C 063 01967 LP: EMI SXLP 30538

Orff

Die Kluge

London May 1956	Role of Peasant's daughter Christ, Cordes, Frick, Prey, Neidlinger, Kusche, Kuen Philharmonia Sawallisch	LP: Columbia 33CX 1446-7/SAX 2257-8 LP: Electrola 1C 137 43291-3 LP: Arabesque 8021-2 CD: EMI CMS 763 7122 Excerpts LP: Columbia 33CX 1810 LP: Electrola 1C 063 00719

Pergolesi

Si tu m'ami

London June 1957	Moore, piano	Columbia unpublished

Puccini

La Bohème: Excerpt (Si, mi chiamano Mimì)

Vienna November 1948	Role of Mimì VPO Karajan	LP: EMI ALP 143 5501 LP: EMI RLS 154 6133 CD: EMI CDM 763 5572
London April 1959	Role of Mimì Philharmonia Rescigno	LP: Columbia CX 5286/SAX 5286 LP: EMI SXDW 3049

La Bohème: Excerpt (Donde lieta uscì)

Vienna November 1948	Role of Mimì VPO Karajan	Columbia unpublished
London May 1950	Role of Mimì Philharmonia Dobrowen	Columbia unpublished
London October 1950	Role of Mimì Philharmonia Galliera	78: Columbia LB 110 45: Columbia SEL 1575 45: Columbia SCD 2141 LP: EMI RLS 763 LP: EMI RLS 154 6133
London April 1959	Role of Mimì Philharmonia Rescigno	Columbia unpublished
London April 1962	Role of Mimì Philharmonia Tonini	Columbia unpublished

Gianni Schicchi: Excerpt (O mio babbino caro)

Vienna November 1948	Role of Lauretta VPO Karajan	78: Columbia LB 85 45: Columbia SEL 1575 LP: Toshiba EAC 30112 LP: EMI RLS 763 LP: EMI RLS 154 6133
London April 1959	Role of Lauretta Philharmonia Rescigno	LP: Columbia CX 5286/SAX 5286 LP: EMI SXDW 3049

Madama Butterfly

London October 1950	Role of Butterfly Philharmonia Galliera	78: Columbia LX 1370 45: Columbia SCD 2076 LP: EMI RLS 763 LP: EMI RLS 154 6133

Madama Butterfly: Excerpts (Bald sind wir auf der Höh'; Eines Tages sehen wir; Ehrenvoll sterbe)

Hamburg 1952	Role of Butterfly NDR Chorus and Orchestra Schüchter Sung in German	LP: Melodram MEL 088

Turandot

Milan July 1957 (Columbia)	Role of Liù Callas, Fernandi, Zaccaria, La Scala Chorus & Orchestra Serafin	LP: Columbia 33CX 1555-7 LP: EMI RLS 741 CD: EMI CDS 747 9718 Excerpts LP: Columbia 33CX 1792 CD: EMI CDM 763 6572/CMS 763 7902

Turandot: Excerpt (Signore, ascolta)

London October 1950 (Columbia)	Role of Liù Philharmonia Galliera	78: Columbia LB 110 45: Columbia SEL 1575 LP: EMI RLS 763
London April 1959 (Columbia)	Role of Liù Philharmonia Rescigno	Columbia unpublished
London April 1962 (Columbia)	Role of Liù Philharmonia Tonini	Columbia unpublished

Turandot: Excerpt (Tu che di gel sei cinta)

Vienna November 1948 (Columbia)	Role of Liù VPO Karajan	Columbia unpublished
Vienna March 1949 (Columbia)	Role of Liù VPO Böhm	78: Columbia LB 85 45: Columbia SEL 1575
London April 1959 (Columbia)	Role of Liù Philharmonia Rescigno	Columbia unpublished
London April 1962 (Columbia)	Role of Liù Philharmonia Tonini	Columbia unpublished

Purcell

Dido and Aeneas

London March 1952	Roles of Belinda, Second Lady and Attendant Spirit Flagstad, Hemsley, Mandikian, Mermaid Singers Philharmonia Jones	LP: HMV ALP 1026 LP: World Records SH 117 LP: EMI 2C 051 03613 CD: EMI CDH 761 0062 All editions name orchestra as Mermaid Orchestra

Music for a while

Berlin 1958	Raucheisen, piano	LP: Melodram MEL 082 Recording incorrectly dated 1953

Rachmaninov

To the children

London January 1958	Moore, piano Sung in English	LP: Columbia CX 5268/SAX 5268

Rameau

Hyppolyte et Aricie: Excerpt (Rossignols amoureux)

Berlin October 1944	Scheck, flute Raucheisen, piano Sung in German	LP: Acanta 40.23557 CD: Acanta 42.43801

Reger

Lieder: Unter den blühenden Linden; Viola d'amour

Berlin October 1944	Raucheisen, piano	LP: Acanta 40.23565 LP: Acanta 40.23557 CD: Acanta 42.43128

Die Verschmähte

Berlin March 1943	Raucheisen, piano	LP: Acanta 40.23565 CD: Acanta 42.43128

Waldseligkeit

Berlin November 1944	Raucheisen, piano	LP: Acanta 40.23565 LP: Acanta 40.23557 CD: Acanta 42.43128

Wiegenlied

Berlin March 1943	Raucheisen, piano	LP: Melodiya M10 41285-6 LP: Discocorp IGI 385 LP: Discocorp RR 208 LP: Acanta 40.23565 LP: Acanta 40.23557 CD: Acanta 42.43801

Rossini

Guilleaume Tell: Excerpt (Sombre forêt)

London April 1962	Role of Mathilde Philharmonia Tonini Sung in Italian	Columbia unpublished

La Danza

Berlin October 1944	Raucheisen, piano	LP: Acanta 40.23557 CD: Acanta 42.43801

Duets: Serate musicali (La regatta veneziana; La pesca); Duetto buffo di due gatti

London February 1967	De los Angeles, Moore, piano	LP: EMI SAN 182-3 LP: EMI SLS 926 CD: EMI CDC 749 2382

Sammartini

Weisse Schäfchen

Berlin October 1944	Raucheisen, piano Sung in German	LP: Acanta 40.23557 CD: Acanta 42.43801

Schubert

An den Frühling

Berlin September 1944	Raucheisen, piano	LP: Acanta 40.23557 CD: Acanta 42.43801

Seligkeit

Vienna October 1946	Hudez, piano	78: Columbia LB 77 LP: EMI RLS 763 LP: EMI RLS 766
London April 1956	Moore, piano	Columbia unpublished
New York November 1956	Reeves, piano	CD: EMI CMS 761 0432
London June 1957	Moore, piano	Columbia unpublished
Strassburg June 1960	Bonneau, piano	CD: Chant du Monde LDC 278.899
Salzburg August 1960	Moore, piano	CD: Stradivarius STR 10009
Hannover March 1962	Reutter, piano	LP: Movimento Musica 02.017 CD: Movimento Musica 051.015 CD: Verona 27075
London April 1964	Moore, piano	Columbia unpublished
Berlin August 1965	Moore, piano	LP: Columbia CX 5268/SAX 5268
Toronto February 1970	Newmark, piano	LP: Rococo 5388

Lieder: Die Vögel; Liebhaber in allen Gestalten

London May 1948	Moore, piano	LP: EMI RLS 766 LP: EMI ALP 143 5501 LP: EMI RLS 154 6133 CD: EMI CDM 763 6562/CMS 763 7902

Die Forelle

Vienna October 1946	Hudez, piano	78: Columbia LB 77 LP: EMI RLS 763 LP: EMI RLS 766
Rome February 1952	Favaretto, piano	CD: Hunt CD 535
London September 1952	Moore, piano	Columbia unpublished
London April 1964	Moore, piano	Columbia unpublished
Berlin August 1965	Moore, piano	LP: Columbia CX 5268/SAX 5268 LP: EMI RLS 154 6133 CD: EMI CDM 763 6562/CMS 763 7902
Toronto February 1970	Newmark, piano	LP: Rococo 5388

Gretchen am Spinnrade

London May 1948	Moore, piano	Columbia unpublished

Der Musensohn

London November 1951	Moore, piano	Columbia unpublished

Wiegenlied

London September 1952	Moore, piano	Columbia unpublished
London April 1964 (Columbia)	Moore, piano	Columbia unpublished

Heidenröslein

London June 1957	Moore, piano	LP: Columbia CX 5268/SAX 5268 LP: EMI RLS 154 6133 CD: EMI CDM 763 6562/CMS 763 7902

Lieder: Ungeduld (Die Schöne Müllerin); Litanei

London   Moore, piano   Columbia unpublished
September 1952

London   Moore, piano   LP: Columbia 33CX 1044
January 1954   LP: EMI RLS 763
                                             LP: EMI RLS 154 6133 (Litanei only)

Lieder: Ungeduld (Die Schöne Müllerin); Auf dem Wasser zu singen; Der Musensohn; Suleika I; Ave Maria

Rome   Favaretto, piano   CD: Hunt CD 535
February 1952

Lieder: 1. Auf dem Wasser zu singen; 2. An Sylvia; 3. An die Musik; 4. Nachtviolen; 5. Die junge Nonne; 6. Nähe des Geliebten; 7. Das Lied im Grünen; 8. Der Musensohn; 9. Gretchen am Spinnrade; 10. Wehmut; 11. Ganymed; 12. Im Frühling

London   Fischer, piano   LP: Columbia 33CX 1040
October 1952   45: Columbia SEL 1564 (2.3.7,9)
                                             45: Columbia SEL 1570 (5,6,10)
                                             45: Columbia SEL 1582 (1,4,8,12)
                                             LP: EMI ALP 3843
                                             LP: Electrola 1C 137 53032-6M
                                             CD: EMI CDC 747 3262

Lieder: An Sylvia; Der Einsame; Romanze aus Rosamunde; Die Vögel; Gretchen am Spinnrade

New York   Reeves, piano   CD: EMI CDH 761 0432
November 1956

Hilversum   De Nobel, piano   CD: Verona 27021
1957

Die Vögel

London   Moore, piano   Columbia unpublished
June 1957

Lieder: An die Musik; Auf dem Wasser zu singen; Fischerweise; Romanze aus Rosamunde; Liebe schwärmt auf allen Wegen; Der Einsame; Du bist die Ruh'

Strassburg   Bonneau, piano   CD: Chant du Monde LDC 278.899
June 1960

Lieder: Fischerweise; An mein Klavier; Das Lied im Grünen

Salzburg August 1960	Moore, piano	CD: Stradivarius STR 10009

Lieder: Liebe schwärmt auf allen Wegen; Lachen und Weinen; Der Jüngling an der Quelle; Du bist die Ruh'; An Sylvia

London January 1961 and March 1962	Moore, piano	Columbia unpublished

Lieder: An die Musik; Der Einsame; Gretchen am Spinnrade

Hannover March 1962	Reutter, piano	LP: Movimento Musica 02.017 CD: Movimento Musica 051.015 CD: Verona 27075

Der Jüngling an der Quelle

London December 1962	Moore, piano	LP: Columbia CX 5268/SAX 5268 CD: EMI CDM 763 6562/CMS 763 7902

Lieder: Der Einsame; Liebe schwärmt auf allen Wegen

Berlin August 1965	Moore, piano	LP: Columbia CX 5268/SAX 5268 LP: EMI RLS 154 6133 CD: EMI CDM 763 6562/CMS 763 7902 CD has Der Einsame only

Lieder: An mein Klavier; Erlkönig

Berlin April 1966	Parsons, piano	LP: EMI ASD 2404 LP: EMI RLS 154 6133 CD: EMI CDM 763 6562/CMS 763 7902

Lieder: Geheimnis; Hänflings Liebeswerbung

Berlin April 1966	Parsons, piano	EMI unpublished

Lieder: Hänflings Liebeswerbung; Suleika I; Suleika II

Berlin October 1968	Parsons, piano	LP: EMI ASD 2634 CD: EMI CDM 763 6562/CMS 763 7902

ROYAL FESTIVAL HALL

(GENERAL MANAGER: JOHN DENISON, CBE)

PHILHARMONIA CONCERT SOCIETY

FOUNDER AND ARTISTIC DIRECTOR:
WALTER LEGGE

IN MEMORIAM
ERNEST NEWMAN

30 November 1868 – 7 July 1959

ELISABETH
SCHWARZKOPF

GEOFFREY PARSONS

Monday 2 December 1968 at 8 pm

Programme Five Shillings

Management: Ibbs & Tillett

BRILLIANT PORTRAYALS BY

Schwarzkopf

FIORDILIGI
in the complete recording of
'COSI FAN TUTTE'
MOZART

33CX1262-3-4 *(Libretto available price 6/-)*
(the cast also includes Nan Merriman,
Lisa Otto, Sesto Bruscantini, Rolando Panerai,
Léopold Simoneau with the Philharmonia Orchestra
conducted by Karajan)

THE COUNTESS
in the complete recording of
'CAPRICCIO'
RICHARD STRAUSS

33CX1600-1-2 *(Libretto available price 7/6)*
(the cast also includes Christa Ludwig,
Nicolai Gedda, Dietrich Fischer-Dieskau,
Hans Hotter with the Philharmonia
Orchestra conducted by Sawallisch)

COLUMBIA
(Regd. Trade Mark of Columbia Graphophone Co. Ltd.)
33⅓ R.P.M. LONG PLAYING RECORDS
E.M.I. RECORDS LTD., 8-11 Great Castle Street, London, W.1

Lieder: 1. Gretchen am Spinnrade; 2. Wehmut; 3. Meeres Stille; 4. An Sylvia; 5. Erntelied

Berlin March 1973	Parsons, piano	LP: EMI ASD 3124 LP: EMI RLS 154 6133 (1,3) CD: EMI CDM 763 6562/CMS 763 7902 (1,3)

An die Musik

Toronto February 1970	Newmark, piano	LP: Rococo 5388

Italian arias: Vedi quanto adoro; Misero pargoletto

Berlin 1958	Raucheisen, piano	LP: Melodram MEL 082 LP: Discocorp RR 208 Recording incorrectly dated 1953

Schumann

Song cycles: Frauenliebe und -leben; Liederkreis op 39

Berlin January and April 1974	Parsons, piano	LP: EMI ASD 3037 Front LP cover incorrectly states Liederkreis op 24

Aufträge

London November 1951	Moore, piano	78: Columbia LB 122 LP: EMI RLS 154 6133
London July 1953	Moore, piano	Columbia unpublished
London January 1954	Moore, piano	LP: Columbia 33CX 1044 LP: EMI RLS 763 CD: EMI CDM 763 6562/CMS 763 7902

Die Kartenlegerin

Berlin October 1967	Parsons, piano	LP: EMI ASD 2404 LP: EMI RLS 154 6133 CD: EMI CDM 763 6562/CMS 763 7902

Der Nussbaum

London November 1951	Moore, piano	78: Columbia LB 122
London January 1954	Moore, piano	LP: Columbia 33CX 1044 LP: EMI RLS 763 LP: EMI RLS 154 6133
New York November 1956	Reeves, piano	CD: EMI CHS 761 0432
Salzburg August 1960	Moore, piano	CD: Stradivarius STR 10009
Toronto February 1970	Newmark, piano	LP: Rococo 5388
Berlin March 1973	Parsons, piano	LP: EMI ASD 3124 CD: EMI CDM 763 6562/CMS 763 7902

2 Venezianische Lieder: Leis' rudern hier; Wenn durch die Piazzetta

Berlin August 1965	Moore, piano	LP: Columbia CX 5268/SAX 5268 LP: EMI ASD 3124 LP: EMI RLS 154 6133 CD: EMI CDM 763 6562/CMS 763 7902

Volksliedchen

Berlin 1945	Raucheisen, piano	LP: Acanta 40.23557 CD: Acanta 42.43801

Widmung

London June 1957	Moore, piano	Columbia unpublished
Berlin August 1965	Moore, piano	LP: Columbia CX 5268/SAX 5268

Wie mit innigstem Behagen (Lied der Suleika)

Berlin August 1965	Moore, piano	LP: EMI ASD 2634 CD: EMI CDM 763 6562/CMS 763 7902

Duets: 1. In der Nacht; 2. Tanzlied; 3. Er und sie; 4. Ich denke dein

London February 1967	Fischer-Dieskau Moore, piano	LP: EMI SAN 182-3 LP: EMI SLS 926 CD: EMI CDC 749 2382 (2,3)

Sibelius

Schilf. Schilf, säusle

London April 1956	Moore, piano Sung in German	LP: Columbia 33CX 1404 45: Columbia SEL 1600 LP: EMI RLS 154 6133

Schwarze Rosen

London April 1956	Moore, piano Sung in German	LP: Columbia 33CX 1404/SAX 2265 45: Columbia SEL 1600/ESR 6274 LP: EMI RLS 154 6133

War es ein Traum?

London April 1956	Moore, piano Sung in German	Columbia unpublished

Sieczynsky

Wien, du Stadt meiner Träume

London July 1957	Philharmonia Ackermann	LP: Columbia 33CX 1570/SAX 2283 LP: EMI ASD 2807 CD: EMI CDC 747 2842

Smetana

The Bartered Bride: Excerpt (Endlich allein)

London December 1956	Role of Marenka Philharmonia Schmidt Sung in German	LP: Columbia CX 5286/SAX 5286 LP: EMI SXDW 3049 CD: EMI CDM 769 5012

Johann Strauss

Casanova: Excerpt (Nuns' Chorus)

London July 1957	Role of Laura Philharmonia Chorus & Orchestra Ackermann	LP: Columbia 33CX 1570/SAX 2283 LP: EMI ASD 2807 CD: EMI CDC 747 2842

Die Fledermaus

London April 1955	Role of Rosalinde Streich, Gedda, Krebs, Christ, Dönch, Chorus Philharmonia Karajan	LP: Columbia 33CX 1309-10 LP: EMI RLS 728 CD: EMI CHS 769 5312 Excerpts LP: Columbia 33CX 1516 LP: Electrola 1C 047 01953 LP: EMI RLS 763 CD: EMI CDM 763 6572/CMS 763 7902

Frühlingsstimmen

Vienna October 1946	VPO Krips	LP: EMI ALP 143 5501 LP: EMI RLS 154 6133 CD: EMI CDM 763 6542/CMS 763 7902 Recording incomplete

G'schichten aus dem Wienerwald

Berlin October 1944	Raucheisen, piano	LP: Acanta 40.23557 CD: Acanta 42.43128

Eine Nacht in Venedig

London May and September 1954	Role of Annina Loose, Gedda, Kunz, Dönch, Chorus Philharmonia Ackermann	LP: Columbia 33CX 1224-5 LP: EMI SXDW 3043 CD: EMI CDH 769 5302 Excerpts LP: EMI RLS 763

Eine Nacht in Venedig: Excerpt (Seht, o seht)

London July 1957	Role of Annina Philharmonia Ackermann	Columbia unpublished

Wiener Blut

London May 1954	Role of Gabriele Köth, Loose, Gedda, Kunz, Dönch, Chorus Philharmonia Ackermann	LP: Columbia 33CX 1186-7 LP: EMI SXDW 3042 CD: EMI CDH 769 5292 Excerpts LP: EMI RLS 763 LP: EMI RLS 154 6133

Wiener Blut: Selection

Berlin 1940	Role of Gabriele Glawitsch, Deutsches Opernhaus Orchestra Otto	78: Telefunken E 3099

Der Zigeunerbaron

London May and September 1954	Role of Saffi Köth, Sinclair, Gedda, Kunz, Prey, Chorus Philharmonia Ackermann	LP: Columbia 33CX 1329-30 LP: EMI SXDW 3046 CD: EMI CHS 769 5262 Excerpts LP: EMI RLS 763

Der Zigeunerbaron: Excerpt (Saffis Lied)

London July 1957	Role of Saffi Philharmonia Ackermann	Columbia unpublished

Richard Strauss

Arabella: Excerpts (1. Ich danke, Fräulein...Aber der Richtige; 2. Mein Elemer; 3. Sie woll'n mich heiraten?; 4. Und jetzt sag' ich ihm Adieu; 5. Das war sehr gut, Mandryka; other excerpt without Schwarzkopf)

London September and October 1954	Role of Arabella Felbermayer, Gedda, Metternich, Berry, Philharmonia Matacic	LP: Columbia 33CX 1226 LP: World Records OH 199 LP: Columbia 33CX 1897 LP: EMI RLS 751 LP: EMI RLS 154 6133 (2,3,5) CD: EMI CDH 761 0012 (1,2,3,5)

Ariadne auf Naxos

London June and July 1954	Role of Ariadne/ Prima Donna Seefried, Streich, Schock, Prey, Dönch, Philharmonia Karajan	LP: Columbia 33CX 1292-4 LP: EMI RLS 760 CD: EMI CMS 769 2962 Excerpt CD: EMI CDM 763 6572/CMS 763 7902

Capriccio

London September 1957	Role of Countess Ludwig, Moffo, Gedda, Hotter, Fischer-Dieskau, Wächter, Schmitt-Walter, Philharmonia Sawallisch	LP: Columbia 33CX 1600-2 LP: World Records OC 230-2 LP: Electrola 143 5243 CD: EMI CDS 749 0148 Excerpts LP: World Records OH 233 CD: EMI CDM 763 6572/CMS 763 7902

Capriccio: Excerpt (Closing Scene)

Watford September 1953	Role of Countess Philharmonia Ackermann	LP: Columbia 33CX 1107 LP: EMI RLS 751 LP: EMI 103 8651 CD: EMI CDH 761 0012

Der Rosenkavalier

London December 1956	Roles of Marschallin & First Noble Orphan Stich-Randall, Ludwig, Edelmann, Wächter, Gedda, Chorus Philharmonia Karajan	LP: Columbia 33CX 1492-5/SAX 2269-72 LP: EMI SLS 810 LP: EMI EX 29 00453 CD: EMI CDS 749 3548 Excerpts LP: Columbia 33CX 1777/SAX 2423 CD: EMI CDM 763 6572/CMS 763 7902
Salzburg August 1960	Role of Marschallin Jurinac, Edelmann, Rothenberger, Kunz, Zampieri, Vienna Opera Chorus VPO Karajan	VHS Video: Rank 7015E
Salzburg August 1963	Role of Marschallin Jurinac, Edelmann, Rothenberger, Dönch, Romani, Vienna Opera Chorus VPO Karajan	LP: Movimento Musica 04.004
New York December 1964	Role of Marschallin Della Casa, Raskin, Edelmann, Dönch, Morell, Metropolitan Opera Chorus & Orchestra Schippers	CD: Claque GM 3010-12

Der Rosenkavalier: Excerpt (Da geht er hin)

Hamburg 1952	Role of Marschallin NDR Orchestra Schüchter	LP: Melodram MEL 088
Toronto February 1970	Role of Marschallin Bible, Canadian RO Rich	LP: Rococo 5388

Der Rosenkavalier: Excerpt (Marie Theres')

Stockholm May 1966	Role of Marschallin Dobbs, Söderström, Stockholm Opera Orchestra Varviso	LP: Legendary LR 168

Der Rosenkavalier: Excerpt (Mir ist die Ehre widerfahren)

Vienna December 1947	Role of Sophie Seefried, VPO Karajan	78: Columbia LX 1225-6 LP: Columbia (USA) ML 2126 LP: World Records SH 286 LP: EMI RLS 763 LP: EMI RLS 154 6133 LP: EMI RLS 7714 CD: EMI CDH 769 7932

4 letzte Lieder

Watford September 1953	Philharmonia Ackermann	LP: Columbia 33CX 1107 LP: EMI RLS 751 LP: EMI 100 8651 CD: EMI CDH 761 0012
London June 1956	Philharmonia Karajan	CD: EMI CDM 763 6552/CMS 763 7902
Salzburg August 1964	BPO Karajan	CD: Paragon PCD 84008 CD: Nuovo Era 2251-2 CD: Virtuoso 269.7152
Berlin September 1965	Berlin RO Szell	LP: Columbia CX 5268/SAX 5268 LP: EMI ASD 2888 CD: EMI CDC 747 2762

Songs with Orchestra: Zueignung; Freundliche Vision; Die heiligen 3 Könige; Muttertändelei; Waldseligkeit

Berlin September 1965	Berlin RO Szell	LP: Columbia CX 5268/SAX 5268 LP: EMI ASD 2888 CD: EMI CDC 747 2762

Songs with Orchestra: Meinem Kinde; Das Rosenband; Das Bächlein; Winterweihe

London March 1968	LSO Szell	LP: EMI ASD 2493 CD: EMI CDC 747 2762

3 Ophelia Lieder

New York January 1966	Gould, piano	LP: CBS 76983 LP: CBS M2X 35914 CD: CBS Sony (Japan) 46DC 5304-5
Berlin October 1967	Parsons, piano	LP: EMI ASD 2634 CD: EMI CDM 763 6562/CMS 763 7902

Lieder: Heimliche Aufforderung; Wer lieben will; Winterweihe

New York January 1966	Gould, piano	CBS unpublished

Wiegenlied

London April 1956	Moore, piano	Columbia unpublished
London May 1956	Moore, piano	LP: Columbia 33CX 1404/SAX 2265 45: Columbia SEL 1588 LP: EMI RLS 154 6133 CD: EMI CDM 763 6562/CMS 763 7902
New York November 1956	Reeves, piano	CD: EMI CHS 761 0432
Hannover March 1962	Reutter, piano	LP: Movimento Musica 02.017
London March 1968	LSO Szell	LP: EMI ASD 2493 CD: EMI CDC 747 2762

Lieder: Wiegenliedchen; Die Nacht; All' mein Gedanken

Berlin October 1968	Parsons, piano	EMI unpublished

Lieder: 1. Wiegenliedchen; 2. Die Nacht

Berlin August and September 1970	Parsons, piano	LP: EMI ASD 2844 LP: EMI RLS 154 6133 (2) CD: EMI CDM 763 6562/CMS 763 7902

Hat gesagt, bleibt's nicht dabei

Berlin January 1945	Raucheisen, piano	LP: Acanta 40.23546 CD: Acanta 42.43128
London November 1951	Moore, piano	Columbia unpublished
London April and September 1952	Moore, piano	Columbia unpublished
London January 1954	Moore, piano	78: Columbia LX 1577 LP: Columbia 33CX 1044 LP: EMI RLS 763 LP: EMI RLS 154 6133 CD: EMI CDM 763 6562/CMS 763 7902
New York November 1956	Reeves, piano	CD: EMI CHS 761 0432
Hilversum 1957	De Nobel, piano	CD: Verona 27021
Berlin 1958	Raucheisen, piano	LP: Melodram MEL 088 <u>Recording incorrectly labelled Einerlei</u> <u>and incorrectly dated 1953</u>
Hannover March 1962	Reutter, piano	LP: Movimento Musica 02.017

Heimkehr

Vienna January 1979	Parsons, piano	Decca unpublished

Schlagende Herzen

Berlin January 1945	Raucheisen, piano	LP: Acanta 40.23546 LP: Acanta 40.23557 CD: Acanta 42.43128

Lieder: 1. Ach, was Kummer; 2. Wer lieben will; 3. Meinem Kinde

Berlin April 1966	Parsons, piano	LP: EMI ASD 2404 CD: EMI CDM 763 6562/CMS 763 7902

Morgen

Berlin January 1945	Raucheisen, piano	LP: Acanta 40.23546 LP: Acanta 40.23557 CD: Acanta 42.43128
New York January 1966	Gould, piano	CBS unpublished
London March 1968	Peinemann, violin LSO Szell	LP: EMI ASD 2493 CD: EMI CDC 747 2762

Heimliche Aufforderung

London May 1959	Moore, piano	Columbia unpublished

Ruhe, meine Seele

London April 1956	Moore, piano	Columbia unpublished
New York November 1956	Reeves, piano	CD: EMI CHS 761 0432
Hilversum 1957	De Nobel, piano	CD: Verona 27021
London May 1959	Moore, piano	Columbia unpublished
Strassburg June 1960	Bonneau, piano	CD: Chant du Monde LDC 278.899
Hannover March 1962	Reutter, piano	CD: Movimento Musica 02.017
London April 1964	Moore, piano	Columbia unpublished
London March 1968	LSO Szell	LP: EMI ASD 2493 CD: EMI CDC 747 2762

Schlechtes Wetter

London November 1951	Moore, piano	Columbia unpublished
London April and September 1952	Moore, piano	Columbia unpublished
London January 1954	Moore, piano	78: Columbia LX 1577 LP: Columbia 33CX 1044 LP: EMI RLS 763 LP: EMI RLS 154 6133 CD: EMI CDM 763 6562/CMS 763 7902
Salzburg August 1956	Moore, piano	CD: Stradivarius STR 10009
New York November 1956	Reeves, piano	CD: EMI CHS 761 0432
Hilversum 1957	De Nobel, piano	CD: Verona 27021
Berlin 1958	Raucheisen, piano	LP: Melodram MEL 088 <u>Recording incorrectly dated 1953</u>
Strassburg June 1960	Bonneau, piano	CD: Chant du Monde LDC 278.899
Hannover March 1962	Reutter, piano	LP: Movimento Musica 02.017

Lieder: Zueignung; Meinem Kinde

Hannover March 1962	Reutter, piano	LP: Movimento Musica 02.017

Lieder: Zueignung; Freundliche Vision

Strassburg June 1960	Bonneau, piano	CD: Chant du Monde LDC 278.899

Zueignung

London June 1957	Moore, piano	Columbia unpublished
London April 1964	Moore, piano	Columbia unpublished

Stravinsky

The Rake's Progress

Venice September 1951	Role of Anne Tourel, Kraus, Rounesville, Arié, La Scala Chorus & Orchestra Stravinsky	LP: Fonit Cetra DOC 29

Pastorale

Berlin October 1967	Parsons, piano	LP: EMI ASD 2404

Suppé

Boccaccio: Excerpt (Hab' ich nur deine Liebe)

London July 1957	Role of Fiametta Philharmonia Ackermann	LP: Columbia 33CX 1570/SAX 2283 LP: EMI ASD 2807 CD: EMI CDC 747 2842

Boccaccio: Selection

Berlin 1940	Role of Fiametta Glawitsch, Deutsches Opernhaus Orchestra Otto	78: Telefunken E 3029

Thursday, 19th January, 1950

LA TRAVIATA

OPERA IN FOUR ACTS

Words by Francesco Maria Piave
from the play " La Dame aux Camèlias "
by Alexandre Dumas the younger

Music by Giuseppe Verdi

English version by Edward J. Dent

Scenery and costumes by Sophie Fedorovitch

CONDUCTOR : REGINALD GOODALL
PRODUCER : TYRONE GUTHRIE

THE COVENT GARDEN OPERA CHORUS
Chorus Master : Douglas Robinson

THE COVENT GARDEN ORCHESTRA
Leader : Joseph Shadwick

GIUSEPPE VERDI, 1813 - 1901

This opera was first produced on 6th March, 1853, at the Teatro La Fenice, Venice, when it was a complete failure. It was subsequently triumphantly received at Venice on 6th May, 1854, and was first performed in England at Her Majesty's, in Italian, on 24th May, 1856, and in English at the Surrey Theatre on 8th June, 1857.

CHARACTERS IN ORDER OF APPEARANCE

Marguerite, a courtesan	ELISABETH SCHWARZKOPF
The Baron, her lover	MARIAN NOWAKOWSKI
Flora, friend of Marguerite	ROSINA RAISBECK
Gaston, a young man of fashion	EDGAR EVANS
Armand Duval, his friend	RUDOLF SCHOCK
The Marquis, an elderly libertine	RONALD LEWIS
The Doctor	ERNEST DAVIES
Annina, Marguerite's maid	ENID STONE
Joseph, Marguerite's servant	DAVID TREE
Georges Duval, Armand's father	JESS WALTERS
A Messenger	ARTHUR KELLET
Flora's Servant	CHARLES MORRIS

The Audience is asked not to applaud at the end of each Act until the Orchestra has finished playing.

Tchaikovsky

Eugene Onegin: Excerpt (Tatiana's Letter Scene)

London September 1966	Role of Tatiana LSO Galliera Sung in German	LP: Columbia CX 5286/SAX 5286 LP: EMI SXDW 3049 CD: EMI CDM 769 5012

None but the lonely heart

London April 1956	Moore, piano Sung in German	LP: Columbia 33CX 1404/SAX 2265 45: Columbia SEL 1600/ESL 6274

Pimpinella

Berlin October 1967 (EMI)	Parsons, piano Sung in Italian	LP: EMI ASD 2404 CD: EMI CDM 763 6542/CMS 763 7902

Trunk

Lieder: Das Hemd; Die Allee

Berlin 1944	Raucheisen, piano	LP: Acanta 40.23557 CD: Acanta 42.43128

4 heitere Lieder: Schlittenfahrt; Vertrag; Menuett; Brautwerbung

Berlin September 1944	Raucheisen, piano	LP: Acanta 40.23557 CD: Acanta 42.43128

Verdi

Falstaff

London June 1956	Role of Alice Moffo, Merriman, Barbieri, Alva, Gobbi, Panerai, Chorus Philharmonia Karajan	LP: Columbia 33CX 1195-6/SAX 2254-6 LP: EMI SLS 5037 LP: EMI SLS 5211 CD: EMI CDS 749 6682 Excerpts LP: Columbia 33CX 1939/SAX 2578
Salzburg August 1957	Role of Alice Moffo, Canali, Simionato, Alva, Gobbi, Panerai, Vienna Opera Chorus VPO Karajan	CD: Hunt CDKAR 226

Otello: Excerpt (Piangea cantando....Ave Maria)

London April 1959	Role of desdemona Elkins, Philharmonia Rescigno	LP: Columbia CX 5286/SAX 5286 LP: EMI SXDW 3049

La Traviata: Excerpt (Ah fors è lui...sempre libera)

London April 1948	Role of Violetta Philharmonia Braithwaite Sung in English	78: Columbia LX 1079

La Traviata: Excerpt (Addio del passato)

London October 1950	Role of Violetta Philharmonia Galliera	78: Columbia LX 1370 45: Columbia SEL 1575 45: Columbia SCD 2076 LP: EMI RLS 763
London April 1959	Role of Violetta Philharmonia Rescigno	Columbia unpublished
London April 1962	Role of Violetta Philharmonia Tonini	Columbia unpublished

La Traviata: Excerpt (Madamigella Valéry....Dite alle giovane)

London October 1953	Role of Violetta Panerai, Philharmonia Galliera	LP: EMI EX 29 10753

Requiem

Milan June 1954	<u>Soprano soloist</u> Dominguez, Di Stefano, Siepi, La Scala Chorus & Orchestra De Sabata	LP: Columbia 33CX 1195-6 LP: EMI RLS 100 9373 <u>Libera me</u> CD: EMI CDM 763 6572/CMS 763 7902
London September 1963 and April 1964	<u>Soprano soloist</u> Ludwig, Gedda, Ghiaurov, Philharmonia Chorus & Orchestra Giulini	LP: EMI AN 133-4/SAN 133-4 LP: EMI SLS 909 CD: EMI CDS 747 2578

Der Schornsteinfeger

Berlin September 1944	Raucheisen, piano <u>Sung in German</u>	LP: Acanta 40.23557 CD: Acanta 42.43801

Wagner

Götterdämmerung

Bayreuth August 1951	Role of Woglinde Varnay, Mödl, Siewert, Aldenhoff, Uhde, Weber, Bayreuth Festival Chorus & Orchestra Karajan	Columbia unpublished
Bayreuth August 1951	Role of Woglinde Varnay, Mödl, Siewert, Aldenhoff, Uhde, Weber, Bayreuth Festival Chorus & Orchestra Knappertsbusch	Decca unpublished

Lohengrin: Excerpt (Einsam in trüben Tagen)

London April 1956	Role of Elsa Philharmonia Susskind	LP: Columbia 33CX 1658/SAX 2300 LP: EMI SXDW 3049 CD: EMI CDM 769 5012

Lohengrin: Excerpt (Euch Lüften, die mein Klagen)

London May 1956	Role of Elsa Hoffman, Czerwenka, Philharmonia Susskind	Columbia unpublished
London May 1958	Role of Elsa Ludwig, Philharmonia Susskind	LP: Columbia 33CX 1658/SAX 2300 LP: EMI SXDW 3049 CD: EMI CDM 769 5012

Die Meistersinger von Nürnberg

Bayreuth July and August 1951	Role of Eva Malaniuk, Hopf, Unger, Edelmann, Dalberg, Kunz, Bayreuth Festival Chorus & Orchestra Karajan	78: Columbia LX 1465-1498/8851-8884 auto LP: Columbia 33CX 1021-5 LP: EMI RLS 7708 LP: EMI RLS 143 3903 CD: EMI CMS 763 5002 CD: Hunt CDKAR 224

Die Meistersinger von Nürnberg: Excerpt (Guten Abend, Meister)

London December 1956	Role of Eva Edelmann, Philharmonia Schmidt	Columbia unpublished

Das Rheingold

Bayreuth August 1951	Role of Woglinde Malaniuk, Siewert, Brivkalne, Fritz, S.Björling, Kuen, Windgassen, Bayreuth Festival Orchestra Karajan	LP: Melodram MEL 516 CD: Melodram MEL 26107 CD: Hunt CDKAR 216 Excerpts LP: Melodram MEL 088
Bayreuth August 1951	Role of Woglinde Malaniuk, Siewert, Brivkalne, Fritz, S.Björling, Kuen, Windgassen, Bayreuth Festival Orchestra Knappertsbusch	Decca unpublished

Das Rheingold: Excerpts (1. Weia! Waga! Woge, du Welle! 2. Lugt, Schwestern 3. Abendlich strahlt...to end)

Berlin 1941	Role of Woglinde Scheppan, Schilp, Nissen, Hann, Aldenhoff, Zimmermann, Deutsches Opernhaus Orchestra Rother	LP: Acanta 22.21486 LP: Acanta 40.23502 LP: Melodram MEL 082 (1) CD: Melodram MEL 16501 (1)

Tannhäuser: Excerpts (Dich teure Halle; Allmächtige Jungfrau)

London April 1956	Role of Elisabeth Philharmonia Susskind	LP: Columbia 33CX 1658/SAX 2300 LP: EMI SXDW 3049 CD: EMI CDM 763 5012

Tristan und Isolde: Excerpt (Tot denn alles)

London September 1951	Role of Brangäne Weber, Philharmonia Schüchter	78: Columbia LX 8892 LP: Electrola 1C 177 00933-4M

Schmerzen; Träume (Wesendonk-Lieder)

London January and February 1961	Moore, piano	Columbia unpublished

Träume (Wesendonk-Lieder)

London December 1962	Moore, piano	LP: EMI SAN 255 LP: EMI RLS 154 6133 CD: EMI CDM 763 6542/CMS 763 7902

Walton

Troilus and Cressida: Excerpts (Is Cressida a slave?; Slowly it all comes back; How can I sleep?; If one last doubt remain; Now close your arms; All's well!; Diomede! Father!)

London April 1955	Role of Cressida Lewis, Sinclair, Philharmonia Walton	LP: Columbia 33CX 1313 LP: World Records OH 217

Weber

Abu Hassan

Berlin 1942	Role of Fatima Witte, Bohnen, Berlin Radio Chorus & Orchestra L.Ludwig	LP: Urania URLP 7029 CD: Urania ULS 5153 Excerpts LP: Melodram MEL 082 CD: Melodram MEL 16501 CD: Forlane UCD 16572 Also issued on Saga and Varèse Sarabande LPs

Der Freischütz: Excerpts (Und ob die Wolke; Leise, leise)

London April 1956	Role of Agathe Philharmonia Susskind	LP: Columbia 33CX 1658/SAX 2300 LP: EMI SXDW 3049 CD: EMI CDM 769 5012

Oberon: Excerpt (Ozean, du Ungeheuer)

London April 1956	Role of Rezia Philharmonia Susskind	Columbia unpublished

3 Italian Duets: 1. Mille volte mio tesoro; 2. Va ti consolo, addio; 3. Se il mio ben

Berlin June 1942	Piltti Raucheisen, piano	LP: Melodiya M10 41285-6 LP: Discocorp IGI 385 LP: Discocorp RR 208 LP: Acanta 40.23566 (3) CD: Acanta 42.43128 (3)

Wolf

Italienisches Liederbuch (complete)

Berlin	Fischer-Dieskau	LP: EMI SAN 210-11
September 1965,	Moore, piano	LP: Electrola 1C 165 01871-2
April 1966,		CD: EMI CDM 763 7322
September and		
October 1967		

Italienisches Liederbuch: Selection (1. Wie lange schon; 2. Was soll der Zorn?; 3. Nein, junger Herr; 4. Mein Liebster hat zu Tische)

Salzburg	Furtwängler, piano	LP: EMI ALP 2114 (2)
August 1953		LP: Electrola 1C 063 01915M (2)
		LP: Seraphim (USA) 60179 (2)
		LP: Fonit Cetra FE 30
		LP: EMI 143 5491
		LP: Melódram MEL 088 (1,3,4)
		LP: Discocorp RR 208 (1,3,4)
		CD: Virtuoso 269.7312

Italienisches Liederbuch: Selection (Man sagt mir; Ich esse nun mein Brot; Mein Liebster hat zu Tische; Du sagst mir, dass ich keine Fürstin; Wohl kenn' ich euren Stand; Was soll ich fröhlich sein?; Was soll der Zorn?; Wenn du, mein Liebster, steigst; Gesegnet sei das Grün; O wär' dein Haus; Schweig' einmal still; Verschling' der Abgrund; Ich hab' in Penna; Auch kleine Dinge; Mir ward gesagt; Wer rief dich denn?; Nun lass' uns Frieden schliessen; Du denkst, mit einem Fädchen; Wie lange schon; Nein, junger Herr; Mein Liebster ist so klein; Ihr jungen Leute; Wir haben beide; Mein Liebster singt)

London	Moore, piano	Columbia unpublished
April, June,		
July and		
September 1954		

Italienisches Liederbuch: Selection (Auch kleine Dinge; Mir ward gesagt; Wer rief dich denn?; Nun lass' uns Frieden schliessen; Du denkst, mit einem Fädchen; Wie lange schon; Nein, junger Herr; Mein Liebster ist so klein; Ihr jungen Leute; Wir haben beide; Mein Liebster singt; Man sagt mir; Ich esse nun mein Brot; Mein Liebster hat zu Tische; Ich liess mir sagen; Du sagst mir, dass ich keine Fürstin; Wohl kenn' ich euren Stand; Was soll ich fröhlich sein?; Was soll der Zorn?; Wenn du, mein Liebster, steigst; Gesegnet sei das Grün; O wär' dein Haus; Schweig' einmal still; Verschling' der Abgrund; Ich hab' in Penna)

London	Moore, piano	LP: Columbia 33CX 1714/SAX 2366
April 1958		
and December		
1959		

Nun lass uns Frieden schliessen (Italienisches Liederbuch)

Berlin	Parsons, piano	EMI unpublished
October 1968		

Spanisches Liederbuch (complete)

Berlin	Fischer-Dieskau	LP: DG SLPEM 139 329-30
December 1966	Moore, piano	LP: DG 2707 035
and January		LP: DG 2726 071
1967		CD: DG 423 9342

Spanisches Liederbuch: Selection (1. Bedeckt mich mit Blumen; 2. Herr, was trägt der Boden?; 3. In dem Schatten meiner Locken; 4. Mögen alle bösen Zungen)

Salzburg	Furtwängler, piano	LP: EMI ALP 2114 (2)
August 1953		LP: Electrola 1C 063 01915M (2)
		LP: Seraphim (USA) 60179 (2)
		LP: Fonit Cetra FE 30
		LP: EMI 143 5491
		LP: Melodram MEL 088 (1,3,4)
		LP: Discocorp IGI 382 (1,3,4)
		LP: Discocorp RR 208 (1,3,4)
		CD: Fonit Cetra CDC 21
		CD: Priceless D 18355
		CD: Virtuoso 269.7312

Spanisches Liederbuch: Bedeckt mich mit Blumen; Herr, was trägt der Boden hier?

Vienna	Parsons, piano	Decca unpublished
January 1979		

Wenn du zu den Blumen gehst (Spanisches Liederbuch)

Berlin	Moore, piano	LP: Columbia CX 5268/SAX 5268
August 1965		CD: EMI CDM 763 6532/CMS 763 7902

Lieder to poems by Goethe: 1. Phänomen; 2. Die Spröde; 3. Die Bekehrte; 4. Anakreons Grab; 5. Blumengruss; 6. Epiphanias

Salzburg   Furtwängler, piano   LP: EMI ALP 2114 (1,2,3,5,6)
August 1953   LP: Electrola 1C 063 01915M (1,2,3,5,6)
                                                   LP: Seraphim (USA) 60179 (1,2,3,5,6)
                                                   LP: Fonit Cetra FE 30
                                                   LP: EMI 143 5491
                                                   LP: Melodram MEL 088 (4)
                                                   LP: Discocoro IGI 382 (4)
                                                   LP: Discocorp RR 208 (4)
                                                   CD: Fonit Cetra CDC 21
                                                   CD: Priceless D 18355
                                                   CD: Virtuoso 269.7152
                                                   CD: Virtuoso 269.7312

Lieder to poems by Goethe: Blumengruss; Frühling übers Jahr; Phänomen; Epiphanias

London   Moore, piano   Columbia unpublished
April 1955

Lieder to poems by Goethe: 1. Philine; 2. Mignon I; 3. Mignon II; 4. Frühling übers Jahr; 5. Gleich und gleich; 6. St Nepomuks Vorabend; 7. Epiphanias; 8. Ganymed

London   Moore, piano   LP: Columbia 33CX 1657/SAX 2333
April 1956   LP: EMI SLS 5197
                                                   LP: EMI RLS 154 6133 (1,2,3)
                                                   CD: EMI CDM 763 6532/CMS 763 7902 (1,2,3,8

Lieder to poems by Goethe: Blumengruss; Mignon III; Phänomen; Die Bekehrte; Die Spröde; Anakreons Grab

London   Moore, piano   Columbia unpublished
April 1956

Lieder to poems by Goethe: Mignon III; Anakreons Grab

London   Moore, piano   Columbia unpublished
July 1956

Lieder to poems by Goethe: 1. Die Bekehrte; 2. Anakreons Grab

London   Moore, piano   LP: Columbia 33CX 1657/SAX 2333
June 1957   LP: EMI SLS 5197
                                                   CD: EMI CDM 763 6532/CMS 763 7902 (1)

Lieder to poems by Goethe: Die Spröde; Mignon III; Der schäfer; Als ich auf dem Euphrat schiffte; Nimmer will ich dich verlieren; Hochbeglückt in deiner Liebe

London   Moore, piano   Columbia unpublished
June 1957

Lieder to poems by Goethe: 1. Die Spröde; 2. Mignon III; 3. Blumengruss

London January 1958	Moore, piano	LP: Columbia 33CX 1657/SAX 2333 LP: EMI SLS 5197 LP: EMI RLS 154 6133 (2) CD: EMI CDM 763 6532/CMS 763 7902 (2)

Lieder to poems by Goethe: Mignon I, II, III; Philine

Hannover March 1962	Reutter, piano	LP: Movimento Musica 02.017 CD: Movimento Musica 051.015
Amsterdam 1962	De Nobel, piano	CD: Verona 27021

Kennst du das Land?

London April and July 1956	Moore, piano	Columbia unpublished
New York November 1956	Reeves, piano	CD: EMI CHS 761 0432
London June 1957	Moore, piano	LP: Columbia 33CX 1657/SAX 2333 LP: EMI SLS 5197 LP: EMI RLS 154 6133 CD: EMI CDM 763 6532/CMS 763 7902
Hannover March 1962	Reutter, piano	LP: Movimento Musica 02.017 CD: Movimento Musica 051.015
Amsterdam 1962	De Nobel, piano	CD: Verona 27021
London February 1967	Moore, piano	LP: EMI SAN 182-3 LP: EMI SLS 926 CD: EMI CDC 749 2382

Philine

Berlin 1958	Raucheisen, piano	LP: Acanta 40.23580

Lieder to poems by Mörike: 1. Im Frühling; 2. Elfenlied; 3. Lebe wohl; 4. Schlafendes Jesuskind

Salzburg August 1953	Furtwängler, piano	LP: EMI ALP 2114 (2,3,4) LP: Electrola 1C 063 01915M (2,3,4) LP: Seraphim (USA) 60179 (2,3,4) LP: Fonit Cetra FE 30 LP: EMI 143 5491 LP: Melodram MEL 088 (1) LP: Discocorp IGI 382 (1) LP: Discocorp RR 208 (1) CD: Fonit Cetra CDC 21 CD: Priceless D 18355 CD: Virtuoso 269.7152 CD: Virtuoso 269.7312

Lieder to poems by Mörike: 1. Auf eine Christblume; 2. Im Frühling

Berlin August and September 1965	Moore, piano	LP: EMI ASD 2844 LP: EMI RLS 154 6133 (2) CD: EMI CDM 763 6532/CMS 763 7902 (2)

Lieder to poems by Mörike: Verborgenheit; Nimmersatte Liebe; Selbstgeständnis

Berlin April 1966	Parsons, piano	LP: EMI ASD 2404

Lieder to poems by Mörike: Das verlassene Mägdlein; Gesang Weylas

Berlin April 1966	Parsons, piano	EMI unpublished

Lieder to poems by Mörike: Denk' es, o Seele; An eine Aeolsharfe

Berlin September 1970	Parsons, piano	LP: EMI ASD 3124 LP: EMI RLS 154 6133 CD: EMI CDM 763 6532/CMS 763 7902

Lieder to poems by Mörike: 1. Auf einen Wanderung; 2. An den Schlaf; 3. Begegnung; 4. Der Gärtner; 5. Auftrag

Berlin March 1973	Parsons, piano	LP: EMI ASD 3124 CD: EMI CDM 763 6532/CMS 763 7902 (1,3)

Lieder to poems by Mörike: Fussreise; Elfenlied; Bei einer Trauung; Jägerlied; Selbstgeständnis; Das verlassene Mägdlein; Auf ein altes Bild; Nimmersatte Liebe

London January 1977	Parsons, piano	LP: Decca SXL 6943 CD: Decca 430 0002

Lieder to poems by Mörike: Nixe Binsenfuss; Heimweh; Schlafendes Jesuskind; Ein Stündlein wohl vor Tag; Gebet

London January 1977	Parsons, piano	Decca unpublished

Lieder to poems by Mörike: Heimweh; Nixe Binsenfuss

Vienna January 1979	Parsons, piano	LP: Decca SXL 6943 CD: Decca 430 0002

Lebe wohl

Berlin October 1967	Parsons, piano	LP: EMI ASD 2404
London January 1977	Parsons, piano	LP: Decca SXL 6943 CD: Decca 430 0002

Storchenbotschaft

London May 1948	Moore, piano	Columbia unpublished
London April 1951	Moore, piano	Columbia unpublished
Berlin October 1968	Parsons, piano	EMI unpublished
London January 1977	Parsons, piano	LP: Decca SXL 6943 CD: Decca 430 0002
Vienna January 1979	Parsons, piano	Decca unpublished

Mausfallensprüchlein

London April and September 1952	Moore, piano	Columbia unpublished
London September and October 1952	Moore, piano	78: Columbia LX 1577
London December 1952 and July 1953	Moore, piano	Columbia unpublished
London January 1954	Moore, piano	LP: Columbia 33CX 1044 LP: EMI RLS 763 LP: EMI RLS 154 6133
Strassburg June 1960	Bonneau, piano	CD: Chant du Monde LDC 278.899
London January 1961	Moore, piano	LP: Columbia 33CX 1946/SAX 2589 LP: EMI SLS 5197 CD: EMI CDM 763 6532/CMS 763 7902
Amsterdam 1962	De Nobel, piano	CD: Verona 27021
London January 1977	Parsons, piano	Decca unpublished
Vienna January 1979	Parsons, piano	LP: Decca SXL 6943 CD: Decca 430 0002

Lieder to poems by Byron: Sonne der Schlummerlosen; Keine gleicht von allen Schönen

Berlin March 1973	Parsons, piano	LP: EMI ASD 3124 Sonne der Schlummerlosen only LP: EMI RLS 154 6133 CD: EMI CDM 763 6532/CMS 763 7902

Alte Weisen: Tretet ein, hoher Krieger; Singt mein Schatz; Wie glänzt der helle Mond; Du milchjunger Knabe; Wandl' ich in dem Morgentau; Das Köhlerweib ist trunken

Salzburg July 1958	Moore, piano	CD: Stradivarius STR 10009

Lieder: Epiphanias; Mein Liebster hat zu Tische; Du denkst, mit einem Fädchen; Schweig' einmal still; Wiegenlied; Im Frühling; Elfenlied; Nixe Binsenfuss; Bedeckt mich mit Blumen; Mögen alle bösen Zungen; In dem Schatten meiner Locken; Wer tat deinem Füsslein weh?; Die Spröde; Die Bekehrte

London April and June 1951	Moore, piano	Columbia unpublished

Lieder: 1. Wie glänzt der helle Mond; 2. Wiegenlied im Sommer

Salzburg August 1953	Furtwängler, piano	LP: EMI ALP 2114 LP: Electrola 1C 063 01915M LP: Seraphim (USA) 60179 LP: Fonit Cetra FE 30 LP: EMI 143 5491 CD: Fonit Cetra CDC 21 CD: Virtuoso 269.7312

Lieder: 1. Elfenlied; 2. In dem Schatten meiner Locken

London April 1956	Moore, piano	LP: Columbia 33CX 1404/SAX 2265 45: Columbia SEL 1588 CD: EMI CDM 763 6532/CMS 763 7902 (1)

Lieder: Ich hab' in Penna; Herr, was trägt der Boden hier?; Bedeckt mich mit Blumen; In dem Schatten meiner Locken; Zum neuen Jahr; Philine; Wir haben beide; Was soll der Zorn?; Wiegenlied im Sommer; Elfenlied

New York November 1956	Reeves, piano	CD: EMI CHS 761 0432

Lieder: Herr, was trägt der Boden hier?; St Nepomuks Vorabend; Nun lass uns Frieden schliessen; In dem Schatten meiner Locken; Wiegenlied im Sommer; Geh, Geliebter

Strassburg June 1960	Bonneau, piano	CD: Chant du Monde LDC 278.899

Lieder: 1. Morgentau; 2. Wandl' ich in dem Morgentau; 3. Singt mein Schatz; 4. Du milchjunger Knabe; 5. Die Spinnerin; 6. Das Vöglein; 7. Wie glänzt der helle Mond; 8. Wiegenlied im Winter; 9. Sonne der Schlummerlosen; 10. Der Schäfer

London January 1961	Moore, piano	LP: Columbia 33CX 1946/SAX 2589 LP: EMI SLS 5197 LP: EMI RLS 154 6133 (7) CD: EMI CDM 763 6532/CMS 763 7902 (1,5,6,7,8)

Lieder: Tretet ein, hoher Krieger; Das Köhlerweib ist trunken; Zur Ruh', zur Ruh'

London January 1961	Moore, piano	Columbia unpublished

Lieder: Hochbeglückt in deiner Liebe; Nimmer will ich dich verlieren

London March and December 1962	Moore, piano	LP: Columbia 33CX 1946/SAX 2589 LP: EMI SLS 5197

Lieder: Herr, was trägt der Boden hier?; Bedeckt mich mit Blumen; In dem Schatten meiner Locken; Wer rief dich denn?; Wiegenlied im Sommer

Hannover March 1962	Reutter, piano	LP: Movimento Musica 02.017 CD: Movimento Musica 051.015

Lieder: Wer rief dich denn?; Nun lass uns Frieden schliessen; Wandl' ich in dem Morgentau; Das Vöglein; Wiegenlied im Sommer; Wiegenlied im Winter

Amsterdam 1962	De Nobel, piano	CD: Verona 27021

Lieder: Tretet ein, hoher Krieger; Als ich auf dem Euphrat schiffte; Das Köhlerweib ist trunken; Wiegenlied im Sommer

London December 1962	Moore, piano	LP: Columbia 33CX 1946/SAX 2589 LP: EMI SLS 5197 Wiegenlied im Sommer only CD: EMI CDM 763 6532/CMS 763 7902

Lieder: Sonne der Schlummerlosen; Das verlassene Mägdlein

London February 1967	Moore, piano	LP: EMI SAN 182-3 LP: EMI SLS 926 CD: EMI CDC 749 2382

Der Genesene an die Hoffnung

London December 1959	Moore, piano	Columbia unpublished
Vienna January 1979	Parsons, piano	Decca unpublished

Wiegenlied im Sommer

London September and October 1952	Moore, piano	78: Columbia LX 1577
London December 1952	Moore, piano	Columbia unpublished
London January 1954	Moore, piano	LP: Columbia 33CX 1044 LP: EMI RLS 763 LP: EMI RLS 154 6133

Nachtzauber

Salzburg August 1953	Furtwängler, piano	LP: EMI ALP 2114 LP: Electrola 1C 063 01915M LP: Seraphim (USA) 60179 LP: Fonit Cetra FE 30 LP: EMI 143 5491 CD: Fonit Cetra CDC 21 CD: Virtuoso 269.7312
London January 1958	Moore, piano	Columbia unpublished
London January 1961 and March 1962	Moore, piano	Columbia unpublished
Hannover March 1962	Reutter, piano	LP: Movimento Musica 02.017 CD: Movimento Musica 051.015

Die Zigeunerin

Salzburg August 1953	Furtwängler, piano	LP: Fonit Cetra FE 30 LP: EMI 143 5491 LP: Melodram MEL 088 LP: Discocorp IGI 382 LP: Discocorp RR 208 CD: Fonit Cetra CDC 21 CD: Virtuoso 269.7312
London April 1956	Moore, piano	Columbia unpublished
New York November 1956	Reeves, piano	CD: EMI CHS 761 0432
Berlin 1958	Raucheisen, piano	LP: Acanta 40.23580
London January 1961, March and December 1962	Moore, piano	Columbia unpublished
Hannover March 1962	Reutter, piano	LP: Movimento Musica 02.017 CD: Movimento Musica 051.015
Amsterdam 1962	De Nobel, piano	CD: Verona 27021
Berlin August 1965	Moore, piano	LP: Columbia CX 5268/SAX 5268 CD: EMI CDM 763 6532/CMS 763 7902
London February 1967	Moore, piano	LP: EMI SAN 182-3 LP: EMI SLS 926 CD: EMI CDC 749 2382

Wolf-Ferrari

7 Songs from the Italian Song Book: Giovanottino che passi per via; Vo' fa' 'na palazzina alla marina; Dio ti facesse star tanto digiuno; Dimmi, bellino mio, com' io ho da fare; Quando a letto vo' la sera; Vado di notte, come fa la luna; Giovanetti, cantate ora che siete

Berlin August 1965	Moore, piano	LP: Columbia CX 5268/SAX 5268 LP: Electrola 1C 187 01307-8 CD: EMI CDM 763 6542/CMS 763 7902 Electrola issue contains an 8th song "Quando sara quel benedetto giorno"

Zeller

Der Obersteiger: Excerpt (Sei nicht bös)

London July 1957	Philharmonia Ackermann	LP: Columbia 33CX 1570/SAX 2283 LP: EMI ASD 2807 CD: EMI CDC 747 2842

Der Vogelhändler: Excerpts (Ich bin die Christel von der Post: Schenkt man sich Rosen in Tirol)

London July 1957	Role of Christel Philharmonia Ackermann	LP: Columbia 33CX 1570/SAX 2283 LP: EMI ASD 2807 CD: EMI CDC 747 2842

Zilcher

Rokoko-Suite: An den Menschen; Der Frühling; Abendständchen; Die Nacht; Die Alte; Mailied; An den Menschen

Berlin November 1944	Richartz, violin Steiner, cello Raucheisen, piano	LP: Acanta 40.23557 CD: Acanta 42.43801

Traditional and folk songs

Alleluia (arr. O'Connor Morris)

London　　　　　　　　Moore, piano　　　　　　　Columbia unpublished
April and
May 1956

Die Beruhigte

Berlin　　　　　　　　Raucheisen, piano　　　　LP: Acanta 40.23557
1944　　　　　　　　　　　　　　　　　　　　　　　CD: Acanta 42.43801

London　　　　　　　　Moore, piano　　　　　　　78: Columbia LB 112
April 1951　　　　　　　　　　　　　　　　　　　LP: EMI ALP 143 5501

Danny Boy (arr. Weatherly)

London　　　　　　　　Moore, piano　　　　　　　LP: Columbia CX 5268/SAX 5268
January 1958　　　　　　　　　　　　　　　　　　LP: EMI RLS 154 6133
　　　　　　　　　　　　　　　　　　　　　　　　CD: EMI CDM 763 6542/CMS 763 7902

Drink to me only (arr. Quilter)

London　　　　　　　　Moore, piano　　　　　　　Columbia unpublished
April 1956

London　　　　　　　　Moore, piano　　　　　　　LP: Columbia 33CX 1404/SAX 2265
May 1956　　　　　　　　　　　　　　　　　　　　45: Columbia SEL 1589/ESL 6255
　　　　　　　　　　　　　　　　　　　　　　　　LP: EMI RLS 154 6133
　　　　　　　　　　　　　　　　　　　　　　　　CD: EMI CDM 763 6542/CMS 763 7902

Berlin　　　　　　　　Raucheisen, piano　　　　LP: Melodram MEL 082
1958　　　　　　　　　　　　　　　　　　　　　　Recording incorrectly dated 1953

Gsätzli

Berlin 1944	Raucheisen, piano	LP: Acanta 40.23557 CD: Acanta 42.43801
London April 1951	Moore, piano	78: Columbia LB 112 LP: EMI ALP 143 5501 LP: EMI RLS 154 6133
London April 1956	Moore, piano	Columbia unpublished
London May 1956	Moore, piano	LP: Columbia 33CX 1404/SAX 2265 45: Columbia SEL 1588 CD: EMI CDM 763 6542/CMS 763 7902
New York November 1956	Reeves, piano	CD: EMI CHS 761 0432

Maria auf dem Berge

London April 1951	Moore, piano	78: Columbia LB 112 LP: EMI ALP 143 5501 LP: EMI RLS 154 6133 CD: EMI CDM 763 6542/CMS 763 7902
London June 1957	Bream, guitar Philharmonia Mackerras	LP: Columbia 33CX 1482 LP: EMI ASD 3798 CD: EMI CDM 763 5742

O du lieb's Aengeli

Berlin 1944	Raucheisen, piano	LP: Acanta 40.23557 CD: Acanta 42.43801
London April 1951	Moore, piano	78: Columbia LB 112 LP: EMI ALP 143 5501 LP: EMI RLS 154 6133
London April 1956	Moore, piano	LP: Columbia 33CX 1404/SAX 2265 45: Columbia SEL 1588 CD: EMI CDM 763 6542/CMS 763 7902

Vesper Hymn (arr. Woodman)

London April and May 1956	Moore, piano	Columbia unpublished

Z' Lauterbach han i mein Strumpf verlor'n

Berlin 1944	Raucheisen, piano	LP: Acanta 40.23557 CD: Acanta 42.43801

Christmas carols

Es ist ein Ros' entsprungen

Vienna March 1949	Vienna Opera Chorus Orchestra	78: International Columbia LC 33

The First Nowell

London October 1952	Covent Garden Chorus Hampstead Parish Church Choir Philharmonia Pritchard	78: Columbia LB 131 45: Columbia SCD 2112 LP: Legendary LR 136
London May 1957	Ambrosian Singers Philharmonia Mackerras	LP: Columbia 33CX 1482 LP: EMI ASD 3798 CD: EMI CDM 763 5742

O come all ye faithful

London October 1952	Covent Garden Chorus Hampstead Parish Church Choir Philharmonia Pritchard	78: Columbia LB 131
London June 1957	Ambrosian Singers Philharmonia Mackerras	LP: Columbia 33CX 1482 LP: EMI ASD 3798 CD: EMI CDM 763 5742

O du fröhliche

Vienna March 1949	Vienna Opera Chorus Orchestra	78: International Columbia LC 33
London May 1957	Ambrosian Singers Philharmonia Mackerras	LP: Columbia 33CX 1482 LP: EMI ASD 3798 CD: EMI CDM 763 5742

O Tannenbaum

Vienna March 1949	Vienna Opera Chorus Orchestra	78: International Columbia LC 32
London June 1957	Philharmonia Mackerras	Columbia unpublished

Stille Nacht, heilige Nacht

Vienna March 1949	Vienna Opera Chorus Orchestra	78: International Columbia LC 32 LP: EMI ALP 143 5501
London October 1952	Covent Garden Chorus Hampstead Parish Church Choir Philharmonia Pritchard <u>Sung in English</u>	78: Columbia LB 131 45: Columbia SCD 2112
London May, June and July 1957	Bream, guitar Ambrosian Singers Philharmonia Mackerras	LP: Columbia 33CX 1482 LP: EMI ASD 3798 CD: EMI CDM 763 5742

Die Lorelei; Ave Maria

London May and June 1957	Philharmonia Mackerras	Columbia unpublished

Sandmännchen; In einem kühlen Grunde; Panis angelicus; In dulci jubilo; Weihnachten; Vom Himmel hoch; I saw three ships; Easter Alleluia

London May and June 1957	Bream, guitar Ambrosian Singers Philharmonia Mackerras	LP: Columbia 33CX 1482 LP: EMI ASD 3798 CD: EMI CDM 763 5742

WIGMORE HALL
Manager : William Lyne

PHILHARMONIA CONCERT SOCIETY LTD.

FOUNDER AND ARTISTIC DIRECTOR:
WALTER LEGGE

HUGO WOLF

SCHWARZKOPF

GEOFFREY PARSONS

Saturday 26 November 1977
at 7.30pm

Management : Margaret Pacy *Programme thirty-five pence*

ROYAL FESTIVAL HALL
GENERAL MANAGER: T. E. BEAN, C.B.E.

PHILHARMONIA CONCERT SOCIETY LTD

ARTISTIC DIRECTOR:
WALTER LEGGE

ELISABETH SCHWARZKOPF

ROYAL PHILHARMONIC ORCHESTRA

LEADER: STEVEN STARYK

HARRY NEWSTONE

GERALD MOORE

Sunday, 18th January 1959, at 3 p.m.

Programme One Shilling

Elisabeth Schwarzkopf: roles performed with the Vienna State Opera

Includes performances with the Vienna company on tour
Figure against each role indicates number of times the part was performed

3	Aennchen (Der Freischütz)
2	Agathe (Der Freischütz)
8	Alice Ford (Falstaff)
2	Blondchen (Die Entführung aus dem Serail)
13	Countess (Capriccio)
20	Countess Almaviva (Le Nozze di Figaro)
29	Donna Elvira (Don Giovanni)
1	Elisabeth (Tannhäuser)
1	Eva (Die Meistersinger von Nürnberg)
17	Fiordiligi (Così fan tutte)
22	Gilda (Rigoletto)
18	Konstanze (Die Entführung aus dem Serail)
2	Liu (Turandot)
20	Marschallin (Der Rosenkavalier)
5	Marzelline (Fidelio)
13	Mimì (La Bohème)
2	Musetta (La Bohème)
3	Nedda (I Pagliacci)
4	Pamina (Die Zauberflöte)
12	Rosina (Il Barbiere di Siviglia)
4	Sophie (Der Rosenkavalier)
7	Susanna (Le Nozze di Figaro)
21	Violetta (La Traviata)
1	Zerbinetta (Ariadne auf Naxos)

Irmgard Seefried
Discography

Compiled by John Hunt
1991

Introduction

It was in 1943, at the tender age of 24, that Irmgard Seefried arrived in Vienna to become a member of the opera company there. She had started in the ensemble at Aachen under Herbert von Karajan, who also invited her for guest performances at the Deutsche Staatsoper in Berlin. But the real choice was between Dresden and Vienna, from whom Seefried received invitations simultaneously. It was a difficult choice to make, both of them being houses with imposing traditions, but after some performances in Dresden, she finally decided on Vienna, perhaps influenced by the fact that Dresden's director, Karl Böhm, was also transferring to Vienna in that same year of 1943. As it was, the young Seefried had enjoyed the privilege of singing in the old opera houses of both cities before their destruction by bombs in the late stages of the war.

Her first task in Vienna was the role of Eva in "Meistersinger", and at the rehearsals she was taken under the wings of Paul Schöffler, who was singing Sachs, and of Max Lorenz, singing the part of Stolzing. The soprano recalls their kindness and understanding, overwhelmed as she was at the time by the size of the stage and orchestra pit and the whole imposing ambience of the house, so different from the small one in Aachen.

How did it feel to be a member of that Vienna Mozart ensemble as it developed immediately after the war ? Seefried feels that it was a matter of the right people, a whole host of talented young singers and experienced conductors, being in the right place at the right time; she also maintains that the deprivations of war, many of which continued in those post-war years in Vienna, helped the artists to get their priorities right. Rivalry there certainly was among the singers, but much greater was the feeling of respect for each others' talents. Seefried and Schwarzkopf, for example, would attune their voices (as in the Letter Duet in "Figaro") to the extent that they could exchange roles if called upon to do so, just as in the male department Erich Kunz and Paul Schöffler could exchange Figaro for the Count, or Leporello for Giovanni. And they were singing actors ("Singschauspieler") rather than just singers, who regarded a recitative and aria as a dramatic entity.

Irmgard Seefried is proud of being the all-round artist, singing opera, oratorio and, in her later years even operetta and straight theatre. Even more important, in her view, is her achievement as a Lieder singer. She helped make the Lieder recital popular not just at home (her very first such recital had been in Vienna's Musikverein in the last dark days of the war) but also in the United States. Her proudest memory is of her very first American concert in New York Town Hall, when, during the intermission, she was visited in her dressing room by a distinguished-looking elderly lady who introduced the singer to her companion with the words "And this is my successor, Irmgard Seefried!". It was not until some minutes later that Seefried realised that her visitor was none other than Elisabeth Schumann!

Her interest in modern music was healthy, and composers wrote works for her and her husband, the violinist Wolfgang Schneiderhan. These included Hindemith (3 Motetten, which Seefried recorded), Henze and Martin. She programmed songs by Bartok, and at her last London concert sang the 4 Housman poems of Vaughan Williams.

The operatic roles which I heard Irmgard Seefried perform (Susanna, Fiordiligi, Octavian and Marie in "The Bartered Bride") remain to this day deeply engraved on my memory, yet even more vivid was her inimitable presence on the Lieder platform, whether it was the Royal Festival Hall or Queen Elizabeth Hall in London, the Salzburg Mozarteum or the Usher Hall in Edinburgh. Fortunately, most of her vividness and warmth comes across in her recorded legacy.

Adapted by John Hunt from an Austrian TV interview given by Irmgard Seefried about 1975

Bach

Saint Matthew Passion

Vienna June 1950	Soprano soloist Ferrier, W.Ludwig, Berry, Edelmann, Schöffler, Vienna Singverein VSO Karajan	LP: Foyer FO 1046 CD: Foyer 3CF-2013 CD: Verona 27070-2 CD: Hunt CDKAR 211 Excerpts CD: Verona 27076
Munich June, July and August 1958	Soprano soloist Töpper, Häfliger, Engen, Proebstl, Fischer-Dieskau, Munich Bach Choir & Orchestra Richter	LP: DG Archiv APM 14 125-8/SAPM 198 009-12 Excerpts LP: DG LPEM 19 233/SLPEM 136 233 LP: DG 2535 220

Saint Matthew Passion: Part 1, Nos 1-33

Vienna April 1952	Soprano soloist Rössl-Majdan, Patzak, Braun, Wiener, Vienna Singakademie VPO Furtwängler	LP: Golden Concert Library (Japan) GCL 5003

Saint Matthew Passion: Excerpts (1. Blute nur, du liebes Herz; 2. Ich will dir mein Herze schenken; 3. So ist nun mein Jesus gefangen...Sind Blitze, sind Donner; 4. Aus Liebe will mein Heiland sterben)

Leipzig December 1955	Soprano soloist Töpper (3), Thomanerchor (3) Leipzig GO Ramin	45: DG Archiv EPA 37 144 (1,2) 45: DG Archiv EPA 37 145 (3,4)

Cantata No 202 "Weichet nur, betrübte Schatten"

Lucerne August 1959	<u>Soprano soloist</u> Lucerne Festival Strings Baumgartner	LP: DG LPM 18606/SLPM 138 086

Cantata No 92: Excerpt (Meinem Hirten bleib' ich treu)

Vienna October 1946	<u>Soprano soloist</u> Schneiderhan, violin Walter, organ	LP: EMI EX 29 10563 LP: EMI EX 29 12363

Cantata No 144: Excerpt (Genügsamkeit ist ein Schatz)

Vienna October 1946	<u>Soprano soloist</u> Schneiderhan, violin Walter, organ	Columbia unpublished

Bartok

<u>Village Scenes</u>

1953	Werba, piano <u>Sung in German</u>	LP: DG LPEM 19 050 LP: DG 410 8471

Beethoven

Fidelio

Vienna May 1944	Role of Marzelline Konetzni, Klein, Ralf, Alsen, Schöffler, Neralcic, Vienna Opera Chorus VPO Böhm	LP: Acanta DE 23.116-7 Excerpts LP: Vox OPL 370/SPOL 5370
Vienna November 1955	Role of Marzelline Mödl, Kmennt, Dermota, Weber, Schöffler, Kamann, Vienna Opera Chorus VPO Böhm	LP: Melodram MEL 008 CD: Memoria CMM 2 CD: Movimento Musica 051.024
Munich June 1957	Role of Marzelline Rysanek, Lenz, Häfliger, Frick, Fischer-Dieskau, Engen, Bavarian State Chorus & Orchestra Fricsay	LP: DG LPM 18 390-1/SLPM 138 390-1 LP: DG 2726 088 LP: DG 2727 006 Excerpts LP: DG LPEM 19 215/SLPEM 136 215 LP: DG 2535 298 LP: DG 2548 118 CD: IMP IMPX 9021 Marzelline's aria only LP: DG LPEM 19 477/SLPEM 136 477 LP: DG 2535 746

Wonne der Wehmut

Vienna October 1957	Werba, piano	LP: DG LPEM 19 115

Symphony No 9 "Choral"

Vienna January 1951	Soprano soloist Anday, Patzak, Edelmann, Vienna Singakademie VPO Furtwängler	LP: Fonit Cetra FE 33 CD: Fonit Cetra CDC 1
Vienna May 1953	Soprano soloist Anday, Dermota, Schöffler, Vienna Singakademie VPO Furtwängler	LP: Discocorp RR 460 LP: German Furtwängler Society F669.056-7 CD: Rodolphe RPC 32456 CD: Hunt CD 532 CD: Nuova Era 013.6301 CD: Virtuoso 269 7202 Hunt issue has incorrect date and soprano soloist incorrectly named
Berlin 1959	Soprano soloist Forrester, Häfliger, Fischer-Dieskau, St Hedwig's Choir BPO Fricsay	LP: DG LPM 18 512-3/SLPM 138 002-3 LP: DG 2700 108 LP: DG 2535 203

Bizet

Carmen: Excerpt (Je dis que rien ne m'épouvante)

Vienna September 1953	Role of Micaela VSO Leitner	LP: DG 410 8471

Brahms

Ein deutsches Requiem

Vienna January 1951	Soprano soloist Fischer-Dieskau, Vienna Singakademie VSO Furtwängler	LP: Furtwängler Series (Japan) AT 01-2
New York 1954	Soprano soloist London, Westminster Choir NYPO Walter	LP: Columbia (USA) ML 4980 LP: Columbia (USA) Y 31015 LP: CBS 61284 LP: CBS M3P 39651 LP: Movimento Musica 02.022 CD: Melodram MEL 18004

Deutsche Volkslieder: Die Sonne scheint micht mehr; Die Schwalbe ziehet fort; Da unten im Tale; Die Trauernde; Mein Mädel hat einen Rosenmund; Schwesterlein; In stiller Nacht; Maria ging aus wandern; Wie komm' ich denn?; Soll sich der Mond nicht heller scheinen; All mein Gedanken

Vienna February 1962	Werba, piano	LP: DG LPEM 19 372/SLPEM 136 372

Deutsche Volkslieder: Da unten im Tale; Die Trauernde

Munich 1970	Werba, piano	LP: Electrola SHZE 281

Liebeslieder op 52

Vienna November 1947	Höngen, Hotter, Meyer-Welfing, Wührer, piano Nordberg, piano	78: Columbia LX 1114-7 LP: World Records SH 373 Excerpts LP: EMI RLS 154 7003 LP: EMI EX 769 7411
Edinburgh September 1952	Ferrier, Patzak, Günter, Curzon, piano Gal, piano	LP: Decca 417 6341
Vienna February 1962	Kostia, Kmennt, Wächter, Werba, piano Weissenborn, piano	LP: DG LPM 18 792/SLPM 138 792

Deutsche Grammophon Gesellschaft

IRMGARD SEEFRIED
with
ERIK WERBA

Bartok
Dorfszenen
Mussorgsky
The Nursery
Songs by Brahms, Schubert, R. Strauss and Wolf
DGM 19050

Cornelius
Christmas Songs, Op. 8
Brahms
Songs and Folk Songs
DG 16077

Songs and Poetry by Schumann and Heine
with Oskar Werner, Speaker
DGM 19067

Recital of Schubert Songs
SLPM 136009 (Stereo)

Recital of Songs by Richard Strauss
• SLPM 136010 (Stereo)

Mozart
9 Songs
Schumann
Frauenliebe und Leben, Op. 42
DGM 19112

DISTINGUISHED COLUMBIA ARTISTS

Irmgard Seefried
AND
Gerald Moore

Ridente la calma, Canzonetta, K.152;
An Chloë, K.524— *Mozart* - - - - LB 116

Unglückliche Liebe, K.520;
Das Traumbild, K.530— *Mozart* - - - - LB 114

Einsam ging ich Jüngst, K.308;
Die kleine Spinnerin, K.531— *Mozart* - - - LB 108

Nacht und Träume, Op. 43, No. 2;
Auf dem Wasser zu singen— *Schubert* - - - LB 106

For details of further recordings, see the Columbia Catalogue.

COLUMBIA
the finest name on record

Lieder: Dein blaues Auge; Ständchen

1953	Werba, piano	LP: DG LPEM 19 050
		LP: DG 410 8471

Lieder: Vergebliches Ständchen; Von ewiger Liebe

Vienna June 1958	Werba, piano	45: DG EPL 30402

Lieder: Wir wandelten; Nicht mehr zu dir zu gehen; Ruhe, Süssliebchen; Die Mainacht; Der Tod, das ist die kühle Nacht; Unbewegte laue Luft; Ständchen

Vienna June 1958	Werba, piano	LP: DG LPEM 19 165/SLPEM 136 010 LP: DG 2548 062

Lieder und Volkslieder: Die Trauernde; Die Schwälble ziehet fort; Feinsliebchen; Schwesterlein; In stiller Nacht; Vergebliches Ständchen

Vienna 1955	Werba, piano	78: DG LVM 72 380 45: DG EPL 30332 LP: DG LP 16 077

Neue Liebeslieder op 65

Vienna February 1962	Kostia, Kmennt, Wächter, Werba, piano Weissenborn, piano	LP: DG LPM 18 792/SLPM 138 792

Neue Liebeslieder op 65: Excerpt (Zum Schluss)

Edinburgh September 1952	Ferrier, Patzak, Günter, Curzon, piano Gal, piano	LP: Decca 417 6341

Wiegenlied

Vienna November 1947	Nordberg, piano	78: Columbia LB 69 LP: EMI RLS 154 7003 LP: EMI EX 29 12363

Bruch

Jubilate op 3

Aachen 1943	Soprano soloist Aachen Cathedral Choir Prussian State Orchestra Rehmann	78: Electrola DB 7655 LP: EMI EX 29 10563 LP: EMI EX 29 12363

Carissimi

4 Cantatas: Detesta la cativa sorte in amore; Lungi omai; Il mio core; A piè d'un verde alloro

London May 1955	Schwarzkopf, Moore, piano	LP: Columbia 33CX 1331 LP: EMI HLM 7267 CD: EMI CDH 769 7932

Cornelius

Weihnachtslieder op 8

Vienna 1955	Werba, piano	78: DG LVM 72 252 45: DG EPL 30327 LP: DG LP 16 077 LP: Decca (USA) DL 9545

Dvorak

Moravian Duets op 32

London May 1955	Schwarzkopf, Moore, piano Sung in German	LP: Columbia 33CX 1331 LP: EMI HLM 7267 CD: EMI CDH 769 7932

Egk

4 Canzoni

Munich 1961	Soprano soloist Bavarian RO Egk	LP: DG LPM 18 759/SLPM 138 759

Flies

Wiegenlied (attrib. Mozart)

Vienna November 1947	Nordberg, piano	78: Columbia LB 69 LP: EMI EX 29 10563 LP: EMI EX 29 12363

Gounod

Saint Cecilia Mass

Prague June 1965	Soprano soloist Stolze, Uhde, Czech Chorus Czech Philharmonic Orchestra Markevitch	LP: DG SLPEM 139 111 CD: DG 427 4092 Excerpt (Gloris in excelsis) LP: DG 410 8471

Handel

Giulio Cesare: Excerpts (1. V'adoro pupille; 2. Tu la mia stella sei; 3. Se pietà; 4. Piangero, la sorte mia; 5. Non e si vago e bella; 6. Più amabile beltà; other excerpts without Seefried)

Berlin April 1960	Role of Cleopatra Fischer-Dieskau, Berlin RO Böhm	LP: DG LPM 18 637/SLPM 138 637 LP: DG LPEM 19 477/SLPEM 136 477 (2) LP: DG 2535 746 (2) LP: DG 410 8471 (2,6)

Giulio Cesare: Excerpt (V'adoro pupille)

Vienna November 1946	Role of Cleopatra VPO Krips	Columbia unpublished

Psalm No 12 "Laudate pueri"

Aachen 1943	Soprano soloist Aachen Cathedral Choir Prussian State Orchestra Rehmann	78: Electrola DB 7703-4 LP: EMI EX 29 10563 LP: EMI EX 29 12363

Haydn

Die Schöpfung

Munich 1952	Soprano soloist W.Ludwig, Hotter, Bavarian Radio Chorus & Orchestra Jochum	LP: Melodram MEL 208
Berlin 1955	Soprano soloist Holm, Borg, St Hedwig's Choir BPO Markevitch	LP: DG NK 551-3/AK 561-3 LP: DG LPM 18 489-90 LP: DG 2700 105

Die Schöpfung: Excerpts (1. Nun beut die Flur; 2. Auf starkem Fittiche)

Vienna November 1946	Soprano soloist VPO Krips	78: Columbia LX 1011 (1) 78: Columbia LX 1245 (2) LP: EMI EX 29 10563 LP: EMI EX 29 12363

Hindemith

3 Geistliche Motetten

Vienna 1954	Werba, piano	78: DG LVM 72328 45: DG NL 32201 LP: Decca (USA) DL 9768

Humperdinck

Hänsel und Gretel

Vienna 1963	Role of Hänsel Rothenberger, Hoffman, Höngen, Maikl, Berry, Vienna Boys Choir VPO Cluytens	LP: Electrola E 91366-7/STE 91366-7 LP: Angel (USA) SBL 3648 Excerpts LP: Electrola 1C 063 00751

Hänsel und Gretel: Excerpts (*Suse, liebe Suse...Brüderchen, komm tanz mit mir; Abends will ich schlafen gehn; other excerpt without Seefried)

London September 1947	Role of Hänsel Schwarzkopf, Philharmonia Krips	78: Columbia LX 1036-7 LP: EMI RLS 763 *CD: EMI CDH 769 7932

Lortzing

Der Wildschütz: Excerpts (1. Auf des Lebens raschen Wogen; 2. Ihr Weib? Mein teures Weib; 3. Ich hab' Nummro Eins; 4. Was seh' ich?; other excerpts without Seefried)

Bamberg September 1965	Role of Baronin Streich, Häfliger, Böhme, Choir Bamberg SO Stepp	LP: DG SLPEM 136 428 LP: DG 2535 429 LP: DG 410 8471 (1,2)

Mahler

Symphony No 4

Salzburg August 1950	Soprano soloist VPO Walter	CD: Varèse Sarabande VCD 47228 CD: MCA Classics MCAD 42337 Also issued on LP by Varèse Sarabande
New York January 1953	Soprano soloist NYPO Walter	LP: King Records (Japan) K22C-182 CD: Music and Arts CD 656

Rheinlegendchen

Munich 1970	Werba, piano	LP: Electrola SHZE 281

Martin

Maria Tryptychon

Geneva September 1970	Soprano soloist Schneiderhan, violin Suisse Romande Orchestra Martin	CD: Jecklin JD 6452

Monteverdi

4 Madrigals: Io son pur vezzosetta pastorella; Ardo e scoprir; Baci cari; Dialogo di ninfa e pastore

London May 1955	Schwarzkopf, Moore, piano	LP: Columbia 33CX 1331 LP: EMI HLM 7267 CD: EMI CDH 769 7932

Mozart

Exsultate jubilate

New York December 1953	<u>Soprano soloist</u> NYPO Walter	CD: Stradivarius STR 10006

Mass in C minor "Great"

Würzburg June 1956	<u>Soprano soloist</u> Kupper, Borg, Fehenberger, Bavarian Radio Chorus & Orchestra Jochum	CD: Orfeo C205 891A

Requiem

Vienna December 1955	<u>Soprano soloist</u> Pitzinger, Holm, Borg, Vienna Opera Chorus VSO Jochum	LP: DG NK 504-5 LP: DG Archiv APM 14 111-2 LP: DG LPM 18 284 LP: DG 89 508 <u>NK 504-5 and APM 14111-2 also include</u> <u>the complete liturgy of the service</u> <u>in St Stephan's Cathedral at which</u> <u>this performance was recorded</u>
New York March 1956	<u>Soprano soloist</u> Tourel, Simoneau, Warfield, Westminster Choir NYPO Walter	LP: Columbia (USA) ML 5012 LP: Columbia (USA) Y 34619 LP: CBS M3P 39651 CD: CBS MPK 45556

Concert Arias: Chi sà, chi sà, qual sia; Vado, ma dove?

London September 1953	London Mozart Players Blech	78: Columbia LX 1596 LP: EMI EX 29 10563 LP: EMI EX 29 12363

Così fan tutte

Berlin December 1962	<u>Role of Fiordiligi</u> Merriman, Köth, Häfliger, Prey, Fischer-Dieskau, RIAS Choir BPO Jochum	LP: DG LPM 18 861-3/SLPM 138 861-3 LP: DG 2728 010 Excerpts LP: DG LPM 18 792/SLPM 138 792 LP: DG LPEM 19 477/SLPEM 136 477 LP: DG 2535 746 LP: DG 410 8471

Così fan tutte: Excerpts (Come scoglio; Per pietà)

Vienna September 1953	<u>Role of Fiordiligi</u> VSO Leitner	LP: DG 410 8471

Don Giovanni

Salzburg July-August 1950	Role of Zerlina Schwarzkopf, Welitsch, Dermota, Gobbi, Greindl, Kunz, Poell, Vienna Opera Chorus VPO Furtwängler	LP: Ed Smith EJS 419 LP: Olympic 9109 LP: Discocorp RR 407 LP: Turnabout THS 65154-6 LP: Melodram MEL 713 CD: Priceless D 16581 CD: Laudis LCD 34001 Part of side 3 of Olympic edition derives from a Furtwängler performance with Erna Berger as Zerlina
Berlin September and October 1958	Role of Zerlina Stader, Jurinac, Fischer-Dieskau, Häfliger, Sardi, Kreppel, RIAS Choir and Orchestra Fricsay	LP: DG LPM 18 580-2/SLPM 138 050-2 LP: DG 2728 003 LP: DG 2730 014 Excerpts LP: DG LPEM 19 224/SLPEM 136 204 LP: DG LPEM 19 477/SLPEM 136 477 LP: DG 2535 746 LP: DG 410 8471

Don Giovanni: Excerpts (1. La ci darem la mano; 2. Batti, batti)

Vienna December 1947	Role of Zerlina Kunz (1), VPO Karajan	78: Columbia LB 76 (2) LP: EMI RLS 764 LP: EMI EX 29 12363

Don Giovanni: Excerpt (La ci darem la mano)

Vienna November 1955	Role of Zerlina London, VPO Böhm Sung in German	LP: Amadeo 412 8211 CD: GDS Records GDS 2204

Idomeneo: Excerpt (Non temer, amato bene)

Vienna September 1953	Role of Ilia VSO Leitner	78: DG LVM 72351 LP: DG NK 558-9 LP: Decca (USA) DL 9768 45: DG EPL 30045

Il Rè Pastore: Excerpt (L'amerò sarò costante)

Vienna September 1953	Role of Aminta VSO Leitner	78: DG LVM 72351 LP: Decca (USA) DL 9768 45: DG EPL 30045 LP: DG 410 8471

SALZBURGER FESTSPIELE 1957

DIE HOCHZEIT DES FIGARO

(IN ITALIENISCHER SPRACHE)

KOMISCHE OPER IN VIER AKTEN NACH BEAUMARCHAIS
VON LORENZO DA PONTE

MUSIK VON
WOLFGANG AMADEUS MOZART

DIRIGENT:
KARL BÖHM

INSZENIERUNG:
GÜNTHER RENNERT

BÜHNENBILD UND KOSTÜME:
ITA MAXIMOWNA

ORCHESTER:
DIE WIENER PHILHARMONIKER
CHOR DER WIENER STAATSOPER

DIE HOCHZEIT DES FIGARO

(In italienischer Sprache)

Komische Oper in vier Akten nach Beaumarchais
von Lorenzo da Ponte

MUSIK VON WOLFGANG AMADEUS MOZART

Graf Almaviva	Dietrich Fischer-Dieskau
Gräfin Almaviva	Elisabeth Schwarzkopf
Susanne, Kammerjungfer der Gräfin	Irmgard Seefried
Figaro, Kammerdiener des Grafen	Erich Kunz
Basilio, Musikmeister	Murray Dickie
Dr. Bartolo, Arzt	Georg Stern
Marcellina	Sieglinde Wagner
Cherubin, Page des Grafen	Christa Ludwig
Antonio, Gärtner, Susannens Oheim	Alois Pernerstorfer
Barbarina, dessen Tochter	Anny Felbermayer
Don Curzio, Richter	Erich Majkut
Erste Brautjungfer	Elfriede Pfleger
Zweite Brautjungfer	Anneliese Fleischmann

Bauern und Bäuerinnen vom Landgut des Grafen

Ballett: Dietlinde Klemisch, Edith Philipp, Karin Wittek,
Wilfried Fränzl, Ludwig Mikura, Konstantin Zajetz

Ort der Handlung: Das Schloß d'Aguas Frescas, drei Stunden
von Sevilla gelegen

Zeit: Achtzehntes Jahrhundert

Nach dem zweiten Akt eine größere Pause

Der offizielle Almanach „Salzburg — Festspiele 1957" ist auch für Sie der unentbehrliche Ratgeber
The official almanac "Salzburg Festivals 1957" is an indispensable guide for all Festival visitors
L'almanach officiel «Salzbourg Festival 1957» est indispensable à tous ceux qui s'intéressent au Festival

Le Nozze di Figaro

Vienna June and October 1950	Role of Susanna Schwarzkopf, Kunz, Jurinac, London, Vienna Opera Chorus VPO Karajan	78: Columbia LWX 410-425 LP: Columbia 33CX 1007-9 LP: Electrola 1C 197 54200-8M CD: EMI CMS 769 6392 Excerpts LP: Columbia 33CX 1558 LP: EMI RLS 764 LP: EMI EX 29 10563	
Salzburg August 1953	Role of Susanna Schwarzkopf, Kunz, Güden, Wagner, Schöffler, Vienna Opera Chorus VPO Furtwängler Sung in German	LP: Ed Smith GMR 999 LP: Discocorp IGI 343 LP: Fonit Cetra LO 8 LP: Fonit Cetra FE 27 CD: Rodolphe RPC 32527-30	
Milan February 1954	Role of Susanna Schwarzkopf, Petri, Jurinac, Panerai, La Scala Chorus and Orchestra Karajan	LP: Fonit Cetra LO 70 CD: Hunt CDKAR 225 CD: Melodram MEL 37075 Excerpts LP: Gioielli della lirica GML 30	
Salzburg July 1957	Role of Susanna Schwarzkopf, Kunz, Ludwig, Wagner, Fischer-Dieskau, Vienna Opera Chorus VPO Böhm	LP: Melodram MEL 709 CD: Di Stefano GDS 31019	
Berlin September 1960	Role of Susanna Stader, Töpper, Capecchi, Fischer-Dieskau, RIAS Choir and Orchestra Fricsay	LP: DG LPM 18 697-9/SLPM 138697-9 LP: DG 2728 004 LP: DG 2730 014 Excerpts LP: DG LPEM 19 272/SLPEM 136 272 LP: DG LPEM 19 477/SLPEM 136 477 LP: DG 2535 746 LP: DG 410 8471	

Le Nozze di Figaro: Excerpts (1. Avanti, avanti, signor uffiziale; 2. Signore, di fuori son già suonatori)

Milan January 1949	Role of Susanna Cebotari, Jurinac, Höfermayer, Taddei, VPO Karajan	LP: Melodram MEL 089 (1) LP: Melodram MEL 087 (2)

Le Nozze di Figaro: Excerpt (Ah! La cieca gelosia)

Milan December 1948	Role of Susanna Schwarzkopf, Höfermayer, VPO Karajan	LP: Melodram MEL 088

Le Nozze di Figaro: Excerpt (Deh vieni, non tardar)

Vienna November 1946	Role of Susanna VPO Krips Without recitative	Columbia unpublished
London September 1947	Role of Susanna Philharmonia Krips	Columbia unpublished
Vienna December 1947	Role of Susanna VPO Karajan	78: Columbia LX 1145 LP: EMI RLS 764 LP: EMI EX 29 12363

Le Nozze di Figaro: Excerpt (Voi che sapete)

Vienna December 1947	Role of Cherubino VPO Karajan	78: Columbia LB 76 LP: EMI RLS 764 LP: EMI EX 29 12363

Zaide: Excerpt (Ruhe sanft, mein holdes Leben)

London September 1953	Role of Zaide London Mozart Players Blech	LP: EMI EX 29 05983 LP: EMI EX 29 10563 LP: EMI EX 29 12363

Die Zauberflöte

Salzburg July 1949	Role of Pamina Lipp, Oravez, W.Ludwig, Greindl, Sohmitt-Walter, Schöffler, Vienna Opera Chorus VPO Furtwängler	LP: Ed Smith EJS 572 LP: Discocorp IGI 337
Vienna November 1950	Role of Pamina Lipp, Loose, Jurinac, Dermota, Kunz, Weber, London, Vienna Singverein VPO Karajan	78: Columbia (Austria) LWX 426-444 LP: Columbia 33CX 1013-5 LP: EMI SLS 5052 LP: Electrola 1C 197 54200-8M CD: EMI CMS 769 6312 Excerpts LP: Columbia 33CX 1572 LP: EMI RLS 764 LP: EMI EX 29 10563
Salzburg August 1951	Role of Pamina Lipp, Oravez, Dermota, Kunz, Greindl, Schöffler, Vienna Opera Chorus VPO Furtwängler	LP: Fonit Cetra LO 9 LP: Foyer FO 1028 LP: Fonit Cetra FE 19 CD: Foyer 3CF-2008 CD: Priceless D 16603 CD: Rodolphe RPC 32527-30

Die Zauberflöte: Excerpt (Ach, ich fühl's)

London September 1947	Role of Pamina Philharmonia Krips	78: Columbia LX 1145 LP: EMI EX 29 12363 EX 29 12363 incorrectly states orchestra to be VPO

Lieder: 1. Die Zufriedenheit; 2. Warnung; 3. Der Zauberer; 4. Das kinderspiel; 5. Das Veilchen; 6. Abendempfindung; 7. Sehnsucht nach dem Frühlinge; 8. Ridente la calma; 9. An Chloe; 10. Als Luise die Briefe; 11. Das Traumbild; 12. Die kleine Spinnerin; 13. Einsam ging ich jüngst

London November 1950	Moore, piano	78: Columbia LX 1543 (1,2,3,4) 78: Columbia LX 1549 (5,6,7) 78: Columbia LB 116 (8,9) 78: Columbia LB 114 (10,11) 78: Columbia LB 108 (12,13) LP: EMI EX 29 10563 LP: EMI EX 29 12363

Lieder: An Chloe; Das Lied der Trennung; Das Kinderspiel; Die Verschweigung; Abendempfindung; Die kleine Spinnerin; Als Luise die Briefe; Einsam ging ich jüngst; Sehnsucht nach dem Frühlinge

Vienna October 1957	Werba, piano	LP: DG LPEM 19 112 LP: DG 410 8471

Das Veilchen

Vienna October 1957	Werba, piano	LP: DG LPEM 19 115 LP: DG 410 8471

Lieder: An Chloe; Abendempfindung; Das Lied der Trennung; Als Luise die Briefe; Warnung

Vienna 1965	Klien, piano	LP: Concert Hall SMSC 2382 LP: Pearl SHE 556-7

Mussorgsky

The Nursery, Song cycle

1953	Werba, piano Sung in German	LP: DG LPEM 19 050 45: DG EPL 30348 LP: DG 410 8471

Reger

Mariä Wiegenlied

Vienna September 1953	Schneiderhan, violin Werba, piano	78: DG L 62893 45: DG NL 32142 LP: Decca (USA) DL 7545
Munich 1970	Schneiderhan, violin Bavarian State Orchestra Heger	LP: Electrola SHZE 281

Respighi

Il Tramonto

Lucerne August 1959	Soprano soloist Lucerne Festival Strings Baumgartner	LP: DG LPM 18 606/SLPM 138 086 LP: DG 410 8471

Rossini

Stabat Mater

Salzburg August 1949	Soprano soloist Anday, Frantz, Fehenberger, Salzburg Cathedral Choir Mozarteum Chorus and Orchestra Messner	LP: Remington R 199 111-2

Schubert

Auf dem Wasser zu singen

Vienna October 1946	Schmidt, piano	Columbia unpublished
Vienna December 1947	Nordberg, piano	Columbia unpublished

Du bist die Ruh'

Vienna October 1946	Schmidt, piano	LP: EMI EX 29 10563 LP: EMI EX 29 12363

Fischerweise

Munich 1970	Werba, piano	LP: Electrola SHZE 281

4 Gretchenlieder: *Der König in Thule; Gretchen am Spinnrade; Gretchens Bitte; Wie anders, Gretchen (Szene aus Faust)

Vienna February 1962	Werba, piano	LP: DG LPEM 19 372/SLPEM 136 372 *LP: DG 410 0471
Vienna 1968	Werba, piano	LP: Concert Hall LP: Pearl SHE 556-7 CD: Adès 13.2272

Nacht und Träume

Vienna November 1946	Schmidt, piano	Columbia unpublished

Lieder: Auf dem Wasser zu singen; Lachen und Weinen

1953	Werba, piano	LP: DG LPEM 19 050 LP: DG 410 8471

Lieder: Ave Maria; Romanze aus Rosamunde; Seligkeit

Vienna 1954	Werba, piano	78: DG LV 36109 45: DG EPL 30128 LP: Decca (USA) DL 9545

UNDER THE PATRONAGE OF HER MAJESTY THE QUEEN
AND HER MAJESTY QUEEN ELIZABETH THE QUEEN MOTHER

Edinburgh International Festival

*In association with the Scottish Committee of
the Arts Council of Great Britain, the British Council
and the Corporation of the City of Edinburgh*

USHER HALL
Saturday, 5th September 1959, at 8 p.m.

Recital

IRMGARD SEEFRIED (*soprano*)

ERIK WERBA (*pianoforte*)

SALZBURGER FESTSPIELE 1958

VIERTER LIEDERABEND

IRMGARD SEEFRIED

DIETRICH FISCHER-DIESKAU

ERIK WERBA
KLAVIER

Lieder: Die Forelle; Auf dem Wasser zu singen; Der Fischer

Vienna	Klien, piano	LP: Concert Hall SMSC 2382
1965		LP: Pearl SHE 556-7

Lieder: Im Frühling; Litanei; Auf dem Wasser zu singen; Ave Maria; Die Liebe hat gelogen; *Fischerweise; *Die junge Nonne; 4 Mignon Lieder; Wiegenlied; *Seligkeit; Lachen und Weinen; *Das Lied im Grünen; *Die Forelle; Liebhaber in allen Gestalten; *An die Musik

Vienna	Werba, piano	LP: DG LPEM 19 164/SLPEM 136 009
June 1958		*LP: DG 410 8471

Lieder: Ganymed; Schäfers Klagelied; Wanderers Nachtlied; Liebhaber in allen Gestalten; Im Frühling; Fischerweise; Widerschein; Der Wanderer an den Mond; Der Tod und das Mädchen; Der Jüngling und der Tod; Das Lied im Grünen; Seligkeit

Vienna	Werba, piano	LP: Pearl SHE 556-7
1968		CD: Adès 13.2272
		Also issued on LP by Concert Hall

Lieder: 1. Nacht und Träume; 2. Auf dem Wasser zu singen

London	Moore, piano	78: Columbia LB 106
April 1948		LP: EMI RLS 766 (2)
		LP: EMI EX 29 10563 (1)
		LP: EMI EX 29 12363

Lieder: 1. Wiegenlied; 2. Heidenröslein

Vienna	Nordberg, piano	78: Columbia LB 78
December 1947		45: Columbia SCD 2158
		LP: EMI RLS 766 (2)
		LP: EMI EX 29 10563 (1)
		LP: EMI EX 29 12363

Lieder to poems by Goethe: Suleika I & II; Heidenröslein; Der König in Thule; Ganymed; Gretchen am Spinnrade

Vienna	Werba, piano	LP: DG LPEM 19 115
October 1957		

Schumann

Frauenliebe und -Leben

Vienna October 1957	Werba, piano	LP: DG LPEM 19 112 LP: DG 410 8471
Vienna 1965	Klien, piano	LP: Concert Hall SMSC 2382 LP: Pearl SHE 556-7

Gedichte der Maria Stuart: Abschied von Frankreich; Nach der Geburt ihres Sohnes; An die Königin Elisabeth; Abschied von der Welt; Gebet

Vienna February 1962	Werba, piano	LP: DG LPEM 19 372/SLPEM 136 372

Lied der Suleika

Vienna October 1957	Werba, piano	LP: DG LPEM 19 115

Lieder to poems by Heine: 1. Die Lotosblume; 2. Was will die einsame Träne; 3. Du bist wie eine Blume; 4. Der Hans und die Grete; 5. In meiner Brust; 6. Der arme Peter; 7. Dein Angesicht; 8. Anfang wollt' ich fast verzagen; 9. Es fiel ein Reif; 10. Mit Myrthen und Rosen; interspersed with other Heine poems read by Oskar Werner

Düsseldorf April 1956	Werner, reciter Werba, piano	LP: DG LPEM 19 067 EP: DG EPL 30324 (1,2,4,5,6,7,8) LP: DG 410 8471 (1,3,10) CD: Amadeo 423 7662

Richard Strauss

Ariadne auf Naxos

Vienna June 1944	Role of Composer Reining, Noni, Lorenz, Kunz, Schöffler, VPO Böhm	LP: DG LPM 18 850-2 LP: Acanta DE 23.309-10 Excerpts LP: DG LPEM 19 477/SLPEM 136 477 LP: DG 2535 746 LP: Acanta DE 23.280-1
London June and July 1954	Role of Composer Schwarzkopf, Streich, Schock, Prey, Dönch, Philharmonia Karajan	LP: Columbia 33CX 1292-4 LP: EMI RLS 760 CD: EMI CMS 769 2962
Salzburg August 1954	Role of Composer Della Casa, Güden, Schock, Poell, Schöffler, VPO Böhm	LP: Melodram MEL 104

Der Rosenkavalier

Dresden December 1958	Role of Octavian Schech, Streich, Böhme, Francl, Fischer-Dieskau, Dresden Opera Chorus and Staatskapelle Böhm	LP: DG LPM 18 570-3/SLPM 138 040-3 LP: DG 2711 001 LP: DG 2721 162 Excerpts LP: DG LPM 18 656/SLPM 138 656 LP: DG LPEM 19 410/SLPEM 136 410 45: DG EPL 30644 LP: DG LPEM 19 477/SLPEM 136 477 LP: DG 2535 746 LP: DG 2537 013 LP: DG 410 8471

Der Rosenkavalier: Excerpt (Mir ist die Ehre widerfahren)

Vienna December 1947	Role of Octavian Schwarzkopf, VPO Karajan	78: Columbia LX 1225-6 LP: Columbia (USA) ML 2126 LP: World Records SH 286 LP: EMI RLS 763 LP: EMI RLS 154 6133 LP: EMI RLS 7714 CD: EMI CDH 769 7932

Lieder: *Morgen; Die Nacht; Du meines Herzens Krönelein; *Allerseelen; Die Georgine; *Meinem Kinde; *Traum durch die Dämmerung; Ständchen

Vienna February 1958	Werba, piano	LP: DG LPEM 19 165/SLPEM 136 010 LP: DG 2548 062 *LP: DG 410 8471

Lieder: Schlechtes Wetter; Wiegenlied

Vienna February 1958	Werba, piano	45: DG EPL 30402

Morgen

Munich 1970	Schneiderhan, violin Bavarian State Orchestra Heger	LP: Electrola SHZE 281

Ständchen

1953	Werba, piano	LP: DG LPEM 19 050 LP: DG 410 8471

Wiegenlied

Munich 1970	Werba, piano	LP: Electrola SHZE 281

Programme

Northern Sinfonia Orchestra
Leader Jack Rothstein

Soloist **Irmgard Seefried**

Soloist/director **Wolfgang Schneiderhan**

Mozart
Adagio in E for violin and orchestra, K 261

Hindemith
Die junge Magd, Op 23, No 2

Bach
Violin concerto in E, BWV 1042

Interval

Vaughan Williams
Four Housman poems for voice and violin

Mozart
Violin concerto in A, K 219

The Northern Sinfonia is in association with
The Arts Council of Great Britain and Northern Arts

Concert in the Queen Elizabeth Hall London 1972

STAATSOPER

Freitag, den 31. März 1967
Im Abonnement VI. Gruppe. Sehr beschr. Kartenverkauf
Preise III

Die verkaufte Braut

Komische Oper in drei Akten
Text von K. Sabina
In der deutschen Übersetzung von Kurt Honolka
Musik von Friedrich Smetana

Dirigent: Berislav Klobučar
Nach einer Inszenierung von Günther Rennert
Bühnenbilder und Kostüme: Leni Bauer-Eczy
Spielleitung: Richard Bletschacher
Einstudierung der Chöre: Richard Rossmayer

Krušina, ein Bauer	Hans Braun
Ludmila, seine Frau	Hilde Konetzni
Marie, beider Tochter	Irmgard Seefried
Micha, Grundbesitzer	Herbert Lackner
Háta, seine Frau	Hilde Rössel-Majdan
Wenzel, beider Sohn	Murray Dickie
Hans, Michas Sohn aus erster Ehe	Ivo Zidek
Kecal, Heiratsvermittler	Oskar Czerwenka
Direktor einer wandernden Künstlertruppe	Erich Kunz
Esmeralda, Tänzerin	Olivera Miljakovic
Muff, ein als Indianer verkleideter Komödiant	Hans Christian

Dorfbewohner — Ort: ein Dorf in Böhmen

Balletteinlagen von Dimitrije Parlic

1. Akt: **P o l k a** : Mädchen: Bach, Coronica, Fränzl El., Gerber, Kozna, Loucky, Stanek, Wittek; Burschen: Dirtl Gerh., Falusy, Haderer, Kastelik, Liederer, Mallek, Minder, Wilhelm
2. Akt: **F u r i a n t** : Mädchen: Dietlinde Klemisch, Erika Zlocha; Burschen: Arnold Jandosch, Herbert Nitsch, Günther Falusy
3. Akt: **Z i r k u s** : Clowns: Dirtl G., Nitsch, Wilhelm, Zajetz; Tänzerin: Haider; Schlange: Lasser; Partner: Hiess; Ringer: Meister, Minder; Frau mit Schlange: Kirnbauer; Frau des Zirkusdirektors: Barteis; Pferdchen: Hauk, Himmelbauer, Wiedermann, Wittek; Jongleur: Stefan Taft

Technische Einrichtung: Hans Felkel — Beleuchtung: Albin Rotter

Nach dem ersten und zweiten Akt eine größere Pause

Anfang 19.30 Uhr   Ende 22.30 Uhr

Preis des Programms S 8,—

Thomas

Mignon: Excerpts(Kennst du das Land?; Ihr Schwalben in den Lüften; *Kam ein armes Kind von fern; *Sie ist da!

Paris November 1963	Role of Mignon Gayer, Häfliger, Engen, Lamoureux Orchestra Fournet Sung in German	LP: DG LPEM 19 418/SLPEM 136 418 *LP: DG 410 8471

Wagner

Die Meistersinger von Nürnberg

Vienna November 1955	Role of Eva Beirer, Schöffler, Anday, Dickie, Frick, Kunz Vienna Opera Chorus VPO Reiner	CD: Melodram CDM 47083

Weber

Der Freischütz

Munich December 1959	Role of Agathe Streich, Holm, Böhme, Wächter, Kreppel, Bavarian Radio Chorus & Orchestra Jochum	LP: DG LPM 18 639-40/SLPM 138 639-40 LP: DG 2707 009 LP: DG 2726 061 Excerpts LP: DG LPEM 19 221/SLPEM 136 221 LP: DG LPEM 19 447/SLPEM 136 477 LP: DG 2535 746 LP: DG 410 8471 CD: DG 423 8692

Wolf

Das verlassene Mägdlein

Vienna November 1946	Schmidt, piano	LP: EMI EX 29 10563 LP: EMI EX 29 12363

Elfenlied

Vienna November 1946	Schmidt, piano	Columbia unpublished

Lieder: Elfenlied; Mausfallensprüchlein

Vienna December 1947	Nordberg, piano	Columbia unpublished
London April 1948	Moore, piano	LP: EMI EX 29 10563 LP: EMI EX 29 12363 LP: EMI EX 769 7411

Schlafendes Jesuskind

Vienna 1953	Werba, piano	78: DG L 62893 45: DG NL 32142 LP: Decca (USA) DL 9545

Lieder: An eine Aeolsharfe; Das verlassene Mägdlein; Begegnung

1953	Werba, piano	LP: DG LPEM 19 050 LP: DG 410 8471

Lieder: Nimmersatte Liebe; Denk es, o Seele

Vienna 1953	Werba, piano	78: DG L 62899 45: DG EPL 30010

Italienisches Liederbuch (complete)

Salzburg August 1958	Fischer-Dieskau Werba, piano	CD: Orfeo C220 901A
Vienna 1959	Fischer-Dieskau Werba, piano Demus, piano	LP: DG LPM 18 568-9/SLPM 138 035-6

Italienisches Liederbuch: Selection (Auch kleine Dinge; Mir ward gesagt; Wer rief dich denn?; Du denst, mit einem Fädchen; Wie lange schon; Nein, junger Herr; Mein Liebster ist so klein; Ihr jungen Leute; Wir haben beide; Mein Liebster singt; Man sagt mir; Mein Liebster hat zu Tische; Du sagst mir, dass ich keine Fürstin sei; Wohl kenn' ich euren Stand; Was soll der Zorn?; Wenn du, mein Liebster, steigst; Gesegnet sei das Grün; O wär dein Haus; Heut' Nacht erhob ich mich; Schweig' einmal still; Verschling' der Abgrund; Ich hab' in Penna

Vienna 1953	Werba, piano	LP: DG LPM 18 192

Spanisches Liederbuch: Selection (Die ihr schwebt um diese Palmen; Ach, des Knaben Augen; Mühvoll komm' ich; Bedeckt mich mit Blumen; In dem Schatten meiner Locken; Geh, Geliebter; Sie blasen zum Abmarsch; Sagt, seid ihr es?; Mögen alle bösen Zungen; Wunden trägst du, Herr (duet); Herr, was trägt der Boden hier (duet); other Lieder sung by Wächter)

Vienna 1960	Wächter Werba, piano	LP: DG LPM 18 591/SLPM 138 059

Lieder to poems by Goethe: Anakreons Grab; Blumengruss; Die Bekehrte; Frühling übers Jahr

Vienna October 1957	Werba, piano	LP: DG LPEM 19 115

3 Mignon-Lieder

Vienna October 1957	Werba, piano	LP: DG LPEM 19 115
Vienna 1965	Klien, piano	LP: Concert Hall SMSC 2382 LP: Pearl SHE 556-7

Lieder to poems by Mörike: Verborgenheit; Ein Stündlein wohl vor Tag; Nimmersatte Liebe; In der Frühe; Agnes; Frage und Antwort; Das verlassene Mägdlein; Gebet; Denk' es, o Seele; Auf ein altes Bild; interspersed with other Mörike poems read by Oskar Werner

Vienna 1959	Werner, reciter Werba, piano	LP: DG LPEM 19 200/SLPEM 136 034 CD: Amadeo 423 7662

Collections

Irmgard Seefried: Erzähltes Leben (The singer talks about her life and career, with musical examples)

1958   Spoken in German   LP: DG LPM 18 729

Nacht voller Wunder: Irmgard Seefried sings and narrates Christmas stories (Nacht voller Wunder; O Tannenbaum; Es hat sich halt eröffnet; Vom Himmel hoch; Kommt, Ihr Hirten; Zu Bethlehem geboren; Heiligste Nacht; Aber Heidschi Bubeidschi; Kling, Glöckchen, kling; Still, still, still; Kindelein zart; In dulci jubilo)

Vienna   Scheit, guitar   LP: Preiser SPR 9955
December 1970

Irmgard Seefried: roles performed with the Vienna State Opera

Includes performances with the Vienna company on tour
Figure against each role indicates number of times the part was performed

57	Antonia/Stella (The Tales of Hoffmann)
9	Baroness (Der Wildschütz)
14	Blanche (The Carmelites)
8	Butterfly (Madama Butterfly)
8	Cleopatra (Giulio Cesare)
6	Countess Almaviva (Le Nozze di Figaro)
37	Composer (Ariadne auf Naxos)
6	Dido (Dido and Aeneas)
29	Eva (Die Meistersinger von Nürnberg)
88	Fiordiligi (Così fan tutte)
3	Giulietta (The Tales of Hoffmann)
1	Kabanicha (Katya Kabanova)
6	Lady (Cardillac)
11	Liu (Turandot)
33	Marie (The Bartered Bride)
2	Marie (Wozzeck)
53	Marzelline (Fidelio)
7	Micaela (Carmen)
16	Musetta (La Bohème)
37	Octavian (Der Rosenkavalier)
2	Olympia (The Tales of Hoffmann)
57	Pamina (Die Zauberflöte)
2	Poppea (L'incoronazione di Poppea)
126	Susanna (Le Nozze di Figaro)
60	Zerlina (Don Giovanni)

Elisabeth Grümmer
Discography

Compiled by John Hunt
1991

Introduction

The most vivid memory of my first visit to the Bayreuth Festival, apart from Wieland Wagner's beautiful production of "Die Meistersinger von Nürnberg", was of the singer of the role of Eva. Elisabeth Grümmer put her pure but mature-sounding lyric soprano voice at the service of Wagner to offer a most winning impersonation of his most endearing and loveable female creation. Grümmer obviously had no difficulty in floating above the Wagner orchestra, but wisely refrained in her career from venturing into the more heroic parts.

Of another Wagner role in her repertoire, I was lucky enough to experience her Elsa in "Lohengrin" when the Hamburg State Opera visited London in 1962. In the admittedly small Sadlers Wells Theatre the Act II encounter between Grümmer's assured Elsa and the Ortrud of the great Astrid Varnay made the most telling impact. It was the only occasion on which I heard an audience burst into cheering and applause in the middle of a Wagner act - to express approval, that is.

When Elisabeth Grümmer came onto the platform for an early-evening Lieder recital organised by the BBC in 1967, she carried an elegant black handbag which was placed on the piano, suggesting almost a business-like approach to her art. Yet there was nothing matter-of-fact about her enraptured delivery of songs by Brahms and Schumann. And her single commercially recorded Lieder recital, accompanied by Gerald Moore, must be a rare gem in many collections, combining directness and commitment with the most feminine purity of line.

Although contracted as an EMI recording artist, it does appear that Grümmer was unfairly neglected by head office in London, many of her operatic excerpt and oratorio performances on record being restricted to the local German market. This was quite unjustified, bearing in mind her contributions to Bach cantatas or her joyous affirmation in the soprano part of Haydn's "Creation".

Impeccable diction, never sacrificed to pure effect or point-making, may have come from her early experience as a theatre actress. It was in Aachen, just before the war, that Herbert von Karajan urged her to put her musical training to practical use by joining his company of singers - another young beginner in that particular company was to be Irmgard Seefried.

Grümmer became an honoured member of the Deutsche Oper Berlin, and among the tapes circulating of her performances there, her Marschallin in "Rosenkavalier" deserves to be issued. From earlier in the 1950s one can hope for issues from broadcasts in which she sang Micaela ("Carmen") and Euridice ("Orfeo ed Euridice").

John Hunt

Bach

Saint Matthew Passion

Vienna April 1954	Soprano soloist Höffgen, Dermota, Fischer-Dieskau, Edelmann, Singakademie VPO Furtwängler	LP: Fonit Cetra LO 508 LP: Movimento Musica 03.008 LP: Fonit Cetra FE 34 CD: Movimento Musica 013.005

Saint John Passion

Berlin 1962	Soprano soloist Ludwig, Traxel, Wunderlich, Kohn, Fischer-Dieskau, St Hedwig's Choir Berlin SO Forster	LP: HMV ALP 1975-7/ASD 526-8 LP: Seraphim SIC 6036 LP: Electrola 1C 147 28589-91 Excerpts: LP: Electrola E/STE 80727 LP: EMI EX 29 12103

Cantata No 11 "Lobet Gott in seinen Reichen"

Leipzig 1960	Soprano soloist Höffgen, Rotzsch, Adam, Thomanerchor Leipzig GO Thomas	LP: Electrola E/STE 60659 LP: HMV ALP 1828

Cantata No 68 "Also hat Gott die Welt geliebt"

Leipzig 1960	Soprano soloist Adam, Thomanerchor Leipzig GO Thomas	LP: Electrola E/STE 80609 Excerpt (Mein gläubiges Herze) LP: Electrola E 70418

Cantata No 111 "Was mein Gott will, das gescheh' allzeit"

Leipzig 1960	Soprano soloist Höffgen, Rotzsch, Adam, Thomanerchor Leipzig GO Thomas	LP: Electrola E/STE 80609

Cantata No 140 "Wachet auf! Ruft uns die Stimme"

Leipzig 1960	Soprano soloist Höffgen, Rotzsch, Adam, Thomanerchor Leipzig GO Thomas	LP: Electrola E/STE 60658 LP: HMV ALP 1828

Beethoven

Symphony No 9 "Choral"

Berlin April 1957	Soprano soloist Höffgen, Häfliger, Frick, St Hedwig's Choir BPO Karajan	LP: Maestri del secolo APE 1209 LP: Movimento Musica 08.001 LP: Replica SRPL 22400 LP: WG Records WG 30009 CD: Artemis CD 710 001

Brahms

Ein deutsches Requiem

Berlin June 1955	Soprano soloist Fischer-Dieskau, St Hedwig's Choir BPO Kempe	LP: HMV ALP 1351-2 LP: HMV XLP 30073-4 LP: Electrola 1C 147 28550-1 Soprano solo only: LP: Electrola E 70418 LP: EMI EX 29 12103
Cologne February 1956	Soprano soloist Prey, WDR Chorus and Orchestra Klemperer	CD: Hunt CD 716

Lieder: 1. Regenlied; 2. Das Mädchen; 3. Geheimnis; 4. Mädchenlied; 5. Wiegenlied

Berlin November 1958	Moore, piano	LP: Electrola E/STE 80437 LP: Electrola 1C 047 29126 LP: EMI EX 29 12103 (2,3,4)

Gounod

Faust: Excerpt (Es war ein König in Thule)

Berlin May 1953	Role of Mararethe Berlin SO Schüchter Sung in German	78: Electrola EH 1434 LP: EMI EX 29 12103* CD: EMI CDM 763 1372

Faust: Excerpt (Valentin's prayer and death)

Berlin 1955	Role of Margarethe Prey, Hildebrand Sung in German	45: Columbia (Germany) C 41007

Grieg

Peer Gynt: Excerpts (Der Winter mag scheiden; Schlaf, du teuerster Knabe mein)

Berlin March 1953	Berlin SO Dietz	78: Electrola EH 1436 LP: EMI EX 29 12103*

Haydn

Die Schöpfung

Berlin January 1960	Soprano soloist Traxel, Frick, St Hedwig's Choir Berlin SO Forster	LP: HMV ALP 1834-6/ASD 409-11 LP: Electrola 1C 147 29144-5 CD: EMI CZS 762 5952 Excerpts LP: Electrola E 70418 LP: Electrola SME 80839 LP: EMI EX 29 12103

Humperdinck

Hänsel und Gretel

London June and July 1953	Role of Hänsel Schwarzkopf, Ilosvay, Schürhoff, Metternich, Choirs Philharmonia Karajan	LP: Columbia 33CX 1096-7 LP: World Records OC 187-8 LP: EMI SLS 5145 CD: EMI CMS 769 2932 Excerpts: LP: Columbia 33CX 1819 LP: World Records OH 189 LP: Electrola 1C 047 28553

Grümmer

MONDAY 3 APRIL 1967
AT 5.45

Queen Elizabeth Hall
GENERAL MANAGER: JOHN DENISON, C.B.E.

BBC MUSIC PROGRAMME PRESENTS

Elisabeth Grümmer (SOPRANO)
Aribert Reimann (PIANO)

Mozart   Das Veilchen
Im Frühlingsanfang
Abendempfindung

Schumann   Frauenliebe und -Leben

Pfitzner   Ich hör' ein Vöglein locken

Brahms   Wie Melodien zieht es mir
Die Mainacht
Der Tod, das ist die kühle Nacht
Wir wandelten, wir zwei zusammen

BERLINER PHILHARMONISCHES ORCHESTER

KONZERTSAAL DER HOCHSCHULE FÜR MUSIK

DONNERSTAG, DEN 25. APRIL 1957, 20 UHR
FREITAG,   DEN 26. APRIL 1957, 20 UHR

FESTKONZERT
aus Anlaß des
75 jährigen Bestehens unseres Orchesters

DIRIGENT
HERBERT VON KARAJAN

SOLISTEN

ELISABETH GRÜMMER, Sopran; MARGA HÖFFGEN, Alt
ERNST HAEFLIGER, Tenor; GOTTLOB FRICK, Baß
DER CHOR DER ST.-HEDWIGS-KATHEDRALE
Leitung: KARL FORSTER

L. V. BEETHOVEN · SYMPHONIE NR. IX D-MOLL OP. 125

ALLEGRO MA NON TROPPO, UN POCO MAESTOSO
MOLTO VIVACE
ADAGIO MOLTO E CANTABILE
FINALE

Mozart

Requiem

Berlin March 1951	Soprano soloist Pitzinger, Krebs, Hotter, St Hedwig's Choir RIAS Choir and Orchestra Fricsay	LP: DG 2535 713
Berlin 1955	Soprano soloist Höffgen, Krebs, Frick. St Hedwig's Choir BPO Kempe	LP: HMV ALP 1444 LP: Electrola 1C 047 00128M

Così fan tutte: Excerpt (Come scoglio)

Berlin 1953	Role of Fiordiligi Berlin RO Rother	LP: Melodram MEL 083
Berlin December 1955	Role of Fiordiligi Berlin SO Schüchter	78: Electrola DB 11596 LP: EMI EX 29 05983 LP: EMI EX 29 12103 CD: EMI CDM 763 1372

Idomeneo

Salzburg July 1961	Role of Electra Lorengar, Kmennt, Häfliger, Capecchi, Wächter, Vienna Opera Chorus VPO Fricsay	LP: Melodram MEL 701

Don Giovanni

Salzburg
July 1953

Role of Donna Anna
Schwarzkopf,
Berger, Dermota,
Siepi, Edelmann,
Arié, Berry,
Vienna Opera Chorus
VPO
Furtwängler

CD: Rodolphe RPC 32527-30
CD: Virtuoso 269.9052

Salzburg
August 1954

Role of Donna Anna
Schwarzkopf,
Berger, Dermota,
Siepi, Edelmann,
Ernster, Berry,
Vienna Opera Chorus
VPO
Furtwängler

LP: Morgan MOR 5302
LP: Discocorp MORG 003
LP: Fonit Cetra LO 7
LP: Foyer FO 1017
LP: Fonit Cetra FE 23
LP: EMI EX 29 06673
CD: Music and Arts CD 003
CD: Hunt CD 509
CD: EMI CMS 763 8602
Excerpts
LP: Gioielli della lirica GML 05
Final scene from this 1954 recording is missing; final scene has been spliced in from the 1953 version

Prolonged confusion over the Austrian Radio tapes of the 1953 and 1954 Salzburg recordings has hopefully been resolved by Edward Chibas in an article in Newsletter No. 105 (December 1990) of the Wilhelm Furtwängler Society UK

Salzburg
July 1956

Role of Donna Anna
Della Casa, Streich,
Simoneau, Siepi,
Corena, Frick,
Vienna Opera Chorus
VPO
Mitropoulos

LP: Replica ARPL 42422
LP: Discoreale DR 10021-3
CD: Hunt CD 552
Early pressings of the Hunt CD contained a 1960 Salzburg performance conducted by Karajan and with a different cast

Don Giovanni: Excerpt (Final scene)

Salzburg
August 1954

Role of Donna Anna
Della Casa, Berger,
Dermota, Siepi,
Edelmann, Berry,
VPO
Furtwängler

LP: Furtwängler Series (Japan) W 28-29
Taken from film soundtrack
(Connoisseur Films/Beta Films)

Don Giovanni: Excerpts (Keine Ruh' bei Tag und Nacht; *Welch ein grauenvolles Bild; Trio Elvira-Anna-Ottavio; other excerpts without Grümmer)

Berlin February 1960	Role of Donna Anna Hillebrecht, Köth, Wunderlich, Kohn, Stewart, Wiemann, Deutsche Oper Chorus, Berlin SO Zanotelli Sung in German	LP: Electrola O/STO 80583 LP: Electrola 1C 063 28418 *CD: EMI CDM 763 1372

Don Giovanni: Excerpts (Du kennst nun den Frevler; Sage nicht, o Heissgeliebter)

Berlin August 1961	Role of Donna Anna Grobe, Deutsche Oper Orchestra Fricsay Sung in German	LP: Melodram MEL 083

Le Nozze di Figaro: Excerpt (Porgi amor)

Berlin October 1955	Role of Countess Berlin SO Schüchter	Version in German language LP: Electrola E 60627 LP: Electrola E 70418 LP: Electrola 1C 047 28553 LP: Electrola 1C 047 28574 Version in Italian language 78: Electrola DB 11590 LP: EMI EX 29 12103 CD: EMI CDM 763 1372

Le Nozze di Figaro: Excerpt (Dove sono)

Cologne 1951	Role of Countess WDR Orchestra Fricsay Sung in German	LP: Melodram MEL 083
Berlin July 1955	Role of Countess Berlin SO Schüchter	Version in German language LP: Electrola 1C 047 28574 Version in Italian language 78: Electrola DB 11596 LP: EMI EX 2912103 CD: EMI CDM 763 1372

Le Nozze di Figaro: Excerpt (Che soave zeffiretti)

Cologne 1951	Role of Countess Güden, WDR Orchestra Fricsay Sung in German	LP: Melodram MEL 083
Berlin October 1955	Role of Countess Berger, Berlin SO Schüchter	Version in German language LP: Electrola E 60627 LP: Electrola E 83384 LP: Electrola 1C 047 28574 LP: Electrola 1C 137 46104-5 Version in Italian language 78: Electrola DB 11590 LP: EMI EX 29 12103 CD: EMI CDM 763 1372 CD: EMI CDM 763 7592

Die Zauberflöte: Excerpts (1. Ach, ich fühl's; 2. Bald prangt der Morgen zu verkünden; other excerpts without Grümmer)

Berlin October 1955	Role of Pamina Regensburger Domspatzen Berlin SO Schüchter	78: Electrola DB 11587 LP: Electrola E 80830 LP: Electrola E 60572 (2) LP: Electrola 1C 047 28575 LP: Electrola 1C 047 28553 (1) LP: EMI EX 29 12103 CD: EMI CDM 763 1372 (2)

Offenbach

The Tales of Hoffmann: Excerpt (Hörst du es tönen)

Berlin 1951	Role of Antonia W. Ludwig, RIAS Orchestra Lehmann Sung in German	LP: Melodram MEL 083

Reger

Mariä Wiegenlied

Berlin January 1948	Dietz, piano	78: Electrola DB 11536 LP: EMI EX 769 7411

Rossini

Stabat Mater

Cologne 1953	Soprano soloist Ilosvay, W.Ludwig, Fehn WDR Chorus and Orchestra Fricsay	CD: Melodram CDM 16523

Schubert

Lieder: Fischerweise; Lachen und Weinen; An der Quelle; An die Nachtigall

Berlin 1956	Klust, piano	LP: Melodram MEL 083

Wie anders, Gretchen (Szene aus Faust)

Berlin 1956	Fischer-Dieskau Klust, piano	LP: Melodram MEL 083

Lieder: 1. Ach um deine feuchten Schwingen; 2. Auf dem Wasser zu singen; 3. Wiegenlied 4. Rastlose Liebe; 5. Vor meiner Wiege; 6. Die Forelle; 7. Fischerweise

Berlin November 1958 (Electrola)	Moore, piano	LP: Electrola E/STE 80437 LP: Electrola 1C 047 29126 LP: EMI EX 29 12103 (2,3,6)

Schumann

Lieder: Die Soldatenbraut; Der Page; Widmung; Der Nussbaum; Volksliedchen

Berlin 1953	Dietz, piano	LP: Melodram MEL 083

Richard Strauss

Der Rosenkavalier: Excerpts (1. Mir ist die Ehre widerfahren; 2. Marie Theres'...; 3. Ist ein Traum, kann nicht wirklich sein; other excerpts without Grümmer)

Berlin October 1955 (Electrola)	Role of Octavian Rysanek, Köth, BPO Schüchter	LP: HMV CLP 1139 LP: Electrola E 60066 LP: Electrola 1C 047 28553 (1 and 3) LP: Electrola 1C 047 38566M LP: EMI MFP 2058 LP: Electrola 1C 147 29150-1M (2) LP: EMI EX 29 12103 (1) CD: EMI CDM 763 1372 (3)

Der Rosenkavalier: Excerpt (Mir ist die Ehre widerfahren)

Munich July 1952	Role of Octavian Berger, Bavarian State Orchestra Kleiber	LP: Orfeo S120 8421

4 letzte Lieder

Berlin 1970	RIAS Orchestra Kraus	CD: Melodram CDM 16523

Tchaikovsky

The Queen of Spades

Berlin April 1947	Role of Lisa Klose, Schock, Prohaska, Nissen, Städtische Oper Chorus Berlin RO Rother Sung in German	LP: Urania URLP 207 Excerpts LP: German Opera Society OPS 125-6 LP: Melodram MEL 083 LP: Acanta 40.23550

Thomas

Mignon: Excerpt (Kennst du das Land ?)

Berlin May 1953	Role of Mignon Berlin SO Schüchter Sung in German	78: Electrola EH 1438 LP: Electrola 1C 047 28553 LP: EMI EX 29 12103 CD: EMI CDM 763 1372

SADLER'S WELLS THEATRE

ROSEBERY AVENUE, E.C.1

(in full assoc. with the Arts Council of Gt. Britain)

Director: Norman Tucker   (Tel.: TER. 1672)   Administrative Director: Stephen Arlen

---

ALFRED DELVAL

(for Alfred Delval Prod. Ltd.)

presents

HAMBURG STATE OPERA

Artistic Director:	Adm. Director:	General Music Director:
Rolf Liebermann	Herbert Paris	Leopold Ludwig

THE HAMBURG PHILHARMONIC STATE ORCHESTRA
and OPERA CHORUS

Conductors:

Leopold Ludwig   Hans Werner Henze   Horst Stein   Albert Bittner

Producers:

Günther Rennert   Wieland Wagner   Helmut Käutner

LOHENGRIN
LULU
DER PRINZ VON HOMBURG
WOZZECK

HAMBURG STATE OPERA
Rolf Liebermann

September 25th, 28th and
October 2nd and 4th
at 7.30 p.m.

LOHENGRIN
by Richard Wagner.

Conductor: Horst Stein
Producer: Wieland Wagner
Costumes and Decors: Wieland Wagner
Stage Director: Ulrich Wenk
Chorus Master: Günther Schmidt-Bohländer

THE HAMBURG PHILHARMONIC STATE ORCHESTRA
THE HAMBURG STATE OPERA CHORUS

Lohengrin, Knight of the Grail	Arturo Sergi
Elsa von Brabant	Elisabeth Grümmer
Friedrich von Telramund	Herbert Fliether
Ortrud, his wife	Astrid Varnay
Henry the Fowler, King of Germany	Ernst Wiemann
The Royal Herald	Tom Krause
Duke Gottfried	Günther Arnold
Four Noblewomen:	Hanna Hienzsch Rosemarie Hartung Ursula Nettling Edith Ochsenreither
Four Noblemen:	Jürgen Förster Georg Mund Jean Pfendt Karl Otto

Interval after the first and second act.

1962

Verdi

Otello: Excerpts (1. Love Duet; 2. Willow Song; 3. Ave Maria; other excerpts without Grümmer)

Berlin November 1957	Role of Desdemona Wagner, Schock, Städtische Oper Orchestra Kraus Sung in German	LP: Electrola E 80031 LP: Electrola E 60045 LP: Electrola 1C 047 26553 (3) LP: EMI EX 29 12103 (2 and 3) CD: EMI CDM 763 1372 (2 and 3) CD: EMI CZS 767 1832 (1)

Wagner

Götterdämmerung

Bayreuth July 1957	Role of Gutrune Varnay, Ilosvay, Windgassen, Uhde, Neidlinger, Greindl, Bayreuth Festival Chorus & Orchestra Knappertsbusch	LP: Discocorp IGI 292 LP: Fonit Cetra LO 61 LP: Melodram MEL 579 CD: Music and Arts CD 256 CD: Laudis LCD 154021
Bayreuth July 1958	Role of Gutrune Varnay, Madeira, Windgassen, Wiener, Andersson, Greindl, Bayreuth Festival Chorus & Orchestra Knappertsbusch	LP: Melodram MEL 589 CD: Hunt CDLSMH 34044

Lohengrin

Bayreuth July 1959	Role of Elsa Gorr, Konya, Crass, Blanc, Bayreuth Festival Chorus & Orchestra Matacic	LP: Melodram MEL 591
Vienna 1963	Role of Elsa Ludwig, Thomas, Fischer-Dieskau, Frick, Vienna Opera Chorus VPO Kempe	LP: EMI AN/SAN 121-5 LP: EMI SLS 5072 LP: EMI EX 29 09553 CD: EMI CDS 749 0178 Excerpts: LP: Electrola SME 80853 LP: Electrola 1C 063 00747 LP: EMI EX 2912103

Die Meistersinger von Nürnberg

Berlin April 1956	Role of Eva Höffgen, Schock, Unger, Frantz, Frick, Kusche, Choirs, BPO Kempe	LP: HMV ALP 1506-10 LP: EMI HQM 1094-8 LP: EMI RLS 740 Excerpts: LP: HMV ALP 2253
Bayreuth July 1957	Role of Eva Milinkovic, Geisler, Stolze, Greindl, Neidlinger, Schmitt-Walter, Bayreuth Festival Chorus & Orchestra Cluytens	LP: Melodram MEL 572
Bayreuth July 1958	Role of Eva Schärtel, Traxel, Stolze, Wiener, Hotter, Blankenheim, Bayreuth Festival Chorus & Orchestra Cluytens	LP: Melodram MEL 582 Excerpt: LP: Melodram MEL 083
Bayreuth July 1959	Role of Eva Schärtel, Schock, Stolze, Wiener, Greindl, Blankenheim, Bayreuth Festival Chorus & Orchestra Leinsdorf	LP: Melodram MEL 592
Bayreuth July 1960	Role of Eva Schärtel, Windgassen, Stolze, Greindl, Adam, Schmitt-Walter, Bayreuth Festival Chorus & Orchestra Knappertsbusch	LP: Melodram MEL 602 CD: Melodram MEL 46103

Die Meistersinger von Nürnberg: Excerpt (Ja, ihr seid es! Nein, du bist es!)

London July 1951	Role of Eva Schacklock, Anders, Hotter, Covent Garden Orchestra Beecham	LP: Melodram MEL 083

Saturday, 7th July, 1951

DIE MEISTERSINGER VON NÜRNBERG

OPERA IN THREE ACTS

Words and Music by Richard Wagner

GUEST CONDUCTOR · SIR THOMAS BEECHAM, BART.

PRODUCER - HEINZ TIETJEN

THE COVENT GARDEN OPERA CHORUS

Chorus Master - Douglas Robinson

THE COVENT GARDEN ORCHESTRA

Leader - Thomas Matthews

RICHARD WAGNER, 1813-1883

This opera was first produced at the Court Theatre, Munich, on 21st June, 1868. First performed in London, in German, at Drury Lane on 30th May, 1882 and in English at the Garrick Theatre on 22nd January, 1897.

CHARACTERS IN ORDER OF APPEARANCE

Eva, daughter of Pogner	ELISABETH GRUMMER
Magdalene, her nurse	CONSTANCE SHACKLOCK
Pogner, a goldsmith	LUDWIG WEBER
Walter von Stolzing, a young knight	PETER ANDERS
David, Sach's apprentice	MURRAY DICKIE

MASTERSINGERS

Sachs, a shoemaker	HANS HOTTER
Beckmesser, the town-clerk	BENNO KUSCHE
Kothner, a baker	RHYDDERCH DAVIES
Nachtigall, a tinsmith	ERNEST DAVIES
Zorn, a pewterer	EMLYN JONES
Eisslinger, a grocer	DENNIS STEPHENSON
Vogelgesang, a furrier	EDGAR EVANS
Moser, a tailor	DAVID TREE
Foltz, a coppersmith	RONALD LEWIS
Ortel, a soap-boiler	MARIAN NOWAKOWSKI
Schwarz, a stocking-weaver	CHARLES MORRIS
Night-Watchman	GERAINT EVANS

The Audience is asked not to applaud at the end of each Act until the Orchestra has finished playing.

Das Rheingold

Rome October 1953	Role of Freia Malaniuk, Frantz, Windgassen, Patzak, Greindl, Rome RAI Orchestra Furtwängler	LP: MRF Records MRF 14 LP: EMI RLS 702 LP: EMI EX 29 06703 CD: Hunt CDWFE 359 CD: EMI CZS 767 1232
Bayreuth July 1957	Role of Freia Milinkovic, Hotter, Suthaus, Kuen, Greindl, Bayreuth Festival Orchestra Knappertsbusch	LP: Discocorp IGI 292 LP: Fonit Cetra LO 50 LP: Melodram MEL 576 CD: Music and Arts CD 253 CD: Laudis LCD 154021
Bayreuth July 1958	Role of Freia Gorr, Hotter, Konya, Saeden, Greindl, Bayreuth Festival Orchestra Knappertsbusch	LP: Melodram MEL 586 CD: Hunt CDLSMH 34041

Tannhäuser

Berlin October 1960	Role of Elisabeth Schech, Hopf, Wunderlich, Frick, Fischer-Dieskau, Deutsche Staatsoper Chorus & Orchestra Konwitschny	LP: HMV ALP 1876-9/ASD 445-8 LP: EMI HQM/HQS 1081-4 CD: EMI CMS 763 2142 Excerpts: LP: HMV ALP 2005/ASD 555 LP: Electrola E 70418 LP: Electrola 1C 047 28553 LP: EMI EX 29 12103 CD: EMI CDM 763 1372

Tannhäuser: Excerpts (Act 2 scenes 1 and 3: Dich, teure Halle...dich treff' ich hier)

Berlin 1959	Role of Elisabeth Frick, Deutsche Staatsoper Chorus & Orchestra Konwitschny	LP: HMV ALP 1784/ASD 363

Tannhäuser: Excerpt (Dich, teure Halle)

Berlin 1953	Role of Elisabeth Berlin RO Rother	LP: Melodram MEL 083

Weber

Der Freischütz

Salzburg July 1954	Role of Agathe Streich, Hopf, Edelmann, Poell, Böhme, Vienna Opera Chorus, VPO Furtwängler	LP: Discocorp IGS 008-10/IGI 338 LP: Fonit Cetra LO 21 LP: Turnabout THS 65148-50 LP: Fonit Cetra FE 24 LP: Robin Hood RHR 522 CD: Rodolphe RPL 32519-20 CD: Nuova Era 013.6324-6 CD: Hunt CDWFE 302 CD: Hunt CDWFE 352 Excerpts: LP: Melodram MEL 083* Some editions incorrectly labelled "stereo"
Cologne 1955	Role of Agathe Streich, Hopf, Pröbstl, Poell, Böhme, WDR Chorus and Orchestra Kleiber	LP: Discocorp IGI 300 LP: Fonit Cetra LO 42 CD: Hunt CDLSMH 34033 Excerpts: LP: Gioielli della lirica GML 74
Berlin April and September 1958 (Electrola)	Role of Agathe Otto, Schock, Prey, Kohn, Frick, Deutsche Staatsoper Chorus, BPO Keilberth	LP: HMV ALP 1752-4/ASD 319-21 LP: EMI HQM/HQS 1031-2 LP: EMI EX 29 06963 CD: EMI CMS 769 3422 Excerpts: LP: Electrola E 70418 LP: Electrola 1C 047 28553 LP: EMI EX 29 12103 CD: EMI CDM 763 1372

Der Freischütz: Excerpt (Schelm, halt fest)

Berlin 1951	Role of Agathe Otto, RIAS Orchestra Rother	LP: Melodram MEL 083

Wolf

Lieder: Ach, des Knaben Augen; Führ mich, Kind, nach Bethlehem; Schlafendes Jesuskind; Auf eine Christblume

Berlin   Dietz, piano   LP: Melodram MEL 083
1953

Traditional

Vom Himmel hoch

Berlin   Dietz, piano   LP: Legendary LR 136
1952

Elisabeth Grümmer:
roles performed with the Vienna State Opera

Includes performances with the Vienna company on tour
Figure against each role indicates number of times the part was performed

1	Agathe (Der Freischütz)
6	Countess Almaviva (Le Nozze di Figaro)
4	Desdemona (Otello)
14	Donna Anna (Don Giovanni)
2	Elsa (Lohengrin)
4	Eva (Die Meistersinger von Nürnberg)
1	5th Maid (Elektra)
1	Margarethe (Faust)
1	Marschallin (Der Rosenkavalier)
2	Micaela (Carmen)
1	Mimì (La Bohème)
3	Octavian (Der Rosenkavalier)
10	Pamina (Die Zauberflöte)

Sena Jurinac
Discography

Compiled by John Hunt
1991

Introduction

You generalise about a singer and a voice at your peril, and reactions must be personal and particular. The first encounter may even prove something of a coup de foudre. I did not hear Sena Jurinac during the Vienna Opera's 1947 visit to London but when I first caught up with her in Salzburg a year later, as Cherubino in The Marriage of Figaro and Amor in Orfeo, she seemed to me immediately a singer of the highest attraction. A strikingly fresh vocal quality, underpinned by quite unusual authority, was immediately apparent, and the same qualities were just as evident when I heard her Dorabella in Florence some months later and of course - pre-eminently, perhaps - when she sang Fiordiligi at Glyndebourne. Fiordiligi's very difficult music was sung with such accuracy and brilliance as to make the bravura as exciting as a coloratura soprano's, with every phrase expressive; this, one felt, was exactly as the composer would have liked to hear it.

From the start, the sound was full and golden, pulsing with vitality - not just a classical vocalist (much as that is to be prized) but something rather more. The clean attack was always a prelude to poised vocalism and elegantly musical phrasing, and that was very much in evidence as Ilia in Idomeneo, also at Glyndebourne. Somehow she seemed to epitomise the post-1945 Viennese school at its best. There was no fuss, no nonsense, no sacrifice to the gods of good taste or contorted inflection, rather a delivery direct to the audience, in a voice that was individual, never to be mistaken for somebody else's.

What struck you at first was the dark, even trafic, resonance in the lower octave. This no doubt made her suitable for lower-based roles like Cherubino, Dorabella - an unsurpassed performance, in my experience - and, of course, Octavian. But you would never associate Donna Elvira, Fiordiligi, Butterfly or Fidelio with a soprano with mezzo-like propensities, however ardent her musicianship, and I checked my tape of her Butterfly performance at Covent Garden in January 1959 to prove that the ringing (optional) C sharp at the end of her entrance was real and not just a product of my imagination. It was, and here again were the Jurinac virtues at their most resplendent - it is all very "straight", honest, almost heroic, but in the final analysis this is the most touching interpreter of the role I have (then or since) encountered.

The Viennese customarily sing Lieder as easily as they sing opera, but Sena Jurinac seemed reluctant to test the theory. Nonetheless, when she tackled the smaller but perhaps subtler form she could reach great heights, and a recording she made in the early 1950s of Schumann's Frauenliebe und -Leben and the greater of his two Liederkreise is a treasured possession, lit by the memory of hearing her do the second of these masterly cycles only ten years ago, the result of much (and for a long time unsuccesful) persuasion.

When I was trying to write about singers a few years ago, I looked up the word "thrilling" in the Shorter Oxford English Dictionary: its definition was "producing a sudden wave of excitement or emotion, piercing the feelings". I can't think of a better definition to describe the effect on most of us of Sena Jurinac's singing.

This article was written by Lord Harewood for the programme book of the 1988 Canterbury Festival and is reproduced here with kind permission

Bach

Magnificat in D BWV243

Munich 1965	Soprano soloist Zareska, Altmeyer, Rehfuss, Munich Pro Arte Chorus & Orchestra, Redel	LP: Philips 835 737 LY LP: Philips 641 737 LL

Beethoven

Fidelio

London March 1961	Role of Leonore Morison, Dobson, Vickers, Frick, Hotter, Robinson, Royal Opera Chorus & Orchestra. Klemperer	LP: Melodram MEL 407 CD: Melodram MEL 27076
Munich 1962	Role of Leonore Stader, Dickie, Peerce, Ernster, Neidlinger, Guthrie, Bavarian State Opera Chorus & Orchestra, Knappertsbusch	LP: Westminster XWN 3319/WST 319 LP: World Records SOC 104-6 LP: Westminster S 1003 CD: MCA Classics MCAD2 9809
Vienna October 1953	Role of Marzelline Mödl, Schock, Windgassen, Frick, Edelmann, Poell, Vienna Opera Chorus VPO Furtwängler	LP: Replica RPL 2439-41 LP: Fonit Cetra FE 8-10 CD: Fonit Cetra CDC 12 CD: Rodolphe RPC 32494
Vienna October 1953	Role of Marzelline Mödl, Schock, Windgassen, Frick, Edelmann, Poell, Vienna Opera Chorus VPO Furtwängler	LP: HMV ALP 1130-2 LP: HMV HQM 1109-10 LP: Electrola 1C 147 01105-7M Excerpts: LP: EMI HQM 1024 LP: Electrola 1C 047 00832 LP: Electrola 1C 047 01444M
Salzburg July 1957	Role of Marzelline Goltz, Kmennt, Zampieri, Edelmann, Schöffler, Zaccaria, Vienna Opera Chorus VPO Karajan	LP: Melodram MEL 040 CD: Hunt CDKAR 222

Bizet

Carmen: Excerpts

Naples
December 1952

<u>Role of Micaela</u>
Simionato, Corelli,
Tagliabue,
San Carlo Chorus
and Orchestra
Rodzinski
<u>Sung in Italian</u>

LP: Edizione Lirica EL 002

Carmen: Excerpt (Wie kommst du von der Mutter)

Baden-Baden
April 1952

<u>Role of Micaela</u>
Anders,
Südwestfunk
Orchestra
Ackermann
<u>Sung in German</u>

LP: Acanta DE 23.116-7

Brahms

Lieder: Nicht mehr zu dir zu gehen; Ach wende diesen Blick; Wie Melodien zieht es mir; Sommerabend; Agnes; Der Jäger; Mädchenlied; Die Trauernde; Maienkätzchen; Vergebliches Ständchen; Alte Liebe; Schön war, das ich dir weihte; Auf dem Kirchhof Wie rafft ich mich auf; 8 Zigeunerlieder

Salzburg
1976

G. Fischer, piano

LP: BASF 25.226700

Cornelius

Der Barbier von Bagdad

Vienna
1952

<u>Role of Margiana</u>
Rössl-Majdan, Schock,
Frick, Poell,
Austrian Radio
Chorus & Orchestra.
Hollreiser

CD: Melodram MEL 27050
CD: Verona 27050

Gluck

Iphigénie en Tauride

Munich
1965

Role of Iphigénie
Fahberg, Wunderlich,
Prey, Engen
Bavarian Radio
Chorus & Orchestra
Kubelik

LP: Melodram
Listed in "Opern auf Schallplatten"
(ECON-Verlag 1983) but catalogue
number not traced; may therefore not
have been published in complete form,
although DG has issued excerpts
featuring Fritz Wunderlich

Orfeo ed Euridice

Salzburg
August 1959

Role of Euridice
Simionato, Sciutti,
Vienna Opera Chorus
VPO
Karajan

LP: Replica RPL 2436-7
LP: Legendary LR 132
CD: Nuova Era 2215-6
Excerpts:
LP: Gioielli della lirica GML 68

Humperdinck

Hänsel und Gretel

Vienna
1979

Role of Witch
Fassbänder,
Gruberova, Prey,
Dernesch,
Choirs
VPO
Solti

VHS Video: Decca 071 1023
Laserdisc: Decca 071 1021

Janacek

Jenufa

Vienna
October 1972

Role of Jenufa
Varnay, Rössl-Majdan,
Konetzni, Cox,
Cochran
Vienna Opera Chorus
VPO
Kulka
Sung in German

LP: Estro Armonico 2EA 061

Kodaly

Te Deum

Vienna 1953	Soprano soloist Wagner, Christ, Poell, Chorus VSO Swoboda	LP: Westminster XWN/ST 18455 LP: Nixa WLP 5001 LP: Westminster W 9729

Krenek

Karl V

Salzburg August 1980	Role of Eleonore Ciesinski, Schwarz, Moser, Schreier. Adam, Austrian Radio Chorus & Orchestra Albrecht	LP: Amadeo AVRS 305

Massenet

Manon: Excerpts (So bleib' ich hier; Letter duet; Gavotte; Leb wohl, mein kleines Tischchen; Saint Sulpice duet)

Hamburg 1950	Role of Manon Dermota, Roth, NDR Orchestra, Schüchter Sung in German	LP: Melodram MEL 089 LP: Melodram MEL 090

Mozart

Requiem

Vienna June 1958	Soprano soloist West, Löffler, Guthrie, Akademiechor, VPO Scherchen	LP: Westminster XWN 2230/WST 205 LP: Westminster XWN 18766 LP: Westminster XAK 28926 LP: World Records ST 140 CD: MCA Classics MCAD 29816

Così fan tutte: Excerpts (1. Ah guarda sorella; 2. Sento, o Dio; 3. Di scrivermi ogni giorno; 4. Soave sia il vento; 5. Come scoglio; 6. Prenderò quel brunettino; 7. Per pietà; 8. Fra gli amplessi; other excerpts without Jurinac)

Glyndebourne July 1950	Role of Fiordiligi Thebom, Lewis, Kunz, Borriello, Glyndebourne Orchestra Busch	78: HMV DB 21116-20 LP: World Records SH 397 LP: EMI 29 05983 (1,4,5,8) CD: EMI CDH 763 1992 (1,5,7)

Idomeneo

London July & August 1956	Role of Ilia Udovick, Lewis, Simoneau, Milligan, McAlpine, Alan, Glyndebourne Chorus and Orchestra Pritchard	LP: HMV ALP 1515-7 LP: Seraphim (USA) SIC 6070 CD: EMI CHS 763 6852 Excerpts LP: HMV ALP 1731

Idomeneo: Excerpts (1. Padre, germani, addio!; 2. Se il padre perdei; 3. Zeffiretti 4. Andrò ramingo e solo; other excerpts without Jurinac)

London July 1951	Role of Ilia McNeil, Lewis, Young, Glyndebourne Chorus and Orchestra Busch	78: HMV DB 21525-7 LP: RCA Victor (USA) LM 1126 LP: Electrola E 80772 LP: HMV ALP 1731 (4) LP: EMI HQM 1024 (1,3) LP: Electrola 1C 047 01444M (1,3) LP: World Records SH 294 LP: EMI 29 05983 (1,2,3) CD: EMI CDH 763 1992 (1,2,3)

Die Zauberflöte

Vienna November 1950	Role of First Lady Seefried, Lipp, Dermota, London, Weber, Vienna Singverein, VPO Karajan	78: Columbia LWX 426-444 LP: Columbia 33CX 1013-5 LP: EMI SLS 5052 LP: Electrola 1C 197 54200-8M CD: EMI CHS 769 6312

Monday, 27th February, 1961

The 93rd performance at the Royal Opera House of

FIDELIO

OPERA IN TWO ACTS

Words by Josef Sonnleithner and G. F. Treitschke
after J. N. Bouilly's libretto
"Leonore, ou l'Amour Conjugal"
(set to music by Pierre Gaveaux, Paris, 1798)

Music by Ludwig van Beethoven

CONDUCTOR — OTTO KLEMPERER

PRODUCER — OTTO KLEMPERER

Associate Producer — CHRISTOPHER WEST

Scenery and costumes by HAINER HILL

Lighting by CHRISTOPHER WEST

THE COVENT GARDEN OPERA CHORUS
Chorus Master — Douglas Robinson

THE COVENT GARDEN ORCHESTRA
Leader — Charles Taylor

CHARACTERS IN ORDER OF APPEARANCE

Jaquino, *a porter* ... ... JOHN DOBSON

Marzelline, *Rocco's daughter* ... ... ELSIE MORISON

Rocco, *a gaoler* ... ... GOTTLOB FRICK

Leonore, *Florestan's wife, disguised as Fidelio, a manservant* ... ... SENA JURINAC

Don Pizarro, *Governor of the Prison* ... HANS HOTTER

First Prisoner ... ... JOSEPH WARD

Second Prisoner ... ... VICTOR GODFREY

Florestan, *a Prisoner of State* ... ... JON VICKERS

Don Fernando, *the Minister* ... ... FORBES ROBINSON

HISTORICAL NOTE

This opera was first performed at Theater an der Wien, Vienna, on 20th November, 1805 with Anna Milder as Leonore and conducted by Beethoven. It was first performed in London at the King's Theatre, Haymarket, on 18th May, 1832 with Wilhelmine Schroeder-Devrient as Leonore. It was given at Covent Garden, in English, in 1835 with Maria Malibran, and in Italian in 1851. Revivals at Covent Garden include 1891 under Mahler with Katherine Klafsky; 1898 with Ternina; 1899 with Lilli Lehmann; 1927 under Bruno Walter with Helene Wildbrunn; 1934 under Beecham with Lotte Lehmann and Franz Voelker; 1938, again under Beecham, with Rose Pauly and Helge Roswaenge. Since the war Leonore has been sung here by Hilde Konetzni, Sylvia Fisher, Kirsten Flagstad, Christel Goltz and Florestan by Julius Patzak, Peter Anders and Thorstein Hannesson.

Don Giovanni

Vienna 1955	Role of Elvira Zadek, Sciutti, London, Simoneau, Weber, Ernster, Vienna Chamber Choir VSO Moralt	LP: Philips ABL 3069-71 LP: Philips GL 5753-5 Mi tradì 45: Philips ABE 10129
Berlin September and October 1958	Role of Anna Stader, Seefried, Fischer-Dieskau, Häfliger, Sardi, Kohn, RIAS Chorus and Orchestra Fricsay	LP: DG LPM 18 580-2/SLPM 138 050-2 LP: DG 2728 003 LP: DG 2730 014 Excerpts LP: DG LPEM 19 224/SLPEM 136 204
London February 1962	Role of Elvira Gencer, Freni, Siepi, Lewis, Evans, Ward, Covent Garden Chorus & Orchestra Solti	CD: GDS Records GDS 31024
Rome May 1970	Role of Elvira Janowitz, Ghiaurov, Miljakovic, Kraus, Bruscantini, Petkov, RAI Rome Chorus & Orchestra Giulini	CD: Hunt CDLSMH 34050 CD: Melodram MEL 37080 CD: Rodolphe RPV 32675-7 CD: Frequenz 043.019

Don Giovanni: Excerpts (Ah taci ingiusto core; Già la mensa e preparata)

Vienna November 1955	Role of Elvira London, Kunz, VPO Böhm Sung in German	CD: GDS Records GDS 2204

Don Giovanni: Excerpts (Ah fuggi il traditor; Don Giovanni, a cenar teco...to end)

Munich August 1962	Role of Elvira Hillebrecht, Rothenberger, London, Gedda, Kusche, Frick, Bavarian State Opera Chorus and Orchestra Keilberth	LP: Orfeo S120.8421

Le Nozze di Figaro

Vienna June and October 1950	Role of Cherubino Schwarzkopf, Kunz, Seefried, London, Vienna Opera Chorus VPO Karajan	78: Columbia LWX 410-425 LP: Columbia 33CX 1007-9 LP: Electrola 1C 197 54200-8M CD: EMI CMS 769 6392 Excerpts: LP: Columbia 33CX 1558 LP: Electrola 1C 047 01444M LP: EMI HQM 1024 CD: EMI CDM 763 5572	
Milan February 1954	Role of Cherubino Schwarzkopf, Petri, Seefried, Panerai, La Scala Chorus & Orchestra Karajan	LP: Fonit Cetra LO 70 CD: Hunt CDKAR 225 CD: Melodram MEL 37075 Excerpts LP: Gioielli della lirica GML 30	
Vienna 1955	Role of Countess Streich, Ludwig, Berry, Schöffler, Vienna Opera Chorus VSO Böhm	LP: Philips A00357-9L LP: Philips GL 5777-9 LP: Philips SFL 14012-4 LP: Philips 6706 006 Dove sono 45: Philips ABE 10129	
London July 1955	Role of Countess Sciutti, Stevens, Bruscantini, Calabrese, Glyndebourne Chorus & Orchestra Gui	LP: HMV ALP 1312-5/ASD 274-7 LP: World Records SOC 168-171 LP: EMI EX 29 00173 Excerpts: LP: EMI HQM 1024 LP: Electrola 1C 047 01444M	

Le Nozze di Figaro: Excerpt (Avanti, avanti, signor uffiziale..Voi che sapete)

Milan January 1949	Role of Cherubino Seefried, Cebotari, VPO Karajan	LP: Melodram MEL 089

Le Nozze di Figaro: Excerpt (Deh vieni, non tardar)

Milan January 1954	Role of Susanna RAI Orchestra Rossi	LP: Fonit Cetra LMR 5018 LP: Melodram MEL 089

Mussorgsky

Boris Godunov

Salzburg July 1965	Role of Marina Ghiaurov, Stolze, Usunov, Ghuselev, Vienna Opera Chorus Zagreb Opera Chorus VPO Karajan	CD: Hunt CDKAR 210 Recording incorrectly dated July 1964
Salzburg July 1966	Role of Marina Ghiaurov, Stolze, Maslennikov, Kelemen, Vienna Opera Chorus Zagreb Opera Chorus VPO Karajan	CD: Nuova Era 6351-3

Pfitzner

The Tales of Hoffmann: Excerpt (Sie entfloh, die Taube so minnig)

Hamburg 1950	Role of Antonia NDR Orchestra Martin Sung in German	LP: Melodram MEL 089

Offenbach

Palestrina

Vienna December 1964	Role of Ighino Wunderlich, Ludwig, Stolze, Frick, Wiener, Berry, Vienna Opera Chorus VPO Heger	LP: Ed Smith EJS 521

Puccini

Madama Butterfly: Excerpts (1. Entrance of Butterfly; 2. Viene la sera; 3. Un bel dì; 4. Che tua madre; 5. Scuoti quella fronda; 6. Con onor muore; other excerpts without Jurinac)

Vienna March 1960	Role of Butterfly Rössl-Majdan, Lorenzi, Paskalis, Vienna Opera Chorus, VPO Klobucar	LP: Gioielli della lirica GML 31 LP: Melodram MEL 089 (2,3,4,6) Melodram incorrectly dated 1957

Madama Butterfly: Excerpts (Entrance of Butterfly; Un bel dì)

London 1959	Role of Butterfly Royal Opera Chorus & Orchestra Balkwill	LP: Legendary LR 105

Madama Butterfly: Excerpt (Mädchen, in deinen Augen liegt ein Zauber)

Baden-Baden April 1952	Role of Butterfly Anders, Südwestfunk Orchestra Ackermann Sung in German	LP: Electrola E 83380 LP: Electrola 1C 047 01444M LP: Electrola 1C 147 29142-3M LP: Acanta 40.23544

La Bohème: Excerpt (Sind wir allein)

Baden-Baden April 1952	Role of Mimi Anders, Südwestfunk Orchestra Ackermann Sung in German	LP: Electrola E 83380 LP: Electrola 1C 147 29142-3M LP: Acanta DE 23.116-7

Tosca: Excerpt (Vissi d'arte)

Hamburg 1950	Role of Tosca NDR Orchestra, Martin	LP: Melodram MEL 089

SENA JURINAC
sings the role of Marzelline in

FIDELIO
Beethoven

Complete recording in German with the Vienna State Opera Chorus and Vienna Philharmonic Orchestra.
Conductor: Furtwängler
ALP 1130-32

and the role of the Countess in

LE NOZZE DI FIGARO
Mozart

Complete recording in Italian with the Glyndebourne Festival Orchestra and Chorus.
Conductor: Vittorio Gui
ALPS1312   ALP1313-5

✳

"HIS MASTER'S VOICE"
LONG PLAY 33⅓ R.P.M. RECORDS

E.M.I. RECORDS LTD · 8-11 GREAT CASTLE STREET · LONDON · W.1

Postage stamp featuring Sena Jurinac, one of a series marking
the centenary of the Vienna State Opera

Respighi

Il Tramonto

Vienna	Barylli String	LP: Westminster XWN/ST 18597
May 1954	Quartet	LP: Westminster WLE 101

Schumann

Song cycles: Frauenliebe und -Leben; Liederkreis op 39

Vienna	Holetschek, piano	LP: Westminster XWN 18493
1954		LP: Westminster WL 5345

Smetana

The Bartered Bride: Excerpt (Endlich allein)

Hamburg	Role of Marenka	LP: Melodram MEL 089
1950	NDR Orchestra	
	Schüchter	
	Sung in German	

London	Role of Marenka	78: HMV DB 21136
September 1950	Philharmonia	LP: HMV HQM 1024
	Braithwaite	LP: Electrola 1C 047 01444M
	Sung in German	CD: EMI CDH 763 1992

The Bartered Bride: Excerpt (Mein lieber Schatz, nun aufgepasst)

Baden-Baden	Role of Marenka	LP: Electrola E 83380
April 1952	Anders,	LP: Electrola 1C 047 01444M
	Südwestfunk	LP: EMI HQM 1024
	Orchestra	
	Ackermann	
	Sung in German	

The Kiss: Excerpt (Wiegenlied)

London	Role of Vendulka	CD: EMI CDH 763 1992
September 1950	Philharmonia	
	Braithwaite	
	Sung in German	

Johann Strauss

Der Zigeunerbaron: Excerpts

Cologne December 1949	Role of Saffi Hollweg, Schröder. Anders, Hann, Schmitt-Walter, Cologne Radio Chorus & Orchestra Marszalek	LP: RCA VL 30310 LP: Electrola E 83740 LP: RCA VL 30310 LP: Acanta 40.22903

Richard Strauss

Vier letzte Lieder

Stockholm May 1951	Stockholm Philharmonic Busch	LP: Discocorp 487 LP: Orfeus 1-73-3 CD: EMI CDH 763 1992
Vienna 1973	Austrian Radio Orchestra Horvat	LP: Rococo 1021

Ariadne auf Naxos

Vienna 1960	Role of Composer Rysanek, Peters, Peerce, Berry, VPO Leinsdorf	LP: RCA RE 25023-5/SER 4523-5 LP: Decca 2BB 112-4

Der Rosenkavalier

Vienna June 1954	Role of Octavian Reining, Güden, Dermota, Weber, Poell, Vienna Opera Chorus, VPO, Kleiber	LP: Decca LXT 2954-7 LP: Decca 4BB 115-8 CD: Decca 425 950-2
Salzburg July 1960	Role of Octavian Della Casa, Güden, Zampieri, Edelmann, Kunz, Vienna Opera Chorus, VPO, Karajan	CD: Hunt CDKAR 213
Salzburg August 1960	Role of Octavian Schwarzkopf, Rothenberger, Zampieri, Edelmann, Kunz. Vienna Opera Chorus, VPO, Karajan	VHS Video: Rank 7015E
Salzburg July 1963	Role of Octavian Schwarzkopf, Rothenberger,
Romani, Edelmann, Dönch, Vienna Opera Chorus, VPO, Karajan	LP: Movimento Musica 04.004

Der Rosenkavalier: Excerpt (Da geht er hin)

Cologne 1975	Role of Marschallin Gürzenich Orchestra, Wallat	LP: Legendary LR 105

Tchaikovsky

Eugene Onegin

Hamburg September 1952	Role of Tatiana Litz, Ilosvay, Schock, Hasslo, Frick, NDR Chorus & Orchestra Schüchter Sung in German	LP: Eurodisc 301 033 435
Vienna January 1961	Role of Tatiana Cvejic, Rössl-Majdan, Dermota, Kreppel, Fischer-Dieskau, Vienna Opera Chorus VPO Matacic Sung in German	LP: Melodram MEL 046 Excerpt (Letter scene): LP: Legendary LR 105

Eugene Onegin: Excerpt (Letter Scene)

Hamburg 1950	Role of Tatiana NDR Orchestra, Martin Sung in German	LP: Melodram MEL 089

Joan of Arc: Excerpt (Lebt wohl, ihr Berge)

London August 1950	Role of Joan Philharmonia, Collingwood Sung in German	LP: HMV HQM 1024 LP: Electrola 1C 047 01444M CD: EMI CDH 763 1992

The Queen of Spades

Florence December 1952	Role of Lisa Pederzini, Poleri, Petri, Bastianini, Maggio Musicale Chorus & Orchestra, Rodzinski Sung in Italian	LP: Fonit Cetra DOC 63

The Queen of Spades: Excerpt (Es geht auf Mitternacht)

London August 1950	Role of Lisa Philharmonia Collingwood Sung in German	LP: EMI EX 769 7411 CD: EMI CDH 763 1992

SENA JURINAC

is featured in

THE DECCA COMPLETE RECORDING OF	THE RCA COMPLETE RECORDING OF
DER ROSENKAVALIER	**ARIADNE AUF NAXOS**
R. Strauss	R. Strauss
with Maria Reining, Hilde Gueden, Ludwig Weber, etc. and The Vienna State Opera Chorus with The Vienna Philharmonic Orchestra conducted by Erich Kleiber	with Roberta Peters, Leonie Rysanek, Jan Peerce, etc. and The Vienna Philharmonic Orchestra conducted by Erich Leinsdorf *(Courtesy Capitol Records)*
ⓜ LXT 2934 7	ⓢ SER-4523 5 ⓜ RE-25023/5
German/English libretto with thematic index 4/6	German/English libretto included with the set

THE DECCA RECORD COMPANY LTD
DECCA HOUSE   ALBERT EMBANKMENT   LONDON SE1

THE HAYDN-MOZART SOCIETY

LONDON MOZART PLAYERS

(Leader - Eli Goren)

Conductor
HARRY BLECH

NATIONAL ANTHEM

Overture and First Scene, Idomeneo	Mozart
Symphony No. 34 in C, K.338 and 409	Mozart

INTERVAL

Concert Aria, 'Bella mia Fiamma', K.528	Mozart
Symphony No. 8 in F	Beethoven

SENA JURINAC
Soprano

THURSDAY, 17 APRIL 1958, at 8 p.m.

IN ACCORDANCE WITH THE REQUIREMENTS OF THE LONDON COUNTY COUNCIL
(i) The public may leave at the end of the performance or exhibition by all exit doors and such doors must at that time be open.
(ii) All gangways, corridors, staircases and external passageways intended for exit shall be kept entirely free from obstruction, whether permanent or temporary.
(iii) Persons shall not be permitted to stand or sit in any of the gangways intersecting the seating, or to sit in any of the other gangways.

The right is reserved to make alterations in the programme if necessary

SMOKING IS NOT PERMITTED IN THE AUDITORIUM

ROYAL FESTIVAL HALL
General Manager—T. E. Bean, C.B.E.

Telemann

Saint Matthew Passion

Lucerne 1960	Soprano soloist Altmeyer, Gunter, Crass, Lucerne Festival Chorus & Orchestra Redel	LP: Philips SAL 3560-1 LP: Philips 835 359-60 AY

Verdi

Aida: Excerpts (Ritorna vincitor; O patria mia)

Hamburg 1950	Role of Aida NDR Orchestra Schüchter	LP: Melodram MEL 089

Un Ballo in Maschera: Excerpts (Ecco l'orrido campo; Morro, ma prima in grazia)

Hamburg 1950	Role of Amelia NDR Orchestra Schüchter	LP: Melodram MEL 089

Don Carlo

Salzburg July 1958	Role of Elisabetta Simionato, Fernandi, Siepi, Bastianini, Stefanoni, Vienna Opera Chorus VPO Karajan	LP: ERR 119 LP: Fonit Cetra LO 72 LP: Foyer FO 1029 CD: Hunt CDKAR 220 Excerpts: LP: Gioielli della lirica GML 19 LP: Legendary LR 105
Salzburg August 1960	Role of Elisabetta Resnik, Fernandi, Christoff, Arié, Bastianini, Vienna Opera Chorus VPO Santi	LP: Melodram MEL 036

La Forza del Destino: Excerpts (Madre, pietosa vergine; Pace, pace)

Edinburgh August 1955	Role of Leonora RPO Pritchard	LP: Legendary LR 105

Otello: Excerpt (Nun in der nächt'gen Stille)

Baden-Baden April 1952	Role of Desdemona Anders, Südwestfunk Orchestra Ackermann Sung in German	LP: Electrola E 83380 LP: Electrola 1C 147 29142-3M LP: Acanta DE 23.116-7

Wagner

Der Ring des Nibelungen

Rome
October and
November 1953

Roles of Woglinde (Das Rheingold); Gutrune & Third Norn (Götterdämmerung)
Mödl, Klose, Suthaus, Greindl, Frick,
Rome RAI Chorus & Orchestra,
Furtwängler

LP: MRF Records MRF 14 (Das Rheingold)
LP: MRF Records MRF 34 (Götterdämmerung)
LP: HMV RLS 702
LP: EMI EX 29 06703
CD: Hunt CDWFE 359
CD: EMI CZS 767 1232

Weber

Der Freischütz : Excerpt (Leise, leise)

Turin
1956

Role of Agathe
RAI Turin Orchestra,
Gui
Sung in Italian

LP: Legendary LR 105

Sena Jurinac:
roles performed with the Vienna State Opera

Includes performances with the Vienna company on tour
Figure against each role indicates number of times the part was performed

48	Antonia/Stella (The Tales of Hoffmann)
40	Butterfly (Madama Butterfly)
131	Cherubino (Le Nozze di Figaro)
58	Composer (Ariadne auf Naxos)
24	Countess Almaviva (Le Nozze di Figaro)
34	Desdemona (Otello)
18	Donna Anna (Don Giovanni)
62	Donna Elvira (Don Giovanni)
5	Dorabella (Così fan tutte)
11	Electra (Idomeneo)
48	Elisabetta (Don Carlo)
9	Euridice (Orpheus in the Underworld)
20	Eva (Die Meistersinger von Nürnberg)
38	Gabriele (Wiener Blut)
23	Giulietta (The Tales of Hoffmann)
21	Ighino (Palestrina)
13	Iphigénie (Iphigénie en Tauride)
32	Jenufa (Jenufa)
13	Kordula (Das Werbekleid)*
19	Kostelnicka (Jenufa)
6	1st Lady (Die Zauberflöte)
21	2nd Lady (Die Zauberflöte)
2	Leonore (Fidelio)

12	5th Maid (Elektra)
18	Manon (Manon)
11	Margiana (Der Barbier von Bagdad)
27	Marie (The Bartered Bride)
18	Marina (Boris Godunov)
49	Marschallin (Der Rosenkavalier)
15	Martha (Der Evangelimann)
16	Marzelline (Fidelio)
33	Micaela (Carmen)
77	Mimì (La Bohème)
82	Octavian (Der Rosenkavalier)
21	Ortlinde (Die Walküre)
11	Pamina (Die Zauberflöte)
18	Poppea (L'incoronazione di Poppea)
25	Rigobert (Die kleine Zauberflöte)**
34	Rosalinde (Die Fledermaus)
8	Rosaura (Die schalkhafte Witwe)***
6	Tatiana (Eugene Onegin)
34	Tosca (Tosca)
8	Wellgunde (Das Rheingold)

*Salmhofer
**Offenbach
***Wolf-Ferrari

Hilde Güden
Discography

Compiled by John Hunt
1991

Introduction

Hilde Güden was, for me, the most elusive of our Viennese ladies.

On the evidence of the recording I was particularly looking forward to hearing her sing Pamina in "Die Zauberflöte" at Salzburg in 1958. Alas, she was unwell on that particular August night and her place was taken by an understudy. My only consolation was that the role of Tamino was being sung by Fritz Wunderlich ! On another occasion the Vienna Philharmonic Orchestra was visiting London to give us one of its delightful Viennese evenings with Willi Boskovsky, and Hilde Güden had been announced as vocal soloist. Again, she was unable to travel and we had a programme without vocal contributions.

However, against these disappointments must be set the occasions when I did hear her, sparkling in the role of Aminta in what was the 1959 Salzburg premiere of Richard Strauss' "Schweigsame Frau", and as Mozart's Countess in "Figaro" on two separate occasions in Salzburg and Vienna.

Güden was a silver soubrette who developed into a golden soprano, although it is in the former category that she is most satisfactorily documented by gramophone recordings. Certainly on her visits to the USA she seems to have enjoyed her greatest successes as Gilda in "Rigoletto", whilst her prime contribution to contemporary opera must be her assumption of Anne Truelove in the American première of Stravinsky's "The Rake's Progress" (recorded by CBS).

Hilde Güden also has importance as being one of the first post-war artists to record what we now know as "crossover" albums: on a visit to London in the 1950s she recorded a selection of music from Ivor Novello and Noel Coward in a far more sincere and genuine manner, in my view, than many of our present-day jet age singers.

At the end of Hilde Güden's discography you will find a not inconsiderable selection of records of traditional Viennese song and operetta. No disrespect is intended if I have not listed all these items under composers' names. In fact, Güden's very important contribution to that area of the repertory, encouraged by her recording company in the early 1950s, underlines the fact that she alone, of our seven "Viennese" sopranos, was born in that very city.

John Hunt

Beethoven

Symphony No 9 "Choral"

Vienna February 1952	<u>Soprano soloist</u> Anday, Patzak, Poell, Singakademie VPO Furtwängler	LP: Rococo 2109
Vienna June 1952	<u>Soprano soloist</u> Wagner, Dermota, Weber, Singverein VPO Kleiber	LP: Decca LXT 2725-6 LP: Decca LXT 5362-3 LP: Decca LXT 5645 LP: Decca ECM 501/ECS 501 CD: Decca 425 9552
Vienna 1955	<u>Soprano soloist</u> Höngen, Majkut, Frick, Vienna Opera Chorus VPO Walter	CD: Nuova Era 2248
Paris 1963	<u>Soprano soloist</u> Heynis, Uhl, Rehfuss, Karlsruhe Choir Lamoureux Orchestra Markevitch	LP: Philips 893 500Y LP: Philips 6580 006

Bizet

Carmen

Vienna October 1954	<u>Role of Micaela</u> Simionato, Gedda, Roux, Singverein VSO Karajan	LP: GOP Dischi GFC 026-8 CD: Melodram MEL 27012
Vienna December 1962	<u>Role of Micaela</u> Resnik, Usunov, Protti, Vienna Opera Chorus VPO Karajan	CD: Hunt CDKAR 201

Debussy

Le Martyre de Saint Sébastien

Philadelphia 1960	Soprano soloist Zorina, Philadelphia Chorus & Orchestra Ormandy	LP: Columbia (USA) ML 5433-4 LP: CBS BRG 72078-9/SBRG 72078-9

Charpentier

Louise: Excerpt (Depuis le jour)

Vienna 1966	Role of Louise VPO Stein	LP: Decca ECS 2122

Donizetti

L'Elisir d'Amore

Florence September 1955	Role of Adina Di Stefano, Capecchi, Corena, Maggio Musicale Chorus & Orchestra Molinari-Pradelli	LP: Decca LXT 5155-7 LP: Decca GOM/GOS 566-7 CD: Decca 411 6992 Excerpts: LP: Decca LXT 5498 LP: Decca BR 3084

Gounod

Faust: Excerpts

Berlin 1962	Role of Margarethe Schock, Frick, Beresford, Deutsche Oper Chorus & Orchestra Schüchter Sung in German	LP: Eurodisc 201.594.250

Gluck

Orfeo ed Euridice

Milan April 1951	Role of Euridice Barbieri, Gabory, La Scala Chorus & Orchestra Furtwängler	LP: Discocorp RR 419 LP: Estro Armonico EA 022 LP: Fonit Cetra LO 19 LP: Turnabout THS 65112-3 LP: Fonit Cetra FE 46 FE 46 incorrectly states that role of Orfeo is sung by Giulietta Simionato
New York April 1955	Role of Euridice Stevens, Hurley, Metropolitan Opera Chorus & Orchestra Monteux	LP: Melodram MEL 438 CD: GDS Records GDS 21018

Haydn

The 7 last words of Christ

Salzburg July 1950	Soprano soloist Oehlschläger, Patzak, Braun Salzburg Cathedral Choir Mozarteum Orchestra Messner	LP: Remington 199-66 Incorrectly dated 1952

Korngold

Die tote Stadt: Excerpt (Marietta-Lied)

Vienna 1966	Role of Marietta VPO Stein	LP: Decca ECS 2122

Lehar

Giuditta

Vienna 1957	Role of Giuditta Loose, Kmennt, Dickie, Berry, Czerwenka, Vienna Opera Chorus & Orchestra Moralt	LP: Decca LK 4238-40 LP: Decca GOS 583-4 Excerpts LP: Decca BR 3035

Die lustige Witwe

Vienna 1958	Role of Hanna Loose, Grunden, Kmennt, Dönch, Vienna Opera Chorus & Orchestra Stolz	LP: Decca LXT 5448-9 LP: Decca SXL 2022-3 LP: Decca ADD/SDD 113-4 Excerpts LP: Decca LXT 5520 LP: Decca SXL 2133 CD: IMPS IMPX 9001

Lortzing

Der Waffenschmied: Selection

Vienna 1963	Role of Marie Kmennt, Wächter, Czerwenka, Vienna Opera Chorus Vienna Volksoper Orchestra Ronnefeld	LP: Decca LXT 6039/SXL 6039

Zar und Zimmermann: Selection

Vienna 1963	Role of Marie Kmennt, Wächter, Czerwenka, Vienna Opera Chorus Vienna Volksoper Orchestra Ronnefeld	LP: Decca LXT 6039/SXL 6039

Millöcker

Der Bettelstudent

Berlin 1962	Role of Laura Schädle, Konetzni, Schock, Minich, Ollendorff, Deutsche Oper Chorus & Orchestra Stolz	LP: Everest S 466 CD: Eurodisc 610.33023 Excerpts LP: Eurodisc IE 89887

Mozart

Requiem

Salzburg August 1950	Soprano soloist Anday, Patzak, Greindl Salzburg Cathedral Choir Mozarteum Orchestra Messner	LP: Remington 199-96 Incorrectly dated 1951

Exsultate, jubilate

Vienna 1955	Soprano soloist VPO Erede	LP: Decca LX 3103 LP: Decca LXT 5242 LP: Decca ECS 557

Don Giovanni

Vienna 1955	Role of Zerlina Danco, Della Casa, Dermota, Siepi, Corena, Böhme, Vienna Opera Chorus VPO Krips	LP: Decca LXT 5103-6 LP: Decca SXL 2117-20 LP: Decca GOS 604-6 CD: Decca 411 6262 Excerpts: LP: Decca LXT 5242 LP: Decca LXT 5443 LP: Decca BR 3025/SWL 8003 LP: Decca SDD 460
Vienna June 1963	Role of Elvira Price, Sciutti, Wunderlich, Berry, Wächter, Kreppel, Vienna Opera Chorus VPO Karajan	CD: Verona 27065-7

Don Giovanni: Excerpt (Vedrai carino)

London 1948	Role of Zerlina LSO Krips	78: Decca K 1861

Don Giovanni: Excerpt (La ci darem la mano)

Hamburg 1951	Role of Zerlina Schöffler, NDR Orchestra L. Ludwig	LP: Melodram MEL 084

Idomeneo: Excerpt (Se il padre perdei)

Vienna 1952	Role of Ilia VPO Krauss	LP: Decca LX 3067 LP: Decca LXT 5242 LP: Decca ECS 557

Idomeneo: Excerpt (Non temer, amato bene)

Vienna 1952	Role of Ilia VPO Krauss	LP: Decca LX 3067 LP: Decca ECS 557

Le Nozze di Figaro

Salzburg August 1953	Role of Cherubino Schwarzkopf, Seefried, Wagner, Kunz, Schöffler, Vienna Opera Chorus VPO Furtwängler Sung in German	LP: Ed Smith GMR 999 LP: Discocorp IGI 343 LP: Fonit Cetra LO 8 LP: Fonit Cetra FE 27 CD: Rodolphe RPC 32527-30*
Vienna 1955	Role of Susanna Della Casa, Danco, Rössl-Majdan, Siepi, Poell, Vienna Opera Chorus VPO Kleiber	LP: Decca LXT 5088-91 LP: Decca SXL 2087-90 LP: Decca GOS 585-7 CD: Decca 417 3152 Excerpts: LP: Decca LXT 5242 LP: Decca LXT 5459 LP: Decca LW 5253 LP: Decca SXL 2035 LP: Decca BR 3026 LP: Decca SDD 237
Salzburg July 1963	Role of Countess Sciutti, Lear, Fischer-Dieskau, Evans, Johnson, Vienna Opera Chorus VPO Maazel	LP: Movimento Musica 03.025 CD: Movimento Musica 013.004
Dresden 1964	Role of Countess Rothenberger, Mathis, Burmeister, Berry, Prey, Dresden Opera Chorus and Staatskapelle Suitner Sung in German	LP: Columbia (Germany) S/STC 91379-81 LP: Seraphim (USA) SIC 6002 LP: Electrola 1C 149 30159-61 Excerpts LP: Columbia (Germany) SMC 80860 LP: Electrola 1C 063 28994

Le Nozze di Figaro: Excerpt (Non so più)

London 1948	Role of Cherubino LSO Krips	78: Decca K 1861

Le Nozze di Figaro: Excerpt (Voi che sapete)

Vienna 1951	Role of Cherubino VPO Krauss	LP: Decca LX 3067 LP: Decca LXT 5242 LP: Decca ECS 557

Le Nozze di Figaro: Excerpts (1. Deh vieni, non tardar; 2. Venite inginocchiatevi)

Vienna 1951	Role of Susanna VPO Krauss	LP: Decca LX 3067 (1) LP: Decca LX 3103 (2) LP: Decca ECS 557

Le Nozze di Figaro: Excerpts (1. Che soave zeffiretto; 2. Crudel, perche finora?)

Cologne 1951	Role of Susanna Grümmer, Schöffler, WDR Orchestra Fricsay Sung in German	LP: Melodram MEL 083 (1) LP: Melodram MEL 084 (2)

Il Rè pastore: Excerpt (L'amerò, sarò costante)

Vienna 1954	Role of Aminta VPO Erede	LP: Decca LX 3103 LP: Decca LXT 5242 LP: Decca ECS 557

Die Zauberflöte

Vienna 1955	Role of Pamina Lipp, Loose, Simoneau, Berry, Böhme, Schöffler, Vienna Opera Chorus VPO Böhm	LP: Decca LXT 5085-7 LP: Decca SXL 2215-7 LP: Decca GOS 501-3 CD: Decca 414 3622 LP: Decca LW 5343 LP: Decca SDD 218

Die Zauberflöte: Excerpt (Ach, ich fühl's)

Vienna 1954	Role of Pamina VPO Erede	LP: Decca LX 3103 LP: Decca LXT 5242 LP: Decca ECS 557

STAATSOPER

WIEDERERÖFFNUNG

Mittwoch, den 1. September 1965
Bei aufgehobenem Abonnement – Beschränkter Kartenverkauf
Preise IV

In italienischer Sprache

Die Hochzeit des Figaro

Komische Oper in vier Akten von Wolfgang Amadeus Mozart
Text nach Beaumarchais von Lorenzo da Ponte

Dirigent: Josef Krips
Inszenierung: Günther Rennert
Spielleitung: Josef Witt
Bühnenbild und Kostüme: Ita Maximowna

Graf Almaviva	Eberhard Wächter
Gräfin Almaviva	Hilde Güden
Susanne, deren Kammermädchen	Graziella Sciutti
Figaro, Kammerdiener des Grafen	Erich Kunz
Cherubino, Page des Grafen	Olivera Miljakovic
Marcelline, Haushälterin im Schlosse des Grafen	Hilde Rössel-Majdan
Basilio, Musikmeister im Dienste des Grafen	Murray Dickie
Don Curzio, Richter	Erich Majkut
Bartolo, Arzt aus Sevilla	Alois Pernerstorfer
Antonio, Gärtner des Grafen und Onkel der Susanne	Ljubo Pantscheff
Barbarina, seine Tochter	Lucia Popp
Erstes Bauernmädchen	Anna Vajda
Zweites Bauernmädchen	Edith Hintermeyer

Ort der Handlung ist das Schloß des Grafen Almaviva

Choreographie: Erika Hanka
Ausführende: Die Damen Fiala, Macholan, Philipp;
die Herren Jandosch, Hiess, Zajetz

Technische Einrichtung: Hans Felkel – Beleuchtung: Albin Rotter

Nach dem zweiten Akt eine größere Pause

Anfang 19 Uhr   Ende nach 22 Uhr

Preis des Programms S 6,–

Puccini

La Bohème

Rome 1951	Role of Musetta Tebaldi, Prandelli, Corena, Arié, Inghilleri, Saint Cecilia Chorus & Orchestra Erede	LP: Decca LXT 2622-3 LP: Decca ACL 121-2 Excerpts: LP: Decca LXT 5387 LP: Decca ACL 186 LP: Decca ECS 2122
New York March 1952	Role of Musetta Albanese, Di Stefano, Guarrera, Siepi, Harvuot, Metropolitan Opera Chorus & Orchestra Erede	LP: GOP Records GFC 021-2
Vienna November 1963	Role of Musetta Freni, Raimondi, Taddei, Panerai, Vinco, Vienna Opera Chorus VPO Karajan	LP: Melodram MEL 414 LP: Movimento Musica 02.020 CD: Melodram MEL 27007 CD: Rodolphe RPC 32513 CD: Curcio OP 1

La Bohème: Excerpts

Berlin 1944	Role of Musetta Eipperle, Anders, Domgraf-Fassbänder, Berlin RO Steinkopf Sung in German	LP: BASF 10.214966

La Bohème: Excerpt (Quando men vo)

London 1948	Role of Musetta LSO Krips	78: Decca M 614

La Bohème: Excerpts (Sì, mi chiamano Mimì; Donde lieta uscì)

London 1948	Role of Mimì LSO Krips	78: Decca X 302

Gianni Schicchi: Excerpt (O mio babbino caro)

London 1948	<u>Role of Lauretta</u> LSO Krips	78: Decca M 614
Rome 1951	<u>Role of Lauretta</u> Saint Cecilia Orchestra Erede	LP: Decca LW 5178 LP: Decca ECS 2122

Turandot: Excerpts (Signore, ascolta; Tu che di gel cinta)

Rome 1951	<u>Role of Liù</u> Saint Cecilia Orchestra Erede	LP: Decca LW 5178 LP: Decca ECS 2122

Schmidt

<u>Das Buch mit sieben Siegeln</u>

Salzburg August 1959	<u>Soprano soloist</u> Malaniuk, Dermota, Wunderlich, Berry, Singverein VPO Mitropoulos	LP: Melodram MEL 705 CD: Melodram MEL 27078

Johann Strauss

Die Fledermaus

Vienna 1950	Role of Rosalinde Lipp, Wagner, Patzak, Dermota, Poell, Preger, Vienna Opera Chorus VPO Krauss	LP: Decca LXT 2550-1 LP: Decca ACL 145-6 LP: Preiser PR 135035-6 Excerpts LP: Decca LXT 2576 LP: Decca ACL 73
Vienna July 1960	Role of Rosalinde Köth, Resnik, Kmennt, Zampieri, Berry, Wächter, Vienna Opera Chorus VPO Karajan	LP: Decca MET/SET 201-3 LP: Decca LXT/SXL 6015-6 LP: Decca D247 D3 CD: Decca 421 0462 Excerpts: LP: Decca LXT/SXL 6155
Vienna December 1960	Role of Rosalinde Streich, Stolze, Kunz, Zampieri, Berry, Kunz, Vienna Opera Chorus VPO Karajan	LP: Foyer FO 1031 CD: Foyer 3CF-2021 CD: Hunt CDKAR 215 Excerpts: LP: Gioielli della lirica GML 25

Die Fledermaus: Excerpts

Vienna 1961	Role of Rosalinde Rothenberger, Terkal, Equiluz, Rössl-Majdan, Vienna Opera Chorus VPO Hollreiser	LP: HMV ALP 1875/ASD 444 LP: EMI CFP 40251

Dorfsschwalben aus Oesterreich

Vienna 1958	VPO Krips	45: Decca CEP 708 LP: Decca ECS 2122

Frühlingsstimmen

Brussels June 1958	VPO Karajan	LP: Movimento Musica 01.039 CD: Movimento Musica 051.030 CD: Hunt CDKAR 215
Vienna 1958	VPO Krips	45: Decca CEP 708 LP: Decca ECS 2122

Der Zigeunerbaron

Vienna
1961

Role of Saffi
Rothenberger,
Rössl-Majdan,
Terkal, Berry,
Kunz,
Singverein
VPO
Hollreiser

LP: HMV ALP 1812-3/ASD 394-5
Excerpts:
LP: HMV ALP 1875/ASD 444
LP: EMI CFP 40251

Wiener Blut

Vienna
June 1965

Role of Gabriele
Lipp, Schramm,
Schock, Gruber,
Kusche,
Chorus
VSO
Stolz

LP: Eurodisc XE 72750-1
Excerpts
LP: Eurodisc IE 89896

Richard Strauss

Arabella

Vienna 1957	Role of Zdenka Della Casa, Malaniuk, London, Dermota, Edelmann, VPO Solti	LP: Decca LXT 5403-6 LP: Decca SXL 2050-3 LP: Decca GOS 571-3

Arabella: Excerpt (Aber der Richtige)

Vienna 1953	Role of Zdenka Della Casa, VPO Moralt	LP: Decca LW 5029 LP: Decca LXT 2865 CD: Decca 425 9592

Ariadne auf Naxos

Salzburg August 1954	Role of Zerbinetta Della Casa, Seefried, Schock, Schöffler, Vienna Opera Chorus VPO Böhm	LP: Melodram MEL 104

Daphne

Vienna June 1964	Role of Daphne Wunderlich, King, Little, Schöffler, Streich, Vienna Opera Chorus VPO Böhm	LP: DG SLPM 138 956-7 LP: DG 2707 019 LP: DG 2726 090 CD: DG 423 5792

Die schweigsame Frau

Salzburg August 1959	Role of Aminta Milinkovic, Prey, Wunderlich, Hotter, Vienna Opera Chorus VPO Böhm	LP: Melodram MEL 105 CD: Melodram MEL 27071

Der Rosenkavalier

Salzburg August 1949	Role of Sophie Reining, Novotna, Roswaenge, Hann, Prohaska, Vienna Opera Chorus VPO Szell	LP: Fonit Cetra LO 69
Vienna June 1954	Role of Sophie Reining, Jurinac, Dermota, Weber, Poell, Vienna Opera Chorus VPO Kleiber	LP: Decca LXT 2954-7 LP: Decca 4BB 115-8 CD: Decca 425 9502
Salzburg July 1960	Role of Sophie Della Casa, Jurinac, Zampieri, Edelmann, Kunz, Vienna Opera Chorus VPO Karajan	CD: Hunt CDKAR 213

Der Rosenkavalier: Excerpts (Mir ist die Ehre widerfahren; Marie Theres'; Ist ein Traum, kann nicht wirklich sein; other excerpts without Güden)

Vienna 1963	Role of Sophie Crespin, Söderström, Holecek, Vienna Opera Chorus VPO Varviso	LP: Decca LXT 6146/SXL 6146 LP: Decca JB 57

Lieder: Einerlei; Schlechtes Wetter; Schlagende Herzen; Befreit

Vienna 1958	Gulda, piano	45: Decca CEP 593 LP: Decca ECS 630 LP: London (USA) R 23212

Lieder: Säusle, liebe Myrthe; Der Stern; Ich wollt' ein Sträusslein binden; Als mir dein Lied erklang; Freundliche Vision; Heimkehr; Die Nacht; Wie sollten wir geheim; Meinem Kinde

Vienna 1958	Gulda, piano	LP: Decca ECS 630 LP: London (USA) R 23212

SALZBURGER FESTSPIELE 1959

DIE SCHWEIGSAME FRAU

KOMISCHE OPER IN DREI AUFZÜGEN
FREI NACH BEN JONSON VON STEFAN ZWEIG

MUSIK VON
RICHARD STRAUSS

DIRIGENT
KARL BÖHM

INSZENIERUNG
GÜNTHER RENNERT

BÜHNENBILD
TEO OTTO

KOSTÜME
ERNI KNIEPERT

ORCHESTER
DIE WIENER PHILHARMONIKER
CHOR DER WIENER STAATSOPER

DIE SCHWEIGSAME FRAU

Komische Oper in drei Aufzügen
Frei nach Ben Jonson von Stefan Zweig
MUSIK VON RICHARD STRAUSS
Opus 80

Sir Morosus	Hans Hotter
Seine Haushälterin	Georgine v. Milinkovic
Der Barbier	Hermann Prey
Henry Morosus	Fritz Wunderlich
Aminta, seine Frau	Hilde Güden
Isotta	Pierette Alarie
Carlotta — Komödianten	Hetty Plümacher
Morbio	Josef Knapp
Vanuzzi	Carl Dönch
Farfallo	Alois Pernerstorfer

Chor der Komödianten und Nachbarn

Ort der Handlung:
Zimmer des Sir Morosus in einem Vorort Londons

Zeit: Nach 1780

Größere Pause nach dem ersten Aufzug

Kleinere Pause nach dem zweiten Aufzug

Der offizielle Almanach „Salzburg — Festspiele 1959" ist auch für Sie der unentbehrliche Ratgeber
The official almanac "Salzburg Festivals 1959" is an indispensable guide for all Festival visitors
L'almanach officiel «Salzbourg Festival 1959» est indispensable à tous ceux qui s'intéressent au Festival

Stravinsky

The Rake's Progress

New York 1953	Role of Anne Thebom, Lipton, Conley, Harrell, Metropolitan Opera Chorus & Orchestra Stravinsky	LP: Philips ABL 3055-7

Verdi

Falstaff: Excerpt (Sul fil d'un soffio etesio)

Rome 1954	Role of Nanetta Saint Cecilia Orchestra Erede	LP: Decca LW 5178 LP: Decca ECS 2122

Rigoletto

New Orleans 1952	Role of Gilda Muhs, Warren, Conley, Wildermann, Chorus & orchestra Herbert	LP: Legendary LR 205
Rome 1954	Role of Gilda Simionato, Protti, Del Monaco, Siepi, Saint Cecilia Chorus & Orchestra Erede	LP: Decca LXT 5006-8 LP: Decca ACL 203-5 Excerpts: LP: Decca LXT 5397 LP: Decca LW 5206 LP: Decca ECS 2122

Rigoletto: Excerpts (Caro nome; Tutte le feste)

Vienna 1951	Role of Gilda VPO Krauss	LP: Decca LX 3067

La Traviata: Excerpts (1. Trinklied; 2. 'S ist seltsam; 3. Unschuldig wie ein Engel; 4. Alfred, ihr hier?; 5. Lebt wohl jetzt; 6. O lass uns fliehen; 7. Nimm es, hier ist dies Bild von mir; other excerpts without Güden)

Munich 1966	Role of Violetta Wunderlich, Fischer-Dieskau, Hellmann, Kohn, Bavarian Radio Chorus & Orchestra Bartoletti Sung in German	LP: DG SLPEM 136 431 LP: DG 2535 322 LP: DG 413 8371 (1,6) CD: DG 423 8732

La Traviata: Excerpt (Sempre libera)

Rome 1954	Role of Violetta Saint Cecilia Orchestra Erede	LP: Decca LW 5178 LP: Decca ECS 2122

Wagner

Die Meistersinger von Nürnberg

Vienna 1950 (Act 2) and 1951 (Acts 1 & 3)	Role of Eva Schürhoff, Treptow, Dermota, Schöffler, Edelmann, Vienna Opera Chorus VPO Knappertsbusch	LP: LXT 2560-1 (Act 2) LP: Decca LXT 2646-7 (Act 1) LP: Decca LXT 2648-50 (Act 3) LP: Decca LXT 2659-64 LP: Decca GOM 535-9 Excerpts: LP: Decca LW 5101 LP: Decca LW 5103 LP: Decca LXT 5544 LP: Decca BR 3089

Weber

Der Freischütz: Excerpt (Einst träumte meiner sel'gen Base...Trübe Augen, blasse Wangen)

Berlin 1944	Orchestra and conductor unknown	LP: DG 88025

Zeller

Der Vogelhändler: Excerpts

Munich 1959	Role of Christel Schädle, Mödl, Minich, Kusche, Bavarian RO Michalski	LP: Telefunken NT 600

Collections

Songs from Viennese operetta: 1. Der Favorit; 2. Clivia; 3. Flucht ins Glück; 4. Paganini; 5. Schwedische Nachtigall; 6. Der Zarewitsch

London	Kingsway Symphony	78: Decca M 666 (1,5)
1948	Orchestra	78: Decca F 9318 (4,6)
	May	LP: Decca LM 4516

Operetta duets with Karl Friedrich: Giuditta; Land des Lächelns; other operetta arias without Güden

Vienna	Friedrich,	LP: Decca LX 3068
1951	VPO	
	Loibner	

Operetta Recital: Die Dubarry; Land des Lächelns; Giuditta; Gräfin Maritza; Paganini; Die Czardasfürstin

Vienna	VPO	LP: Decca LX 3071
1951	Loibner	

This is my Vienna: O du lieber Augustin; Brüderlein fein; Die Banda kommt; S'Mailüfterl Wenn die Geigen heimlich streicheln; Wiener Künstler; Das ist mein Wien; Kunst und Natur; Ich und der Mond; Wien, Weib, Wein; S'Herz von an echten Weana; Vogerl, flieg in d'Welt hinaus; Wie sich der Wiener den Himmel vorstellt; Wienerwald; Herrgott, wie schön bist du, Wien

Vienna	Orchestra	LP: Decca LX 3108
1953	Adler	

Christmas Songs: 1. O du fröhliche; 2. O Tannenbaum; 3. Was soll das bedeuten? 4. Es blühen die Maien; 5. Es ist ein Ros' entsprungen; 6. Es hat sich halt eröffnet; 7. Süsser die Glocken nie klingen; 8. Stille Nacht, heilige Nacht

Vienna	VPO	LP: Decca LX 3117
1953	Rossmayr	45: Decca CEP 520 (1,2,5,8)

Operetta Recital: Wiener Blut; Sissy; Gräfin Maritza; Der tapfere Soldat; Madame Pompadour; Zigeunerliebe

Vienna	Vienna Opera Chorus	LP: Decca LW 5126
1954	VPO	LP: Decca LXT 5033
	Schönherr	LP: Decca PA 52/SPA 52

Operetta Recital: Hoheit tanzt Walzer; Der Zarewitsch; Schön ist die Welt; Die
lustige Witwe; Ein Walzertraum; Die Tänzerin Fanny Elssler

Vienna	Vienna Opera Chorus	LP: Decca LW 5133
1954	VPO	LP: Decca LXT 5033
	Schönherr	LP: Decca PA 52/SPA 52

Hilde Güden sings Noel Coward and Ivor Novello: Music in May; I'll follow my secret
heart; Zigeuner; Some day my heart will awake; I can give you the starlight; Waltz
of my heart; I'll see you again; A violin began to play; Some day I'll find you;
Glamorous night

London	Chorus & Orchestra	LP: Decca LK 4196
1955	Black	

Operetta Evergreens: 1. Gräfin Maritza; 2. Im weissen Rössl; 3. Der Zarewitsch;
4. Madame Pompadour; 5. Casanova; 6. Zigeunerliebe; 7. Der Favorit; 8. Die Fledermaus;
9. Der Obersteiger; 10. Wiener Blut; 11. Der tapfere Soldat

Vienna	VPO	LP: Decca LXT 5658
1961	Stolz	LP: Decca SXL 2295
		LP: Telefunken AF 628.228 (1)
		LP: Decca 414 1761
		CD: IMP IMPX 9001 (5,8)

Viennese Roundabout: Im Prater blüh'n wieder die Bäume; Draussen in Sievering; Wien,
Wien, nur du allein; Wiener Blut; other items with other artists

Vienna	Orchestra	LP: Telefunken GMA 77
1963		Im Prater blüh'n wieder die Bäume
		LP: Telefunken 628.303

Königin der Operette: Madame Pompadour; Ball im Savoy; Cagliostro; Die Dubarry;
Frühjahrsparade; Sissy; Der Zarewitsch; Rund um die Liebe; Gitta entdeckt ihr Herz;
Die Czardasfürstin

Vienna	Vienna Volksoper	LP: Telefunken SLK 16622
1965	Orchestra	LP: Telefunken AF 622.228 (Czardasfürstin)
	Paulik	

Das Wiener Lied mit Hilde Güden: So war's Anno '30 in Wien; Das Glück is' a Vogerl;
Ja, das ist halt so; O du lieber Augustin; Stadt der Lieder; Wenn's Mailüfterl weht;
Vogerl fliagst in d' Welt hinaus; Brüderlein fein

Vienna	Orchestra	LP: Polydor 2371 057
1966	Carste	

Childrens' Songs from many lands

Vienna	Vienna Volksoper	LP: Decca SXL 6424
1968	Orchestra	
	G. Fischer	

Hilde Güden:
roles performed with the Vienna State Opera

Includes performances with the Vienna company on tour
Figure against each role indicates number of times the part was performed

11	Alice Ford (Falstaff)
9	Cherubino (Le Nozze di Figaro)
44	Countess Almaviva (Le Nozze di Figaro)
5	Daphne (Daphne)
6	Despina (Così fan tutte)
28	Donna Elvira (Don Giovanni)
9	Fiordiligi (Così fan tutte)
6	2nd Flower Maiden (Parsifal)
39	Gilda (Rigoletto)
22	Liù (Turandot)
8	Margarethe (Faust)
25	Marzelline (Fidelio)
8	Mélisande (Pelléas et Mélisande)
61	Micaela (Carmen)
54	Mimì (La Bohème)
2	Musetta (La Bohème)
72	Pamina (Die Zauberflöte)
59	Rosalinde (Die Fledermaus)
60	Sophie (Der Rosenkavalier)
46	Susanna (Le Nozze di Figaro)
38	Violetta (La Traviata)
9	Zerbinetta (Ariadne auf Naxos)
53	Zerlina (Don Giovanni)

Lisa Della Casa
Discography

Compiled by John Hunt
1991

Introduction

The nobility of Lisa Della Casa's voice and her physical appearance always brought international critical acclaim. This applied equally to her operatic and her concert performances. The great conductors appreciated her musicianship, which was legendary. Fritz Reiner said to her during a recording session in Chicago "Lisa, you know I don't like singers, but you're not a singer - you are a musician!"

She was the most noted interpreter of Richard Strauss in her time and had the privilege of entering musical history, while still artistically active and famous, as Arabella, and also as the Marschallin, Octavian, Ariadne, the Countess in "Capriccio", Chrysothemis and Salome.

But her fame was not limited to Richard Strauss, for she was also considered an ideal Mozart singer. The Countess in "Figaro" was one of her most frequently sung parts. She sang Donna Anna in 1955 at the reopening of the Vienna State Opera and Donna Elvira at the opening of the new Met and, years earlier, in the film of the outstanding Salzburg production under Furtwängler's direction. Her Fiordiligi, Countess and Elvira are immortalised on records (the last two each recorded twice).

As a result of her extraordinary technique she was able to sing both lyrical and dramatic works up to the end of her career, frequently alternating roles within the same week. Her repertoire ranged from Bach and Handel, through Puccini, Wagner and Hindemith, to Gottfried von Einem: in the premiere of "Der Prozess" in 1953 in Salzburg she sang all three female parts.

Lisa Della Casa was also a frequent Lieder singer. Extensive tours took her to the most important countries and cities of Europe, North and South America, Australia and Japan. In Lieder too she maintained her individuality: she would make neither compromise nor concession in the planning of her programmes and her interpretations.

At the 1970 World Fair in Japan she represented her homeland, Switzerland, performing Richard Strauss' "4 Last Songs" and making her last public appearance as a Lieder singer (this recital was recorded and later issued by Relief Records).

Kammersängerin Lisa Della Casa ended her 31-year stage career at the end of November 1973, Arabella being her last public performance. There were no prior announcements and no farwell performances. True to her character and her resolution to retire whilst still in possession of her full powers, she made her decision spontaneously and privately.

Edited version of an article by Rico Leitner

Bach

Ave Maria (arr. Gounod)

Hamburg 1960	Hamburg State Chorus & Orchestra Hertel	LP: Telefunken 628.303 45: Decca (Germany) 45-23370

Beethoven

Fidelio

Salzburg August 1948	Role of Marzelline Schlüter, Patzak, Schock, Alsen, Frantz, Edelmann, Vienna Opera Chorus VPO Furtwängler	LP: Rococo 1012 Nos. 5-8 missing from recording

Brahms

Lieder: Wie Melodien; Immer leiser wird mein Schlummer; Von ewiger Liebe; Ständchen

Vienna 1957	Hudez, piano	LP: Decca LXT 5258

Lieder: Wie Melodien; Die Mainacht; Auf dem Kirchhofe; Mein' Lieb ist ein Jäger; Brauner Bursche; Vergebliches Ständchen

Tokyo May 1970	Kobayashi, piano	LP: Relief RL 825 CD: Relief CR 1825

Dvorak

Zigeunerlieder

Tokyo May 1970	Kobayashi, piano	LP: Relief RL 825 CD: Relief CR 1825

Orfeo ed Euridice

Rome 1956	Role of Euridice Stevens, Peters, Rome Opera Chorus & Orchestra Monteux	LP: RCA RB 16058-60

Handel

Giulio Cesare: Excerpts (1. Hast du mich ganz berauscht; 2. Es blaut die Nacht; 3. Breite aus die gnädigen Hände; 4. Weine nur, klage nur; 5. Heil und sicher kam dein Nachen)

Vienna 1956	Role of Cleopatra VPO Hollreiser	LP: Decca LXT 5277 45: Decca CEP 595/SEC 5017 (3,4) LP: Decca SDD 288

Nelson Mass

Vienna 1951	Soprano soloist Höngen, Taubmann, London, Akademiechor VSO Sternberg	LP: Haydn Society HSLP 2004 Also published on Nixa label

Lehar

Der Graf von Luxemburg: Excerpt (Bist du's, lachendes Glück)

Zürich 1946	Role of Angèle Roswaenge, Tonhalle Orchestra Reinshagen	78: Decca K 2181 LP: Decca LM 5420 45: Decca 45-71134 LP: London (USA) R 23253

Die lustige Witwe (Abridged version)

New York 1961	Role of Hanna Hurley, Reardon, Davis, American Opera Society Chorus and Orchestra Allers Sung in English	LP: CBS OL 2280/OS 2280 LP: CBS 61833

Der Zarewitsch (Abridged version)

Zürich 1946	Role of Sonia Funk, Roswaenge, Jungwirth, Zürich Choir, Tonhalle Orchestra Reinshagen	LP: Decca LK 4033 LP: Relief RL 826 Excerpts: LP: Decca BR 3034

Mahler

Symphony No 4

Chicago 1959	Soprano soloist Chicago SO Reiner	LP: RCA RB 16205/SB 2081 LP: RCA AGL1-5256 CD: RCA (USA) 5722-2 RC

Lieder: Rheinlegendchen; Hans und Grete; Ich ging mit Lust; Ich bin der Welt abhanden gekommen

Tokyo May 1970	Kobayashi, piano	LP: Relief RL 825 CD: Relief CR 1825

Mozart

Requiem

Salzburg
July 1956

Soprano soloist
Malaniuk,
Dermota, Siepi,
Vienna Opera Chorus
VPO
Walter

LP: Fonit Cetra LO 516
CD: Nuova Era 2209

Così fan tutte

Vienna
1954

Role of Fiordiligi
Ludwig, Loose,
Dermota, Kunz,
Schöffler,
Vienna Opera Chorus
VPO
Böhm

LP: Decca LXT 5107-9
LP: Decca GOM/GOS 543-5
Excerpts:
LP: Decca LXT 5277
LP: Decca LXT 5511
LP: Decca SXL 2058
EP: Decca CEP 572
LP: Decca BR 3085
LP: Decca SDD 288

Don Giovanni

Vienna
1955

Role of Elvira
Danco, Güden,
Dermota, Siepi,
Corena, Böhme,
Vienna Opera Chorus
VPO
Krips

LP: Decca LXT 5103-6
LP: Decca SXL 2117-20
LP: Decca GOS 604-6
CD: Decca 411 6262
Excerpts:
LP: Decca LXT 5277
LP: Decca LXT 5443
LP: Decca BR 3025/SWL 8003
LP: Decca SDD 288
LP: Decca SDD 460

Salzburg
July 1956

Role of Elvira
Grümmer, Streich,
Simoneau, Siepi,
Corena, Frick,
Vienna Opera Chorus
VPO
Mitropoulos

LP: Replica ARPL 42422
LP: Discoreale DR 10021-3
CD: Hunt CD 552
Early pressings of the Hunt CD
contained a 1960 Salzburg
performance conducted by Karajan
and with a different cast

Don Giovanni: Excerpt (Final scene)

Salzburg
August 1954

Role of Elvira
Grümmer, Berger,
Dermota, Siepi,
Edelmann, Berry,
VPO
Furtwängler

LP: Furtwängler Series (Japan) W 28-29
Taken from film soundtrack
(Connoisseur Films/Beta Films)

Don Giovanni: Excerpt (Fuggi, crudele, fuggi....Or sai che l'onore)

Vienna
November 1955

Role of Anna
Dermota
VPO
Böhm
Sung in German

CD: Melodram CDM 26522

Le Nozze di Figaro

Vienna 1955	Role of Countess Güden, Danco, Rössl-Majdan, Siepi, Poell, Vienna Opera Chorus VPO Kleiber	LP: Decca LXT 5088-91 LP: Decca SXL 2087-90 LP: Decca GOS 585-7 CD: Decca 417 3152 Excerpts: LP: Decca LXT 5277 LP: Decca LXT 5459 LP: Decca LW 5253 LP: Decca SXL 2035 LP: Decca BR 3026 LP: Decca SDD 237 LP: Decca SDD 288
Vienna 1959	Role of Countess Peters, Elias, Warfield, Tozzi, London, Vienna Opera Chorus VPO Leinsdorf	LP: RCA RE 25009-12/SB 4508-11 LP: Decca ECS 743-5

Le Nozze di Figaro: Excerpt (Voi che sapete)

Geneva 1951	Role of Cherubino Suisse Romande Orchestra Reinshagen	LP: Decca LXT 2685

Die Zauberflöte

Salzburg July 1959	Role of Pamina Sciutti, Köth, Simoneau, Böhme, Hotter, Vienna Opera Chorus VPO Szell	LP: Melodram MEL 007 CD: Melodram MEL 27505

Die Zauberflöte: Excerpt (Ach, ich fühl's)

Geneva 1951	Role of Pamina Suisse Romande Orchestra Reinshagen	LP: Decca LXT 2685

SALZBURGER FESTSPIELE 1959

DIE ZAUBERFLÖTE

OPER IN ZWEI AUFZÜGEN
TEXT VON EMANUEL SCHIKANEDER

MUSIK VON
WOLFGANG AMADEUS MOZART

DIRIGENT
GEORGE SZELL

INSZENIERUNG
GÜNTHER RENNERT

BÜHNENBILD UND KOSTÜME
ITA MAXIMOWNA

ORCHESTER
DIE WIENER PHILHARMONIKER
CHOR DER WIENER STAATSOPER

DIE ZAUBERFLÖTE

Oper in zwei Aufzügen
Text von Emanuel Schikaneder
MUSIK VON WOLFGANG AMADEUS MOZART

Sarastro	Kurt Böhme
Tamino	Leopold Simoneau
Sprecher	Hans Hotter
Erster Priester	Erich Majkut
Zweiter Priester	Alfred Jerger
Königin der Nacht	Erika Köth
Pamina, ihre Tochter	Lisa Della Casa
Erste Dame	Friederike Sailer
Zweite Dame	Hetty Plümacher
Dritte Dame	Sieglinde Wagner
Papageno	Walter Berry
Papagena	Graziella Sciutti
Monostatos, ein Mohr	Carl Dönch
Erster Knabe	
Zweiter Knabe	Drei Wiener Sängerknaben
Dritter Knabe	
Erster Geharnischter	Robert Charlebois
Zweiter Geharnischter	Alois Pernerstorfer

Priester, Sklaven, Gefolge

Schlußbild des zweiten Aufzuges nach Oscar Strnad

Nach dem ersten Aufzug eine größere Pause

Der offizielle Almanach „Salzburg — Festspiele 1959" ist auch für Sie der unentbehrliche Ratgeber
The official almanac "Salzburg Festivals 1959" is an indispensable guide for all Festival visitors
L'almanach officiel «Salzbourg Festival 1959» est indispensable à tous ceux qui s'intéressent au Festival

Offenbach

La Vie Parisienne

Berlin February 1968	Role of Metella Hallstein, Schramm, Schock, Gruber, Unger, Wächter, Böhme, Deutsche Staatsoper Chorus Berlin SO Allers Sung in German	LP: Eurodisc XE 77485 Excerpts LP: Eurodisc IE 89889 CD: RCA GD 69028

Puccini

La Bohème: Excerpt (O soave fanciulla...to end Act 1)

Hollywood 1962	Role of Mimi Gedda Hollywood Bowl Orchestra Conductor unknown	LP: Melodram MEL 659

Tosca: Excerpts

Berlin September 1959	Role of Tosca Schock, Metternich, Deutsche Oper Chorus Berlin SO Klobucar Sung in German	LP: Electrola SME 80538

Schubert

Lieder Recital: Auf dem Wasser zu singen; Im Frühling; Du bist die Ruh'; Gretchen am Spinnrade

Vienna 1957	Hudez, piano	LP: Decca LXT 5258

Ave Maria

Hamburg 1960	Hamburg State Chorus & Orchestra Hertel	45: Decca (Germany) 45-23370

Schumann

Frauenliebe und -Leben

1963	Peschko, piano	LP: HMV ALP 2044/ASD 593

434   Della Casa

Johann Strauss

Der Zigeunerbaron: Excerpt (Wer uns getraut)

Zürich 1946	Role of Saffi Roswaenge, Tonhalle Orchestra Reinshagen	78: Decca K 2181 LP: Decca LM 4520 45: Decca 45-71134 LP: London (USA) R 23253

Richard Strauss

4 letzte Lieder

Vienna 1953	VPO Böhm	LP: Decca LXT 2865 LP: Decca LW 5056 LP: Decca LXT 5403-6 LP: Decca ACL 318 LP: Decca BR 3100 LP: Decca ECM 778 LP: Decca 411 6601 CD: Decca 425 9592
Munich 1971	Bavarian State Orchestra Rieger	LP: Discocorp IGI 301

Ariadne auf Naxos

Salzburg August 1954	Role of Ariadne Güden, Seefried, Schock, Schöffler, VPO Böhm	LP: Melodram MEL 104

Ariadne auf Naxos: Excerpts (Es gibt ein Reich; Closing Scene; other excerpts without Della Casa)

Berlin June 1959	Role of Ariadne Köth, Schock, BPO Erede	LP: Electrola E 80503/STE 80503

Ariadne auf Naxos: Excerpt (Es gibt ein Reich)

Vienna 1954	Role of Ariadne VPO Hollreiser	LP: Decca LXT 5017 LP: Decca ECM 778 LP: Decca ECS 812 LP: Decca 411 6601 CD: Decca 425 9592

Arabella

Vienna 1957	Role of Arabella Güden, Malaniuk, London, Dermota, Edelmann VPO Solti	LP: Decca LXT 540306 LP: Decca SXL 2050-3 LP: Decca GOS 571-3
Munich July 1963	Role of Arabella Rothenberger, Malaniuk, Kohn, Fischer-Dieskau, Bavarian State Orchestra Keilberth	LP: DG LPM 18883-5/SLPM 138 883-5 LP: DG 2709 013 LP: DG 2721 163 Excerpts: LP: DG SLPEM 136 419
Salzburg August 1947	Role of Zdenka Reining, Anday, Hotter, Hann, VPO Böhm	LP: Melodram MEL 101

Arabella: Excerpt (Aber der Richtige)

Vienna 1953	Role of Arabella Güden, VPO Moralt	LP: Decca LXT 2865 LP: Decca LW 5029 CD: Decca 425 9592
Dresden 1965	Role of Arabella Rothenberger, Dresden Staatskapelle Neuhaus	LP: Eterna (East Germany) 825 638

Arabella: Excerpt (Und du wirst mein Gebieter sein)

London 1953	Role of Arabella Uhde, Bavarian State Orchestra Kempe	LP: Melodram MEL 094
Vienna 1954	Role of Arabella Schöffler, VPO Hollreiser	LP: Decca LXT 5017 LP: Decca 414 4531 CD: Decca 425 9592

Arabella: Excerpt (Das war sehr gut, Mandryka)

Vienna 1953	Role of Arabella Poell, VPO Moralt	LP: Decca LXT 2865 LP: Decca LW 5029 CD: Decca 425 9592

Capriccio

Munich July 1960	Role of Countess Köth, Litz, Holm, Prey, Böhme, Bavarian State Orchestra Heger	LP: Melodram MEL 110

Capriccio: Excerpt (Closing Scene)

Vienna 1954	Role of Countess VPO Hollreiser	LP: Decca LXT 5017 LP: Decca BR 3100 LP: Decca ECM 778 LP: Decca ECS 812 LP: Decca 411 6601 CD: Decca 425 9592

Elektra

Salzburg July 1957	Role of Chrysothemis Borkh, Madeira, Lorenz, Böhme, Vienna Opera Chorus, VPO Mitropoulos	LP: Discocorp BWS 731 LP: Fonit Cetra LO 83 CD: Nuova Era 2241-2

Der Rosenkavalier

Salzburg July 1960	Role of Marschallin Jurinac, Güden, Zampieri, Kunz, Edelmann, Vienna Opera Chorus VPO Karajan	CD: Hunt CDKAR 213
New York December 1964	Role of Octavian Schwarzkopf, Raskin, Edelmann, Dönch, Morell, Metropolitan Opera Chorus & Orchestra Schippers	CD: Claque GM 3010-12

Der Rosenkavalier: Excerpts (*Da geht er hin; Mir ist die Ehre widerfahren; Zu ihm hätt' ich ein Zutraun; Ist ein Traum, kann nicht wirklich sein)

Dresden 1965	Roles of *Marschallin and Octavian Rothenberger, Leib, Dresden State Orchestra Neuhaus	LP: HMV ASD 2335

Thursday, 21st March, 1968

The 154th performance at the Royal Opera House of

Der Rosenkavalier

Comedy for music

Words by HUGO VON HOFMANNSTHAL

Music by RICHARD STRAUSS

Producer LUCHINO VISCONTI

Production rehearsed by JOHN COPLEY

Scenery designed by LUCHINO VISCONTI and FERDINANDO SCARFIOTTI

Costumes designed by VERA MARZOT

Lighting by LUCHINO VISCONTI and BILL McGEE

Conductor GEORG SOLTI

THE COVENT GARDEN OPERA CHORUS
Chorus Master Douglas Robinson

THE COVENT GARDEN ORCHESTRA
Leader Charles Taylor

THE FELDMARSCHALLIN PRINCESS OF WERDENBERG	LISA DELLA CASA
OCTAVIAN, called Quinquin, a young gentleman of noble family	YVONNE MINTON
BLACK PAGE TO THE PRINCESS	OLCIAN LEWIS
THE PRINCESS'S FOOTMEN	STANLEY COOPER WILFRED JONES CLIFFORD STARR DAVID WINNARD
BARON OCHS auf LERCHENAU	MICHAEL LANGDON
MAJOR-DOMO TO THE PRINCESS	MALCOLM CAMPBELL
A NOBLE WIDOW	NADA POBJOY
THREE NOBLE ORPHANS	MARYBELLE OAKES ELIZABETH SHELLEY MARGARET SMITH
A MILLINER	GWYNNETH PRICE
AN ANIMAL SELLER	DANIEL McCOSHAN
A HAIRDRESSER	DOREEN ROBERTSON
AN ATTORNEY	DENNIS WICKS
VALZACCHI, an Intriguer	JOHN DOBSON
ANNINA, his accomplice	ANNE HOWELLS
A TENOR	KENNETH MACDONALD
A FLUTE PLAYER	ERNEST ROSSER
LEOPOLD	EDGAR BONIFACE
HERR VON FANINAL, a rich merchant, newly ennobled	GWYN GRIFFITHS
SOPHIE, his daughter	ELIZABETH ROBSON
MARIANNE LEITMETZERIN, Sophie's Duenna	MARGARET KINGSLEY
MAJOR-DOMO TO FANINAL	ARTHUR COBBIN
BARON OCHS' RETINUE	KEITH RAGGETT ANDREW SELLARS PAUL STATHAM GLYNNE THOMAS
A DOCTOR	IGNATIUS McFADYEN
A LANDLORD	DAVID LENNOX
WAITERS	ARTHUR COBBIN ALAN JONES KEITH RAGGETT DAVID WINNARD
A COMMISSIONER OF POLICE	ERIC GARRETT

A Scholar, a Cook and Assistant, Maidservants, Footmen, Suspicious Personages, Children, Musicians, Coachmen and Constables

Master Olcian Lewis and all the children are members of Tollington Park School and have been coached for the Opera House by Jean Povey

Lieder: Einerlei; Ich wollt' ein Sträusslein binden; Schlechtes Wetter; Befreit

Vienna	Hudez, piano	LP: Decca LXT 5258
1957		LP: Decca ECM 778
		LP: Decca 411 6601

Lieder: Morgen; Einerlei; Waldseligkeit; Hat gesagt; Seitdem dein Aug' in meines schaute; Schlechtes Wetter; Befreit

1963   Peschko, piano   LP: HMV ALP 2044/ASD 593

Lieder: Ständchen; Ich wollt' ein Sträusslein binden; Allerseelen; Für fünfzehn Pfennige; Ich trage meine Minne; Nichts; Die Nacht; Wiegenlied; Der Stern; Nur Mut; Lob des Leidens; Zueignung; Mein Herz ist stumm; Herr Lenz; Ach Lieb', ich muss nun scheiden; Das Geheimnis; Ruhe, meine Seele

1962   Sandor, piano   LP: RCA RB 6590/SB 6590

Lieder: Morgen; Befreit; Hat gesagt; Ach Lieb', ich muss nun scheiden

Tokyo	Kobayashi, piano	LP: Relief RL 825
May 1970		CD: Relief CR 1825

Wagner

Die Meistersinger von Nürnberg

Bayreuth July 1952	Role of Eva Malaniuk, Unger, Hopf, Edelmann, Böhme, Bayreuth Festival Chorus & Orchestra Knappertsbusch	LP: Melodram MEL 522 CD: Hunt CDLSMH 34040 Excerpts from Meistersinger on Gioielli della lirica GML 37 is labelled "Bayreuth 1952", but in fact contains excerpts from a 1949 Munich performance with Annelies Kupper in the role of Eva

Die Meistersinger von Nürnberg: Excerpt (Guten Abend, Meister)

New York January 1956	Role of Eva Schöffler, Metropolitan Opera Orchestra Kempe	LP: Melodram MEL 084

Wolf

Lieder: Der Gärtner; Geh, Geliebter; Er ist's

Vienna 1957	Hudez, piano	LP: Decca LXT 5258

Lieder: Der Gärtner; Fussreise; Begegnung; So ist die Lieb'

Tokyo May 1970	Kobayashi, piano	LP: Relief RL 825 CD: Relief CR 1825

Collections

Lisa della Casa und Vico Torriani singen Lieder aus unserer Heimat (Swiss songs and duets): Le vieux chalet; Gsätzli; Vieni sulla barchetta; Chanson du chevrier; Im Aargäu sind zwei Liebi; O du liebs Aengeli; Chanzun da sot; Ninna, Nanna; others without della Casa

Zürich 1971	Orchestra Rehbein	LP: Philips 844 324

Lisa Della Casa:
roles performed with the Vienna State Opera

Includes performances with the Vienna company on tour
Figure against each role indicates number of times the part was performed

32	Arabella (Arabella)
40	Ariadne (Ariadne auf Naxos)
12	Butterfly (Madama Butterfly)
4	Chrysothemis (Elektra)
20	Countess (Capriccio)
64	Countess Almaviva (Le Nozze di Figaro)
6	Donna Anna (Don Giovanni)
33	Donna Elvira (Don Giovanni)
16	Eva (Die Meistersinger von Nürnberg)
9	Fiordiligi (Così fan tutte)
3	Frl.Bürstner/Gerichtsdieners Frau/Leni (Der Prozess)*
9	Frau Fluth (The Merry Wives of Windsor)
5	Gilda (Rigoletto)
6	Ilia (Idomeneo)
22	Laura (Der Bettelstudent)
5	Lucille (Dantons Tod)*
2	Marie (The Bartered Bride)
43	Marschallin (Der Rosenkavalier)
6	Marzelline (Fidelio)
13	Mimì (La Bohème)
10	Nedda (I Pagliacci)
7	Octavian (Der Rosenkavalier)
38	Pamina (Die Zauberflöte)
3	Queen of Night (Die Zauberflöte)
14	Sophie (Der Rosenkavalier)
3	Ursula (Mathis der Maler)

*Von Einem

Rita Streich
Discography

Compiled by John Hunt
1991

Introduction

Rita Streich, in a career spanning from the mid 1940s until the early 1980s, followed in the lyric coloratura tradition of Maria Ivogün and Erna Berger, with both of whom she studied.

Like most of the singers in our survey, the central composers in her repertoire were Mozart and Strauss, yet we must not overlook an incredibly wide range of recordings from the Slav, Italian and French opera (she sang, and spoke fluently, at least half a dozen languages). She also possessed the widest possible repertory of operettas, recording extensively in that field with a succession of outstanding tenors - Peter Anders, Rudolf Schock, Fritz Wunderlich and Nicolai Gedda.

Rita Streich's voice was far from large and many listeners felt that she was heard to better advantage on recordings than in the theatre. Nonetheless, stage presence and projection were warm and compelling, standing the singer in good stead on the concert platform: there she relied much more on beauty of tone than on plumbing great psychological depths in the songs which she performed - composers like Mozart, Schubert and Mendelssohn benefited especially from this.

The soprano was proud of her association with "Die Zauberflöte", beginning her Mozart career with the small role of Papagena, then for many years dominating the international scene as Queen of Night, whilst in later years taking the role of Pamina. However, only the Queen of Night was recorded.

An interesting aspect of Rita Streich's busy recording career in the 1950s was the recording of operatic arias from her repertory for 78 rpm discs and 45 rpm EPs, then very popular. At many of these sessions a version in the original language was recorded, followed by a version in German for the domestic market. Sadly, this policy was abandoned as the LP recital began to come into its own.

Many of us in London have vivid memories of Rita Streich from when, late in her career, she often came to London to delight a faithful audience in the intimate surroundings of the Wigmore Hall or the Purcell Room.

John Hunt

Auber

Fra Diavolo: Excerpts (Erblickt auf Felsenhöhn; Nur unbesorgt, Mylord)

Berlin 1957	Role of Zerline Berlin RO Gaebel Sung in German	45: DG EPL 30299

Bellini

I Capuleti e i Montecchi: Excerpt (O quante volte)

Berlin May 1965	Role of Giulietta Deutsche Oper Orchestra Peters	LP: DG LPEM 19 368/SLPEM 136 368 LP: DG 2548 057 LP: DG 413 8241

Bizet

Les Pêcheurs de Perles: Excerpt (Me voilà seule dans la nuit)

Berlin May and June 1965	Role of Léila Deutsche Oper Orchestra Peters	LP: DG SLPEM 136 495 LP: DG 2548 057 LP: DG 413 8241

Brahms

Lieder: 1. Auf dem Schiffe; 2. Trennung; 3. Das Mädchen spricht; 4. Geheimnis; 5. 3 Mädchenlieder; 6. Vergebliches Ständchen; 7. Wiegenlied; 8. Ständchen

Vienna April 1961	Weissenborn, piano	LP: DG LPM 18 716/SLPM 138 716 LP: DG 413 8241 (4,5,6,7,8)

Duets: Die Meere; Phänomen; Am Strande; Die Schwestern

Paris September 1979	Forrester, Machwilsky, piano	LP: Etcetera ETC 1010 CD: Etcetera KTC 1010

Czernik

Chi sa?

Berlin September 1951	Städtische Oper Orchestra Lenzer	LP: Urania URLP 209 45: Nixa EP 751
Berlin 1956	RIAS Orchestra Gaebel	45: DG NL 32119

Delibes

Lakmé: Excerpts (Les fleurs me paraissent plus belles; Ou va la jeune hindoue?)

Berlin May and June 1965	Role of Lakmé Deutsche Oper Orchestra Peters	LP: DG SLPEM 136 495 LP: DG 2548 057 LP: DG 413 8241

Donizetti

Don Pasquale: Excerpts (1. Auch unter allen Blicken; 2. Auch ich versteh' die feine Kunst; 3. Les' ich in deinen Blicken; other excerpts without Streich)

Munich April 1955	Role of Adina Wehofschitz, Bavarian RO Lehmann	LP: DG LPE 17053 LP: DG LPE 17074 (1 and 2) 45: DG NL 32112 (3) 45: DG EPL 30275 (1 and 2) Versions in Italian language LP: DG LPM 19137 (1) 45: DG NL 32113 (3) 45: DG EPL 30225 (1 and 2) LP: DG 413 8241 (2)

Linda di Chamonix: Excerpt (O luce di quest' anima)

Berlin May 1965	Role of Linda Deutsche Oper Orchestra Peters	LP: DG SLPEM 136 495 LP: DG 413 8241

Lucia di Lammermoor: Excerpts (Regnava nel silenzio; Il dolce suono)

Berlin April 1962	Role of Lucia Berlin RO Gaebel	LP: DG LPEM 19 368/SLPEM 136 368 LP: DG 2548 057 LP: DG 413 8241

Dvorak

Rusalka: Excerpt (O silver moon)

Berlin May 1958	Role of Rusalka Berlin RO, Gaebel Sung in Czech	LP: LPEM 19 161/SLPEM 136 011 LP: DG 2535 367 LP: DG 2535 644

Gluck

Orfeo ed Euridice

Berlin 1953	Role of Amor Klose, Berger, Städtische Oper Chorus & Orchestra Rother	LP: Urania US 5223 LP: Acanta FA 22140
Berlin 1956	Role of Amor Stader, Fischer-Dieskau, RIAS Choir, Berlin RO, Fricsay Sung in German	LP: DG LPM 18345-6 LP: DG 2700 103 Excerpts LP: DG LPM 19 411

Orfeo ed Euridice: Excerpt (Mit Freuden den Willen der Götter erfüllen; other excerpts without Streich)

Munich 1954	Role of Amor Schlemm, Klose, Bavarian Radio Choir, Munich PO, Rother Sung in German	LP: DG LPEM 19 053 LP: DG 478 128

Heuberger

Der Opernball: Excerpt (Im chambre séparée)

Berlin 1954	Anders Operetten-Orchester Marszalek	45: Polydor NH 22260

E.T.A. Hoffmann

Undine

Munich Recording date uncertain ? 1960s	Role of Undine Muszely, Grumbach, Proebstl, Engen, Kohn Bavarian Radio Chorus & Orchestra Koertsier	LP: Voce VOCE 101

Humperdinck

Hänsel und Gretel

Munich 1954	Role of Gretel Litz, Schech, Günter, Choir, Munich Philharmonic Lehmann	LP: DG LPM 18 215-6 Excerpts: LP: DG LPEM 19 407

Lehar

Eva: Excerpt (Wär' es auch nicht ein Traum vom Glück)

London 1974	Role of Eva Symphonica of London Morris	LP: Pye TPLS 13064

Die lustige Witwe: Excerpt (Vilja-Lied)

London 1974	Role of Hanna Symphonica of London Morris	LP: Pye TPLS 13064

Der Zarewitsch

Munich 1968	Role of Sonja Gedda, Söhnker, Bavarian Radio Choir, Graunke Orchestra Mattes	LP: Electrola 1C 163 29020-21 CD: EMI CMS 769 3662 Excerpts LP: Electrola 1C 061 28073 CD: EMI CDM 769 6012

Lortzing

Undine: Excerpt (Nun ist's vollbracht)

Berlin April 1953	Role of Undine Fischer-Dieskau Choir & Orchestra Schüchter	LP: Electrola 1C 047 28181M

Der Wildschütz: Excerpts (Lass' Er doch hören ; Was seh' ich ?; other excerpts without Streich)

Bamberg September 1965	Role of Gretchen Seefried, Böhme, Häfliger, Choir, Bamberg SO Stepp	LP: DG SLPEM 136 428 LP: DG 2535 429

Maillart

Das Glöckchen des Eremiten: Excerpt (Er liebt mich)

Berlin 1957	Role of Rose RIAS Orchestra Gaebel	45: DG EPL 30299

Marchesi

La Folletta

Berlin 1956	RIAS Orchestra Gaebel	45: DG NL 32119

Massenet

Manon: Excerpts (Gavotte; Adieu, notre petite table)

Berlin May and June 1965	Role of Manon Deutsche Oper Chorus & Orchestra Peters	LP: DG SLPEM 136 495 LP: DG 2548 057 LP: DG 413 8241

Mendelssohn

A Midsummer Night's Dream, Incidental Music

Berlin June 1950	Soprano soloist Eustrati, RIAS CHoir, Fricsay	LP: DG LPM 18 001 LP: DG 2548 201 LP: DG 2535 736

Lieder: Auf Flügeln des Gesanges; Neue Liebe; Hexenlied

Berlin 1968	Parsons, piano	LP: Electrola 1C 063 28995

Duets: Ich wollt', meine Liebe ergösse sich; Abschiedslied der Zugvögel; Gruss; Herbstlied; Abendlied; Lied aus Ruy Blas

Paris September 1979	Forrester, Machwilsky, piano	LP: Etcetera ETC 1010 CD: Etcetera KTC 1010

Meyerbeer

Les Huguenots: Excerpt (Nobles seigneurs)

Berlin	Role of Urbain	78: DG L 62924
October 1953	RIAS Orchestra	LP: DG LPM 19 137
	Leitner	45: DG NL 32011
		45: DG EPL 30464
		LP: DG 413 8241
		Version in German language
		45: DG NL 32013

Dinorah: Excerpt (Ombra leggiera)

Berlin	Role of Dinorah	LP: DG LPM 19 161/SLPM 136 011
May 1958	Berlin RO	LP: DG 2535 367
	Gaebel	LP: DG 2535 644
		LP: DG 413 8241

Milhaud

4 Chansons de Ronsard; 3 Chansons populaires

Munich	Werba, piano	LP: DG LPEM 19 103
August 1957		LP: DG 413 8241

Millöcker

Der Bettelstudent

Munich	Role of Laura	LP: Electrola 1C 191 30162-3
1968	Litz, Gedda,	CD: EMI CMS 769 6782
	Holm, Unger,	Excerpts
	Prey,	LP: Electrola 1C 061 28199
	Bavarian	CD: EMI CDM 769 6022
	Radio Chorus,	
	Graunke Orchestra	
	Allers	

Der Bettelstudent: Selection

Berlin	Role of Laura	LP: Polydor LPH 45040
1954	Anders, Witsch,	LP: Polydor LPH 46664
	Schneider,	45: Polydor EPH 20042
	Capellman,	LP: DG 478 109
	Orchestra	
	Marszalek	

Mozart

Bastien und Bastienne

Munich 1955	Role of Bastienne Holm, Blankenheim, Munich CO Stepp	LP: DG LPM 18 280 LP: DG 89 736

Così fan tutte: Excerpt (Una donna a quindici anni)

Berlin January 1955	Role of Despina RIAS Orchestra Sandberg	45: DG NL 32029 LP: DG 413 8241 Version in German language 45: DG NL 32028

Don Giovanni

Cologne May 1955	Role of Zerlina Cunitz, Zadek, Simoneau, London, Kusche, Weber, WDR Chorus and Orchestra Klemperer	LP: Discocorp RR 478 CD: Frequenz CMA 3
Salzburg July 1956	Role of Zerlina Grümmer, Della Casa, Simoneau, Siepi, Corena, Frick, Vienna Opera Chorus, VPO Mitropoulos	LP: Replica ARPL 42422 LP: Discoreale DR 10021-3 CD: Hunt CD 552 Early pressings of the Hunt CD contained a 1960 Salzburg performance conducted by Karajan and with a different cast

Don Giovanni: Excerpts (1. Ich weiss ein Mittel; 2. Reich' mir die Hand, mein Leben; other excerpts without Streich)

Berlin February 1963	Role of Zerline Fischer-Dieskau, Berlin RO Löwlein Sung in German	LP: DG LPEM 19 415/SLPEM 136 415 LP: DG 2535 278 LP: DG 2535 627 (2) LP: DG 2548 230 LP: DG 413 8241

Die Entführung aus dem Serail

Berlin December 1949	Role of Blondchen Barabas, Dermota, Krebs, Greindl, RIAS Choir and Orchestra Fricsay	LP: Movimento Musica 02.001
Berlin May 1954	Role of Blondchen Stader, Häfliger, Greindl, Vantin, RIAS Choir and Orchestra Fricsay	LP: DG LPM 18 197-8/LPM 18 184-5 LP: DG 2700 010 LP: DG 2730 014 Excerpts LP: DG LPM 19 409 LP: DG 413 8241

Idomeneo: Excerpt (Zeffiretti lusinghieri)

Berlin November 1955	Role of Ilia Berlin RO Rother	45: DG EPL 30217 Version in German language 45: DG EPL 30216

Il Rè Pastore: Excerpt (L'amerò sarò costante)

London 1974	Role of Aminta Symphonica of London Morris	LP: Pye TPLS 13064

Il Rè Pastore: Excerpt (Alessandro lo confesso)

Salzburg May 1962	Role of Aminta Camerata Academica Paumgartner	LP: DG LPM 18 695/SLPM 138 695 LP: DG 199 032

Le Nozze di Figaro

Vienna	Role of Susanna	LP: Philips A00357-9L
1955	Jurinac, Ludwig,	LP: Philips GL 5777-9
	Berry, Schöffler,	LP: Philips SFL 14012-4
	Vienna Opera Chorus,	LP: Philips 6706 006
	VSO	
	Böhm	

Le Nozze di Figaro: Excerpt (Venite inginocchiatevi)

London	Role of Susanna	LP: Pve TPLS 13064
1974	Symphonica	
	of London	
	Morris	

Le Nozze di Figaro: Excerpt (Deh vieni, non tardar)

Berlin	Role of Susanna	LP: DG LPEM 19 368/SLPEM 136 368
April 1962	Berlin RO	LP: DG 413 8241
	Gaebel	

London	Role of Susanna	LP: Pye TPLS 13064
1974	Symphonica	
	of London	
	Morris	

Le Nozze di Figaro: Excerpts (Fünfe, zehne; Sollt' einst die Gräfin; Warum gabst du bis heute; Wenn die sanften Abendlüfte; O säume länger nicht; other excerpts without Streich)

Berlin	Role of Susanna	LP: DG LPEM 19 406/SLPEM 136 406
1961	Stader, Berry,	LP: DG 2535 279
	Fischer-Dieskau,	CD: DG 423 8742
	BPO	
	Leitner	
	Sung in German	

Zaide: Excerpt (Ruhe sanft)

Berlin	Role of Zaide	45: DG EPL 30216/EPL 30217
November 1955	Berlin RO	
	Rother	

Die Zauberflöte

Rome December 1953	Role of Queen Schwarzkopf, Noni, Gedda, Taddei, Clabassi, Petri, RAI Rome Chorus and Orchestra Karajan Sung in Italian	CD: Myto MCD 89007
Berlin June 1955	Role of Queen Stader, Otto, Fischer-Dieskau, Häfliger, Greindl, RIAS Choir and Orchestra Fricsay	LP: DG LPM 18264-6/LPM 18267-9 LP: DG 2701 003 LP: DG 2728 009 LP: DG 2730 014 Excerpts LP: DG LPEM 19 194 LP: DG LPE 17 074 LP: DG 413 8241
Buenos Aires September 1958	Role of Queen Lorengar, Chelavine, Berry, Dermota, Van Mill, Teatro Colon Chorus & Orchestra Beecham	LP: Melodram MEL 462

Concert Arias: Ah se in ciel, benigne stelle; Vado, ma dove ?; Popoli di Tessaglia; Vorrei spiegarvi; No che non sei capace; Mia speranza adorata

Munich September 1958	Bavarian RO Mackerras	LP: DG LPEM 19 183/SLPEM 136 028 Vorrei spiegarvi only LP: DG 413 8241

Concert Aria: Non so d'onde viene

Salzburg May 1962	Camerata Academica Paumgartner	LP: DG LPM 18 695/SLPM 138 695 LP: DG 199 032

Lieder: Die Zufriedenheit; Geheime Liebe; Wie unglücklich bin ich nit; Ridente la calma; Abendempfindung; An die Einsamkeit; Warnung

Berlin May 1956	Werba, piano	LP: DG LPEM 19 080

Lieder: Un moto di gioia; Oiseaux, si tous les ans; Dans un bois solitaire; Das Kinderspiel; Das Lied der trennung; Die kleine Spinnerin; Das Veilchen; Der Zauberer; An Chloë; Die Verschweigung; Sehnsucht nach dem Frühlinge

Berlin May 1956	Werba, piano	LP: DG LPEM 19 080 LP: DG 413 8241

Mussorgsky

The Nursery, song cycle

Berlin 1968	Parsons, piano	LP: Electrola 1C 063 28995

Nicolai

The Merry Wives of Windsor: Excerpt (Nun eilt herbei)

Berlin April 1962	Role of Alice Berlin RO Gaebel	LP: DG LPEM 19 368/SLPEM 136 368 LP: DG 413 8241

Variations on Weber's "Schlaf, Herzenssöhnchen"

Munich 1957	Werba, piano	LP: DG LPEM 19 103

Offenbach

The Tales of Hoffmann

Berlin July 1946	Role of Olympia Berger, Klein, Klose, Anders, Prohaska, Berlin Radio Choir Berlin RO Rother Sung in German	LP: BASF 22.218042 LP: Acanta 40.21804 Excerpts LP: Saga XID 2133

The Tales of Hoffmann: Excerpts (Phöbus stolz im Sonnenwagen; Schöne Nacht, du Liebesnacht; Leise klingt mir im Gemüt; other excerpts without Streich)

Berlin November 1954	Roles of Olympia, Giulietta & Antonia Schock, Wagner, Klose, Metternich, Deutsche Oper Choir Orchestra Schüchter Sung in German	LP: Electrola E60061 LP: Electrola 1C 047 28181M LP: Electrola 1C 047 28577 Olympia & Giulietta excerpts only LP: Electrola E60053

The Tales of Hoffmann: Excerpt (Les oiseaux dans la charmille)

Berlin June 1960	Role of Olympia RIAS Choir Berlin RO Kraus	LP: DG LPEM 19 368/SLPEM 138 368 LP: DG SLPEM 136 404 LP: DG 135 020 LP: DG 413 8241

Don Giovanni

OPERA IN TWO ACTS

Libretto by Lorenzo da Ponte
Music by Wolfgang Amadeus Mozart

Don Giovanni	GEORGE LONDON
The Commendatore	LUDWIG WEBER
Donna Anna, *his daughter*	ELISABETH GRÜMMER
Don Ottavio, *betrothed to Donna Anna*	LÉOPOLD SIMONEAU
Donna Elvira, *a Lady from Burgos abandoned by Don Giovanni*	SENA JURINAC
Leporello, *servant to Don Giovanni*	ERICH KUNZ
Zerlina, *a peasant girl*	RITA STREICH
Masetto, *betrothed to Zerlina*	WALTER BERRY

Staging: OSCAR FRITZ SCHUH
Stage Direction: JOSEF WITT
Scenery and Costumes: ROBERT KAUTSKY
Chorus Master: DR. R. ROSSMAYER

THE VIENNA PHILHARMONIC ORCHESTRA
Musical Direction: KARL BÖHM

ACT I

Scene 1—Outside the Commendatore's House
Scene 2—A Street
Scene 3—Garden Entrance to Don Giovanni's Palazzo
Scene 4—A Room in Don Giovanni's Palazzo
Scene 5—Don Giovanni's Garden
Scene 6—The Ballroom in Don Giovanni's Palazzo

INTERVAL OF TWENTY MINUTES

ACT II

Scene 1—A Street outside Donna Elvira's Lodging
Scene 2—A Courtyard in Donna Anna's House
Scene 3—A Cemetery
Scene 4—A Room in Donna Anna's House
Scene 5—Supper Room in Don Giovanni's Palazzo

TUESDAY, 14 SEPTEMBER, 1954, at 7.15 p.m.

Vienna State Opera visit to London 1954

SALZBURGER FESTSPIELE 1957

SAMSTAG, DEN 24. AUGUST 1957, 11 UHR VORMITTAGS
IM GROSSEN SAAL DES MOZARTEUMS

VIERTE
MOZART-MATINEE

DIE CAMERATA ACADEMICA DES MOZARTEUMS

Dirigent:
BERNHARD PAUMGARTNER

Solisten:

RITA STREICH　　**CHRISTA RICHTER-STEINER**
Sopran　　　　　　　Violine

PAUL DOKTOR
Viola

Pfitzner

Palestrina: Excerpt (Allein in dunkler Tiefe)

Munich 1955	Role of Angel Schlemm, Trötschel, Fehenberger, Bavarian RO Lehmann	78: DG LM 68420 45: DG NL 32204

Poulenc

Airs chantés

Berlin 1968	Parsons, piano	LP: Electrola 1C 063 28995

Puccini

Gianni Schicchi: Excerpt (O mio babbino caro)

Berlin May 1965	Role of Lauretta Deutsche Oper Orchestra Peters	LP: DG SLPEM 136 495 LP: DG 2548 057 LP: DG 413 8241

La Bohème

Berlin 1960	Role of Musetta Lorengar, Konya, Fischer-Dieskau, Günter, Bertram, Deutsche Staatsoper Chorus & Orchestra Erede Sung in German	LP: DG LPM 18 720-1/SLPM 138 720-1 LP: DG 2726 059 Excerpts LP: DG SLPEM 136 404 LP: DG 2535 427 LP: DG 2537 007 CD: DG 423 8752

La Bohème: Excerpt (Lebt wohl, ihr süssen Stunden)

Stuttgart 1954	Role of Musetta Trötschel, Fehenberger, Fischer-Dieskau, Württemberg State Orchestra Leitner	45: DG NL 32048

Turandot: Excerpt (Signore, ascolta)

Berlin May 1965	Role of Liù Deutsche Oper Orchestra Peters	LP: DG SLPEM 136 495 LP: DG 2548 057 LP: DG 413 8241

Rheinberger

The Star of Bethlehem

Munich 1968	Soprano soloist Fischer-Dieskau, Bavarian Radio Choir, Graunke Orchestra Heger	LP: EMI ASD 2630 LP: Electrola 146 7951 CD: Carus (USA) 83111

Rimsky-Korsakov

The Golden Cockerel: Excerpt (Hymn to the Sun)

Berlin April 1962	Role of Queen of Shemakha Berlin RO Gaebel Sung in Russian	LP: DG LPEM 19 368/SLPEM 136 368 ~~LP: DG 2548 057~~ LP: DG 413 8241

Rossini

Il Barbiere di Siviglia: Excerpts (Frag' ich mein beklommnes Herz; Also ich? Meinst du es wirklich?; Ist er's wirklich?; Nur Mut und List und Liebe; other excerpts without Streich)

Berlin 1963	Role of Rosina Häfliger, Sardi, Grumbach, Borg. RIAS Choir, Deutsche Oper Orchestra Peters Sung in German	LP: DG SLPEM 136 423 LP: DG 2535 374

Il Barbiere di Siviglia: Excerpt (Una voce poco fà)

Berlin October 1953	Role of Rosina RIAS Orchestra Leitner	78: DG LVM 72446 45: DG EPL 30052 LP: DG 413 8241 Version in German language 78: DG LVM 72445 LP: DG LPE 17 074 45: DG EPL 30051

Semiramide: Excerpt (Bel raggio lusinghier)

Munich April 1955	Role of Semiramis Bavarian RO Lehmann	45: DG EPL 30225

Schubert

Lieder: Die Forelle; Auf dem Wasser zu singen; Seligkeit; Heidenröslein

Munich August 1957	Werba, piano	LP: DG LPEM 19 103 LP: DG 413 8241

Lieder: Heidenröslein; Liebe schwärmt auf allen Wegen; Schweizerlied; Liebhaber in allen Gestalten; Auf dem Wasser zu singen; An die Nachtigall; Wiegenlied; Nachtviolen; Seligkeit; Die Vögel; *Nähe des Geliebten; *Das Lied im Grünen; *Der Schmetterling; *An den Mond; *Der Hirt auf dem Felsen; *Lied der Mignon; Die Forelle

Berlin April 1959	Werba, piano Geuser, clarinet (Hirt auf dem Felsen)	LP: DG LPM 18 585/SLPM 138 047 LP: DG 2548 136 *LP: DG 413 8241

Lieder: Der Wanderer an den Mond; Geheimes; Die Liebende schreibt; Der Jüngling an der Quelle; Liebhaber in allen Gestalten

Berlin 1968	Parsons, piano	LP: Electrola 1C 063 28995

Schumann

Lieder: Schneeglöckchen; *Aufträge; *Der Nussbaum; *Die Stille; *Die Lotosblume

Vienna April 1961	Weissenborn, piano	LP: DG LPM 18 716/SLPM 138 716 *LP: DG 413 8241

Duets: Wenn ich ein Vöglein wär'; Herbstlied; Schön Blümelein; Erste Begegnung; Liebesgram; An den Abendstern; Mailied; Sommerruh'

Paris September 1979	Forrester, Machwilsky, piano	LP: Etcetera ETC 1010 CD: Etcetera KTC 1010

Johann Strauss

Die Fledermaus

Berlin November 1949	Role of Adele Schlemm, Anders, Krebs, Brauer Chorus Berlin RO Fricsay	CD: Melodram MEL 29001
London April 1955	Role of Adele Schwarzkopf, Gedda, Krebs, Christ, Dönch, Chorus, Philharmonia Karajan	LP: Columbia 33CX 1309-10 LP: EMI RLS 728 CD: EMI CHS 769 5312 Excerpts LP: Columbia 33CX 1516 LP: Electrola 1C 047 01953 LP: Electrola 1C 047 28181M
Vienna December 1960	Role of Adele Güden, Zampieri, Stolze, Berry, Kunz, Vienna Opera Chorus, VPO Karajan	LP: Foyer FO 1031 CD: Foyer 3CF 2021 CD: Hunt CDKAR 215 Excerpts LP: Gioielli della lirica GML 25

Die Fledermaus: Selection

Berlin 1954	Role of Adele Trötschel, Anders, Hofmann, Schneider, Operetta Chorus & Orchestra Marszalek	LP: Polydor LPH 45025 LP: Polydor LPH 46664 45: Polydor EPH 20038

Die Fledermaus: Excerpts (Mein Herr Marquis; Spiel' ich die Unschuld vom Lande)

Berlin May 1958	Role of Adele Berlin RO Gaebel	LP: DG LPEM 19 161/SLPEM 136 011 LP: DG 2535 644 LP: DG 413 8241

Die Fledermaus: Excerpt (Mein Herr Marquis)

London 1974	Role of Adele Symphonica of London Morris	LP: Pye TPLS 13064

1001 Nacht: Excerpts (Komm' in die Gondel; Niemals kann man die vergessen)

Hamburg 1952	NDR Orchestra Stephan	LP: Acanta 40.22903

Eine Nacht in Venedig

Munich 1966	Role of Annina Rothenberger, Litz, Gedda, Curzi, Prey, Bavarian Radio Chorus, Graunke Orchestra Allers	LP: Electrola SME 81051-2 LP: Electrola 1C 163 29095-6 CD: EMI CMS 769 3632 Excerpts LP: Electrola 1C 061 28200 CD: EMI CDM 769 6082

Eine Nacht in Venedig: Selection

Berlin 1954	Role of Ciboletta Weigelt, Schulz, Anders, Hofmann, Operetta Chorus & Orchestra Marszalek	LP: Polydor LPH 45067 LP: Polydor LPH 46664 45: Polydor EPH 20052

Wiener Blut

Berlin September 1951	Role of Pepi Richter, Beilke, Hauser, Hoppe, Städtische Oper Chorus & Orchestra Lenzer	LP: Urania URLP 209 LP: RCA VL 30313 Excerpts 45: Nixa EP 751

Der Zigeunerbaron

Munich 1965	Role of Arsena Bumbry, Litz, Gedda, Anheisser, Prey, Böhme, Bavarian Radio Chorus & Orchestra Allers	LP: Electrola 1C 163 28354-5 Excerpts LP: Electrola 1C 061 28820

Der Zigeunerbaron: Excerpt (Wer uns getraut)

Berlin 1954	Role of Saffi Anders, Grosses Operetten-Orchester Marszalek	LP: Polydor LPH 45064 45: Polydor NH 22260 45: Polydor EPH 20153

Richard Strauss

Ariadne auf Naxos

London June and July 1954	Role of Zerbinetta Schwarzkopf, Seefried, Schock, Prey, Philharmonia Karajan	LP: Columbia 33CX 1292-4 LP: EMI RLS 760 CD: EMI CMS 769 2962 Excerpts LP: Electrola 1C 047 28181M
Salzburg August 1954	Role of Najad Della Casa, Güden, Seefried, Schock, Schöffler, VPO Böhm	LP: Melodram MEL 104

Daphne

Vienna June 1964	Role of 1st Maid Güden, Little, Wunderlich, King, Schöffler, Vienna Opera Chorus VSO Böhm	LP: DG SLPM 138 956-7 LP: DG 2707 019 LP: DG 2726 090 CD: DG 423 5792

Der Rosenkavalier

Dresden December 1958	Role of Sophie Schech, Seefried, Böhme, Francl, Fischer-Dieskau, Dresden Opera Chorus and Staatskapelle Böhm	LP: DG LPM 18 570-3/SLPM 138 040-3 LP: DG 2711 001 LP: DG 2721 162 Excerpts LP: DG LPM 18 656/SLPM 138 656 LP: DG LPEM 19 410/SLPEM 136 410 LP: DG LPEM 19 477/SLPEM 136 477 LP: DG 2535 746 LP: DG 2537 013 LP: DG 410 8471

Lieder: *Der Stern; *Schlechtes Wetter; Einerlei

Munich August 1957	Werba, piano	LP: DG LPEM 19 103 *LP: DG 413 8241

Lieder: Als mir dein Lied erklang; Amor; Schlechtes Wetter; *Schlagende Herzen; *Wiegenlied; *An die Nacht

Vienna April 1961	Weissenborn, piano	LP: DG LPM 18 716/SLPM 138 716 *LP: DG 413 8241

In the original German

Ariadne auf Naxos
(New Version)

OPER IN EINEM AUFZUG NEBST EINEM VORSPIEL

Text nach Hugo von Hofmannsthal   Musik von Richard Strauss

The Major Domo	James Atkins (*English*)
A Music Master	Thomas Hemsley (*English*)
The Composer	Elisabeth Söderström (*Swedish*)
Bacchus	David Lloyd (*American*)
An Officer	John Carolan (*Irish*)
A Dancing Master	Hugues Cuenod (*Swiss*)
A Wig Maker	Gwyn Griffiths (*Welsh*)
A Lackey	Frederick Westcott (*English*)
Zerbinetta	Rita Streich (*German*)
Ariadne	Lucine Amara (*American*)
Harlekin	Heinz Blankenburg (*American*)
Scaramuccio	Kevin Miller (*Australian*)
Truffaldin	Peter Lagger (*Swiss*)
Brighella	Edward Byles (*Welsh*)
Naiade	Rosl Schwaiger (*Austrian*)
Dryade	Monica Sinclair (*English*)
Echo	Pilar Lorengar (*Spanish*)

Conductor: JOHN PRITCHARD   Producer: CARL EBERT

Designer: OLIVER MESSEL

THE ROYAL PHILHARMONIC ORCHESTRA

Pianoforte: Kyla Greenbaum

Scenery built by THE RINGMER BUILDING WORKS LTD. *under the supervision of* R. W. GOUGH *and* S. ZEAL
and by THE AMBASSADORS SCENIC STUDIOS
Scenery painted by THE AMBASSADORS SCENIC STUDIOS *under the supervision of* CHARLES BRAVERY
Costumes made by B. J. SIMMONS *and at the* GLYNDEBOURNE OPERA WARDROBE
Head-dresses and special properties made by HUGH SKILLEN
Jewellery by DEBORA JONES   *Chariot modelled by* WILLI SUKOP
Wigs by WIG CREATIONS LTD.   *Shoes by* GAMBA

Ariadne auf Naxos (original version) was first presented by the Glyndebourne Opera at the Edinburgh Festival of 1950, and the scenery and costumes, the property of the Edinburgh Festival Society Ltd., are here used by arrangement with the Society.

DATES OF PERFORMANCE: July 5 · 7 · 12 · 14 · 16 · 18 · 23

Glyndebourne Festival 1955

Suppé

Boccaccio

Hamburg October 1949	Role of Fiametta Jung, Kind, Glawitsch, Günter, Neidlinger NDR Chorus and Orchestra Schüchter	LP: RCA VL 30404

Boccaccio: Excerpt (Hab' ich nur deine Liebe)

Berlin May 1958	Role of Fiametta Berlin RO Gaebel	LP: DG LPEM 19 161/SLPEM 136 011 LP: DG 2535 367

Thomas

Mignon: Excerpt (Ja, für den Abend bin ich Königin der Feen; other excerpts without Streich)

Stuttgart 1954	Role of Philine Schlemm, Fehenberger, Blankenheim, Württemberg State Orchestra Leitner Sung in German	LP: DG LPEM 19 004

Verdi

Un Ballo in Maschera: Excerpts (1. Volta la terrea; 2. Sapper vorreste)

Berlin October 1953	Role of Oscar RIAS Orchestra Leitner	78: DG L 62924 45: DG NL 32011 45: DG EPL 30464 LP: DG 413 8241 (1) Versions in German language 45: DG NL 32013 (1) LP: DG LPE 17074 (2)

Falstaff: Excerpt (Sul fil d'un soffio)

Berlin May 1965	Role of Nanetta Deutsche Oper Chorus & Orchestra Peters	LP: DG SLPEM 136 495 LP: DG 2548 057 LP: DG 413 8241

Rigoletto: Excerpts (1. Caro nome; 2. Tutte le feste; other excerpts without Streich)

Berlin October 1953	Role of Gilda Munteanu, Uhde, Böhme, RIAS Orchestra, Leitner	78: DG LVM 72446 (1) LP: DG LPE 17 011 45: DG EPL 30052 (1) LP: DG LPEM 19 043 (2) LP: DG LPEM 19 137 (1) LP: DG 413 8241 (1) Version of "Caro nome" in German language 78: DG LVM 72445 LP: DG LPE 17074 45: DG EPL 30051

I Vespri Siciliani: Excerpt (Mercè, dilette amiche)

Berlin February 1958	Role of Elena Berlin RO Märzendorfer	45: DG EPL 30464 LP: DG LPEM 19 137

Wagner

Parsifal

Bayreuth July 1953	Role of Flower Maiden Mödl, Vinay, Weber, Greindl, Uhde, Bayreuth Festival Chorus & Orchestra Krauss	LP: Documents OR 305 LP: Melodram MEL 533 CD: Rodolphe RPC 32516-7

Siegfried

Bayreuth July 1953	Role of Woodbird Varnay, Ilosvay, Windgassen, Kuen, Neidlinger, Hotter, Greindl, Bayreuth Festival Chorus & Orchestra Krauss	LP: Allegro-Elite 3133-7 LP: Melodram MEL 538 LP: Foyer FO 1010 CD: Laudis LCD 44004 CD: Foyer 3CF-2009 CD: Rodolphe RPC 32503-9 Allegro-Elite edition names conductor incorrectly as Keilberth

Tannhäuser

Munich 1951	Role of Shepherd Schech, Bäumer, Seider, Paul, Rohr, Bavarian State Opera Chorus & Orchestra Heger	LP: Artia ALS 506 LP: Acanta HB 23129-32 Also issued on Urania & Nixa labels

Weber

Der Freischütz

Salzburg July 1954	Role of Aennchen Grümmer, Hopf, Edlemann, Poell, Böhme, Vienna Opera Chorus VPO Furtwängler	LP: Discocorp IGS 008-10/IGI 338 LP: Fonit Cetra LO 21 LP: Turnabout THS 65148-50 LP: Fonit Cetra FE 24 CD: Rodolphe RPL 32519-20 CD: Movimento Musica 013.6324-6 CD: Hunt CDWFE 302 CD: Hunt CDWFE 352 Some editions incorrectly labelled "stereo"
Cologne 1955	Role of Aennchen Grümmer, Hopf, Pröbstl, Poell, Böhme, WDR Chorus and Orchestra Kleiber	LP: Discocorp IGI 300 LP: Fonit Cetra LO 42 CD: Hunt CDLSMH 34033 Excerpts LP: Gioielli della lirica GML 74
Munich December 1959	Role of Aennchen Seefried, Holm, Böhme, Wächter, Kreppel, Bavarian Radio Chorus & Orchestra Jochum	LP: DG LPM 18 639-40/SLPM 138 639-40 LP: DG 2707 009 LP: DG 2726 061 Excerpts LP: DG LPEM 19 221/SLPEM 136 221 LP: DG 2535 280 LP: DG 413 8241 CD: DG 423 8692

Der Freischütz: Excerpts (1.Kommt ein schlanker Bursch'; 2.Einst träumte meiner seligen Base; other excerpts without Streich)

Stuttgart 1954	Role of Aennchen Schlemm, Windgassen, Württemberg State Chorus & Orchestra Leitner	45: DG NL 32028 (1) LP: DG LPE 17 074 LP: DG LPEM 19 013 LP: DG LPEM 19 015 (2) 45: DG EPL 30275 (2)

Wolf

Lieder: Nachtgruss; Wiegenlied; *Wohin mit der Freud'; *Die Kleine

Munich	Werba, piano	LP: DG LPEM 19 103
August 1957		*LP: DG 413 8241

Lieder: Tretet ein, hoher Krieger; Verschwiegene Liebe; Gleich und gleich; Die Spröde; Die Bekehrte; Wiegenlied im Sommer; Der Gärtner; Zitronenfalter im April; Mausfallensprüchlein; Elfenlied; Zum neuen Jahr; Du denkst mit einem Fädchen; Mein Liebster ist so klein; Wie lange schon; Wer rief dich denn?; Nun lass uns Frieden schliessen; Nein junger Herr; O wär' dein Haus; Auch kleine Dinge; Trau' nicht der Liebe; Köpfchen, nicht gewimmert; Bedeckt mich mit Blumen; In dem Schatten meiner Locken

Vienna	Werba, piano	LP: DG LPM 18 641/SLPM 138 641
1960		

Lieder: Die Spröde; Die Bekehrte; Wiegenlied

Berlin	Parsons, piano	LP: Electrola 1C 063 28995
1968		

Collections

Von Hirten und der Heiligen Nacht: Rita Streich singt Weihnachtslieder (Alle Jahre wieder; Maria auf dem Berge; Ihr Kindelein kommt; Echolied der Hirten; O du fröhliche; Es ist ein' Ros' entsprungen; Vom Himmel hoch; Die Hirten auf dem Felde; Maria ging durch ein'n Dornwald; Still, still, still; Süsser die Glocken; Stille Nacht)

Berlin 1954	RIAS Boys Choir and Orchestra Gaebel	78: DG LVM 72442 45: DG EPL 30062

Rita Streich singt unvergängliche Melodien (*Voices of Spring; Mein Herr Marquis; Spiel' ich die Unschuld vom Lande; Hab' ich nur deine Liebe; Lied an den Mond; Schattentanz; *Tales from the Vienna Woods; *Le rossignol et la rose; *Lo spazzocamino; *Parla Waltz; *Berceuse de Jocelyn)

Berlin May 1958	Berlin RO RIAS Choir Gaebel	LP: LPEM 19 161/SLPEM 136 011 LP: DG 2535 644 *LP: DG 413 8241

Rita Streich singt Walzer und Kanzonen (Dorfschwalben aus Oesterreich; Die Nachtigall; Die Mädchen von Cadiz; Last Rose of Summer; Vilanelle; Draussen in Sievering; Il bacio)

Berlin 1953	RIAS Orchestra Gaebel	Version with "Die Nachtigall" and "Last Rose of Summer" in German LP: DG LPE 17 051 Version with "Die Nachtigall" in Russian and "Last Rose of Summer" in English LP: DG LPE 17 052

Folk Songs (Gsätzli; When love is kind; Canto delle risaioli; Au clair de la lune; Z' Lauterbach)

Munich August 1957	Werba, piano	LP: DG LPEM 19 103

Folksongs of the World (Du, du liegst mir im Herzen; O du liabs Aengeli; Frère Jacques; L'amour de moi; Canto delle risaioli; Z'Lauterbach; Schlof sche, mein Vogele; Drink to me only; Nobody knows the trouble; Sakura-sakura; Tschubtschiki; Spi mladenez; In mezzo al mar; Der Mond ist aufgegangen; Wenn ich ein Vöglein wär'; Muss i denn)

Munich 1962	Rudolf Lamy Choir, Instrumental Ensemble Michalski	LP: DG LPEM 19 376/SLPM 136 376

Folksongs and Lullabies (Weisst du, wie viele Sterne stehen; O wie wohl ist mir am Abend; Wo e kleins Hüttle steht; All mein Gedanken; Glockenruf; Der Bürgermester von Wesel; Der Wechsel der Jahreszeiten; Schlaf, Herzenssöhnchen; Schlafe, mein Prinzchen; Sandmännchen; Der Kuckuck; Schwesterlein; Ach Modr ich will en Ding han; In der Fruah; Abendlied; Ave Maria)

Munich 1963	Regensburger Domspatzen, Bavarian RO Gaebel	LP: DG LPEM 19 462/SLPEM 136 462

Rita Streich singt die erfolgreichsten Melodien aus dem Gitta-Alpar-Repertoire: Was kann so scön sein wie deine Liebe?; Dort wo die Wälder grün; Ich hab' einen Mann, der mich liebt; Liebe kleine Jeanne; Wenn man sein Herz verliert; Sag' armes Herzchen; Toujours l'amour; Es lockt die Nacht; Wenn du liebst, dann scheint die Sonne; Heut' hab' ich Glück; Du Veilchen von Montmartre; Bin verliebt, bin so verliebt

Berlin 1965	Grosses Berliner Promenaden- Orchester Carste	LP: Polydor 237 280

Rita Streich: Erzähltes Leben (The singer talks about her life and career, with musical examples)

1958	Spoken in German	LP: DG LPM (number not known)

Augsburgisches Tafelkonfekt: vocal works by lesser-known pre-classical German composers

Munich 1970	Soprano soloist Anheisser, Frick, Brokmeier Munich Instrumental Soloists Neumeyer	LP: Electrola 1C 187 30198-9

Rita Streich:
roles performed with the Vienna State Opera

Includes performances with the Vienna company on tour
Figure against each role indicates number of times the part was performed

9	Adele (Die Fledermaus)
21	Blondchen (Die Entführung aus dem Serail)
18	Despina (Così fan tutte)
6	1st Angel (Palestrina)
3	Gilda (Rigoletto)
3	Girofle-Girofla (Girofle-Girofla)*
7	Konstanze (Die Entführung aus dem Serail)
5	1st Maid (Daphne)
11	Olympia (The Tales of Hoffmann)
8	Oscar (Un ballo in maschera)
3	Papagena (Die Zauberflöte)
6	Queen of Night (Die Zauberflöte)
6	Rosina (Il Barbiere di Siviglia)
4	Shepherd (Tannhäuser)
12	Italian Singer (Capriccio)
12	Sophie (Der Rosenkavalier)
35	Susanna (Le Nozze di Figaro)
3	Woodbird (Siegfried)
11	Zerbinetta (Ariadne auf Naxos)
14	Zerlina (Don Giovanni)

*Offenbach

Dr. Elisabeth Legge-Schwarzkopf, Kammersängerin

Mr. John Hunt BA
Flat 6, 37 Chester Way
London SE 11 4 UR / England

15.3.90

Dear Mr. Hunt,

I want to thank you from the bottom of my heart to let me enjoy your marvellous discography of Wilhelm Furtwängler.

The memory of the performances with that gigantic artist is one of the most precious things in my life.

Many thanks again,

Yours

Elisabeth Legge Schwarzkopf

Still available

Price £11 (£14 outside UK)
Cheque payable to Wilhelm Furtwangler
Society UK. Available from John Hunt,
Flat 6, 37 Chester Way, London SE11 4UR

Still available

The Furtwängler Sound, 2nd edition (1985)
incorporating
Furtwängler and Great Britain
Survey of the conductor's British appearances, with extensive press comments and reviews.

Price £5 (£7 outside UK)
Cheque payable to Wilhelm Furtwängler Society UK

Philharmonia Orchestra: Complete discography and
The Recordings of Herbert von Karajan
2 separate discographies in 1 volume (537 pages)

Price £9 (£13 outside UK)
Cheque payable to John Hunt

Both available from:
John Hunt
Flat 6
37 Chester Way
London SE11 4UR

Discographies by Travis & Emery:
Discographies by John Hunt.

1987: 978-1-906857-14-1: From Adam to Webern: the Recordings of von Karajan.

1991: 978-0-951026-83-0: 3 Italian Conductors and 7 Viennese Sopranos: 10 Discographies: Arturo Toscanini, Guido Cantelli, Carlo Maria Giulini, Elisabeth Schwarzkopf, Irmgard Seefried, Elisabeth Gruemmer, Sena Jurinac, Hilde Gueden, Lisa Della Casa, Rita Streich.

1992: 978-0-951026-85-4: Mid-Century Conductors and More Viennese Singers: 10 Discographies: Karl Boehm, Victor De Sabata, Hans Knappertsbusch, Tullio Serafin, Clemens Krauss, Anton Dermota, Leonie Rysanek, Eberhard Waechter, Maria Reining, Erich Kunz.

1993: 978-0-951026-87-8: More 20th Century Conductors: 7 Discographies: Eugen Jochum, Ferenc Fricsay, Carl Schuricht, Felix Weingartner, Josef Krips, Otto Klemperer, Erich Kleiber.

1994: 978-0-951026-88-5: Giants of the Keyboard: 6 Discographies: Wilhelm Kempff, Walter Gieseking, Edwin Fischer, Clara Haskil, Wilhelm Backhaus, Artur Schnabel.

1994: 978-0-951026-89-2: Six Wagnerian Sopranos: 6 Discographies: Frieda Leider, Kirsten Flagstad, Astrid Varnay, Martha Moedl, Birgit Nilsson, Gwyneth Jones.

1995: 978-0-952582-70-0: Musical Knights: 6 Discographies: Henry Wood, Thomas Beecham, Adrian Boult, John Barbirolli, Reginald Goodall, Malcolm Sargent.

1995: 978-0-952582-71-7: A Notable Quartet: 4 Discographies: Gundula Janowitz, Christa Ludwig, Nicolai Gedda, Dietrich Fischer-Dieskau.

1996: 978-0-952582-72-4: The Post-War German Tradition: 5 Discographies: Rudolf Kempe, Joseph Keilberth, Wolfgang Sawallisch, Rafael Kubelik, Andre Cluytens.

1996: 978-0-952582-73-1: Teachers and Pupils: 7 Discographies: Elisabeth Schwarzkopf, Maria Ivoguen, Maria Cebotari, Meta Seinemeyer, Ljuba Welitsch, Rita Streich, Erna Berger.

1996: 978-0-952582-77-9: Tenors in a Lyric Tradition: 3 Discographies: Peter anders, Walther Ludwig, Fritz Wunderlich.

1997: 978-0-952582-78-6: The Lyric Baritone: 5 Discographies: Hans Reinmar, Gerhard Huesch, Josef Metternich, Hermann Uhde, Eberhard Waechter.

1997: 978-0-952582-79-3: Hungarians in Exile: 3 Discographies: Fritz Reiner, Antal Dorati, George Szell.

1997: 978-1-901395-00-6: The Art of the Diva: 3 Discographies: Claudia Muzio, Maria Callas, Magda Olivero.

1997: 978-1-901395-01-3: Metropolitan Sopranos: 4 Discographies: Rosa Ponselle, Eleanor Steber, Zinka Milanov, Leontyne Price.

1997: 978-1-901395-02-0: Back From The Shadows: 4 Discographies: Willem Mengelberg, Dimitri Mitropoulos, Hermann Abendroth, Eduard Van Beinum.

1997: 978-1-901395-03-7: More Musical Knights: 4 Discographies: Hamilton Harty, Charles Mackerras, Simon Rattle, John Pritchard.

1998: 978-1-901395-94-5: Conductors On The Yellow Label: 8 Discographies: Fritz Lehmann, Ferdinand Leitner, Ferenc Fricsay, Eugen Jochum, Leopold Ludwig, Artur Rother, Franz Konwitschny, Igor Markevitch.

1998: 978-1-901395-95-2: More Giants of the Keyboard: 5 Discographies: Claudio Arrau, Gyorgy Cziffra, Vladimir Horowitz, Dinu Lipatti, Artur Rubinstein.

1998: 978-1-901395-96-9: Mezzo and Contraltos: 5 Discographies: Janet Baker, Margarete Klose, Kathleen Ferrier, Giulietta Simionato, Elisabeth Hoengen.

1999: 978-1-901395-97-6: The Furtwaengler Sound Sixth Edition: Discography and Concert Listing.
1999: 978-1-901395-98-3: The Great Dictators: 3 Discographies: Evgeny Mravinsky, Artur Rodzinski, Sergiu Celibidache.
1999: 978-1-901395-99-0: Sviatoslav Richter: Pianist of the Century: Discography.
2000: 978-1-901395-04-4: Philharmonic Autocrat 1: Discography of: Herbert Von Karajan [Third Edition].
2000: 978-1-901395-05-1: Wiener Philharmoniker 1 - Vienna Philharmonic and Vienna State Opera Orchestras: Discography Part 1 1905-1954.
2000: 978-1-901395-06-8: Wiener Philharmoniker 2 - Vienna Philharmonic and Vienna State Opera Orchestras: Discography Part 2 1954-1989.
2001: 978-1-901395-07-5: Gramophone Stalwarts: 3 Separate Discographies: Bruno Walter, Erich Leinsdorf, Georg Solti.
2001: 978-1-901395-08-2: Singers of the Third Reich: 5 Discographies: Helge Roswaenge, Tiana Lemnitz, Franz Voelker, Maria Mueller, Max Lorenz.
2001: 978-1-901395-09-9: Philharmonic Autocrat 2: Concert Register of Herbert Von Karajan Second Edition.
2002: 978-1-901395-10-5: Sächsische Staatskapelle Dresden: Complete Discography.
2002: 978-1-901395-11-2: Carlo Maria Giulini: Discography and Concert Register.
2002: 978-1-901395-12-9: Pianists For The Connoisseur: 6 Discographies: Arturo Benedetti Michelangeli, Alfred Cortot, Alexis Weissenberg, Clifford Curzon, Solomon, Elly Ney.
2003: 978-1-901395-14-3: Singers on the Yellow Label: 7 Discographies: Maria Stader, Elfriede Troetschel, Annelies Kupper, Wolfgang Windgassen, Ernst Haefliger, Josef Greindl, Kim Borg.
2003: 978-1-901395-15-0: A Gallic Trio: 3 Discographies: Charles Muench, Paul Paray, Pierre Monteux.
2004: 978-1-901395-16-7: Antal Dorati 1906-1988: Discography and Concert Register.
2004: 978-1-901395-17-4: Columbia 33CX Label Discography.
2004: 978-1-901395-18-1: Great Violinists: 3 Discographies: David Oistrakh, Wolfgang Schneiderhan, Arthur Grumiaux.
2006: 978-1-901395-19-8: Leopold Stokowski: Second Edition of the Discography.
2006: 978-1-901395-20-4: Wagner Im Festspielhaus: Discography of the Bayreuth Festival.
2006: 978-1-901395-21-1: Her Master's Voice: Concert Register and Discography of Dame Elisabeth Schwarzkopf [Third Edition].
2007: 978-1-901395-22-8: Hans Knappertsbusch: Kna: Concert Register and Discography of Hans Knappertsbusch, 1888-1965. Second Edition.
2008: 978-1-901395-23-5: Philips Minigroove: Second Extended Version of the European Discography.
2009: 978-1-901395--24-2: American Classics: The Discographies of Leonard Bernstein and Eugene Ormandy.

Discography by Stephen J. Pettitt, edited by John Hunt:
1987: 978-1-906857-16-5: Philharmonia Orchestra: Complete Discography 1945-1987

Available from: Travis & Emery at 17 Cecil Court, London, UK. (+44) 20 7 240 2129. email on sales@travis-and-emery.com .

© Travis & Emery 2009

Music and Books published by Travis & Emery Music Bookshop:
Anon.: Hymnarium Sarisburiense, cum Rubricis et Notis Musicis.
Agricola, Johann Friedrich from Tosi: Anleitung zur Singkunst.
Bach, C.P.E.: edited W. Emery: Nekrolog or Obituary Notice of J.S. Bach.
Bateson, Naomi Judith: Alcock of Salisbury
Bathe, William: A Briefe Introduction to the Skill of Song
Bax, Arnold: Symphony #5, Arranged for Piano Four Hands by Walter Emery
Burney, Charles: The Present State of Music in France and Italy
Burney, Charles: The Present State of Music in Germany, The Netherlands ...
Burney, Charles: An Account of the Musical Performances ... Handel
Burney, Karl: Nachricht von Georg Friedrich Handel's Lebensumstanden.
Cobbett, W.W.: Cobbett's Cyclopedic Survey of Chamber Music. (2 vols.)
Corrette, Michel: Le Maitre de Clavecin
Crimp, Bryan: Dear Mr. Rosenthal ... Dear Mr. Gaisberg ...
Crimp, Bryan: Solo: The Biography of Solomon
d'Indy, Vincent: Beethoven: Biographie Critique
d'Indy, Vincent: Beethoven: A Critical Biography
d'Indy, Vincent: César Franck (in French)
Frescobaldi, Girolamo: D'Arie Musicali per Cantarsi. Primo & Secondo Libro.
Geminiani, Francesco: The Art of Playing the Violin.
Handel; Purcell; Boyce; Geene et al: Calliope or English Harmony: Volume First.
Häuser: Musikalisches Lexikon. 2 vols in one.
Hawkins, John: A General History of the Science and Practice of Music (5 vols.)
Herbert-Caesari, Edgar: The Science and Sensations of Vocal Tone
Herbert-Caesari, Edgar: Vocal Truth
Hopkins and Rimboult: The Organ. Its History and Construction.
Hunt, John: Adam to Webern: the recordings of von Karajan
Isaacs, Lewis: Hänsel and Gretel. A Guide to Humperdinck's Opera.
Isaacs, Lewis: Königskinder (Royal Children) A Guide to Humperdinck's Opera.
Kastner: Manuel Général de Musique Militaire
Lacassagne, M. l'Abbé Joseph : Traité Général des élémens du Chant.
Lascelles (née Catley), Anne: The Life of Miss Anne Catley.
Mainwaring, John: Memoirs of the Life of the Late George Frederic Handel
Malcolm, Alexander: A Treaty of Music: Speculative, Practical and Historical
Marx, Adolph Bernhard: Die Kunst des Gesanges, Theoretisch-Practisch
May, Florence: The Life of Brahms
May, Florence: The Girlhood Of Clara Schumann: Clara Wieck And Her Time.
Mellers, Wilfrid: Angels of the Night: Popular Female Singers of Our Time
Mellers, Wilfrid: Bach and the Dance of God
Mellers, Wilfrid: Beethoven and the Voice of God
Mellers, Wilfrid: Caliban Reborn - Renewal in Twentieth Century Music

Music and Books published by Travis & Emery Music Bookshop:
Mellers, Wilfrid: François Couperin and the French Classical Tradition
Mellers, Wilfrid: Harmonious Meeting
Mellers, Wilfrid: Le Jardin Retrouvé, The Music of Frederic Mompou
Mellers, Wilfrid: Music and Society, England and the European Tradition
Mellers, Wilfrid: Music in a New Found Land: ... ... American Music
Mellers, Wilfrid: Romanticism and the Twentieth Century (from 1800)
Mellers, Wilfrid: The Masks of Orpheus: ...... the Story of European Music.
Mellers, Wilfrid: The Sonata Principle (from c. 1750)
Mellers, Wilfrid: Vaughan Williams and the Vision of Albion
Panchianio, Cattuffio: Rutzvanscad Il Giovine
Pearce, Charles: Sims Reeves, Fifty Years of Music in England.
Playford, John: An Introduction to the Skill of Musick.
Purcell, Henry et al: Harmonia Sacra ... The First Book, (1726)
Purcell, Henry et al: Harmonia Sacra ... Book II (1726)
Quantz, Johann: Versuch einer Anweisung die Flöte traversiere zu spielen.
Rameau, Jean-Philippe: Code de Musique Pratique, ou Methodes.
Rastall, Richard: The Notation of Western Music.
Rimbault, Edward: The Pianoforte, Its Origins, Progress, and Construction.
Rousseau, Jean Jacques: Dictionnaire de Musique
Rubinstein, Anton : Guide to the proper use of the Pianoforte Pedals.
Sainsbury, John S.: Dictionary of Musicians. Vol. 1. (1825). 2 vols.
Serré de Rieux, Jean de : Les dons des Enfans de Latone
Simpson, Christopher: A Compendium of Practical Musick in Five Parts
Spohr, Louis: Autobiography
Spohr, Louis: Grand Violin School
Tans'ur, William: A New Musical Grammar; or The Harmonical Spectator
Terry, Charles Sanford: J.S. Bach's Original Hymn-Tunes for Congregational Use.
Terry, Charles Sanford: Four-Part Chorals of J.S. Bach. (German & English)
Terry, Charles Sanford: Joh. Seb. Bach, Cantata Texts, Sacred and Secular.
Terry, Charles Sanford: The Origins of the Family of Bach Musicians.
Tosi, Pierfrancesco: Opinioni de' Cantori Antichi, e Moderni
Van der Straeten, Edmund: History of the Violoncello, The Viol da Gamba ...
Van der Straeten, Edmund: History of the Violin, Its Ancestors... (2 vols.)
Waltern: Musikalisches Lexicon
Walther, J. G.: Musicalisches Lexikon ober Musicalische Bibliothec

Travis & Emery Music Bookshop
17 Cecil Court, London, WC2N 4EZ, United Kingdom.
Tel. (+44) 20 7240 2129

© Travis & Emery 2009

www.ingramcontent.com/pod-product-compliance
Lightning Source LLC
Chambersburg PA
CBHW071233300426
44116CB00008B/1011